Bertolt B~
Colle~

The Good
The Resistib
Mr Puntila

The sixth volume of Brecht's C~ ~~d Plays contains three plays he wrote while on the run in the early stages of the Second World War. In *The Good Person of Szechwan*, the gods come to earth in search of a thoroughly good person. They find Shen Teh, a good-hearted prostitute, but she has to disguise herself as a man in order to muster sufficient ruthlessness to survive in an evil world.

The Resistible Rise of Arturo Ui is a witty and savage satire on the rise of Hitler – recast by Brecht in terms of a small-time Chicago gangster's takeover of the city's greengrocery trade. This translation by Ralph Manheim won the 1976 Schlegel-Tieck prize.

Mr Puntila and his Man Matti, one of Brecht's finest comedies, is built around the dual personality of its central character. When drunk Puntila is human and humane; when sober, surly and self-centred. Oscillating unsteadily between these two poles, he plays havoc with his workmen, his women and the loyalty of his sardonic chauffeur, Matti.

Edited by John Willett and Ralph Manheim, the volume includes Brecht's own notes and relevant texts as well as an extensive introduction and commentary.

Bertolt Brecht was born in Augsburg on 10 February 1898 and died in Berlin on 14 August 1956. He grew to maturity as a playwright in the frenetic years of the twenties and early thirties, with such plays as *Man equals Man*, *The Threepenny Opera* and *The Mother*. He left Germany when Hitler came to power in 1933, eventually reaching the United States in 1941, where he remained until 1947. It was during this period of exile that such masterpieces as *Life of Galileo*, *Mother Courage* and *The Caucasian Chalk Circle* were written. Shortly after his return to Europe in 1947 he founded the Berliner Ensemble, and from then until his death was mainly occupied in producing his own plays.

BRECHT COLLECTED PLAYS
Series Editors: John Willett, Ralph Manheim and Tom Kuhn

Brecht Collected Plays: One
Baal
Drums in the Night
In the Jungle of Cities
The Life of Edward II of England
A Respectable Wedding
The Beggar or The Dead Dog
Driving Out a Devil
Lux in Tenebris
The Catch

Brecht Collected Plays: Two
Man Equals Man
The Elephant Calf
The Threepenny Opera
The Rise and Fall of the City of Mahagonny
The Seven Deadly Sins

Brecht Collected Plays: Three
Lindbergh's Flight
The Baden-Baden Lesson on Consent
He Said Yes/He Said No
The Decision
The Mother
The Exception and the Rule
The Horatians and the Curiatians
St Joan of the Stockyards

Brecht Collected Plays: Four
Round Heads and Pointed Heads
Dansen
How Much Is Your Iron?
The Trial of Lucullus
Fear and Misery of the Third Reich
Señora Carrar's Rifles

Brecht Collected Plays: Five
Life of Galileo
Mother Courage and her Children

Brecht Collected Plays: Six
The Good Person of Szechwan
The Resistible Rise of Arturo Ui
Mr Puntila and his Man Matti

Brecht Collected Plays: Seven
The Visions of Simone Machard
Schweyk in the Second World War
The Caucasian Chalk Circle
The Duchess of Malfi

Brecht Collected Plays: Eight
The Antigone of Sophocles
The Days of the Commune
Turandot or The Whitewasher's Congress

BERTOLT BRECHT

Collected Plays: Six

The Good Person of Szechwan
translated by John Willett

Original work entitled:
Der Gute Mensch von Setzuan

The Resistible Rise of Arturo Ui
translated by Ralph Manheim

Original work entitled:
Der Aufhaltsame Aufstieg des Arturo Ui

Mr Puntila and his Man Matti
translated by John Willett

Original work entitled:
Herr Puntila und sein Knecht Matti

Edited and introduced by
John Willett and Ralph Manheim

Bloomsbury Methuen Drama
An imprint of Bloomsbury Publishing Plc

B L O O M S B U R Y
LONDON · NEW DELHI · NEW YORK · SYDNEY

Bloomsbury Methuen Drama
An imprint of Bloomsbury Publishing Plc

Imprint previously known as Methuen Drama

50 Bedford Square   1385 Broadway
London   New York
WC1B 3DP   NY 10018
UK   USA

www.bloomsbury.com

This edition first published in Great Britain in 1994 by Methuen Drama by arrangement with Suhrkamp Verlag,
Frankfurt am Main
Reissued with a new cover 1998
Reprinted by Bloomsbury Methuen Drama 2014

Methuen Drama series editor for Bertolt Brecht: Tom Kuhn

British Library Cataloguing-in-Publication Data
A catalogue record for this book is available from the British Library.

ISBN: PB: 978-0-4136-8580-3
ePDF: 978-1-4081-7743-3
ePUB: 978-0-4136-8580-3

Library of Congress Cataloging-in-Publication Data
A catalog record for this book is available from the Library of Congress.

Series: World Classics

Printed and bound in Great Britain

Contents

Introduction

Following *Galileo* (first version, Denmark, 1938) and *Mother Courage* (Sweden, 1939), in which Brecht had first turned away from day-to-day politics and any immediate possibilities of production, the present volume contains the three works written in Finland after the end of the 'phoney war' while the family was waiting to move on a stage further, to the United States. One play, *The Good Person of Szechwan*, had been in his mind for a long time, and demanded constant reworking. One was the product of his Finnish experiences (which also inspired a new vein of poetry) and grew from a draft comedy by his hostess there. The third was written in haste, meant to be staged in America once their precarious journey had been achieved. All three demanded large casts. And none could be performed as Brecht himself wanted until after his return to Europe in 1947.

Like *The Caucasian Chalk Circle* later, *The Good Person of Szechwan* stands out from his more didactic and politically committed works by being conceived as a 'parable' – a description not previously used for his plays – with ethical problems as its main concern. More than once in his journal he complains about its complicated history: conceived some ten years before he began serious work on it, then worked on successively in Denmark, Sweden and Finland till he reluctantly undertook a last revision at the beginning of 1941, he was never able to give it the final test by staging it under his own direction. At bottom the problem was how to maintain the original social point when the Chinese setting risked becoming (as he noted in mid-1940) a 'mere disguise, and a ragged disguise at that'. For the short play which he had sketched in 1930 as *Die Ware Liebe* (a pun roughly equivalent to 'Love is the Goods') was on a theme close to that of his story 'The Job' (*Short Stories 1921–1946*, p. 112): a society where women's role was to be sold, but salesmen had to be men. This, rather than the ambiguities of good and evil, is what suggested that the Person should be a whore.

Just when Brecht first thought of locating the play in China we do not know, but it must have been at some point between Piscator's production of Friedrich Wolf's *Tai Yang Wakes Up* (a counter-play to

Klabund's 1924 *Chalk Circle*) and the first reference to it in his journal
for March 1939, by which time it was already an unfinished fragment
consisting of five scenes under its present title. 'A thin structure of
steel', he called it, and clearly he did not wish it to have an exotic
flavour:

> the girl must be a big powerful person. the city must be a big, dusty
> uninhabitable place. [. . .] some attention must be paid to counter-
> ing the risk of chinoiserie. the vision is of a chinese city's outskirts
> with cement works and so on. there are still gods around but
> aeroplanes have come in. perhaps the lover should be an
> unemployed pilot?

Repeatedly he seems to have become uneasy about the local colour
and the degree of realism needed: was Shen Teh, for instance, to give
her impoverished neighbours bread, or milk, or rice? Originally a
vague name for the city, Szechwan itself, which is more properly the
name of a province, became specified in the stage directions as 'The
capital of Szechwan, which has been semi-europeanised'. This would-
be precision, which contrasts oddly with his later insistence that
Szechwan stands indifferently for 'all those places where man is
exploited by man', is less vivid in the end than some of Brecht's wilder
flights of geographical fantasy, for instance in *Man equals Man*. Even
then his use of Chinese theatrical techniques had to be accentuated
during the last laborious revisions before the play was duplicated. This
was done so as to 'add a poetic element', making it lighter and more
entertaining in an effort to compensate for its undue length.

。　　　。　　　。

Duplicated scripts went off early in 1941 to Piscator and Kurt Weill in
the United States, as well as to recipients in Sweden and Switzerland,
the latter including the Zurich Schauspielhaus, who were even then
preparing the world première of *Mother Courage*. Piscator seems to
have been the first to react, and within a few weeks of Brecht's arrival
in California on 21 July 1941 he responded enthusiastically, saying
that he had begun negotiating about a possible production with the
Theatre Guild; moreover the poet John Latouche, author of the
patriotic-progressive 'Ballad for Americans', was interested in trans-
lating the play. Brecht however was not prepared to be hurried,
preferring to wait until he knew whether he himself would be coming
to New York, and meanwhile suggesting to Piscator that *Arturo Ui*
would be a simpler play to mount. Whether he had already heard
about the productions of Piscator's Dramatic Workshop at the New

School is not clear, but they had featured a version of the Klabund
Chalk Circle that March starring Dolly Haas (of *Broken Blossoms* fame)
as the heroine, a performance which the *New York Post* praised for its
'quaintness and delicacy'; and soon the poet Hoffman Hays was
warning Brecht that Piscator's errors of judgement might harm him
with the Guild. It may have been as a result of this that he now began
looking elsewhere for the possibility of a production, showing the
script to Elisabeth Bergner, who knew his work from Munich and
Berlin and was predisposed to help. Not only had she had one of her
great successes in Klabund's play in 1924, but she was now told by
Brecht that he had written *The Good Person* specifically for her to act
(though all the early scripts carry a dedication to Helene Weigel), and
what she heard of its story clearly intrigued her. On reading it however
she found it boring and guessed that others would as well, while the
film actress Anna May Wong – yet another who had acted in the
Klabund play, this time in London in 1931 – seems to have lost
interest after a first meeting in Hollywood engineered by Alexander
Granach, another of Brecht's Berlin friends.

The sole effect of these approaches to actresses, then, was to enrage
Piscator, who saw that he was being neglected and by-passed and felt
that this was a poor reward for all his efforts to get Brecht invited to the
United States in the first place. It looks as if Brecht then shunted the
play into the sidings while he concentrated on the writing of Fritz
Lang's Czech resistance film *Hangmen Also Die*. One night in August
1942 however his old friend the novelist Lion Feuchtwanger telephoned to say that he had heard from Zurich that the Schauspielhaus
there wanted to produce the script which Brecht had sent them before
leaving Europe. This decision came at a crucial turning point in the
military fortunes of the Allies, shortly before the victories of Alamein
and Stalingrad, and from then on Zurich became for some years
Brecht's European base. Naturally he was not yet able to see any
productions there, let alone to exert any kind of influence on the
interpretation of his plays, and it is difficult even now to judge how far
the committedly anti-Nazi Schauspielhaus company managed to grasp
all his ideas. But at least its initial reception, unlike that of *Mother
Courage* and (later) *Puntila*, never led Brecht to make any corrective
changes to the text, which accordingly became the authorised version
as we now have it.

And yet within a matter of weeks Brecht was planning a major
rewrite which was to lead – as later in the case of *Galileo* – to the
making of a shorter, tighter and in some ways stronger 'version for
here', i.e. for the American stage. This originated in Kurt Weill's

reaction to the script that Brecht had sent him, which the now successful composer wanted to make into a (presumably musical) play for Broadway production. During a long visit to New York (February to May inclusive) Brecht therefore spent a week with the Weills, establishing the outline given on pp. 325–30 of our notes. This, it seems, was to form the basis for a production to be set up some while after that of the *Schweik* musical which they were planning at the same time and hoped to have ready by the autumn. The full script must then have been written during the summer of 1943, after the completion of *Schweyk in the Second World War*: typed by Brecht, it is headed '1943 version' and datelined 'Santa Monica 1943'. It eliminates two scenes and five characters and is roughly two-thirds of the length of the Zurich (authorised) version; and it can be reconstructed from the passages quoted on pp. 336–51. Probably this is the version which Brecht gave Christopher Isherwood to read that September in the hope that he might translate it; however, only 'a few polite compliments' resulted. Weill anyway wanted a more radical adaptation by an American writer, possibly the black poet Langston Hughes, who later wrote the adaptation of *Street Scene* for him. By November it seems that the new Brecht version had been shelved, and that winter a contract was made giving Weill the right to choose his own librettist and lyric writer, along with exclusive production rights for the next two and a half years. By then he had come round to the idea of a 'semi-opera' – the term which he had used of *Silver Lake* in 1933, with its separate musical 'numbers'. (He never entirely abandoned the idea, but the work had still not been started when he died in 1950.)

For at least a year Weill's interest put a stopper on any further production plans, and although Brecht speculated about the possibility of setting the play in Jamaica with an all black cast (and a translation by Auden) it never rose to the surface of his concerns again until he left America for Switzerland in November 1947. It was only after that point that a wave of American college and university productions began, using the *Two Parables* translation which Eric and Maya Bentley had made at Brecht's request on the basis of the 1940 text. Perhaps it was this that once again aroused Broadway's interest, but by now Brecht was quite as reluctant to commit himself as he had been in the case of Piscator and the Theatre Guild. In particular he did not want any experimental productions in New York; Shen Teh must be played by 'an artiste of the first rank' (Jessica Tandy for example); while Bentley himself should not venture to direct in 'the hopeless atmosphere of Broadway' without first gaining experience with Brecht's own company in Berlin. As a result it was only after the writer's death in August 1956 that the play finally reached New York, when T.E. Hambleton put on a production that December at the Phoenix Theatre, directed by Bentley with Uta Hagen as Shen Teh. Two months earlier George Devine had staged it at the Royal Court Theatre in London with Peggy Ashcroft, after visiting Brecht earlier in the year and gaining his approval. Both these first productions had music by Paul Dessau and sets by Teo Otto, friends and accepted interpreters of Brecht.

How highly did Brecht himself rank the play? Certainly he never gave it a particularly high priority where German productions were concerned, and it seems that Brecht still regarded *The Good Person* as an unusually difficult play to deal with, for all the apparent ease of its acceptance at college level. Nor were matters helped by the fact that its first professional postwar production was licensed and prepared without his being consulted; indeed the Brecht literature generally ignores it. This took place at Max Reinhardt's former Vienna theatre, the eighteenth-century Theater in der Josefstadt, where there was a production by Rudolf Steinböck in March 1946 with the outstanding actress Paula Wessely as Shen Teh; conservative Austrian critics felt she was too cold. It was another six years before Harry Buckwitz in Frankfurt mounted the first West German production, a somewhat dragging affair with Solveig Thomas as a clearly much sweeter and daintier Shen Teh. A number of other West German performances followed before Brecht, who had spent four days with Buckwitz in Frankfurt trying 'to infuse ease and clarity into the production', gave his young Swiss assistant Benno Besson the task of directing the play's East German première at Rostock. With Käthe Reichel as a dialect-ically polarised Shen Teh this laboured the play's antitheses and stressed the links between the Chinese city and Western capitalism. It was conceived as a pilot production for Besson and Reichel to develop eighteen months later at the Berliner Ensemble.

·   ·   ·

Despite its obvious attractions *The Good Person of Szechwan* is made up of too many conflicting layers simply to convey the thin steely strength or the clarity and ease for which Brecht variously aimed. The difficulty is that despite Brecht's warnings against a fancy-dress orientalising approach there is some danger of sentimentality and prettification in the play as he left it to us; indeed the example of the *Chalk Circle* (or *Circle of Chalk* in James Laver's 1931 translation) is hard to shake off. Perhaps because of this the actresses who have been tempted to play Shen Teh – even, it seems, when Brecht himself did the tempting –

have started with an idealised model of the oriental 'good woman' before them, an image only slightly spiced up by her description as a prostitute. At the same time the social relevance of the original *Love is the Goods* story is not so much 'alienated' by the Szechwan setting as diffused and diluted by it. 'We had in mind a sort of golden myth' says the speaker of the epilogue, and this comforting interpretation is now available from the first appearance of the three hopelessly unserious gods.

Obviously Brecht in this play was concerned with something more than sharp formulations of the 'Food is the first thing. Morals follow on' variety. Not only had he been reading Chinese philosophy, but his journal shows that he had begun holding discussions about Marxist ethics with the actor Hermann Greid and other friends. In the *Flüchtlingsgespräche* or *Conversations between Exiles*, which he was writing in Finland around the same time, he deals with the concepts of good and evil in a comic-paradoxical way, showing in a long 'Parade of the Vices and Virtues' how both these opposites can 'identify themselves as the servants of *Oppression*'. The play however is dialectical rather than paradoxical, and by splitting the central character down the middle into two irreconcilable parts it can easily cut away the point, which is that in aggressive and unjust societies good can only survive by means of evil. Nor is it ever made clear enough that the root of this ethical duplicity is not simply poverty, such as can afflict any form of society; indeed only the 'Song of Green Cheese' at the end of scene 6 suggests that a better society can be conceived at all, and it does so in the most unreal fairy-story terms. Brecht, in other words, had only himself to blame if audiences applauded him for modifying his previously 'political' approach, and instead tackling the eternal problem of 'humanity as such'. The feeling with which they are most likely to be left by the play is one of generalised discontent.

Such problems of focus are built into *The Good Person of Szechwan*, and it could accordingly be argued that a faithful production is one that simply allows them to emerge. There are however ways of blocking some of the dangers against which Brecht warned us: by casting a 'big, powerful' Shen Teh for instance, or by eliminating the Chinese setting altogether as did Giorgio Strehler, who in his 1981 Milan production dropped it in favour of an Italian shanty town with filthy puddles everywhere. What seems rather surprising, in view of the high risk of having Shen Teh interpreted as a sweet-natured oriental waif, is that Brecht's experience of Chinese acting, which so influenced him in other respects, never led him to propose giving the dual role to a man. This would instantly correct any undue softness that may stem from the sexually loaded 'good woman' image; moreover it seems to make it easier to see elements of Shui Ta in Shen Teh and vice versa, as the parable surely demands; nor is there anything in the text to rule it out. Brecht, it is true, spoke of the part from the first as being 'for a woman', but this, like her designation as a prostitute, is traceable back to the original pre-1933 story. It is not specifically demanded by the 1940 play.

The relative strength of the 'Americanised' version of 1943 is that it is both tougher and more topically relevant to our societies today, for the 'tobacco' in the sacks which the visiting family of scene 1 leave in Shen Teh's shop turns out to be opium. What is more, Shen Teh's evident complicity in this traffic, once Shui Ta begins selling the stuff, makes the good person's dependence on evil actions seem that much more real and less schematic. At the same time the puzzling financial complexities of the old people's loan, the highly improbable blank cheque from the barber and the proceeds of the sale both of the tobacco and the shop, which in the 1940 version were too much for Brecht ever to straighten out convincingly, are greatly simplified by the elimination of both loan and cheque: a definite gain. This generally faster-moving version was used in David Thompson's Greenwich Theatre production of May 1977 and gave a much clearer line to the story, though at the cost of losing two individually effective scenes: the wedding in the restaurant and the factory scene with its brutal 'Song of the Eighth Elephant'. In particular Sun, by ending up as an enfeebled addict, is much more convincingly 'broken-down' than the bowler-hatted 'charming manager' of the standard text.

.   .   .

In April 1940 when Hitler's armies invaded Denmark and Norway the Brechts felt they must move quickly. From Sweden, where they were living temporarily on the island of Lidingo near Stockholm, they wrote to the Finnish playwright Hella Wuolijoki asking her to send them an invitation which would help them to enter her country. There they hoped to catch a ship to America from the arctic port of Petsamo before the next winter set in. Wuolijoki knew her prime minister well enough to persuade him to admit the author of *The Threepenny Opera* – a play that he had enjoyed – and by the end of April the extended family had arrived and found a temporary home in the Tölö district of Helsinki. Then Wuolijoki invited them to spend the summer in her country house at Marlebäck in Tavasthus province to the north of the capital, where she farmed a twelve-hundred-acre estate. And there, while France was being assimilated and the Battle of Britain fought, Brecht began that short but intense love affair with the Finnish countryside which started a new phase in his work.

Their hostess was then in her mid-fifties, an old supporter of the 1905 and Bolshevik revolutions who was at the same time not only the successful author of some thirty plays but also a leading business woman, founder of two timber firms during the 1920s boom and thereafter chairman of the Finnish petrol company Suomen Nafta until 1938. She had been born in Estonia, one of those three small Baltic states which the Russians re-annexed soon after the Brechts' arrival at Marlebäck, but completed her studies in Helsinki where she met her future husband. Sulo Wuolijoki was then a leader of the Social-Democratic Student Union along with Otto Kuusinen, later to become the leader of the Finnish Communist Party and its represent-ative on the Comintern in Moscow. With them she took part in the revolutionary movement, and when after the October Revolution the Communists lost Helsinki to the Whites the Wuolijokis were arrested and their house searched. The marriage did not last long after that: Sulo Wuolijoki, it appears, became an alcoholic; he was a big landowner and vile when drunk. His wife in turn lost much of her political idealism when the First World War broke out, so she later told Lion Feuchtwanger, and bought the Marlebäck estate independ-ently with her wartime profits; she also visited Berlin where she met Gorky, Walter Rathenau and Gerhart Hauptmann, and was a close friend of Ivan Maisky, who was to become the Soviet Ambassador to London during the Second World War.

Having done her university research on Estonian folk poetry she wrote her first play in that largely suppressed language in 1912, only to have it banned by the Tsarist censorship. Later she wrote in Finnish (though she is said also to have been fluent in Russian, Swedish, French, German and English) and during the 1930s had particular success with her cycle of five naturalistic plays about *Niiskavuoren naiset*, the Women of Niskavuori, of which one was performed successfully in the Hamburg State Theatre in 1938 – until the Nazis learnt of her political record. These and other plays of Finnish country life and women's role in it became the mainstay of the repertoire of the Helsinki People's Theatre (Kansanteatteri) directed by Eino Salmelai-nen. And by the time of her meeting with Brecht in 1940 she had also written a still unperformed play·called *Sahanpuruprinsessa* or Sawdust Princess, which Suomi-Film was hoping to make into a film. This was based on an earlier story of hers which told of an authentic incident of rural life that took place on her fortieth birthday, in 1926. Now reproduced on pp. 371–80, it was called 'A Finnish Bacchus' and featured the large-scale farmer Johannes Punttila (*sic*).

Brecht arrived on her estate on 5 July 1940 and was captivated by its calm beauty. Thus his first entry in his journal:

> drove with HELLA WUOLIJOKI to marlebäk (kausala). she is letting us have a villa surrounded by lovely birch trees. we discuss the quietness out here. but it isn't quiet; it's just that the noises are so much more natural, the wind in the trees, the rustle of grass, the twittering and the sound of water. the white manor house with its two rows each of eight large windows is over 100 years old, built in empire style. the rooms would not disgrace a museum. alongside it lies a huge stone building for the cows (some 80 head) with openings for fodder overhead for the forage lorry to drive to . . . helli is going to have difficulty cooking, i'm afraid, the stove needs to be kept in and the water supply is outdoors. but the people are very friendly and h.w. has an unending fund of stories.

Already this sets the scene for a certain return to nature in Brecht's writing, and three days later he is visibly infected with the mood of *Puntila* and the Finnish poems (e.g. *Poems 1913–1956* pp. 352–3):

> it's not hard to see why people in these parts love their landscape. it is so very opulent and widely varied. the waters stocked with fish and the woods full of beautiful trees with their scent of berries and birches. the immense summers that irrupt overnight following endless winters. extreme heat following extreme cold, and as the winter day dwindles so does the summer night. then the air is so strong and good to the taste that it is almost enough to satisfy the appetite. and the music that fills that clear sky! nearly all the time there is a wind, and because it blows on many different plants, grasses, corn, bushes and forests the result is a gentle harmony that rises and falls, virtually imperceptible yet always there.

Everything was combining to reintroduce the author of 'A Reader for Those who Live in Cities' to that mixture of humour, harshness and simple beauty that he had absorbed so productively in the Bavaria of his youth. These he could find again in the landscape and people of the Tavast country, thanks to his hostess's shrewd eye and vivid gift of narration.

*   *   *

Hella Wuolijoki was not merely a knowledgeable guide to the new surroundings in which Brecht found himself but a writer who had managed in her own plays and stories to set down something of their essence. Above all she was a raconteur whose language and style exactly suited his socio-aesthetic tastes. 'marvellous, the stories wuolijoki tells', he noted at the end of July:

> about the people on the estate, in the forests where she used to own big sawmills in the heroic period. she looks wise and lovely as she tells of the tricks of simple people and the stupidity of the upper crust, shaking with perpetual laughter and now and again looking at you through cunningly screwed-up eyes as she accompanies the various personages' remarks by epic, fluid movements of her lovely fat hands as though beating time to some music that nobody else can hear. (loose-wristed, she beats a horizontal figure of eight.)

Margarete Steffin and Brecht began to transcribe her remarks and to help with the translation of some of her writings, which she seems to have been very ready to go over with the former. Thus there is a German version by Steffin of *The Young Mistress of Niskavuori*, one of the cycle already mentioned, which begins with Loviisa the young mistress and Liisu the maid carrying a big water bucket into 'an imposing farm kitchen built of wooden beams'.

The plan for making a collection of her oral stories came to nothing, since (in Steffin's words) 'If one takes down HW's stories in shorthand and then sees them in black and white it is remarkable how they lose their sparkle. Much of their charm is due to the repetitions and the lively play of her features, also to the beautiful way in which her gestures accompany them.' But in addition to the Niskavuori play Wuolijoki now decided to make a German translation of her as yet unperformed *Sahanpuruprinsessa*, which she dictated to Steffin, it seems, during August. Here was the Puntila figure whom she had termed the 'Finnish Bacchus': in real life Roope Juntula, a cousin of her former husband's who had indeed once driven his Buick away recklessly in the middle of the night to get legal alcohol very much as in scene 3 of the present play; he had also, like Puntila, got engaged to three village women, though this was omitted from her written version of the story. A number of other incidents or passages of dialogue in Brecht's text coincide more or less closely with various lesser plays and jottings of hers, notably Matti's harangue to the herring (pp. 286–7) which occurs in a short piece called *Tramps' Waltz*. There is no doubt that these and the Puntila character, along with her vivid way of expressing his remarks, are at the root of the play which we print.

It was in the second half of August that Wuolijoki first began

discussing plans with Brecht. The previous year the Finnish Dramatists' League, with ministerial backing, had announced a competition
for a 'people's play' to be submitted by the end of the coming October.
Wuolijoki now suggested to Brecht that perhaps they might collaborate on an entry, and got Steffin to show him the new German version
of *The Sawdust Princess*. This was not exactly the 'draft play'
subsequently mentioned by him in his prefatory note (p. 215), since it
was by no means just a first sketch but the result of much preparatory
work. None the less he saw it as technically old-fashioned and wanted
to rebuild it along his own lines.

> what i have to do is to bring out the underlying farce, dismantle the
> psychological discussions so as to make place for tales from finnish
> popular life or statements of opinion, find a theatrical form for the
> master/man contradiction, and give the theme back its poetic and
> comic aspects. this theme shows how in spite of all her cleverness,
> her experience, her vitality and her gifts as a writer h.w. is
> hampered by her conventional dramatic technique.

It was not just a matter of making use of her play's local colour and
characters. He must dismantle its structure so as to avoid banal
conventions (like the absurd happy ending), reveal the other side of
the central Puntila figure, and infiltrate some of those spontaneous
anecdotes which she herself would think hopelessly undramatic.

Brecht started revising and rewriting her script on 2 September, and
within three weeks had typed out what he called 'a fat little calf of a
play. it contains more landscape than any other of my plays except
perhaps BAAL.' What he had done to change it, the stages through
which he worked and the amendments which he made later, are all
outlined in our editorial notes (pp. 399–426), whose main gist is that
he made it into a rambling epic play rather than a 'well-made' one on
Aristotelian principles, virtually eliminating the major character of
'Aunt Hanna' (though she still haunts scene 2 rather awkwardly in the
form of the absent Mrs Klinkmann), and strengthening the element of
class self-interest in Puntila so as to offset his drunken benevolence.
He also brought in the stories told by the four village women as a result
of the landowner's hostile behaviour (scene 8 arising out of scene 7)
and gave Wuolijoki's cosy plot a downbeat ending by resigning Matti
to the impossibility of natural human relations across such socio-
economic barriers, except when saturated with alcohol. Alcoholism
then, from being a national Finnish problem (which is how Wuolijoki
seems to have encountered it in her own life), becomes an aspect of
the class war, if still a broadly farcical one.

Not surprisingly, the initial impact on Wuolijoki of Brecht's alterations was a shock, for he had in effect taken over her play and in many cases her actual words, and turned them into something recognisably of his own: epic, Schweikian, schematically Marxist and in her view un-Finnish. But he managed to argue her out of such strictures, persuading her to translate the play back into Finnish and submit it for the competition, where it won no kind of prize. Thereafter they came to an agreement in effect to go their own separate ways. That is to say that Wuolijoki could dispose of the Finnish version throughout Scandinavia, making whatever changes she wished; thus she renamed the principal figure 'Johannes Iso-Heikkilä' to make him less identifiable with the still living (but now anti-alcoholic) Mr Juntula, and subtitled the play 'A comic tale of Tavastland drunkenness in nine scenes'. Brecht for his part could negotiate performances of his distinctly less jovial version anywhere else in the world, apparently without naming Wuolijoki as co-author, though he agreed that they should split the royalties equally. Yet he always regarded the play's Finnish setting, its relation to the Tavast landscape and its living legends, and its permeation (à la *Schweik*) with digressive anecdotes as essential to it. And if it owes its lovely background, its main characters and much of its humour to the warm personality of Brecht's hostess it also owes something to those anonymous figures whose photographs appear at the end of his and Steffin's typescripts: the Finnish farmworkers with their flat fields and wooden cottages, the women in headscarves at work in the meadows and the woods.

.   .   .

By the end of that September Hella Wuolijoki had made up her mind to sell the estate, which wartime transport difficulties were making increasingly difficult to run. By 7 October the family were back in Helsinki, where they moved into three rooms near the harbour to await their American visas. These finally came through, along with a tourist visa for the tubercular Margarete Steffin, at the beginning of May 1942; she was described as Hella Wuolijoki's secretary. Brecht by then had completed the troublesome *Good Person of Szechwan*, written a new play in the form of *The Resistible Rise of Arturo Ui* and heard of the première, in distant Zurich, of *Mother Courage*, a work which he had vainly hoped might be staged in Stockholm or in Helsinki. At a late stage he had yet again to ask for Wuolijoki's help, this time in finding out about the cargo ships that might be able to take them to America from a Soviet port, whether Murmansk on the Arctic,

Odessa on the Black Sea or Vladivostok in the Far East. On 14 May she and other Finnish friends gave the Brechts a farewell dinner in a Helsinki restaurant. The following day they left for Leningrad.

This was barely a month before the German invasion of the USSR, and once again the Brechts got away only just in time. For back in Finland the situation quickly changed as Hitler advanced through the Baltic republics and the Finns became his allies. In Karelia the Finnish army attacked, and by early September Leningrad was under siege. Wuolijoki, who had been involved in a last-minute attempt to keep her country out of the war, was now suspect as a Communist, a negotiator with the Russians, and a friend of Alexandra Kollontai, the old bolshevik Soviet ambassador to Sweden. She was arrested in 1942, when she was accused of giving help to a Soviet parachutist, the daughter of her childhood friend Santeri Nuorteva who, like Kuusinen, had been living in exile in the USSR ever since 1918. Kuusinen's daughter too, who had been working for the Soviet embassy in Helsinki, remained underground in Finland. Thanks to such associations Wuolijoki was tried for treason and imprisoned; she was all but sentenced to death – 'even though I worked far too little against the war', says an autobiographical sketch quoted by Manfred Peter Hein. Released after the ceasefire of 1944, she re-entered active politics, helping Herta Kuusinen to establish the Popular Front and herself becoming one of its deputies. She was head of the Finnish radio from 1945 to 1949, came to Berlin and saw Brecht's *Puntila* production with the Berliner Ensemble, and died on 2 February 1954 in her sixty-eighth year.

Brecht never seems to have made any attempt to get this play staged during his ensuing years in the United States, though as soon as he returned to Europe in 1947 it became one of his first priorities, initially in Zurich where he helped direct its world première at the Schauspielhaus (though for legal reasons he could not be named in the programme), then in East Berlin where he directed it in collaboration with Erich Engel as the opening production of the new Berliner Ensemble. The main adjustments made for the Zurich production were the introduction of the 'Plum Song' for Therese Giehse as Sly Grog Emma to sing in scene 3 (to the tune of 'When it's springtime in the Rockies' by Robert Sauer, 1927) and the virtual loss of the Hiring Fair scene; while from Brecht's notes on p. 385 it appears that he already saw the danger of allowing the audience to be so captivated by Puntila's drunken antics as to side with him against Matti. In the Berliner Ensemble production that followed, where the Puntila part was again played by the same actor, Leonard Steckel, Brecht took special measures to alienate him from the German audience, prescribing masks for him and all the other representatives of the bourgeoisie; later he re-cast the production with the smaller and more agile comedian Curt Bois in the title part, to reduce the old sozzler's human appeal still further. In addition the thinly schematic character of Red Surkkala was introduced as offering a 'positive', proletarian element to offset the much more interesting ambiguities of Matti. The linking 'Puntila Song' too was written for Berlin, where Paul Dessau for the first time wrote the music (after Brecht's death he was to develop this into an opera), while Caspar Neher came in instead of Teo Otto as the scene designer, contributing almost incidentally a series of splendidly lively watercolours of the play's main incidents as well as pen drawings intended apparently for projection between the scenes. This was the production that was seen by Wuolijoki and led her to tell Brecht in a letter:

> . . . and as for what you have made of Puntila, here we would never have known how to put him on the stage . . .

Indeed the Wuolijoki–Brecht version, though published soon after the end of the war, remained unperformed in any Scandinavian country until the year of Wuolijoki's death.

.   .   .

What Brecht had managed to do was to assimilate his own revived feeling for the unspoiled countryside, together with Wuolijoki's sense of anecdote and rustic expressiveness, into a thoughtful (and necessarily Marxist) analysis of the limitations of human geniality, of superficial warmth. To anyone familiar with the German theatre in Brecht's day it must recall *Der fröhliche Weinberg*, The Cheerful Vineyard, that notoriously jolly play with which Carl Zuckmayer in 1925 broke away from the prevalent Expressionism and at the same time distanced himself from the rebelliousness of his close colleague Brecht. There too a gifted dramatist had conjured up the beauties of the landscape, the vitality of an ageing farmer, the rejection by the farmer's daughter of an upper-class lover in favour of a man of the people, and even the humanising influence of drink; and had done so both decently (in the moral-political sense) and with great commercial success. Whether or not Brecht saw the analogy at the outset he must have realised that his had to be something of a 'counter-play' to this. And all the more so since Zuckmayer's great post-1945 hit *The Devil's General*, performed by the Zurich company eighteen months before the *Puntila* première, showed how easily the German theatre prefers any jovial, full-blooded autocrat to his unforthcoming opponent, whether in the person of Brecht's ironic driver, Matti, or of Zuckmayer's inconspicuous saboteur. No wonder Brecht was so worried about what he came to see as Puntila's dangerous charm. Behind this Finnish Faust with his two souls, as also behind Zuckmayer's wine-grower and his Luftwaffe General, lurks the shadow of that spuriously genial, murderously popular figure Hermann Göring.

Contradiction, then, is the essence of this play, so that the great challenge for any director must be how to balance its conflicting elements against one another, thereby forcing the audience to discount the comedy and make a considered judgement. It is all the more difficult today since the Finland of the 1920s, which is where its original incidents were set, seems on the face of it so very remote from our world of seventy years later: remote from modern Finland, remoter still from Germany, whether East or West, and (of course) very remote indeed from Broadway and Shaftesbury Avenue. This was already one of the main objections raised in 1950 by the East German theatre critics, who forced Brecht into the kind of defence expressed by him on p. 394: the story, he claimed, was still relevant, even in a radically reformed society whose big landowners had been expropriated, because there too one could learn from 'the history of the struggle' and (rather more plausibly) 'because past eras leave a deposit in men's minds'. Yet are these characters and their conflicts really so very much in the past? In Texas, for example, or in Australia?

Certainly *Puntila* is a play that needs rescuing. For it is not a jolly romp with some amusing lines and characters. It is not a women's magazine story about the love of an only daughter for her father's chauffeur. It is not, whatever Brecht says in the prologue, a reconstruction of an extinct monster known to science as 'Estatium possessor', but deals with live issues. It is not a schematic conflict between ugly masked capitalists and open-faced workers. It is not a celebration of the Finnish national character, much though Wuolijoki would have liked it to be. It is something altogether subtler and more complicated than any of these things: a jumble of criss-crossing contradictions – Naturalism and epic theatre, the warmth and coldness of the two authors, the drunkenness and sobriety of their hero, the Finnish master and his strikingly un-Finnish employee, tranquillity in wartime, country beauties seen through a city-dweller's eye, farcical episodes making serious points – the dialectical list can, and perhaps should, be prolonged by anyone seriously concerned with its performance.

This is not to pretend that it is not also a very funny play. Unhappily in the present state of our world and our country's role in it, where we have an uneasy sense of fiddling before some great disaster comes, the British obsession with comedy has become neurotic. Today, as the media are continually letting us know, jokeyness is all; nothing like a good laugh, is there? – as if we were determined to go down the plughole not with a bang but a titter. Here however is a 'people's' comedy where the laughs are set against the dangers of the larger-than-lifesize personality, so as to remind us (among other things) of the other side of the folksy politician's television act. The play is unique in Brecht's work, and its balancing act between the farcical and the deeply serious is of a kind that ought to suit the British theatre better than it has so far done. Perhaps it is no coincidence that Brecht worked on it at a time when, for all his hostility to the British class system (and it is noticeable that he never seems to have applied for any permit to settle in England or the Commonwealth), he was reading a good deal of previously unfamiliar English literature – Boswell, Macaulay, Wordsworth, Arnold and Lytton Strachey all being discussed in his journal. This made him aware, apparently for the first time, of the great richness of the English literary and educational tradition as against the German, nor was it possible not to relate them in some measure to Britain's situation as the last country then holding out against Hitler. *Puntila* was actually written as the Battle of Britain was being fought, with London in flames. Thanks to its unforced humour, at once dry and warm, it has emerged as the most 'English' in feeling of all his plays.

·   ·   ·

The Resistible Rise of Arturo Ui is the last of those great plays of Brecht's Scandinavian exile whose rich variety led him to note that

> the plays tend to fly apart like constellations in the new physics, as though here too some kind of dramaturgical core had exploded.

True as this is of his oeuvre from *Fear and Misery of the Third Reich* (1937–38) right up to his departure for America in May 1941, *Ui* was perhaps the most clearly centrifugal of them all, for it was dashed off as an afterthought in a mere three weeks following the completion of *Puntila* and *The Good Person of Szechwan* while his household was waiting in Helsinki for United States visas to come through. Conceived with a view to the American stage – Brecht did not envisage any German-language production at the time – it seems like an unplanned, high-spirited appendix to his most isolated, yet also most fruitful years.

Only two months earlier, in March 1941, the American stage designer Mordecai Gorelik had sent Brecht a copy of his book *New Theatres for Old*, a general survey of the modern theatre whose emphasis on the 'epic' approach owed much to Brecht's ideas. Before that, in 1935, when the playwright had paid his only prewar visit to the U.S., Gorelik's sets had provided the one redeeming feature of that New York production of *The Mother* which Brecht and Hanns Eisler had vainly tried to direct along their own lines; since then Gorelik had visited the Brechts in Denmark and been invited to form part of that Diderot Society or 'Society for Theatrical Science' which Brecht was hoping to set up as an antidote to the Stanislavsky-based 'Method' style of naturalistic acting. Now, reading Gorelik's book and reconsidering the possibilities of the epic (or loosely narrative) structure – thinking no doubt also about the American theatre and his own possible role in it – Brecht was transported back to his earlier American experiences and

> again struck by the idea i once had in new york, of writing a gangster play that would recall certain events familiar to us all. (*the gangster play we know.*)

– this last phrase being set down in English, a language in which he would increasingly have to think.

Executive as ever, within a few days he had sketched out the plan of the play, noting in his journal that 'of course it will have to be written in the grand style'. That was on 10 March. On the 28th – 'in the midst of all the commotion about visas and the chances of our making the journey' – the play was complete except for the last scene. Then four days later he was already looking back at the finished job and starting to revise it. It 'ought really to stand a chance on the U.S. stage', so he told Gorelik, and he had clearly enjoyed himself writing it. Once again – and for the last time – he had returned to the largely mythical America of his earlier plays, filling it out with his and his family's accumulated knowledge of gangster movies and lore, and linking it to unremitting ridicule of the still victorious Nazis. In this critical moment of history – critical not only for the world but also for his own safety – he had reacted by writing very largely for fun.

·   ·   ·

Brecht's obsession with the American setting – and specifically with Chicago – was an old one, going right back to the writing of his third

play *In the Jungle* and of the poem 'Epistle to the Chicagoans' in the
chilly Berlin of winter 1921–22. Starting as a form of fashionable
exoticism, with strange underworld characters called Skinny, Worm
and Baboon snuffling around in front of a backdrop largely derived
from Upton Sinclair, it served even then as a cloak to distance
German audiences from what were really parables about their own
society. By the end of the 1920s the device was no longer quite so
effective, and Brecht on second thoughts joined with Weill to have
the American names in their opera *Mahagonny* replaced by German
ones. None the less his preoccupation with the U.S. survived his
conversion to Marxism, to take on a new socio-economic emphasis as
he began studying the great capitalist trusts and tycoons, immortalised
by him in the Faustian character of the millionaire Pierpont Mauler in
St Joan of the Stockyards. By then the gangster world too had begun to
fascinate him, thanks no doubt to his addictive reading of crime
stories, and something of this fascination seeped into the London
world of *The Threepenny Opera*, where gangster and businessman were
shown to be brothers under the skin, linked by the same unscrupulous
morality. A year later the same recipe was less successfully repeated in
Happy End, though here the setting was a crudely depicted Chicago
peopled by fantastic criminals: an ex-boxer, an ex-clergyman, a
Japanese pickpocket (played by Peter Lorre) and a policeman's
mysterious widow known as 'The Fly' or 'The Lady in Grey'.

   Then with the 1930s came the talking film, notably the great
gangster movies associated with such actors as Humphrey Bogart,
James Cagney, Paul Muni, Bruce Cabot and Edward G. Robinson.
Brecht loved these, and it must have been their impact which made *Ui*
so much more vivid and dynamic a play than its precursors (this is
most visible perhaps in scenes 10 and 11, the hotel and garage scenes).
What is not certain is whether he knew the stage or film version of
Winterset (first produced in 1935), the gangster play by Kurt Weill's
new collaborator Maxwell Anderson (whom he was subsequently to
meet – and offend – in New York), though clearly its application of
verse forms to such a theme would have intrigued him. Following *St
Joan of the Stockyards*, with its allusions to Goethe and Schiller and its
use of blank verse for the Chicago milieu, he himself had used a quasi-
Shakespearean structure and diction for *The Round Heads and the
Pointed Heads*, his anti-Nazi parable of the mid-thirties which he set in
an unconvincing Brechtian Ruritania. This conflict of levels was
originally intended not so much as a deliberate experiment in
incongruity (or 'alienation') but as a by-product of that play's origins
in an adaptation of *Measure for Measure*. But he already saw something

of the same bloodshed and violence in Elizabethan high drama or Roman history (the setting of his first tentative 'Ui' story, as outlined on pp. 366–7) as in Chicago gang warfare or the Nazi street fighting of Hitler's rise to power. To him there was nothing inappropriate in using the same 'grand style' for all these things, and if it disconcerted the audience so much the better.

In 1940 Brecht's favourite film actor guyed Hitler and Mussolini in *The Great Dictator*, and if the war removed much of the daring and outrage of Chaplin's original conception it also made it a lot easier to get such satires shown. So Brecht too could now take Hitler and some of his chief associates (Göring, Goebbels, Von Papen, Röhm – though not Heinrich Himmler), and present them as protection-racket gangsters straight from the Al Capone-like milieu so brilliantly popularised by Warner Brothers and First National, while at the same time making them talk like characters out of Shakespeare. There was a double alienation at work here; first the events of Hitler's rise to power became transposed into the setting of (say) Dashiell Hammett's 'The Big Knockover', while secondly the underworld characters, with their talk of Brownings and the Bronx, moved into conscious parody of the high poetic drama: the Garden Scene from Goethe's *Faust* for instance in the rhymed couplets of scene 12, Mark Antony's speech in that with the old Shakespearean actor, the second scene of *Richard III* in Ui's wooing of the widow Dullfeet in scene 13. Both aspects of this operation presented new and intriguing problems to Brecht. On the one hand he had to establish the historical analogies without reducing the outward and visible gangster story to a lifeless parable; which meant striking a happy compromise (as it were) between *Scarface* and *Mein Kampf*, and taking the lumbering epic theatre for an unprecedentedly fast gallop over ground normally associated with gun battles and car chases. On the other, the grand style of the language had to go slumming, as in Ragg's speech of regret for the fading gang leader –

Yesterday's hero has been long forgotten
His mug-shot gathers dust in ancient files

– culminating in the ironic explosion of 'Oh, lousy world!' The gratifying thing to him about this inconsistency of style and level was that it not only brought out 'the inadequacy of [the Nazis'] masterful pose' but also, by its wilful manhandling of the blank verse form, seemed to generate 'new formal material for a modern verse with irregular rhythms, which could lead to great things'.

•   •   •

It must be remembered that Brecht was writing before the time of the 'Final Solution', and many of the horrors which we now associate with the Third Reich were still to come. Even such historical events as are covered by the play had to be cut and compressed, and the 'certain incidents in the recent past' which loom up relentlessly at the end of each scene are far from giving a complete picture of the period: in other words Hitler's triumphant career from 1932, the last year of the Weimar Republic, up to his unopposed takeover of Austria in 1938. It would be wrong to attribute the gaps in this story primarily to shortcomings in Brecht's own understanding of events, since it is generally accepted (and borne out by the *Fear and Misery* sketches and such poems as 'The Last Wish', written in 1935), that he made a relentless effort to keep himself informed.

Among his more substantial sources would probably have been Konrad Heiden's pioneering life of Hitler, which appeared in Switzerland in 1936, but above all the remarkably detailed and well-illustrated 'Brown Books' compiled in Paris by the brilliant Comintern propagandist Willi Muenzenberg and a whole team of writers including Arthur Koestler and the clever but untrustworthy Otto Katz, former business manager of the Piscator company with which Brecht had been associated in Berlin. The first of these documents appeared as early as 1933, and made a strong case against the Nazis – and particularly Göring – for having themselves originated the Reichstag Fire. The second dealt with the trial of the alleged Communist arsonists, the third with the Nazi subversion and propaganda network in Austria and other countries subsequently swallowed by Hitler. All three contained liberal evidence of beatings and murders, already naming Oranienburg, Buchenwald, Dachau and other now notorious concentration camps.

What Brecht left out of his historical outline, as appended on p. 213, was in the first place the role played by the Bulgarian Communist Georgi Dimitrov, who with two of his compatriots was among those framed in the show trial before the Leipzig Supreme Court. This is surprising since Dimitrov became a great left-wing hero as a result of his accusatory confrontation with Göring; he was the principal figure of the second Brown Book. Propaganda value apart, however, this episode was less important than the previous dismantling by Von Papen of the Socialist-run Prussian provincial government and state apparatus: a crucial step in smoothing the way for a right-wing dictatorship which Brecht, once again, curiously omits. Yet neither of these points seems to have disturbed his critics so much as his failure to refer to Hitler's persecution of the Jews or to allow for any kind of resistance by the German people. Not that the latter omission should surprise anyone today, when a more realistic view is taken of popular support for the Nazis than prevailed among their opponents at the time. But the decision to say nothing whatever about the racial issue does seem a little odd considering the big part which it had played five years before in *The Round Heads and the Pointed Heads*.

Otherwise the analogies set out in the outline are pretty well correct. The Dock Aid scandal of the early scenes refers to the *Osthilfe*, a form of state subsidy to the Junkers or East German landowners – Brecht's Cauliflower Trust – one of whom, a baron Von Oldenburg-Januschau, was a friend and neighbour of President Hindenburg and had got up the subscription to buy him the former family estate of Neudeck – the country house of scene 4 – as a tribute for his eightieth birthday in 1929. For tax reasons this was put in the name of Colonel Oskar von Hindenburg, the old man's son and heir. Late in 1932, during the chancellorship of Oskar's slippery friend Franz von Papen – Clark of the Trust – the facts leaked out and threatened to upset Hindenburg's system of government by like-minded ex-officers and gentlemen, industrialists and landowners, by-passing the Reichstag thanks to his use of presidential decrees.

Hitler – Ui – whose party had been returned with 38% of the seats in the July Reichstag elections, was at that time still regarded by the president as a pretentious (non-commissioned) upstart unfit for high office; moreover by that autumn even his popular support showed symptoms of decline – the occasion for Ragg's mock-lamentations. Papen however had legalised the SA, Hitler's brown-shirted private army under the leadership of Ernst Röhm – Roma – the former officer who was the party's 'Chief of Staff'. The gang was again free to threaten and brawl, while their leader started canvassing the industrialists and other influential conservatives on behalf of his precariously-financed party. That winter, with Papen and his successor Schleicher both unable to govern, Hitler's chancellorship appeared the only practical solution, so long as he and Göring could be contained within a cabinet of Papen and other orthodox nationalists. So enter Ui in scene 5, with his 'Hi, Clark! Hi, Dogsborough! Hi, everybody!' The upstart was on top.

Within a month of Hitler's appointment as chancellor on 30 January 1933 the now largely inoperative Reichstag building – the warehouse of scene 7 – had burned down: pretext for a wave of repression against the left wing, who were held responsible. The Communist view at that time was that the only one of the accused to be involved was the half-crazy unemployed Dutch youth Marinus van der Lubbe – Fish in scene 8 – who was caught on the premises, having supposedly been introduced by the real incendiaries, led by a particularly vile SA officer named Heines, through an underground passage from the house of Göring, the Reichstag president. This version is now generally accepted by historians, though a book by Fritz Tobias has argued that Van der Lubbe did the job entirely on his own. What is certain is that the suppression of all opposition and union activity within Germany dates from the fire; hence the Brechts' own departure on the following day, and hence also the symbolism of the Woman's speech of terror in scene 9a (though originally this was placed at the end of the play).

Next came the suppression of the quasi-revolutionary element within Hitler's own party – interpreted by Brecht, like Konrad Heiden before him, as the Nazi leader's attempt to legitimise himself as the declining Hindenburg's inevitable successor. On 30 June 1934 Hitler went to attend a conference of SA commanders called by Röhm at Bad Wiessee in Bavaria – the garage of scene 11 – taking Goebbels with him; they arrived with old party friends in an armoured column. Heines was shot out of hand, Röhm arrested and later shot in a prison cell; a total of 122 dead was later reported, while another 150 or so were executed under Göring's orders in Berlin and other, smaller, operations were simultaneously carried out elsewhere. Less than a month later, the Austrian chancellor Engelbert Dollfuss – 'a very small man' like Brecht's Ignatius Dullfeet – was also murdered by SS men as part of an unsuccessful Nazi coup against this Catholic-dominated country. He too had been a right-wing dictator with few humanitarian inhibitions, and although he was prepared to negotiate with the Nazis he would never do the same with the Left. For four years after his death the Austrians tried to play off Hitler against Mussolini before being finally absorbed by the former in the *Anschluss* (or reunification) of 1938, after which the seizure of Czechoslovakia and the German wartime conquests followed – the Washington, Milwaukee, Detroit and so on of Ui's closing speech. All the same, the play effectively follows events only up to 1935, the year of its original conception, and Brecht never wrote 'the utterly and universally unperformable' sequel which he felt the itch to start in April 1941 as soon as he had finished revising: '*Ui Part Two*, spain/munich/poland/france'. The real scale of Hitler's triumphs remains only as a prophetic threat.

.   .   .

Ui was not written for the desk drawer but, said Brecht, 'with the possibility of a production continually before my eyes; and that's the main reason why I so enjoyed it'. And yet only a few months after his arrival in California in July 1941 this possibility somehow slid out of reach, to be relegated to a remote corner of the back of his mind. What happened was that, having already failed to find any takers for Reyher's translation of the *Fear and Misery* scenes (under the title *The Devil's Sunday*), he almost at once proposed the new play to Piscator in New York with the suggestion that Oscar Homolka, then finding few satisfactory parts in Hollywood, should play the title part. Piscator and Hanns Eisler together persuaded H. R. Hays to make a rapid translation, arguing that they had got trade union support for a production. The translation was done by the end of September, and the script sent off to Louis Shaffer, director of Labor Stage. Shaffer however (in a letter quoted by James Lyon in *Brecht in America*) turned it down, saying, 'I gave the play to several people to read, and the opinion is, including my own, that it is not advisable to produce it.'

This was of course before the United States entered the war, and in any case Hays was doubtful about giving the play to Piscator at all, and warned Brecht with some justification that his old colleague's first New York productions had been far from successful. However, as it turned out, the money was never raised; Hays lost interest when Brecht gave up answering his letters; and Brecht, though at some point he evidently resumed his revision of the play, soon put it away and seemingly forgot it. Only a cutting in his journal for January 1942 recalls his interest: this reproduced a cartoon captioned 'Murder Inc.', with Hitler as a gangster, smoking pistol in his hand, followed by his henchmen 'The Monk' and 'Benny the Fat'. 'See *Rise of Arturo Ui*!' says a handwritten note by Brecht, who also gummed the picture into his own copy of the script.

There the matter rested for the next ten years or so. There is no sign of any further interest in an English-language production, and the question of a German one still did not arise. For the only theatre which might have wished to put the play on in the war years was the Zurich Schauspielhaus, and for that company, with its large complement of refugee German actors, it would have been politically impossible: there is no evidence that Brecht ever bothered to submit it. Nor would he have trusted any postwar German theatre company to stage a play on such a sensitive subject except under his own direction, even supposing that he had thought its satire appropriate to the immediate aftermath of defeat. So there was no question of bringing the play out again until after his return to Germany and the setting up of the Berliner Ensemble in 1949, and even then there were at least half-a-dozen other major plays which he wanted to stage himself and get properly established first. *Ui* was a problematic work, near the bottom of a very substantial pile. No part of it had been published in any form or discussed in the press, and not many people can even have known of its existence.

He first seems to have dug it out and shown it to a slightly wider circle in the second half of 1953: a time when the events of 17 June – the street riots in Berlin and the intervention of the Russian tanks – had forced him to take stock of his country with its Nazi survivals and Communist mistakes. That autumn he wrote the cycle of short, closely compressed 'Buckow Elegies', balancing half-veiled criticisms of the continuing Stalinism of the regime against uncomfortable glimpses of the Nazi heritage, seen in the shifty attitude of the village tradespeople, the military walk, the sudden upraised arm. It was in such a mood of renewed suspicion of his own people that he discussed the script with a group of writers along the lines suggested on pp. 357–358 and also (we don't quite know when) found himself explaining to his younger collaborators – dramaturgs and directors – why he did not think that it could yet be performed. His feeling, in effect, was that they were not mature enough to stand seeing Hitler mocked; the old sentiments were still too close to the surface. He told them that *Fear and Misery of the Third Reich* would have to be shown first: in other words that they could not stage *Ui* until they and their audience had taken the trouble to see exactly what they were mocking.

Early in 1957 five of the Ensemble's young assistant directors – Peter Palitzsch, Lothar Bellag, Käthe Rülicke, Carl Weber and the Pole Konrad Swinarski – staged scenes from *Fear and Misery of the Third Reich* against projections of historical photographs. The following year Palitzsch directed *Ui*'s world première in Stuttgart, West Germany, provoking his Ensemble colleague Manfred Wekwerth to the criticisms here reprinted on pp. 359–62: there was also a very interesting review by the leading West German critic Siegfried Melchinger which called the play 'a brilliant miscarriage' and took up the East German writer's point that the German people had been omitted, but then stood this argument on its head by complaining that Brecht had failed to show how a majority of them had voted Hitler into power; i.e. how *Ui* was not a mere creature of the trusts.

Four months later the Ensemble launched its own trumphal production – one of its outstanding box-office successes, and the first real demonstration of Brecht's continuing vitality after 1956 – with Palitzsch and Wekwerth as co-directors. This was staged in fairground style, with ruthless verve and brassy vulgarity, and it centred on one of

the great acting performances of the past thirty-five years: Ekkehard
Schall's clowning, acrobatic yet chillingly serious interpretation of the
ghastly red-eyed, mackintoshed ham rhetorician Arturo Ui. Seen in
Berlin, London and the Paris International Theatre Festival, it was
one of the great proofs of Brecht's theatricality, for nobody reading the
play, with its crude and obviously rather dated mockery of such
(happily) defunct mass-murderers, could imagine that it would be so
amusing, let alone so compelling to watch. And yet it caught the
spectator up and propelled him along the curves and gradients of its
rickety-looking structure, for all the world like a giant switchback.
The experience was inspiring: theatres and television channels in one
country after another tried to emulate it, as a succession of outstanding
actors tackled the Ui role: Leonard Rossiter and Antony Sher on stage
and Nicol Williamson on television in Britain, Jean Vilar in Paris,
John Bell in Sydney, Christopher Plummer and Al Pacino in the
United States. Who would have thought the old man had so much
blood in him?

.   .   .

Whether Brecht himself would have approved of the play's delayed
success is another matter. Always liable to say the unexpected yet
blindingly obvious, he might well have been disconcerted by the
happy relief with which middle-class audiences everywhere fell on this
apparent evidence that the monsters who fifty years ago quite truly
'almost won the world' were only overgrown mobsters after all,
something to laugh at and forget. Brecht had wanted to make his
spectators feel uncomfortable, even as they noted the ridiculous
disproportion between the stature of the Nazi leaders and the scale of
their crimes; but certainly his play never achieved this in anything like
the same measure as such inferior pieces of writing as *Holocaust* and
The Diary of Anne Frank; moreover the parable might be expected to
lose its sting progressively as the real-life events on which it reposes
fade from the public mind. This is the dilemma facing any would-be
director of *The Resistible Rise of Arturo Ui* today: he may be able to
make a powerful theatrical event of it, but as he looks at Brecht's
ingeniously self-justificatory notes on pp. 355–8 he is likely – if he has
any kind of political conscience – to wonder whether it is nowadays
possible to make it anything more.

The objects of Brecht's satire are dead, and neither their surviving
followers nor their more ignorant imitators have been able to recreate
anything resembling their reign. For whatever we may think of the
reactionary regimes still to be found in the civilised world today no

great technologically and administratively advanced country is now open to the unchecked rule of demagogues propelled by expansionist ambition and what the Nazis termed 'thinking with one's blood'. Modern right-wing or totalitarian governments are not in the same league as Hitler's Reich. But what does live on is the mindless violence of the hoodlum, which has now spread a great deal further within those very societies, to haunt the football terraces, the film and television screens and the imaginations of the elderly, sometimes gratuitously, sometimes under the guise of legitimate social or political grievance.

So the alienating devices can change their function, as Brecht's big plays come to convey a very different message from the one they were planned to carry. *Galileo* becomes a defence of sceptical human reason against imposed systems of thought; *Ui* a blasting attack on the banal irrationality which can lead in certain circumstances to psychopathic government. Such works in other words are continually shifting in relation to our times; they are still in motion. In that sense they do indeed seem like the dispersed fragments of some great explosion which took place about fifty years ago. But at the moment they may still be tending to come together again.

THE EDITORS

Chronology

1898   10 February: Eugen Berthold Friedrich Brecht born in Augsburg.
1917   Autumn: Bolshevik revolution in Russia. Brecht to Munich university.
1918   Work on his first play, *Baal*. In Augsburg Brecht is called up as medical orderly till end of year. Elected to Soldiers' Council as Independent Socialist (USPD) following Armistice.
1919   Brecht writing second play *Drums in the Night*. In January Spartacist Rising in Berlin. Rosa Luxemburg murdered. April–May: Bavarian Soviet. Summer: Weimer Republic constituted. Birth of Brecht's illegitimate son Frank Banholzer.
1920   May: death of Brecht's mother in Augsburg.
1921   Brecht leaves university without a degree. Reads Rimbaud.
1922   A turning point in the arts. End of utopian Expressionism; new concern with technology. Brecht's first visit to Berlin, seeing theatres, actors, publishers and cabaret. He writes 'Of Poor BB' on the return journey. Autumn: becomes a dramaturg in Munich. Première of *Drums in the Night*, a prize-winning national success. Marries Marianne Zoff, an opera singer.
1923   Galloping German inflation stabilised by November currency reform. In Munich Hitler's new National Socialist party stages unsuccessful 'beer-cellar putsch'.
1924   'Neue Sachlichkeit' exhibition at Mannheim gives its name to the new sobriety in the arts. Brecht to Berlin as assistant in Max Reinhardt's Deutsches Theater.
1925   Field-Marshal von Hindenburg becomes President. Elisabeth Hauptmann starts working with Brecht. Two seminal films: Chaplin's *The Gold Rush* and Eisenstein's *The Battleship Potemkin*. Brecht writes birthday tribute to Bernard Shaw.
1926   Première of *Man equals Man* in Darmstadt. Now a freelance; starts reading Marx. His first book of poems, the *Devotions*, includes the 'Legend of the Dead Soldier'.
1927   After reviewing the poems and a broadcast of *Man equals Man*, Kurt Weill approaches Brecht for a libretto. Result is the text

of *Mahagonny*, whose 'Songspiel' version is performed in a boxing-ring at Hindemith's Baden-Baden music festival in July. In Berlin he helps adapt *The Good Soldier Schweik* for Piscator's high-tech theatre.

1928   August 31: première of *The Threepenny Opera* by Brecht and Weill, based on Gay's *The Beggar's Opera*.

1929   Start of Stalin's policy of 'socialism in one country'. Divorced from Marianne, Brecht now marries the actress Helene Weigel. May 1: Berlin police break up banned KPD demonstration, witnessed by Brecht. Summer: Brecht writes two didactic music-theatre pieces with Weill and Hindemith, and neglects *The Threepenny Opera*'s successor *Happy End*, which is a flop. From now on he stands by the KPD. Autumn: Wall Street crash initiates world economic crisis. Cuts in German arts budgets combine with renewed nationalism to create cultural backlash.

1930   Nazi election successes; end of parliamentary government. Unemployed 3 million in first quarter, about 5 million at end of the year. March: première of the full-scale *Mahagonny* opera in Leipzig Opera House.

1931   German crisis intensifies. Aggressive KPD arts policy: agitprop theatre, marching songs, political photomontage. In Moscow the Comintern forms international associations of revolutionary artists, writers, musicians and theatre people.

1932   Première of Brecht's agitational play *The Mother* (after Gorky) with Eisler's music. *Kuhle Wampe*, his militant film with Eisler, is held up by the censors. He meets Sergei Tretiakov at the film's première in Moscow. Summer: the Nationalist Von Papen is made Chancellor. He denounces 'cultural bolshevism', and deposes the SPD-led Prussian administration.

1933   January 30: Hitler becomes Chancellor with Papen as his deputy. The Prussian Academy is purged; Goering becomes Prussian premier. A month later the Reichstag is burnt down, the KPD outlawed. The Brechts instantly leave via Prague; at first homeless. Eisler is in Vienna, Weill in Paris, where he agrees to compose a ballet with song texts by Brecht: *The Seven Deadly Sins*, premièred there in June. In Germany Nazi students burn books; all parties and trade unions banned; first measures against the Jews. Summer: Brecht in Paris works on anti-Nazi publications. With the advance on his *Threepenny Novel*, he buys a house on Fyn island, Denmark, overlooking the Svendborg Sound, where the family will spend the next six years. Margarete Steffin, a young Berlin Communist, goes with them. Autumn: he meets the Danish Communist actress Ruth Berlau, a doctor's wife.

1934   Spring: suppression of Socialist rising in Austria. Eisler stays with Brecht to work on *Round Heads and Pointed Heads* songs. Summer: Brecht misses the first Congress of Soviet Writers, chaired by Zhdanov along the twin lines of Socialist Realism and Revolutionary Romanticism. October: in London with Eisler.

1935   Italy invades Ethiopia. Hitler enacts the Nuremberg Laws against the Jews. March–May: Brecht to Moscow for international theatre conference. Meets Kun and Knorin of Comintern Executive. Eisler becomes president of the International Music Bureau. At the 7th Comintern Congress Dimitrov calls for all antifascist parties to unite in Popular Fronts against Hitler and Mussolini. Autumn: Brecht with Eisler to New York for Theatre Union production of *The Mother*.

1936   Soviet purges lead to arrests of many Germans in USSR, most of them Communists; among them Carola Neher and Ernst Ottwalt, friends of the Brechts. International cultural associations closed down. Official campaign against 'Formalism' in the arts. Mikhail Koltsov, the Soviet journalist, founds *Das Wort* as a literary magazine for the German emigration, with Brecht as one of the editors. Popular Front government in Spain resisted by Franco and other generals, with the support of the Catholic hierarchy. The Spanish Civil War becomes a great international cause.

1937   Summer: in Munich, opening of Hitler's House of German Art. Formally, the officially approved art is closely akin to Russian 'Socialist Realism'. In Russia Tretiakov is arrested as a Japanese spy, interned in Siberia and later shot. October: Brecht's Spanish war play *Señora Carrar's Rifles*, with Weigel in the title part, is performed in Paris, and taken up by antifascist and amateur groups in many countries.

1938   January: in Moscow Meyerhold's avant-garde theatre is abolished. March: Hitler takes over Austria without resistance. It becomes part of Germany. May 21: première of scenes from Brecht's *Fear and Misery of the Third Reich* in a Paris hall. Autumn: Munich Agreement, by which Britain, France and Italy force Czechoslovakia to accept Hitler's demands. In Denmark Brecht writes the first version of *Galileo*. In Moscow Koltsov disappears into arrest after returning from Spain.

1939   March: Hitler takes over Prague and the rest of the Czech
territories. Madrid surrenders to Franco; end of the Civil War.
Eisler has emigrated to New York. April: the Brechts leave
Denmark for Stockholm. Steffin follows. May: Brecht's
Svendborg Poems published. His father dies in Germany.
Denmark accepts Hitler's offer of a Non-Aggression Pact.
August 23: Ribbentrop and Molotov agree Nazi-Soviet Pact.
September 1: Hitler attacks Poland and unleashes Second
World War. Stalin occupies Eastern Poland, completing its
defeat in less than three weeks. All quiet in the West.
Autumn: Brecht writes *Mother Courage* and the radio play
Lucullus in little over a month. November: Stalin attacks
Finland.

1940   Spring: Hitler invades Norway and Denmark. In May his
armies enter France through the Low Countries, taking Paris
in mid-June. The Brechts hurriedly leave for Finland, taking
Steffin with them. They aim to travel on to the US, where
Brecht has been offered a teaching job in New York at the New
School. July: the Finnish writer Hella Wuolijoki invites them
to her country estate, which becomes the setting for *Puntila*,
the comedy she and Brecht write there.

1941   April: première of *Mother Courage* in Zurich. May: he gets US
visas for the family and a tourist visa for Steffin. On 15th they
leave with Berlau for Moscow to take the Trans-Siberian
railway. In Vladivostok they catch a Swedish ship for Los
Angeles, leaving just nine days before Hitler, in alliance with
Finland, invades Russia. June: Steffin dies of tuberculosis in a
Moscow sanatorium, where they have had to leave her. July:
once in Los Angeles, the Brechts decide to stay there in the
hope of film work. December: Japanese attack on Pearl Harbor
brings the US into the war. The Brechts become 'enemy
aliens'.

1942   Spring: Eisler arrives from New York. He and Brecht work on
Fritz Lang's film *Hangmen Also Die*. Brecht and Feuchtwanger
write *The Visions of Simone Machard*; sell rights to MGM. Ruth
Berlau takes a job in New York. August: the Brechts rent a
pleasant house and garden in Santa Monica. Autumn: Germans defeated at Stalingrad and El Alamein. Turning point of
World War 2.

1943   Spring: Brecht goes to New York for three months – first visit
since 1935 – where he stays with Berlau till May and plans a
wartime *Schweik* play with Kurt Weill. In Zurich the Schau-

spielhaus gives world premières of *The Good Person of Szechwan* and *Galileo*. November: his first son Frank is killed on the Russian front.

1944   British and Americans land in Normandy (June); Germans driven out of France by end of the year. Heavy bombing of Berlin, Hamburg and other German cities. Brecht works on *The Caucasian Chalk Circle*, and with H.R. Hays on *The Duchess of Malfi*. His son by Ruth Berlau, born prematurely in Los Angeles, lives only a few days. Start of collaboration with Charles Laughton on English version of *Galileo*.

1945   Spring: Russians enter Vienna and Berlin. German surrender; suicide of Hitler; Allied military occupation of Germany and Austria, each divided into four Zones. Roosevelt dies; succeeded by Truman; Churchill loses elections to Attlee. June: *Private Life of the Master Race* (wartime adaptation of *Fear and Misery* scenes) staged in New York. August: US drops atomic bombs on Hiroshima and Nagasaki. Japan surrenders. Brecht and Laughton start discussing production of *Galileo*.

1946   Ruth Berlau taken to hospital after a violent breakdown in New York. Work with Auden on *Duchess of Malfi*, which is finally staged there in mid-October – not well received. The Brechts have decided to return to Germany. Summer: A.A. Zhdanov reaffirms Stalinist art policies: Formalism bad, Socialist Realism good. Eisler's brother Gerhart summoned to appear before the House Un-American Activities Committee. November: the Republicans win a majority in the House. Cold War impending.

1947   FBI file on Brecht reopened in May. Rehearsals begin for Los Angeles production of *Galileo*, with Laughton in the title part and music by Eisler; opens July 31. Brecht's HUAC hearing October 30; a day later he leaves the US for Zurich.

1948   In Zurich renewed collaboration with Caspar Neher. Production of *Antigone* in Chur, with Weigel. Berlau arrives from US. Summer: *Puntila* world première at Zurich Schauspielhaus. Brecht completes his chief theoretical work, the *Short Organum*. Travel plans hampered because he is not allowed to enter US Zone (which includes Augsburg and Munich). Russians block all land access to Berlin. October: the Brechts to Berlin via Prague, to establish contacts and prepare production of *Mother Courage*.

1949   January: success of *Mother Courage* leads to establishment of the Berliner Ensemble. Collapse of Berlin blockade in May followed by establishment of West and East German states. Eisler, Dessau and Elisabeth Hauptmann arrive from US and join the Ensemble.

1950 Brecht gets Austrian nationality in connection with plan to involve him in Salzburg Festival. Long drawn-out scheme for *Mother Courage* film. Spring: he and Neher direct Lenz's *The Tutor* with the Ensemble. Autumn: he directs *Mother Courage* in Munich; at the end of the year *The Mother* with Weigel, Ernst Busch and the Ensemble.

1951 Selection of *A Hundred Poems* is published in East Berlin. Brecht beats off Stalinist campaign to stop production of Dessau's opera version of *Lucullus*.

1952 Summer: at Buckow, east of Berlin, Brecht starts planning a production of *Coriolanus* and discusses Eisler's project for a *Faust* opera.

1953 Spring: Stalin dies, aged 73. A 'Stanislavsky conference' in the East German Academy, to promote Socialist Realism in the theatre, is followed by meetings to discredit Eisler's libretto for the *Faust* opera. June: quickly suppressed rising against the East German government in Berlin and elsewhere. Brecht at Buckow notes that 'the whole of existence has been alienated' for him by this. Khrushchev becomes Stalin's successor.

1954 January: Brecht becomes an adviser to the new East German Ministry of Culture. March: the Ensemble at last gets its own theatre on the Schiffbauerdamm. July: its production of *Mother Courage* staged in Paris. December: Brecht awarded a Stalin Peace Prize by the USSR.

1955 August: Shooting at last begins on *Mother Courage* film, but is broken off after ten days and the project abandoned. Brecht in poor health.

1956 Khrushchev denounces Stalin's dictatorial methods and abuses of power to the Twentieth Party Congress in Moscow. A copy of his speech reaches Brecht. May: Brecht in the Charité hospital to shake off influenza. August 14: he dies in the Charité of a heart infarct.

1957 *The Resistible Rise of Arturo Ui*, *The Visions of Simone Machard* and *Schweyk in the Second World War* produced for the first time in Stuttgart, Frankfurt and Warsaw respectively.

The Good Person of Szechwan
A parable play

Collaborators: R. BERLAU AND M. STEFFIN

Music: PAUL DESSAU

Translator: JOHN WILLETT

Written in 1938–41. First produced in the Zürich Schauspielhaus on 4 February 1943

Characters
WANG, *a water-seller*
SHEN TEH-SHUI TA
YANG SUN, *an unemployed airman*
MRS YANG, *his mother*
MRS SHIN, *a widow*
THE FAMILY OF EIGHT
LIN TO, *a carpenter*
MRS MI TZU, *a property owner*
THE POLICEMAN
THE CARPET-DEALER AND HIS WIFE
THE YOUNG PROSTITUTE
SHU FU, *the barber*
THE PRIEST
THE UNEMPLOYED MAN
THE WAITER
Passers-by of the Prologue

Prologue

A Street in the Capital of Szechwan

It is evening. Wang, the water-seller, introduces himself to the audience.

WANG: I am a water-seller in the capital of Szechwan province. My job is tedious. When water is short I have to go far for it. And when it is plentiful I earn nothing. But utter poverty is the rule in our province. All agree that only the gods can help us. To my inexpressible joy a widely-travelled cattle dealer has told me that some of the highest gods are already on their way, and that Szechwan may see them too. They say that the heavens are deeply disturbed by the many complaints that have been going up. For the last three days I have waited at this entrance to the city, especially towards evening, so that I may be the first to greet them. There will hardly be a chance for me later; they will be surrounded by important people and there will be far too many demands on them. But shall I be able to recognise them? They may not arrive in a group. Perhaps they will come singly, so as not to attract attention. It cannot be those men – *he studies some workmen passing by* – they are coming away from work. Their shoulders are bent by the burdens they have to carry. That fellow is no god either, he has inky fingers. At most he may be some kind of clerk in a cement works. I would not take those gentlemen – *two gentlemen walk past* – for gods even: they have the brutal faces of men who beat people, and the gods find that unnecessary. But look at these three! They seem very different. They are well nourished, show no evidence of any kind of employment, and have dust on their shoes, so they must have travelled far. It is them! Yours to command, Illustrious Ones!

He flings himself to the ground.

THE FIRST GOD, *pleased*: Have you been expecting us?

WANG *gives them a drink*: For a long while. But only I knew that you were coming.

THE FIRST GOD: We must find a lodging for tonight. Do you know of one?

WANG: One? Lots! The city is at your service, O Illustrious Ones. Where do you wish to stay?

The gods exchange significant looks.

THE FIRST GOD: Try the first house, my son. Take the very first one first.

WANG: I only fear that I may attract the enmity of the powerful, if I give one of them the preference.

THE FIRST GOD: Then take it as an order: try the first one.

WANG: That's Mr Fo opposite. One moment.

He runs to a house and hammers on the door. It opens, but one can see him being turned away. He comes hesitantly back.

WANG: How stupid. Mr Fo happens to be out just now, and his servants dare not take the responsibility, as he is very strict. Won't he be angry when he finds who has been turned away!

THE GODS, *smiling*: Indeed.

WANG: Another moment then! The house next door is the widow Su's. She will be beside herself with joy.

He runs there, but is apparently turned away once more.

I shall have to ask across the road. She says she has only one very small room, and it's in no fit state. I will go straight to Mr Cheng's.

THE SECOND GOD: But a small room is all we need. Tell her that we are coming.

WANG: Even if it has not been cleaned? Suppose it is crawling with spiders?

THE SECOND GOD: No matter. The more spiders, the fewer flies.

THE THIRD GOD, *in an amiable way*: Try Mr Cheng or anybody else you like, my son. I admit I find spiders a little unattractive.

Wang knocks at another door and is admitted.

A VOICE FROM THE HOUSE: Get away with your gods! We've got enough troubles of our own.

WANG, *returning to the gods*: Mr Cheng is extremely sorry, he has his whole house full of relatives and dare not appear before you, Illustrious Ones. Between ourselves, I think there are evil men among them whom he would prefer you not to see. He is much too frightened of your judgement. That must be it.

THE THIRD GOD: Are we all that frightening?

WANG: Only to evil people, isn't it? We all know that Kwan province has suffered from floods for years.

THE SECOND GOD: Oh? And why is that?

WANG: Because they are not god-fearing people, I suppose.

THE SECOND GOD: Rubbish. Because they didn't look after the dam properly.

THE FIRST GOD: Sh! *To Wang*: Any other prospects, my son?

WANG: How can you ask? I have only to go to the next house, and I can have my pick. They are all falling over each other to entertain you. An unlucky combination of circumstances, you understand. Half a minute.

He walks away hesitantly and stands in the street unable to make up his mind.

THE SECOND GOD: What did I tell you?

THE THIRD GOD: It may just be circumstances.

THE SECOND GOD: Circumstances in Shun, circumstances in Kwan, and now circumstances in Szechwan. There are no god-fearing people left: that is the naked truth which you will not recognize. Our mission is hopeless, and you had better admit it.

THE FIRST GOD: We may still come across good people at any moment. We cannot expect to have things all our own way.

THE THIRD GOD: The resolution says: the world can go on as it is if we find enough good people, able to lead a decent human existence. The water-seller himself is such a person, if I am not deceived.

He goes up to Wang, who is still standing uncertain.

THE SECOND GOD: He is always deceived. When the water man let us drink out of his measure I saw something. Look. *He shows it to the first god.*

THE FIRST GOD: It has got a false bottom.

THE SECOND GOD: A swindler.

THE FIRST GOD: Very well, we strike him out. But what does it matter if one man is corrupted? We shall soon find plenty who fulfil the conditions. We must find someone. For two thousand years we have been hearing the same complaint, that the world cannot go on as it is. No one can stay on earth and remain good. We must at last be able to show some people who are in a position to keep our commandments.

THE THIRD GOD, *to Wang*: Is it too difficult for you to find us a place?

WANG: Such guests as you? What are you thinking of? It is my fault that you were not taken in immediately; I am a bad guide.

THE THIRD GOD: Not that, certainly.

He turns back to the others.

WANG: They have begun to realise. *He accosts a gentleman*: Honoured sir, forgive me for addressing you, but three of the highest gods, whose impending advent has been the talk of all Szechwan for years, have now really arrived and are looking for a place to spend the night. Don't walk away. Look for yourself. One glance will convince you. For heaven's sake do something about it. It's the chance of a lifetime! Invite the gods to visit your home before someone else snaps them up; they are sure to accept.

The gentleman has walked on. Wang turns to another.

You, sir, you heard what it's about. Have you any room? It needn't be palatial. The intention is what matters.

THE GENTLEMAN: How am I to tell what sort of gods yours are? Heaven knows who I might be letting into my house. *He goes into a tobacconist's. Wang runs back to the three.*

WANG: I have found somebody who is sure to take you.

He sees his measure on the ground, looks embarrassedly at the gods, picks it up and runs back again.

THE FIRST GOD: That does not sound encouraging.

WANG, *as the man steps out of the shop*: What about the accommodation?

THE GENTLEMAN: How do you know I'm not living in rooms myself?

THE FIRST GOD: He will find nothing. We had better write Szechwan off too.

WANG: It's three of the chief gods. Truly. Their images in the temples are just like them. If you get your invitation in now they might perhaps accept.

THE GENTLEMAN *laughs*: I suppose they're a lot of prize swindlers you're trying to foist off on someone.

Off.

WANG, *shouting after him*: You swivel-eyed chiseller! Have you no reverence? You'll all roast in brimstone for your lack of interest. The gods crap on the lot of you. And you'll be sorry for it. You shall pay for it unto the fourth generation. You have disgraced the whole province. *Pause.* That leaves us with Shen Teh the prostitute; she can't refuse.

He calls 'Shen Teh!' Shen Teh looks out of the window above.

They've arrived, and I can't find them a room. Could you possibly have them for one night?

SHEN TEH: Not much hope, Wang. I am expecting someone. But how is it that you can't find a room for them?

WANG: I can't explain now. Szechwan is nothing but one big muck-heap.

SHEN TEH: I should have to hide when he arrives. Then he might go away. He was supposed to be taking me out.

WANG: Can we come up in the meantime?

SHEN TEH: If you don't talk too loudly. Do I have to be careful what I say?

WANG: Very. They mustn't find out how you earn your living.

We had better wait downstairs. But you won't be going off with him, will you?

SHEN TEH: I've had no luck lately, and if I can't find the rent by tomorrow they'll throw me out.

WANG: You shouldn't think of money at a moment like this.

SHEN TEH: I don't know: I'm afraid that a rumbling stomach is no respecter of persons. But very well, I will take them in.

She is seen to put out her light.

THE FIRST GOD: It looks hopeless to me.

They go up to Wang.

WANG, *startled to see them standing behind him*: You are fixed up for the night.

He wipes the sweat off his face.

THE GODS: Really? Then let us go.

WANG: There is no great hurry. Take your time. The room is not quite ready.

THE THIRD GOD: Very good, we will sit here and wait.

WANG: But isn't there too much traffic here? Let's cross the road.

THE SECOND GOD: We like looking at people. That is exactly what we came for.

WANG: It's a windy spot.

THE THIRD GOD: Does this seem all right to you?

They sit on a doorstep. Wang sits on the ground somewhat to one side.

WANG, *with a rush*: You are lodging with a girl who lives on her own. She is the best person in Szechwan.

THE THIRD GOD: That is gratifying.

WANG, *to the audience*: When I picked up my mug just then they gave me a peculiar look. Do you think they noticed anything? I daren't look them in the face any longer.

THE THIRD GOD: You seem exhausted.

WANG: A little. I have been running.

THE FIRST GOD: Do people here find life very hard?

WANG: Good people do.

THE FIRST GOD, *seriously*: Do you?

WANG: I know what you mean. I am not good. But I too find life hard.

Meanwhile a gentleman has appeared in front of Shen Teh's house and whistled a number of times. Each time Wang gives a nervous jerk.

THE THIRD GOD, *in an undertone to Wang*: It looks as if he has given up.

WANG, *confused*: It does.

He jumps up and runs into the open, leaving his carrying-pole behind. But the following has occurred: the man waiting has gone off and Sheh Teh, after opening the door quietly and calling 'Wang!' in a low voice, has gone down the street in search of Wang. When Wang in turn calls 'Shen Teh!' in a low voice he gets no reply.

WANG: She has let me down. She has gone off to get the money for the rent, and I have no place for the Illustrious Ones. They are waiting there, exhausted. I cannot go back yet again and tell them: no good, sorry. My own sleeping place under the culvert is out of the question. And I am sure the gods would not care to lodge with a man whose dirty business they have seen through. I would not go back for anything in the world. But my carrying-pole is still there. What shall I do? I dare not fetch it. I shall leave the capital and find somewhere where I can hide from their eyes, for I failed to do anything to help those I honour.

He hurries away. As soon as he has gone, Shen Teh returns, searches for him on the opposite side and sees the gods.

SHEN TEH: Are you the Illustrious Ones? My name is Shen Teh. I should be happy if you consented to make do with my small room.

THE THIRD GOD: But where has the water-seller disappeared to?

SHEN TEH: I must have missed him.

THE FIRST GOD: He probably thought you were not coming, and then felt too scared to come back to us.

THE THIRD GOD *picks up the carrying-pole*: We will ask you to look after it. He needs it.

They enter the house led by Shen Teh. It grows dusk, then light again. In the half-light of the dawn the gods again leave the door, led by Shen Teh guiding them with a lantern. They take their leave.

THE FIRST GOD: Dear Shen Teh, we are grateful for your hospitality. We shall not forget that it was you who took us in. Will you give the water-seller his pole back? And tell him that we are grateful to him too for having shown us a good person.

SHEN TEH: I am not good. I have an admission to make: when Wang asked me if I could shelter you I had hesitations.

THE FIRST GOD: Hesitations do not count if you overcome them. Know that you gave us more than a lodging. There are many, including even certain of us gods, who have begun to doubt whether such a thing as a good person still exists. To check up was the main object of our journey. We are now happy to continue it, for we have succeeded in finding one. Farewell.

SHEN TEH: Wait, Illustrious Ones. I am by no means sure that I am good. I should certainly like to be, but how am I to pay the rent? Let me admit: I sell myself in order to live, and even so I cannot manage, for there are so many forced to do this. I would take on anything, but who would not? Of course I should like to obey the commandments: to honour my parents and respect the truth. Not to covet my neighbour's house would be a joy to me, and to love, honour and cherish a husband would be very pleasant. Nor do I wish to exploit other men or to rob the defenceless. But how can it be done? Even by breaking one or two of the commandments I can barely manage.

THE FIRST GOD: All these, Shen Teh, are but the doubts of a good person.

THE THIRD GOD: Goodbye, Shen Teh. And give our warmest greetings to the water-seller. He was a good friend to us.

THE SECOND GOD: I fear we did but little good to him.

THE THIRD GOD: The best of luck.

THE FIRST GOD: Above all, be good, Shen Teh. Goodbye.

They turn to go. They begin to wave goodbye.

SHEN TEH, *nervously*: But I am not certain of myself, Illustrious Ones. How can I be good when everything is so expensive?

THE SECOND GOD: Alas, that is beyond our powers. We cannot meddle in the sphere of economics.

THE THIRD GOD: Wait! Just a minute. If she were better provided she might stand more chance.

THE SECOND GOD: We cannot give her anything. We could not answer for it up there.

THE FIRST GOD: Why not?

They put their heads together and confer animatedly.

THE FIRST GOD, *awkwardly, to Shen Teh*: We understand that you have no money for the rent. We are not poor people, so it is natural that we should pay for our lodging. Here you are. *He gives her money.* But please let nobody know that we paid. It might be misinterpreted.

THE SECOND GOD: Only too easily.

THE THIRD GOD: No, it is permissible. We can quite well pay for our lodging. There was nothing against it in the resolution. So fare you well.

The gods exeunt rapidly.

I

A small Tobacconist's

The shop is not yet properly installed, and not yet open.

SHEN TEH, *to the audience*: It is now three days since the gods left. They told me they wanted to pay for their lodgings. And when I looked at what they had given me I saw that it was more than a thousand silver dollars. I have used the money to buy a tobacconist's business. I moved in here yesterday, and now I hope to be able to do a great deal of good. Look at Mrs Shin, for instance, the old owner of the shop. Yesterday she came to ask for rice for her children. And today I again see her bringing her pot across the square. *Enter Mrs Shin. The women bow to one another.*

SHEN TEH: Good evening, Mrs Shin.

MRS SHIN: Good evening, Miss Shen Teh. What do you think of your new home?

SHEN TEH: I like it. How did the children spend the night?

MRS SHIN: Oh, in someone's house, if you can call that shack a house. The baby's started coughing.

SHEN TEH: That's bad.

MRS SHIN: You don't know what's bad. You've got it good. But you'll find plenty to learn in a dump like this. The whole district's a slum.

SHEN TEH: That is right what you told me, though? That the cement workers call in here at midday?

MRS SHIN: But not a customer otherwise, not even the locals.

SHEN TEH: You didn't tell me that when you sold me the business.

MRS SHIN: That's right: throw it in my face. First you take the roof away over the children's heads, and then it's nothing but dump and slum. It's more than I can bear.
She weeps.

SHEN TEH, *quickly*: I'll get your rice.

MRS SHIN: I was going to ask you if you could lend me some money.

SHEN TEH, *as she pours rice into her bowl*: I can't do that. I haven't sold anything yet.

MRS SHIN: But I need it. What am I to live on? You've taken everything I've got. Now you're cutting my throat. I'll leave my children on your door-step, you bloodsucker!
She snatches the pot from her hands.

SHEN TEH: Don't be so bad-tempered. You'll spill your rice.
Enter an elderly couple and a shabbily dressed man.

THE WOMAN: Ah, Shen Teh, my dear, we heard you were doing so nicely now. Why, you've set up in business! Just fancy, we're without a home. Our tobacconist's shop has folded up. We wondered if we mightn't spend a night with you. You know my nephew? He can't abide being separated from us.

THE NEPHEW, *looking round*: Smashing shop.

MRS SHIN: Who's this lot?

SHEN TEH: When I arrived here from the country they were my first landlords. *To the audience*: When my small funds ran out they threw me on the street. They are probably frightened that I will say no. They are poor.

They have no shelter.
They have no friends.
They need someone.
How can they be refused?

Addressing the woman in a friendly voice: Welcome to you, I will gladly give you lodging. But all I have is a tiny room at the back of the shop.

THE MAN: That'll do us. Don't you worry. *While Shen Teh fetches them tea*: We'd better move in behind here, so as not to be in your way. I suppose you picked on a tobacconist's to remind you of your first home? We'll be able to give you one or two tips. That's another reason for coming to you.

MRS SHIN, *sardonically*: Let's hope one or two customers come too.

THE WOMAN: Is that meant for us?

THE MAN: Sh. Here's a customer already.

Enter a tattered man.

THE UNEMPLOYED MAN: Excuse me, miss, I'm out of a job.

Mrs Shin laughs.

SHEN TEH: What can I do for you?

THE UNEMPLOYED MAN: They say you're opening up tomorrow. I thought people sometimes find things in bad condition when they unpack them. Can you spare a fag?

THE WOMAN: What cheek, begging for tobacco. 'Tisn't as if it had been bread.

THE UNEMPLOYED MAN: Bread's expensive. A few puffs at a fag and I'm a new man. I'm so done in.

SHEN TEH *gives him cigarettes*: That's very important, being a new man. I shall open up with you, you'll bring me luck.

The unemployed man hastily lights a cigarette, inhales and goes off coughing.

THE WOMAN: Was that wise, my dear?

MRS SHIN: If that's how you open up you'll be closing down before three days are out.

THE MAN: I bet he had money on him all right.

SHEN TEH: But he said he hadn't anything.

THE NEPHEW: How do you know he wasn't having you on?

SHEN TEH, *worked up*: How do I know he was having me on?

THE WOMAN, *shaking her head*: She can't say no. You're too good, Shen Teh. If you want to hang on to your shop you'd better be able to refuse sometimes.

THE MAN: Say it isn't yours. Say it belongs to a relation and he insists on strict accounts. Why not try it?

MRS SHIN: Anyone would who didn't always want to play Lady Bountiful.

SHEN TEH *laughs*: Grumble away. The room won't be available and the rice goes back in the sack.

THE WOMAN, *shocked*: Is the rice yours too?

SHEN TEH, *to the audience*:
> They are bad.
> They are no man's friend.
> They grudge even a bowl of rice.
> They need it all themselves.
> How can they be blamed?

Enter a little man.

MRS SHIN *sees him and leaves hurriedly*: I'll look in tomorrow then. *Off.*

THE LITTLE MAN *starts after her*: Hey, Mrs Shin! Just the person I want.

THE WOMAN: Does she come regularly? Has she got some claim on you?

SHEN TEH: No claim, but she's hungry: and that's more important.

THE LITTLE MAN: She knows why she's running away. Are you the new proprietress? I see you're stocking up your shelves. But they aren't yours, let me tell you. Unless you pay for them. That old ragamuffin who was squatting here didn't pay. *To the others*: I'm the carpenter, see?

SHEN TEH: But I thought that was part of the fittings I paid for.

THE CARPENTER: Crooks. A pack of crooks. You and this Mrs Shin are thick as thieves. I want my 100 silver dollars, or my name's not Lin To.

SHEN TEH: How can I pay? I've got no money left.

THE CARPENTER: Then I'll have you sold up! On the spot. Pay on the spot or you'll be sold up.

THE MAN *prompts Shen Teh*: Your cousin . . .

SHEN TEH: Can't you make it next month?

THE CARPENTER, *shouting*: No.

SHEN TEH: Don't be too hard, Mr Lin To. I can't satisfy all demands at once. *To the audience*:
> A slight connivance, and one's powers are doubled.

Look how the cart-horse stops before a tuft of grass:
Wink one eye for an instant and the horse pulls better.
Show but a little patience in June and the tree
By August is sagging with peaches. How
But for patience could we live together?
A brief postponement
Brings the most distant goal within reach.

To the carpenter: Please be patient, just a little, Mr Lin To.

THE CARPENTER: And who is going to be patient with me and my family? *He pulls some of the shelving away from the wall, as if to take it down.* You pay, else I take the shelves with me.

THE WOMAN: My dear Shen Teh, why don't you refer the whole thing to your cousin? *To the carpenter*: Put your claim in writing, and Miss Shen Teh's cousin will pay.

THE CARPENTER: We all know those cousins.

THE NEPHEW: Don't stand there laughing like an idiot. He's a personal friend of mine.

THE MAN: He's sharp as a knife.

THE CARPENTER: All right, he'll get my bill.

He tips the shelving over, sits down on it and writes out his bill.

THE WOMAN: He'll have the clothes off your back for his rotten old planks if you don't stop him. My advice is never admit a claim, right or wrong, or you'll be smothered in claims, right or wrong. Throw a bit of meat in your dustbin, and every mongrel in the place will be at each other's throats in your back yard. What are solicitors for?

SHEN TEH: He has done some work and can't go away with nothing. He has a family too. It's dreadful that I can't pay him. What will the gods say?

THE MAN: You did your bit when you took us in, that's more than enough.

Enter a limping man and a pregnant woman.

THE LIMPING MAN, *to the couple*: So there you are. A credit to the family, I don't think. Going and leaving us waiting at the corner.

THE WOMAN, *embarrassed*: This is my brother Wung and my sister-in-law. *To the two*: Stop nagging and sit quietly out of the way, and don't bother our old friend Miss Shen Teh. *To Shen Teh*: We ought to take them both in, I think, what with my sister-in-law being four months gone. Or are you against it?

SHEN TEH: You are welcome.

THE WOMAN: Thank her. The cups are over there. *To Shen Teh*: They would never have known where to go. Just as well you've got this shop.

SHEN TEH, *laughing to the audience as she brings tea*: Yes, just as well I have got it.

Enter Mrs Mi Tzu, the proprietress, with a document in her hand.

MRS MI TZU: Miss Shen Teh, I am Mrs Mi Tzu, the proprietress of this building. I hope we will get on together. Here is the agreement for the lease. *While Shen Teh studies the agreement*: An auspicious moment, do you not think, gentlemen, when a small business is opened? *She looks round her.* A few gaps on the shelves still, but it will do. I suppose you can provide me with one or two references?

SHEN TEH: Is that necessary?

MRS MI TZU: You see, I have really no idea who you are.

THE MAN: Can we vouch for Miss Shen Teh, maybe? We've known her ever since she first came to town, and we'd cut off our right hands for her.

MRS MI TZU: And who are you?

THE MAN: I am Ma Fu, tobacconist.

MRS MI TZU: Where's your shop?

THE MAN: I haven't got a shop at the moment. It's like this: I've just sold it.

MRS MI TZU: Aha. *To Shen Teh*: And is there no one else who can give me any information about you?

THE WOMAN, *prompting*: Cousin . . . your cousin . . .

MRS MI TZU: But you must have someone who can tell me what.

kind of tenant I'm getting in my house. This is a respectable house, my dear. I can't sign any agreement with you otherwise.

SHEN TEH, *slowly, with lowered eyes*: I have got a cousin.

MRS MI TZU: Oh, so you've got a cousin? Round here? We could go straight over now. What is he?

SHEN TEH: He doesn't live here; he's in another town.

THE WOMAN: In Shung, weren't you saying?

SHEN TEH: Mr Shui Ta. In Shung.

THE MAN: But of course I know him. Tall, skinny.

THE NEPHEW, *to the carpenter*: You've had to do with Miss Shen Teh's cousin too, chum. Over the shelving.

THE CARPENTER, *grumpily*: I'm just making out his bill. There you are. *He hands it over.* I'll be back first thing in the morning. *Exit.*

THE NEPHEW, *calling after him, for the proprietress's benefit*: Don't you worry. Her cousin will pay.

MRS MI TZU, *with a keen look at Shen Teh*: Well, I shall also be glad to meet him. Good evening, madam. *Exit.*

THE WOMAN, *after an interval*: It's bound to come out now. You can bet she'll know all about you by the morning.

THE SISTER-IN-LAW, *quietly to the nephew*: This set-up won't last long!

Enter an old man, guided by a boy.

THE BOY, *calling back*: Here they are.

THE WOMAN: Hello, grandpa. *To Shen Teh*: The dear old man. He must have been worrying about us. And the youngster, look how he's grown. He eats like an ostrich. Who else have you got with you?

THE MAN, *looking out*: Only your niece. *To Shen Teh*: A young relation up from the country. I hope we aren't too many for you. We weren't such a big family when you used to live with us, were we? Ah yes, we grew and grew. The worse it got, the more of us there seemed to be. And the more of us there were the worse it got. But we'd better lock up or we'll have no peace.

She shuts the door and all sit down.

THE WOMAN: The great thing is, we mustn't get in your way in the shop. It's up to you to keep the home fires burning. We planned it like this: the kids'll be out during the day, and only grandpa and my sister-in-law will stay, and perhaps me. The others will just be looking in once or twice during the daytime, see? Light that lamp, boys, and make yourselves at home.

THE NEPHEW, *facetiously*: I hope that cousin doesn't blow in tonight, tough old Mr Shui Ta! *The sister-in-law laughs.*

THE BROTHER, *reaching for a cigarette*: One more or less won't matter.

THE MAN: You bet.

They all help themselves to something to smoke. The brother hands round a jug of wine.

THE NEPHEW: Drinks on old cousin!

THE GRANDFATHER, *solemnly to Shen Teh*: Hullo!

Shen Teh is confused by this delayed greeting, and bows. In one hand she holds the carpenter's bill, in the other the agreement for the lease.

THE WOMAN: Can't you people sing something to entertain our hostess?

THE NEPHEW: Grandpa can kick off.

They sing:

SONG OF THE SMOKE

THE GRANDFATHER:

> Once I believed intelligence would aid me
> I was an optimist when I was younger
> Now that I'm old I see it hasn't paid me:
> How can intelligence compete with hunger?
>> And so I said: drop it!
>> Like smoke twisting grey
>> Into ever colder coldness you'll
>> Blow away.

THE MAN:

> I saw the conscientious man get nowhere
> And so I tried the crooked path instead
> But crookedness makes our sort travel slower.
> There seems to be no way to get ahead.
>> Likewise I say: drop it!
>> Like smoke twisting grey
>> Into ever colder coldness you'll
>> Blow away.

THE NIECE:

> The old, they say, find little fun in hoping.
> Time's what they need, and time begins to press.
> But for the young, they say, the gates are open.
> They open, so they say, on nothingness.
>> And I too say: drop it!
>> Like smoke twisting grey
>> Into ever colder coldness you'll
>> Blow away.

THE NEPHEW: Where did that wine come from?

THE SISTER-IN-LAW: He pawned the sack of tobacco.

THE MAN: What? That tobacco was all we had left. We didn't touch it even to get a bed. You dirty bastard!

THE BROTHER: Call me a bastard just because my wife's half frozen? And who's been drinking it? Give me that jug.

They struggle. The shelves collapse.

SHEN TEH *touches them*: O look out for the shop, don't smash everything! It's a gift of the gods. Take whatever's there if you want, but don't smash it!

THE WOMAN, *sceptically*: It's a smaller shop than I thought. A pity we went and told Aunty and the others. If they turn up too there won't be much room.

THE SISTER-IN-LAW: Our hostess is getting a bit frosty too.

There are voices outside, and a knocking on the door.

CRIES: Open up! It's us!

THE WOMAN: Is that you, Aunty? How are we going to manage now?

SHEN TEH: My beautiful shop! Oh, such hopes! No sooner opened, than it is no more. *To the audience*:
   The dinghy which might save us
   Is straightway sucked into the depths:
   Too many of the drowning
   Snatch greedily at it.

CRIES *from outside*: Open up!

Interlude

Under a Bridge
The water-seller is crouching by the stream.

WANG, *looking round*: All quiet. That makes four days I have been hiding. They won't find me, I've got my eyes open. I took the same direction as them on purpose. The second day they crossed the bridge; I heard their footsteps overhead. By now they must be a long way off; I have nothing more to fear.
He has leant back and gone to sleep. Music. The slope becomes transparent, and the gods appear.

WANG, *holding his arm in front of his face, as though he were about to be struck*: Don't say anything! I know! I failed to find anybody who would take you into his house! Now I have told you! Now go your way!

THE FIRST GOD: No, you did find somebody. As you left they came up. They took us in for the night; they watched over our sleep; and they lighted our way next morning when we left them. You had told us that she was a good person, and she was good.

WANG: So it was Shen Teh who lodged you?

THE THIRD GOD: Of course.

WANG: And I ran away, I had so little faith! Just because I thought she couldn't come. Because she had been down on her luck she couldn't come.

THE GODS:

> O feeble one!
> Well-meaning but feeble man!
> Where hardship is, he thinks there is no goodness.
> Where danger lies, he thinks there is no courage.
> O feebleness, that believes no good whatever!
> O hasty judgement! O premature despair!

WANG: I am deeply ashamed, Illustrious Ones.

THE FIRST GOD: And now, O water-seller, be so good as to return quickly to the city and look to dear Shen Teh, so that you can keep us posted about her. She is doing well now. She is said to have acquired the money to set up a small shop, so she can freely follow the impulses of her gentle heart. Show some interest in her goodness, for no one can be good for long if goodness is not demanded of him. We for our part wish to travel further and continue our search, and discover still more people like our good person in Szechwan, so that we can put a stop to the rumour which says that the good have found our earth impossible to live on.

They vanish.

2

The Tobacconist's

Sleeping bodies everywhere. The lamp is still burning. A knock.

THE WOMAN *raises herself, drunk with sleep.* Shen Teh! Somebody knocking! Where has the girl got to?

THE NEPHEW: Getting breakfast, I expect. It's on her cousin. *The women laughs and slouches to the door. Enter a young gentleman, the carpenter behind him.*

THE YOUNG GENTLEMAN: I am her cousin.

THE WOMAN, *falling from the clouds*: What did you say you were?

THE YOUNG GENTLEMAN: My name is Shui Ta.

THE FAMILY, *shaking one another awake*: Her cousin! But it was all a joke, she's got no cousin! But here's someone who says he's her cousin! Don't tell me, and at this hour of the day!

THE NEPHEW: If you're our hostess's cousin, mister, get us some breakfast right away, will you?

SHUI TA, *turning out the lamp*: The first customers will be arriving any moment. Please be quick and get dressed so that I can open up my shop.

THE MAN: Your shop? I fancy this shop belongs to our friend Shen Teh? *Shui Ta shakes his head.* What, do you mean to say it's not her shop at all?

THE SISTER-IN-LAW: So she's been having us on. Where's she slunk off to?

SHUI TA: She has been detained. She wishes me to tell you that now I am here she can no longer do anything for you.

THE WOMAN, *shaken*: And we thought she was such a good person.

THE NEPHEW: Don't you believe him! Go and look for her!

THE MAN: Right, we will. *He organises them*: You and you and you and you, go and comb the place for her. Grandpa and us will stay here and hold the fort. The boy can go and find us something to eat. *To the body*: See that baker's at the corner. Nip over and stuff your shirt full.

THE SISTER-IN-LAW: And don't forget some of those little round cakes.

THE MAN: But mind the baker doesn't catch you. And keep clear of the policeman!

The boy nods and goes off. The others get fully dressed.

SHUI TA: Won't cake-stealing damage the reputation of the shop which has given you refuge?

THE NEPHEW: Don't mind him, we'll soon find her. She'll tell him what's what.

Exeunt nephew, brother, sister-in-law and niece.

THE SISTER-IN-LAW, *as she goes*: Leave us a bit of breakfast.

SHUI TA, *calmly*: You won't find her. My cousin naturally regrets being unable to make unbounded concessions to the laws of hospitality. But I fear you are too numerous. This is a tobacconist's, and it is Miss Shen Teh's livelihood.

THE MAN: Our Shen Teh could never bring herself to say such things.

SHUI TA: You may be right. *To the carpenter*: The unfortunate fact is that the poverty in this city is too much for any individual to correct. Alas, nothing has changed in the eleven centuries since a poet wrote:

That so many of the poor should suffer from cold what can we do to prevent!

To bring warmth to a single body is not much use.

I wish I had a big rug ten thousand feet long,

Which at one time could cover up every inch of the City.*

He starts clearing up the shop.

THE CARPENTER: I see you are trying to straighten out your cousin's affairs. There is a small bill to be settled for the shelves; she has admitted it before witnesses. 100 silver dollars.

SHUI TA, *drawing the bill out of his pocket, not unkindly*: Wouldn't you say that 100 silver dollars was rather much?

THE CARPENTER: No. I can't do it for less. I've a wife and family to look after.

SHUI TA, *hard*: How many children?

THE CARPENTER: Four.

SHUI TA: Then my offer is 20 silver dollars.

---

* 'The Big Rug', from *170 Chinese Poems* by Arthur Waley.

THE CARPENTER *laughs*: Are you crazy? These shelves are walnut.

SHUI TA: Then take them away.

THE CARPENTER: What do you mean?

SHUI TA: I can't afford it. I suggest you take your walnut shelves away.

THE WOMAN: One up to you. *She in turn laughs.*

THE CARPENTER, *uncertainly*: I would like Miss Shen Teh to be fetched. She seems to be a decent person, unlike you.

SHUI TA: Obviously. She is ruined.

THE CARPENTER *resolutely seizes some shelving and takes it to the door*: You can stack your goods on the floor then. It doesn't matter to me.

SHUI TA, *to the man*: Give him a hand.

THE MAN *takes some more shelving and takes it to the door with a grin*: Here we go. Chuck the lot out!

THE CARPENTER: You bastard. Do you want my family to starve?

SHUI TA: Let me repeat my offer: you can have 20 silver dollars, to save me stacking my goods on the floor.

THE CARPENTER: 100.

Shui Ta looks indifferently out of the window. The man sets about removing the shelves.

THE CARPENTER: Anyway, don't smash them into the door-post, you fool! *In confusion*: But they're made to fit. They won't go anywhere else. The boards had to be cut to size, sir.

SHUI TA: Exactly. That's why I can't offer you more than 20 silver dollars. Because the boards were cut to size.

The woman squeals with delight.

THE CARPENTER *suddenly decides he has had enough*: I can't go on. Keep the shelves and pay me what you like.

SHUI TA: 20 silver dollars.

He lays two big coins on the table. The carpenter takes them.

THE MAN, *bringing back the shelves*: Good enough for a lot of cut-up boards!

THE CARPENTER: About good enough to get drunk on! *Exit.*

THE MAN: Good riddance!

THE WOMAN, *wiping away tears of laughter*: 'But they're walnut!' – 'Take them away!' – '100 silver dollars, I've got four children!' – 'Then I'll pay 20!' – 'But they've been cut to fit!' – 'Exactly, 20 silver dollars!' That's the way to deal with his sort!

SHUI TA: Yes. *Seriously*: Leave here at once.

THE MAN: What, us?

SHUI TA: Yes, you. You are thieves and parasites. Leave at once, waste no time in arguing, and you can still save your skins.

THE MAN: It is better not to take any notice of him. No arguing on an empty stomach. I wonder where the nipper is?

SHUI TA: Yes, where is he? I told you I will not have him here with stolen cakes. *Suddenly shouting*: For the second time. Get out!

They remain seated.

SHUI TA, *calm once more*: All right then.

He walks to the door and bows deeply to someone outside. A policeman looms up in the doorway.

SHUI TA: I take it I am addressing the police representative for this district?

THE POLICEMAN: You are, Mr . . .

SHUI TA: Shui Ta. *They exchange smiles.* Pleasant weather today!

THE POLICEMAN: A trifle warm, perhaps.

SHUI TA: Perhaps a trifle warm.

THE MAN, *softly to his wife*: If he goes on gassing till the kid gets back we'll be done for.

He tries to make Shui Ta a surreptitious sign.

SHUI TA, *without noticing*: It all depends whether one is contemplating the weather from a cool establishment like this or from the dusty street.

THE POLICEMAN: It certainly does.

THE WOMAN: Don't worry. He'll keep away when he sees the copper standing in the door.

SHUI TA: But do come in. It really is cooler here. My cousin and I have opened a shop. Let me tell you that we consider it highly important to be on good terms with the authorities.

THE POLICEMAN *enters*: That is very kind of you, sir. Why yes, it really is cooler in here.

THE MAN, *softly*: He's asked him in just so the kid won't see him.

SHUI TA: Some guests. Distant acquaintances of my cousin's, apparently. They have a journey to make. *Bows are exchanged.* We were just saying goodbye.

THE MAN, *hoarsely*: All right then, we'll be going.

SHUI TA: I will tell my cousin that you thanked her for her hospitality, but could not wait for her return.
Noises from the street and cries of 'Stop thief!'

THE POLICEMAN: What's that about?
The boy appears in the door. Cakes and rolls are tumbling out of his shirt. The woman motions him desperately to get out. He turns and tries to go off.

THE POLICEMAN: You stay here. *He catches hold of him.* Where d'you get those cakes from?

THE BOY: Over there.

THE POLICEMAN: Aha. Stolen, eh?

THE WOMAN: We knew nothing about it. It was the boy's own idea. Little wretch.

THE POLICEMAN: Mr Shui Ta, can you throw any light on this?
Shui Ta remains silent.

THE POLICEMAN: Right. You all come along to the station with me.

SHUI TA: I am exceedingly sorry that anything like this should happen in my shop.

THE WOMAN: He watched the boy go off!

SHUI TA: I can assure you, officer, that I should hardly have invited you in if I had been wanting to conceal a robbery.

THE POLICEMAN: I quite see. You realise I'm only doing my duty, Mr Shui Ta, in taking these persons in custody. *Shui*

Ta bows. Get moving, you! *He pushes them out.*

THE GRANDFATHER, *peacefully from the doorway*: Hullo.
Exeunt all except Shui Ta. Enter Mrs Mi Tzu.

MRS MI TZU: So you are the cousin I've heard about? How do the police come to be escorting people away from my building? What does your cousin mean by starting a boarding-house here? That's what comes of taking in people who a moment ago were in cheap digs, begging for crusts from the baker on the corner. I know all about it, you see.

SHUI TA: I do see. People have been speaking against my cousin. They have blamed her for being hungry! She has a bad name for living in poverty. Her reputation is the worst possible: she was down and out!

MRS MI TZU: She was a commom or garden . . .

SHUI TA: Pauper; let's say the nasty word aloud.

MRS MI TZU: Oh, don't try and play on my feelings. I am speaking of her way of life, not her income. I have no doubt there was an income from somewhere, or she would hardly have started this shop. No doubt one or two elderly gentlemen looked after that. How does one get hold of a shop? This is a respectable house, sir. The tenants here aren't paying to live under the same roof as that sort of person: no, sir. *Pause.* I am not inhuman, but I have got my obligations.

SHUI TA, *coldly*: Mrs Mi Tzu, I'm a busy man. Just tell me what it will cost to live in this highly respectable house.

MRS MI TZU: Well, you are a cold fish, I'll give you that!

SHUI TA *takes the form of agreement out of the drawer*: It is a very high rent. I take it from this agreement that it is to be paid monthly?

MRS MI TZU, *quickly*: Not for your cousin's sort.

SHUI TA: What does that mean?

MRS MI TZU: That means that people like your cousin have to pay six months' rent in advance: 200 silver dollars.

SHUI TA: 200 silver dollars! That is plain murder! Where am I to find that much? I cannot count on a big turnover here. My one hope is the girls who sew sacks in the cement works, who are supposed to smoke a lot because they find the work so exhausting. But they are badly paid.

MRS MI TZU: You should have thought of that sooner.

SHUI TA: Mrs Mi Tzu, please have a heart! I realise that my cousin made the unforgiveable mistake of giving shelter to some unfortunates. But she will learn. I shall see that she learns. Against that, where could you find a better tenant than one who knows the gutter because he came from there? He'll work his fingers to the bone to pay his rent punctually, he'll do anything, go without anything, sell anything, stick at nothing, and at the same time be as quiet as a mouse, gentle as a fly, submit to you utterly rather than return there. A tenant like that is worth his weight in gold.

MRS MI TZU: 200 silver dollars in advance, or she goes back on the street, where she came from.

Enter the policeman.

THE POLICEMAN: Don't let me disturb you, Mr Shui Ta!

MRS MI TZU: The police really seem remarkably interested in this shop.

THE POLICEMAN: Mrs Mi Tzu, I hope you haven't got a wrong impression. Mr Shui Ta did us a service, and I have come in the name of the police to thank him.

MRS MI TZU: Well, that's no affair of mine. Mr Shui Ta, I trust my proposition will be agreeable to your cousin. I like to be on good terms with my tenants. Good morning, gentlemen. *Exit.*

SHUI TA: Good morning, Mrs Mi Tzu.

THE POLICEMAN: Have you been having trouble with Mrs Mi Tzu?

SHUI TA: She is demanding the rent in advance, as she doesn't think my cousin is respectable.

THE POLICEMAN: And can't you raise the money? *Shui Ta remains silent.* But Mr Shui Ta, surely someone like you ought to be able to get credit.

SHUI TA: I dare say. But how is someone like Shen Teh to get credit?

THE POLICEMAN: Are you not staying here then?

SHUI TA: No. And I shall not be able to come again. I could only give her a hand because I was passing through; I just saved her from the worst. Any minute she will be thrown back on her own resources. I am worried as to what will happen.

THE POLICEMAN: Mr Shui Ta, I am sorry to hear that you are having trouble over the rent. I must admit that we began by viewing this shop with mixed feelings, but your decisive action just now showed us the sort of man you are. Speaking for the authorities, we soon find out who we can rely on as a friend of law and order.

SHUI TA, *bitterly*: To save this little shop, officer, which my cousin regards as a gift of the gods, I am prepared to go to the utmost limits of the law. But toughness and duplicity will serve only against one's inferiors, for those limits have been cleverly defined. I am in the position of a man who has just got the rats out of his cellar, when along come the floods. *After a short pause*: Do you smoke?

THE POLICEMAN, *putting two cigars in his pocket*: Our station would be sorry to see you go, Mr Shui Ta. But you've got to understand Mrs Mi Tzu's point of view. Shen Teh, let's face it, lived by selling herself to men. You may ask, what else was she to do? For instance, how was she to pay her rent? But the fact remains: it is not respectable. Why not? A: you can't earn your living by love, or it becomes immoral earnings. B: respectability means, not with the man who can pay, but with the man one loves. C: it mustn't be for a handful of rice but for love. All right, you may say: what's the good of being so clever over spilt milk? What's she to do? When she has to find six months' rent? Mr Shui Ta, I must admit I don't know. *He thinks hard*. Mr Shui Ta, I have got it! All you need do is to find a husband for her.

Enter a little old woman.

THE OLD WOMAN: I want a good cheap cigar for my husband. Tomorrow is our fortieth wedding anniversary, you see, and we are having a little celebration.

SHUI TA, *politely*: Forty years, and still something to celebrate!

THE OLD WOMAN: As far as our means allow! That's our carpet shop over the way. I hope we are going to be good neighbours, it's important in these hard times.

SHUI TA *spreads various boxes before her*: Two very familiar words, I'm afraid.

THE POLICEMAN: Mr Shui Ta, what we need is capital. So I suggest a marriage.

SHUI TA, *excusing himself to the old woman*: I have been allowing myself to tell the officer some of my private troubles.

THE POLICEMAN: We've got to find six months' rent. Right, we marry a bit of money.

SHUI TA: That will not be easy.

THE POLICEMAN: Why not? She's a good match. She owns a small and promising business. *To the old woman*: What do you think?

THE OLD WOMAN, *doubtfully*: Well . . .

THE POLICEMAN: An advertisement in the personal column.

THE OLD WOMAN, *reluctant*: If the young lady agrees . . .

THE POLICEMAN: Why shouldn't she agree? I'll draft it out for you. One good turn deserves another. Don't think the authorities have no sympathy for the small and struggling shopkeeper. You play along with us, and in return we draft your matrimonial advertisement! Hahaha!

He hastens to pull out his notebook, licks his pencil stump and starts writing.

SHUI TA, *slowly*: It's not a bad idea.

THE POLICEMAN: 'What respectable gentleman . . . small capital . . . widower considered . . . desires marriage . . . into progressive tobacconist's?' And then we'll add: 'With charming attractive brunette.' How's that?

SHUI TA: You don't feel that's overstating it?

THE OLD WOMAN, *kindly*: Certainly not. I have seen her.

The policeman tears the page out of his notebook and hands it to Shui Ta.

SHUI TA: With horror I begin to realise how much luck one needs to avoid being crushed! What brilliant ideas! What faithful friends! *To the policeman*: Thus for all my decisiveness I was at my wit's end over the rent. And then you came along and helped me with good advice. I really begin to see a way out.

3

Evening in a Public Park

A young man in tattered clothes is watching an aeroplane, which is evidently making a high sweep over the park. He takes a rope from his pocket and looks round him for something. He is making for a big willow-tree, when two prostitutes come up to him. One of them is old, the other is the niece from the family of eight.

THE YOUNG ONE: Evening, young fellow. Coming home with me, dear?

SUN: It could be done, ladies, if you'll stand me a meal.

THE OLD ONE: Are you nuts? *To the young one*: Come on, love. He's just a waste of time. That's that out-of-work pilot.

THE YOUNG ONE: But there won't be a soul in the park now, it's going to rain.

THE OLD ONE: There's always a chance.

They walk on. Sun looks round him, pulls out his rope and throws it over a branch of a willow tree. But he is interrupted again. The two prostitutes return rapidly. They do not see him.

THE YOUNG ONE: It's going to pelt with rain.

Shen Teh is walking up.

THE OLD ONE: Hullo, here she is, the bitch! She got your lot into trouble all right!

THE YOUNG ONE: Not her. It was her cousin. She took us in, and in the end she offered to pay for the cakes. I haven't any bone to pick with her.

THE OLD ONE: I have. *Loudly*: Why, there's our fancy friend with all the money. She's got a shop, but she still wants to pinch our boys off us.

SHEN TEH: Don't jump down my throat! I'm going down to the teahouse by the lake.

THE YOUNG ONE: Is it true you're marrying a widower with three children?

SHEN TEH: Yes, I'm meeting him there.

SUN, *impatiently*: Do your cackling somewhere else, will you? Isn't there anywhere one can get a bit of peace?

THE OLD ONE: Shut up!

Exeunt the two prostitutes.

SUN *calls after them*: Scavengers! *To the audience*: Even in this remote spot they fish tirelessly for victims, even in the thickets, in the rain, they pursue their desperate hunt for custom.

SHEN TEH, *angry*: What call have you got to slang them? *She sees the rope.* Oh!

SUN: What are you gooping at?

SHEN TEH: What's that rope for?

SUN: Move on, sister, move on! I've got no money, nothing, not a copper. And if I had I'd buy a drink of water, not you. *It starts raining.*

SHEN TEH: What's that rope for? You're not to do it!

SUN: Mind your own business! And get out of the way!

SHEN TEH: It's raining.

SUN: Don't you try sheltering under my tree.

SHEN TEH *remains motionless in the rain*: No.

SUN: Why not give up, sister, it's no use. You can't do business with me. Besides, you're too ugly, Bandy legs.

SHEN TEH: That's not true.

SUN: I don't want to see them! All right, come under the bloody tree, since it's raining!

She approaches slowly and sits down under the tree.

SHEN TEH: Why do you want to do that?

SUN: Would you like to know? Then I'll tell you, so as to be rid of you. *Pause.* Do you know what an airman is?

SHEN TEH: Yes, I once saw some airmen in a teahouse.

SUN: Oh no you didn't. One or two windy idiots in flying helmets, I expect: the sort who's got no ear for his engine and no feeling for his machine. Gets into a kite by bribing the hangar superintendent. Tell a type like that: now stall your crate at 2,000, down through the clouds, then catch her up with the flick of the stick, and he'll say: But that's not in the book. If you can't land your kite gently as lowering your bottom you're not an airman, you're an idiot. Me, I'm an airman. And yet I'm the biggest idiot of the lot, because I read all the manuals in flying school at Pekin. But just one page of one manual I happened to miss, the one where it says Airmen Not Wanted. And so I became an airman without an aircraft, a mail pilot without mail. What that means you wouldn't understand.

SHEN TEH: I think I do understand all the same.

SUN: No, I'm telling you you can't understand. And that means you can't understand.

SHEN TEH, *half laughing, half crying*: When we were children we had a crane with a broken wing. He was very tame and didn't mind our teasing him, and used to come strutting after us and scream if we went too fast for him. But in the autumn and the spring, when the great flocks of birds flew over our village, he became very restless, and I could understand why.

SUN: Stop crying.

SHEN TEH: Yes.

SUN: It's bad for the complexion.

SHEN TEH: I'm stopping.

She dries her tears on her sleeve. Leaning against the tree, but without turning towards her, he reaches for her face.

SUN: You don't even know how to wipe your face properly.
He wipes it for her with a handkerchief.

SUN: If you've got to sit there and stop me from hanging myself
you might at least say something.

SHEN TEH: I don't know what.

SUN: Why do you want to hack me down, sister, as a matter of
interest?

SHEN TEH: It frightens me. I'm sure you only felt like that
because the evening's so dreary. *To the audience.*

> In our country
> There should be no dreary evenings
> Or tall bridges over rivers
> Even the hour between night and morning
> And the whole winter season too, that is dangerous.
> For in face of misery
> Only a little is needed
> Before men start throwing
> Their unbearable life away.

SUN: Tell me about yourself.

SHEN TEH: What is there? I've got a small shop.

SUN, *ironically*: Oh, so you haven't got a flat, you've got a
shop!

SHEN TEH, *firmly*: I've got a shop, but before that I was on the
streets.

SUN: And the shop, I take it, was a gift of the gods?

SHEN TEH: Yes.

SUN: One fine evening they stood before you and said: Here's
some money for you.

SHEN TEH, *laughing quietly*: One morning.

SUN: You're not exactly entertaining.

SHEN TEH, *after a pause*: I can play the zither a bit, and do
imitations. *In a deep voice she imitates a dignified gentleman*: 'How idiotic, I must have come without my wallet!'
But then I got the shop. The first thing I did was give away
my zither. From now on, I told myself, you can be a

complete jellyfish and it won't matter.

How rich I am, I told myself.
I walk alone. I sleep alone.
For one whole year, I told myself
I'll have no dealings with a man.

SUN: But now you're going to marry one? The one in the teahouse by the lake.

Shen Teh says nothing.

SUN: As a matter of interest, what do you know of love?

SHEN TEH: Everything.

SUN: Nothing, sister. Or was it perhaps pleasant?

SHEN TEH: No.

Sun strokes her face, without turning towards her.

SUN: Is that pleasant?

SHEN TEH: Yes.

SUN: Easily satisfied, you are. God, what a town.

SHEN TEH: Haven't you got friends?

SUN: A whole lot, but none that like hearing that I'm still out of a job. They make a face as if someone were complaining that the sea's wet. Have you got a friend, if it comes to that?

SHEN TEH, *hesitantly*: A cousin.

SUN: Then don't you trust him an inch.

SHEN TEH: He was only here once. Now he has gone off and is never coming back. But why do you talk as if you'd given up hope? They say: to give up hope, is to give up kindness.

SUN: Just talk on! At least it's something to hear a human voice.

SHEN TEH, *eagerly*: There are still friendly people, for all our wretchedness. When I was little once I was carrying a bundle of sticks and fell. An old man helped me up and even gave me a penny. I have often thought of it. Those who have least to eat give most gladly. I suppose people just like showing what they are good at; and how can they do it better than by being friendly? Crossness is just a way of being inefficient. Whenever someone is singing a song or building a machine or planting rice it is really friendliness. You are friendly too.

SUN: It doesn't seem hard by your definition.

SHEN TEH: And that was a raindrop.

SUN: Where?

SHEN TEH: Between my eyes.

SUN: More to the left or more to the right?

SHEN TEH: More to the left.

SUN: Good. *After a moment, sleepily*: So you're through with men?

SHEN TEH, *smiling*: But my legs aren't bandy.

SUN: Perhaps not.

SHEN TEH: Definitely not.

SUN, *wearily leaning back against the tree*: But as I haven't eaten for two days or drunk for one, I couldn't love you, sister, even if I wanted.

SHEN TEH: It is good in the rain.

Wang, the water-seller appears. He sings.

WANG:

THE WATER-SELLER'S SONG IN THE RAIN

I sell water. Who will taste it?
– Who would want to in this weather?
All my labour has been wasted
Fetching these few pints together.
I stand shouting Buy my Water!
And nobody thinks it
Worth stopping and buying
Or greedily drinks it.
(Buy water, you devils!)

O to stop the leaky heaven
Hoard what stock I've got remaining:
Recently I dreamt that seven
Years went by without it raining.
How they'd all shout Give me Water!
How they'd fight for my good graces

And I'd make their further treatment
Go by how I liked their faces.
(Stay thirsty, you devils!)

Wretched weeds, you're through with thirsting
Heaven must have heard you praying.
You can drink until you're bursting
Never bother about paying.
I'm left shouting Buy my Water!
And nobody thinks it
Worth stopping and buying
Or greedily drinks it.
(Buy water, you devils!)

The rain has stopped. Shen Teh sees Wang and runs towards him.

SHEN TEH: Oh Wang, so you have come back. I have looked after your pole for you.

WANG: Thank you for taking care of it! How are you, Shen Teh?

SHEN TEH: Well. I have got to know a very brave and clever person. And I should like to buy a cup of your water.

WANG: Throw your head back and open your mouth, and you can have as much water as you want. The willow tree is still dripping.

SHEN TEH:

But I want your water, Wang.
Laboriously carried
Exhausting to its bearer
And hard to sell, because it is raining.
And I need it for the man over yonder.
He is an airman. An airman
Is braver than other humans. With the clouds for
companions
Daring enormous tempests
He flies through the heavens and brings

To friends in far countries
The friendly post.
She pays and runs over to Sun with the cup.
SHEN TEH *calls back to Wang, laughing*: He has fallen asleep.
Hopelessness and the rain and I have tired him out.

Interlude

Wang's sleeping-place under a Culvert

The water-seller is asleep. Music. The culvert becomes transparent, and the gods appear to him as he dreams.

WANG, *beaming*: I have seen her, O Illustrious Ones! She has not changed.
THE FIRST GOD: That gives us pleasure.
WANG: She is in love! She showed me her friend. Truly things are going well for her.
THE FIRST GOD: That is good to hear. Let us hope that she will be strengthened in her pursuit of goodness.
WANG: Indeed yes! She is performing all the charitable deeds she can.
THE FIRST GOD: Charitable deeds? What sort? Tell us about them, dear Wang.
WANG: She has a friendly word for everyone.
THE FIRST GOD, *keenly*: What else?
WANG: It is rare that a man is allowed to leave her shop without something to smoke, just for lack of money.
THE FIRST GOD: That sounds satisfactory. Any more?
WANG: She has taken in a family of eight.
THE FIRST GOD, *triumphantly to the second*: Eight, indeed! *To Wang*: Have you anything else you can tell us?
WANG: Although it was raining she bought a cup of water from me.

THE FIRST GOD: Yes, minor charities of that sort. Of course.

WANG: But they eat into the money. A small business doesn't make all that much.

THE FIRST GOD: True, true! But a prudent gardener can work wonders with his little patch.

WANG: That is just what she does! Every morning she distributes rice; believe me, it must cost more than half her earnings!

THE FIRST GOD, *slightly disappointed*: I am not denying it. I am not displeased with her start.

WANG: Remember, times are not easy! She had to call in a cousin once, as her shop was getting into difficulties.

> Hardly was a shelter erected against the wind
> Than the ruffled birds of the whole wintry heaven
> Came tumbling flying and
> Squabbled for a place and the hungry fox gnawed through
> The flimsy wall and the one-legged wolf
> Knocked the little rice-bowl over.

In other words the business was too much for her to manage. But everyone agrees that she is a good girl. They have begun to call her 'The Angel of the Slums'. So much good goes out from her shop. Whatever Lin To the carpenter may say!

THE FIRST GOD: What's that? Does Lin To the carpenter speak ill of her?

WANG: Oh, he only says the shelving in the shop wasn't quite paid for.

THE SECOND GOD: What are you telling us? A carpenter not paid? In Shen Teh's shop? How could she permit that?

WANG: I suppose she didn't have the money.

THE SECOND GOD: No matter: one pays one's debts. One cannot afford even the appearance of irregularity. The letter of the law has first to be fulfilled; then its spirit.

WANG: But Illustrious Ones, it was only her cousin, not herself.

THE SECOND GOD: Then that cousin must never again enter her door.

WANG, *dejected*: I have understood, Illustrious One! But in Shen Teh's defence let me just say that her cousin is supposed to be a most reputable businessman. Even the police respect him.

THE FIRST GOD: This cousin will not be condemned without a hearing either. I know nothing of business, I admit; perhaps we ought to find out what is thought usual in such matters. But business indeed! Is it so very necessary? Nowadays there is nothing but business. Were the Seven Good Kings in business? Did Kung the Just sell fish? What has business to do with an upright and honourable life?

THE SECOND GOD, *with a bad cold*: In any case it must not be allowed to occur again.

He turns to leave. The other two gods likewise turn.

THE THIRD GOD, *the last to leave, embarrassedly*: Forgive our rather sharp tone today! We are very tired, and we have slept too little. Oh, those nights! The well-off give us the best possible recommendations to the poor, but the poor have too few rooms.

THE GODS *grumble as they move off*: Broken reeds, even the best of them! Nothing conclusive! Pitiful, pitiful! All from the heart, of course, but it adds up to nothing! At least she ought to . . .

They can no longer be heard.

WANG *calls after them*: Do not be too hard on us, O Illustrious Ones! Do not ask for everything at once!

4

Square in front of Shen Teh's Shop

A barber's, a carpet shop and Shen Teh's tobacconist's shop. It is Monday. Outside Shen Teh's shop wait two survivors of the family of eight – the grandfather and the sister-in-law. Also the unemployed man and Mrs Shin.

SISTER-IN-LAW: She never came home last night!

MRS SHIN: Astonishing behaviour! We manage to get rid of this maniac of a cousin and there's nothing to stop her having a little rice to spare now and again, when off she goes for the night chasing around God knows where!

Loud voices are heard from the barber's. Wang staggers out followed by Mr Shu Fu, the stout barber, with a heavy pair of curling tongs in his hand.

MR SHU FU: I'll teach you to come bothering my customers with your stinking water! Take your mug and get out!

Wang reaches for the mug which Mr Shu Fu is holding out to him, and gets a blow on the hand with the curling-tongs, so that he screams.

MR SHU FU: Take that! Let that be a lesson to you.

He puffs back to his shop.

THE UNEMPLOYED MAN *picks up the mug and hands it to Wang*: You can have him up for hitting you.

WANG: My hand's gone.

THE UNEMPLOYED MAN: Any bones broken?

WANG: I can't move it.

THE UNEMPLOYED MAN: Sit down and bathe it a bit.

MRS SHIN: The water won't cost you much, anyway.

THE SISTER-IN-LAW: Eight o'clock already, and one can't even lay hands on a bit of rag here. She has to go gallivanting off! A disgrace!

MRS SHIN, *darkly*: She's forgotten us, that's what!

Shen Teh comes down the street carrying a pot of rice.

SHEN TEH, *to the audience*: I had never seen the city at dawn. These were the hours when I used to lie with my filthy blanket over my head, terrified to wake up. Today I mixed with the newsboys, with the men who were washing down the streets, with the ox-carts bringing fresh vegetables in from the fields. It was a long walk from Sun's neighbourhood to here, but with every step I grew happier. I had always been told that when one is in love one walks on air, but the wonderful thing is that one walks on earth, on tarmac. I tell you, at dawn the blocks of buildings are like rubbish heaps with little lights glowing in them; the sky is pink but still transparent, clear of dust. I tell you, you miss a great deal if you are not in love and cannot see your city at that hour when she rises from her couch like a sober old craftsman, filling his lungs with fresh air and reaching for his tools, as the poets have it. *To the group waiting*: Good morning! Here is your rice! *She shares it out, then notices Wang*: Good morning, Wang. I am light-headed today. All along the way I looked at my reflection in the shop windows, and now I would like to buy myself a shawl. *After a short hesitation*: I should so like to look beautiful.

She turns quickly into the carpet shop.

MR SHU FU, *who is again standing in his doorway, to the audience*: I am smitten today with the beauty of Miss Shen Teh, the owner of the tobacconist's opposite, whom I have never previously noticed. I have watched her for three minutes, and I believe I am already in love. An infinitely charming person! *To Wang*: Get to hell, you lout!

He turns back into the barber's shop. Shen Teh and an extremely old couple, the carpet-dealer and his wife, come out of the carpet-shop. Shen Teh is carrying a shawl, the carpet-dealer a mirror.

THE OLD WOMAN: It's very pretty and not at all dear; there's a small hole at the bottom.

SHEN TEH, *trying the shawl on the old woman's arm*: I like the green one too.

THE OLD WOMAN, *smiling*: But I'm afraid it's in perfect condition.

SHEN TEH: Yes, a pity. I cannot undertake too much with my shop. The income is small, and there are many expenses.

THE OLD WOMAN: For charity; don't you do so much. When you are starting every bowl of rice counts, eh?

SHEN TEH *tries on the shawl with the hole in it*: Except that I have to; only at present I'm light-headed. Do you think the colour suits me?

THE OLD WOMAN: You had better ask a man that question.

SHEN TEH *calls to the old man*: Does it suit me?

THE OLD MAN: Why don't you ask . . .

SHEN TEH, *very politely*: No, I am asking you.

THE OLD MAN, *equally politely*: The shawl suits you. But wear it dull side out.

Shen Teh pays.

THE OLD WOMAN: If you don't like it I will always change it for another. *Draws her aside*: Has he any money?

SHEN TEH, *laughing*: O goodness no.

THE OLD WOMAN: Will you be able to pay your half-year's rent?

SHEN TEH: The rent! It had clean gone out of my mind!

THE OLD WOMAN: I thought it had! And Monday will be the first of the month. I have something to suggest. You know: my husband and I were a little doubtful about the marriage advertisement once we had got to know you. We decided we'd help you out if need be. We've put something by, and we can lend you the 200 silver dollars. If you like you can make over your stock to us as security. But of course we don't need anything in writing.

SHEN TEH: Would you really lend money to such a scatter-brained person?

THE OLD WOMAN: To be honest, we'd think twice about lending it to your cousin, who is definitely not scatter-brained, but we'd gladly lend it to you.

THE OLD MAN *comes up*: All fixed?

SHEN TEH: I wish the gods could have heard your wife just then, Mr Deng. They are looking for good and happy people. And I'm sure you must be happy, to be helping me out of the troubles that love has brought me.

The two old people smile at one another.

THE OLD MAN: Here is the money.

He hands her an envelope. Shen Teh accepts it and bows. The old people bow too. They go back to their shop.

SHEN TEH, *to Wang, holding up the envelope*: This is six

months' rent. Isn't that a miracle? And Wang, what do you think of my new shawl?

WANG: Did you buy it for the man I saw in the park?

Shen Teh nods.

MRS SHIN: You might choose to look at his hand instead of retailing your shady adventures!

SHEN TEH, *alarmed*: What's the matter with your hand?

MRS SHIN: The barber smashed it with his curling tongs in front of our eyes.

SHEN TEH, *horrified at her heedlessness*: And I didn't notice! You must go to the doctor at once, or your hand will go stiff and you'll never be able to work properly again. It's a frightful disaster. Come on, get up! Hurry!

THE UNEMPLOYED MAN: He doesn't want the doctor; he wants the magistrate! The barber's a rich man, and he ought to get compensation.

WANG: Do you think there's a chance?

MRS SHIN: If you really can't use it. Can you?

WANG: I don't think so. It's already very swollen. Would it mean a pension for life?

MRS SHIN: You need a witness, of course.

WANG: But you all saw! You can all of you bear me out.

He looks round. Unemployed man, grandfather, sister-in-law: all are sitting against the wall and eating. No one looks up.

SHEN TEH, *to Mrs Shin*: You yourself saw it, didn't you?

MRS SHIN: I don't want to get mixed up with the police.

SHEN TEH, *to the sister-in-law*: What about you then?

THE SISTER-IN-LAW: Me? I wasn't looking!

MRS SHIN: Of course you were looking. I saw you looking! You're just scared because the barber's got too much pull.

SHEN TEH, *to the grandfather*: I am sure that you will confirm what happened.

THE SISTER-IN-LAW: They wouldn't listen to him. He's gaga.

SHEN TEH, *to the unemployed man*: It may mean a pension for life.

THE UNEMPLOYED MAN: They've taken my name twice for begging. It won't do him much good if I give evidence.

SHEN TEH, *incredulous*: Do you mean to say that not one of you will say what happened? His hand gets broken in full daylight, in front of you all, and not one will open his mouth.

Angrily:

O you unfortunates!

Your brother is mishandled before you, and you just shut your eyes.

Injured, he screams aloud, and you keep mum.

The bully swaggers round, picks out his victim

And you say: he'll spare us, for we hide our displeasure.

What sort of a town is that, what sort of humans are you?

When an injustice takes place in a town there must be an uproar

And where there is no uproar it is better the town disappears

In flames before the night falls.

Wang, if nobody who saw it will be your witness, then I will be your witness and say that I saw it.

MRS SHIN: It'll be perjury.

WANG: I don't know if I can allow that. But perhaps I have to allow it. *Looking anxiously at his hand*: Do you think it has swollen enough? It looks to me as if it has started to go down?

THE UNEMPLOYED MAN, *calming him*: No, it certainly hasn't gone down.

WANG: Are you sure? Ah yes, I do believe it's swelling a bit more. Possibly my wrist is broken! I'd better go straight to the magistrate.

Holding his hand carefully and still looking at it, he hurries off. Mrs Shin enters the barber's shop.

THE UNEMPLOYED MAN: She's gone to the barber's to butter him up.

THE SISTER-IN-LAW: It's not for us to change the world.

SHEN TEH, *discouraged*: I didn't mean to be rude to you. It's just that I was shocked. No, I did mean to be rude to you. Get out of my sight!

The unemployed man, the sister-in-law and the grandfather go off eating and grumbling.

SHEN TEH, *to the audience*:

They cannot respond. Where they are stationed
They stay put, and when turned away
They quickly yield place!
Nothing now moves them. Only
The smell of cooking will make them look up.

An old woman comes hurrying up. It is Sun's mother, Mrs Yang.

MRS YANG, *out of breath*: Are you Miss Shen Teh? My son has told me everything. I am Sun's mother, Mrs Yang. Think of it, he has got the chance of a job as a pilot! He got a letter from Pekin this morning, just now. From one of the superintendents in the postal service.

SHEN TEH: That means he can fly again? Oh, Mrs Yang!

MRS YANG: But it will cost a lot: 500 silver dollars.

SHEN TEH: That's a great deal, but money must not stand in his way. After all, I've got the shop.

MRS YANG: If you could only do something!

SHEN TEH *embraces her*: If I could help him!

MRS YANG: You would be giving a chance to a very gifted individual!

SHEN TEH: Why should they stop a man from applying his gifts? *After a pause*: Except that I shall not get enough for the shop, and the 200 silver dollars which I have got in cash are only a loan. Of course you can have those now. I will sell my stock and pay them back out of that.

She gives her the old couple's money.

MRS YANG: O Miss Shen Teh, a friend in need is a friend indeed. And they were all calling him the dead pilot, because they said he has as much chance of flying again as a corpse.

SHEN TEH: We still need 300 silver dollars for the job, though. Mrs Yang, we must think. *Slowly*: I know someone who might perhaps help. Someone who has advised me before. I didn't really want to have to resort to him again; he is too smart and too tough. This will definitely be the last time. But a pilot has got to fly, that is obvious.
Sound of engines in the distance.

MRS YANG: If your friend could only raise the money! Look, there goes the morning mail service to Pekin!

SHEN TEH, *with determination*: Wave to it, Mrs Yang. I'm sure the pilot can see us! *She waves her shawl.* Go on, wave!

MRS YANG, *waving*: Do you know the pilot?

SHEN TEH: No. I know a pilot. For the man without hope shall fly, Mrs Yang. One of us at least shall be able to fly above all this wretchedness; one at least shall rise above us all!
To the audience:

> Yang Sun, my loved one, with the clouds for companions!
> Daring enormous tempests
> Flying through the heavens and bringing
> To friends in far countries
> The friendly post.

Interlude
in front of the curtain

Shen Teh enters, carrying Shui Ta's mask and costume, and sings the

SONG OF THE DEFENCELESSNESS OF THE GOOD AND THE GODS

SHEN TEH:
> In our country

The capable man needs luck. Only
If he has mighty backers
Can he prove his capacity.
The good
Have no means of helping themselves and the gods are
    powerless.

> So why can't the gods launch a great operation
> With bombers and battleships, tanks and destroyers
> And rescue the good by a ruthless invasion?
> Then maybe the wicked would cease to annoy us.

She puts on Shui Ta's costume and takes a few steps in his way of walking.

The good
Cannot remain good for long in our country
Where cupboards are bare, housewives start to squabble.
Oh, the divine commandments
Are not much use against hunger.

> So why can't the gods share out what they've created
> Come down and distribute the bounties of nature
> And allow us, once hunger and thirst have been sated
> To mix with each other in friendship and pleasure?

She dons Shui Ta's mask and sings on in his voice.

In order to win one's mid-day meal
One needs the toughness which elsewhere builds empires.
Except twelve others be trampled down
The unfortunate cannot be helped.

> So why can't the gods make a simple decision
> That goodness must conquer in spite of its weak-
>   ness? –
> Then back up the good with an armoured division
> Command it to: 'fire!' and not tolerate meekness?

5

The Tobacconist's

Shui Ta sits behind the counter and reads the paper. He takes no notice of Mrs Shin, who is cleaning the place and talking.

MRS SHIN: A small business like this soon goes downhill, believe me, once certain rumours get around locally. This shady affair between the young lady and that fellow Yang Sun from the Yellow Alley, it was high time a proper gentleman like you came and cleared it up. Don't forget that Mr Shu Fu, the hairdresser next door, a gentleman who owns twelve houses and has only one wife, and an old one at that, hinted to me yesterday that he took a rather flattering interest in the young lady. He went so far as to ask about her financial standing. I'd say that showed real partiality.
Getting no answer, she finally leaves with her bucket.
SUN'S VOICE, *from outside*: Is this Miss Shen Teh's shop?
MRS SHIN'S VOICE: Yes. But her cousin's there today.
Shui Ta runs to a mirror, with Shen Teh's light steps, and is just beginning to arrange his hair when he realises his mistake. He turns away with a soft laugh. Enter Yang Sun. Behind him appears the inquisitive Mrs Shin. She goes past him into the back of the shop.
SUN: I am Yang Sun. *Shui Ta bows.* Is Shen Teh in?
SHUI TA: No, she is not in.
SUN: But I expect you're in the picture about me and her? *He begins to take stock of the shop.* A real shop, large as life. I always thought she was putting it on a bit. *He examines the boxes and china pots with satisfaction.* Oh boy, I'm going to be flying again. *He helps himself to a cigar, and Shui Ta gives him a light.* Do you think we can squeeze another 300 dollars out of the business?

SHUI TA: May I ask: is it your intention to proceed to an immediate sale?

SUN: Why? Have we got the 300 in cash? *Shui Ta shakes his head.* It was good of her to produce the 200 at once. But I've got to have the other 300 or I'm stuck.

SHUI TA: Perhaps she was a bit hasty in offering you the money. It may cost her her business. They say, haste is the wind that blew the house down.

SUN: I need it now or not at all. And the girl's not one to hesitate when it's a question of giving. Between ourselves, she hasn't hesitated much so far.

SHUI TA: Really?

SUN: All to her credit, of course.

SHUI TA: May I ask how the 500 dollars will be used?

SUN: Why not? As you seem to be checking up on me. The airport superintendent in Pekin is a friend of mine from flying school, and he can get me the job if I cough up 500 silver dollars.

SHUI TA: Isn't that an unusually large sum?

SUN: No. He has got to prove negligence against a highly conscientious pilot with a large family. You get me? That's between us, by the way, and there's no need for Shen Teh to know.

SHUI TA: Perhaps not. One point though: won't the superintendent be selling you up the river a month later?

SUN: Not me. No negligence with me. I've been long enough without a job.

SHUI TA *nods*: It is the hungry dog who pulls the cart home quickest. *He studies him for a moment or two*: That's a very big responsibility. You are asking my cousin, Mr Yang Sun, to give up her small property and all her friends in this town, and to place herself entirely in your hands. I take it your intention is to marry Shen Teh?

SUN: I'd be prepared to.

SHUI TA: Then wouldn't it be a pity to let the business go for a few silver dollars? You won't get much for a quick sale. The

200 silver dollars that you've already got would guarantee the rent for six months. Do you not feel at all tempted to carry on the tobacconist's business?

SUN: What, me? Have people see Yang Sun the pilot serving behind a counter? 'Good morning, sir; do you prefer Turkish or Virginia?' That's no career for Yang Suns, not in the twentieth century!

SHUI TA: And is flying a career, may I ask?

SUN *takes a letter from his pocket*: They're paying me 250 silver dollars a month, sir. Here is the letter; see for yourself. Look at the stamp, postmarked Pekin.

SHUI TA: 250 silver dollars? That is a lot.

SUN: Do you think I'd fly for nothing?

SHUI TA: It sounds like a good job. Mr Yang Sun, my cousin has asked me to help you get this pilot's job which means so much to you. Looking at it from her point of view I see no insuperable objection to her following the bidding of her heart. She is fully entitled to share in the delights of love. I am prepared to realise everything here. Here comes Mrs Mi Tzu, the landlady; I will ask her advice about the sale.

MRS MI TZU *enters*: Good morning, Mr Shui Ta. I suppose it's about your rent that's due the day after tomorrow?

SHUI TA: Mrs Mi Tzu, circumstances have arisen which make it doubtful whether my cousin will carry on with the business. She is contemplating marriage, and her future husband – *he introduces Yang Sun* – Mr Yang Sun, is taking her to Pekin where they wish to start a new life. If I can get a good price for my tobacco I shall sell it.

MRS MI TZU: How much do you need?

SUN: 300 in cash.

SHUI TA, *quickly*: No, no. 500!

MRS MI TZU, *to Sun*: Perhaps I can help you out. How much did your stock cost?

SHUI TA: My cousin originally paid 1000 silver dollars, and very little of it has been sold.

MRS MI TZU: 1000 silver dollars! She was swindled, of course.

I'll make you an offer: you can have 300 silver dollars for the whole business, if you move out the day after tomorrow.

SUN: All right. That's it, old boy!

SHUI TA: It's too little!

SUN: It's enough!

SHUI TA: I must have at least 500.

SUN: What for?

SHUI TA: May I just discuss something with my cousin's fiancé? *Aside to Sun*: All this stock of tobacco is pledged to two old people against the 200 silver dollars which you got yesterday.

SUN, *slowly*: Is there anything about it in writing?

SHUI TA: No.

SUN, *to Mrs Mi Tzu after a short pause*: 300 will do us.

MRS MI TZU: But I have to be sure that the business has no outstanding debts.

SUN: You answer.

SHUI TA: The business has no outstanding debts.

SUN: How soon can we have the 300?

MRS MI TZU: The day after tomorrow, and you had better think it over. Put the sale off for a month and you will get more. I can offer you 300, and that's only because I'm glad to help where it seems to be a case of young love. *Exit.*

SUN, *calling after her*: It's a deal! Lock, stock and barrel for 300, and our troubles are over. *To Shui Ta*: I suppose we might get a better offer in the next two days? Then we could even pay back the 200.

SHUI TA: Not in the time. We shan't get a single dollar over Mrs Mi Tzu's 300. Have you got the money for both your tickets, and enough to tide you over?

SUN: Sure.

SHUI TA: How much?

SUN: Anyway, I'll raise it even if I have to steal it!

SHUI TA: Oh, so that's another sum that has to be raised?

SUN: Don't worry, old boy. I'll get to Pekin all right.

SHUI TA: It costs quite a bit for two.

SUN: Two? I'm leaving the girl here. She'd only be a liability at first.

SHUI TA: I see.

SUN: Why do you look at me as if I was something the cat had brought in? Beggars can't be choosers.

SHUI TA: And what is my cousin to live on?

SUN: Can't you do something for her?

SHUI TA: I will look into it. *Pause.* I should like you to hand me back the 200 silver dollars, Mr Yang Sun, and leave them with me until you are in a position to show me two tickets to Pekin.

SUN: My dear cousin, I should like you to mind your own business.

SHUI TA: Miss Shen Teh . . .

SUN: You just leave her to me.

SHUI TA: . . . may not wish to proceed with the sale of her business when she hears . . .

SUN: O yes she will.

SHUI TA: And you are not afraid of what I may have to say against it?

SUN: My dear man!

SHUI TA: You seem to forget that she is flesh and blood, and has a mind of her own.

SUN, *amused*: It astounds me what people imagine about their female relations and the effect of sensible argument. Haven't they ever told you about the power of love, the twitching of the flesh? You want to appeal to her reason? She hasn't any reason! All she's had is a life-time of ill-treatment, poor thing! If I put my hand on her shoulder and say 'You're coming with me,' she'll hear bells and not recognise her own mother.

SHUI TA, *laboriously*: My Yang Sun!

SUN: Mr . . . whatever your name is!

SHUI TA: My cousin is indebted to you because . . .

SUN: Let's say because I've got my hand inside her blouse? Stuff that in your pipe and smoke it! *He takes another cigar, then sticks a few in his pocket, and finally puts the box under his arm.* You're not to go to her empty-handed: we're getting married, and that's settled. And she'll bring the 300 with her or else you will: either her or you. *Exit.*

MRS SHIN *sticks her head out of the back room*: How very disagreeable! And the whole Yellow Alley knows that he's got the girl exactly where he wants her.

SHUI TA, *crying out*: The business has gone! He's not in love. This means ruin. I am lost! *He begins to rush round like a captive animal, continually repeating, 'The business has gone!' – until he suddenly stops and addresses Mrs Shin*: Mrs Shin, you grew up in the gutter and so did I. Are we irresponsible? No. Do we lack the necessary brutality? No. I am ready to take you by the scruff of the neck and shake you until you spit out the farthing you stole from me, and you know it. Times are frightful, the town is hell, but we scrabble up the naked walls. Then one of us is overcome by disaster: he is in love. That is enough, he is lost. A single weakness, and you can be shovelled away. How can one remain free of every weakness, above all of the most deadly, of love? It is intolerable! It costs too much! Tell me, has one got to spend one's whole life on the look-out? What sort of world do we live in?

Love's caresses merge in strangulation.
Love's sighs grow into a scream of fear.
What are the vultures hovering for?
A girl is keeping an appointment.

MRS SHIN: I think I had better fetch the barber. You must talk to the barber. He is a man of honour. The barber: that's the right man for your cousin.

Getting no answer, she hurries away. Shui Ta continues rushing around until Mr Shu Fu enters, followed by Mrs Shin, who however is forced to withdraw at a gesture from Mr Shu Fu.

SHUI TA *turns to him*: My dear sir, rumour has it that you have shown a certain interest in my cousin. You must allow me to set aside the laws of propriety, which call for a measure of reserve, for the young lady is at the moment in great danger.

MR SHU FU: Oh!

SHUI TA: Proprietress of her own business until a few hours ago, my cousin is now little more than a beggar. Mr Shu Fu, this shop is bankrupt.

MR SHU FU: Mr Shui Ta, Miss Shen Teh's attraction lies less in the soundness of her business than in the goodness of her heart. You can tell a lot from the name they give the young lady around here: The Angel of the Slums!

SHUI TA: My dear sir, this goodness has cost my cousin 200 silver dollars in a single day! There are limits.

MR SHU FU: Allow me to put forward a different opinion: is it not time that all limits to this goodness were removed? It is the young lady's nature to do good. What is the sense of her feeding four people, as she so moves me by doing every morning! Why should she not feed four hundred? I hear for instance that she is desperate to find shelter for a few homeless. My buildings across the cattleyard are unoccupied. They are at her disposal. And so on and so forth. Mr Shui Ta, have I the right to hope that such thoughts as these which I have lately been entertaining may find a willing listener in Miss Shen Teh?

SHUI TA: Mr Shu Fu, she will listen with admiration to such lofty thoughts.

Enter Wang with the policeman. Mr Shu Fu turns round and examines the shelves.

WANG: Is Miss Shen Teh here?

SHUI TA: No.

WANG: I am Wang, the water-seller. I suppose you are Mr Shui Ta?

SHUI TA: Quite correct. Good morning, Wang.

WANG: I am a friend of Shen Teh's.

SHUI TA: I know that you are one of her closest friends.

WANG, *to the policeman*: See? *To Shui Ta*: I have come about my hand.

THE POLICEMAN: He can't use it, there's no denying.

SHUI TA, *quickly*: I see you want a sling for your arm. *He fetches a shawl from the back room and tosses it to Wang.*

WANG: But that's her new shawl.

SHUI TA: She won't need it.

WANG: But she bought it specially to please a particular person.

SHUI TA: As things have turned out that is no longer necessary.

WANG *makes a sling out of the shawl*: She is my only witness.

THE POLICEMAN: Your cousin is supposed to have seen Shu Fu the barber strike the water-carrier with his curling-tongs. Do you know anything about that?

SHUI TA: I only know that my cousin was not present when this slight incident took place.

WANG: It's a misunderstanding! When Shen Teh comes she will clear it all up. Shen Teh will bear me out. Where is she?

SHUI TA, *seriously*: Mr Wang, you call yourself my cousin's friend. At the moment my cousin has really serious worries. She has been disgracefully exploited on all sides. From now on she cannot permit herself the slightest weakness. I am convinced that you will not ask her to ruin herself utterly by testifying in your case to anything but the truth.

WANG, *puzzled*: But she told me to go to the magistrate.

SHUI TA: Was the magistrate supposed to cure your hand?

THE POLICEMAN: No. But he was to make the barber pay up.

Mr Shu Fu turns round.

SHUI TA: Mr Wang, one of my principles is never to interfere in a dispute between my friends.

Shui Ta bows to Mr Shu Fu, who bows back.

WANG, *sadly, as he takes off the sling and puts it back*: I see.

THE POLICEMAN: Which means I can go, eh? You tried your game on the wrong man, on a proper gentleman that is. You be a bit more careful with your complaints next time, fellow. If Mr Shu Fu doesn't choose to waive his legal rights you can still land in the cells for defamation. Get moving!

Both exeunt.

SHUI TA: I beg you to excuse this episode.

MR SHU FU: It is excused. *Urgently*: And this business about a 'particular person'? *He points to the shawl*. Is it really over? Finished and done with?

SHUI TA: Completely. She has seen through him. Of course, it will take time for it all to heal.

MR SHU FU: One will be careful, considerate.

SHUI TA: Her wounds are fresh.

MR SHU FU: She will go away to the country.

SHUI TA: For a few weeks. But she will be glad to talk things over first with someone she can trust.

MR SHU FU: Over a little supper, in a small but good restaurant.

SHUI TA: Discreetly. I shall hasten to inform my cousin. She will show her good sense. She is greatly upset about her business, which she regards as a gift from the gods. Please be so good as to wait for a few minutes. *Exit into the back room.*

MRS SHIN *sticks her head in*: Can we congratulate you?

MR SHU FU: You can. Mrs Shin, will you tell Shen Teh's dependants from me before tonight that I am giving them shelter in my buildings across the yard?
She grins and nods.

MR SHU FU, *standing up, to the audience*: What do you think of me, ladies and gentlemen? Could one do more? Could one be more unselfish? More delicate? More far-sighted? A little supper. How crude and vulgar that would normally sound. Yet there will be nothing of that kind, not a thing. No contact, not even an apparently accidental touch when passing the salt. All that will happen will be an exchange of ideas. Two souls will discover one another, across the flowers on the table – white chrysanthemums, by the way. *He notes it down*. No, this will be no exploiting of an unfortunate situation, no profiting from a disappointment. Understanding and assistance will be offered, but almost unspoken. By a glance alone will they be acknowledged, a glance that can also signify rather more.

MRS SHIN: Has it all turned out as you wanted, Mr Shu Fu?

MR SHU FU: Oh, quite as I wanted. You can take it that there will be changes in this neighbourhood. A certain character has been sent packing, and one or two hostile movements against this shop are due to be foiled. Certain persons who have no hesitation in trampling on the good name of the most respectable girl in this town will in future have me to deal with. What do you know about this Yang Sun?

MRS SHIN: He is the idlest, dirtiest . . .

MR SHU FU: He is nothing. He does not exist. He is simply not present, Mrs Shin.

Enter Sun.

SUN: What's this about?

MRS SHIN: Would you like me to call Mr Shui Ta, sir? He won't like strangers wandering round the shop.

MR SHU FU: Miss Shen Teh is having an important discussion with Mr Shui Ta, and they cannot be interrupted.

SUN: She's here, is she? I didn't see her go in! What are they discussing? They can't leave me out!

MR SHU FU *prevents him from going into the back room*: You will have to be patient, sir. I think I know who you are. Kindly take note that Miss Shen Teh and I are about to announce our engagement.

SUN: What?

MRS SHIN: That is a surprise for you, isn't it?

Sun struggles with the barber in an effort to get into the back room; Shen Teh emerges.

MR SHU FU: Forgive us, my dear Shen Teh. Perhaps you will explain.

SUN: What's up, Shen Teh? Have you gone crazy?

SHEN TEH, *breathlessly*: Sun, Mr Shu Fu and my cousin have agreed that I ought to listen to Mr Shu Fu's ideas of how to help the people round here. *Pause.* My cousin is against our relationship.

SUN: And you have agreed?

SHEN TEH: Yes.

Pause.

SUN: Have they told you I'm a bad character?
Shen Teh remains silent.

SUN: Perhaps I am, Shen Teh. And that is why I need you. I am
a debased character. No capital, no manners. But I can put
up a fight. They're wrecking your life, Shen Teh. *He goes up
to her, subdued*: Just look at him! Haven't you got eyes in
your head? *Putting his hand on her shoulder*: Poor creature,
what are they trying to shove you into now? Into a sensible
marriage! If it weren't for me they would simply have put
you out of your misery. Tell me yourself: but for me,
wouldn't you have gone off with him?

SHEN TEH: Yes.

SUN: A man you don't love!

SHEN TEH: Yes.

SUN: Have you completely forgotten? The rain?

SHEN TEH: No.

SUN: How you hacked me down from the tree, how you
brought me a glass of water, how you promised me the
money so I could fly again?

SHEN TEH, *trembling*: What do you want?

SUN: Come away with me.

SHEN TEH: Mr Shu Fu, forgive me, I want to go away with
Sun.

SUN: We are in love, you know. *He escorts her to the door.*
Have you got the key of the shop? *He takes it from her and
gives it to Mrs Shin.* Put it on the step when you've finished.
Come, Shen Teh.

MR SHU FU: But this is rape! *He shouts into the back room*: Mr
Shui Ta!

SUN: Tell him not to make so much row here.

SHEN TEH: Please don't call my cousin, Mr Shu Fu. We are not
of one mind, I know. But he is not in the right, I can sense it.
To the audience:
    I would go with the man whom I love.
    I would not reckon what it costs me.

I would not consider what is wiser.
I would not know whether he loves me.
I would go with the man whom I love.
SUN: Just like that.
Both walk off.

Interlude
in front of the curtain

Shen Teh in her wedding clothes, on her way to the wedding, turns and addresses the audience.

SHEN TEH: I have had a fearful experience. As I stepped out of the door, joyous and full of expectation, I found the carpet-dealer's old wife standing in the street, shakily telling me that her husband was so excited and troubled about the money she lent me that he had fallen ill. She thought it best for me in any case to give her back the money. Of course I promised. She was greatly relieved and, weeping, gave me her good wishes, begging me to excuse her for not completely trusting my cousin, nor, alas, Sun. I had to sit down on the steps when she left, I had so scared myself. In the tumult of my feelings I had thrown myself once more into Yang Sun's arms. I could resist neither his voice nor his caresses. The evil that he had spoken to Shui Ta could not teach Shen Teh a lesson. Sinking into his arms, I still thought: the gods wanted me to be kind to myself too.

To let none go to waste, not oneself either
To bring happiness to all, even oneself, that
Is good.

How could I simply have forgotten the two good old people? Like a small hurricane Sun just swept my shop off in the direction of Pekin, and with it all my friends. But he is

not evil, and he loves me. As long as I am near him he will do nothing wicked; what a man tells other men means nothing. He wants to seem big and strong then, and particularly hard-boiled. If I tell him that the old people cannot pay their taxes he will understand. He would rather get a job at the cement works than owe his flying to a wrong action. True, flying is a tremendous passion with him. Shall I be strong enough to call out the goodness in him? At the moment, on the way to my wedding, I am hovering between fear and joy.
She goes off quickly.

6

Private Room in a cheap Suburban Restaurant

A waiter is pouring out wine for the wedding guests. Round Shen Teh stand the grandfather, the sister-in-law, the niece, Mrs Shin and the unemployed man. A priest stands by himself in a corner. Sun is talking to his mother, Mrs Yang, in front. He is wearing a dinner jacket.

SUN: Bad news, mother. She just told me, oh so innocently, that she can't sell the shop for me. Some people are dunning her to pay back those 200 silver dollars she gave you. Though her cousin says there's nothing about it in writing.

MRS YANG: What did you say to her? You can't marry her, of course.

SUN: There's no point in discussing all that with her; she is too pig-headed. I have sent for her cousin.

MRS YANG: But he wants to get her married to the barber.

SUN: I've dealt with that marriage. The barber has been seen off. Her cousin will soon realise the business has gone if I don't produce the two hundred, as the creditors will seize it, but that the job's gone too if I don't get the 300 on top.

MRS YANG: I'll go and look for him outside. Go and talk to your bride now, Sun!

SHEN TEH, *to the audience as she pours out wine*: I was not mistaken in him. Not a line of his face betrayed disappointment. Despite the heavy blow that it must have been to renounce his flying he is perfectly cheerful. I love him very much. *She motions Sun to come to her.* Sun, you have not yet drunk with the bride!

SUN: What shall we drink to?

SHEN TEH: Let it be to the future.

They drink.

SUN: When the bridegroom's dinner jacket is his own!

SHEN TEH: But the bride's dress is still sometimes exposed to the rain.

SUN: To all we want for ourselves!

SHEN TEH: May it come soon!

MRS YANG, *to Mrs Shin as she leaves*: I am delighted with my son. I've always tried to make him realise that he can get any girl he wants. Him, a trained pilot and mechanic. And what does he go and tell me now? I am marrying for love, mother, he says. Money isn't everything. It's a love match! *To the sister-in-law*: Sooner or later these things have to happen, don't they? But it's hard on a mother, very hard. *Calling to the priest*: Don't cut it too short. If you take as long over the ceremony as you did arguing about the fee, that will make it nice and dignified. *To Shen Teh*: We shall have to hold things up a bit, my dear. One of our most valued guests has still to arrive. *To all*: Please excuse us. *Exit.*

THE SISTER-IN-LAW: It's a pleasure to be patient as long as there's something to drink.

They sit down.

THE UNEMPLOYED MAN: We're not missing much.

SUN, *loudly and facetiously in front of the guests*: Before the ceremony starts I ought to give you a little test. There's some point when the wedding's at such short notice. *To the guests*: I have no idea what sort of wife I'm going to get. It's most disturbing. For instance, can you use three tea-leaves to make five cups of tea?

SHEN TEH: No.

SUN: Then I shan't be getting any tea. Can you sleep on a straw mattress the size of that book the priest's reading?

SHEN TEH: Double?

SUN: Single.

SHEN TEH: In that case, no.

SUN: Dreadful, what a wife I'm getting.

All laugh. Behind Shen Teh Mrs Yang appears in the doorway. She shrugs her shoulders to tell Sun that the expected guest is not to be seen.

MRS YANG, *to the priest, who is pointing to his watch*: Don't be in such a hurry. It can't be more than a matter of minutes. There they are, all drinking and smoking, and none of them's in a hurry. *She sits down with her guests.*

SHEN TEH: But oughtn't we to discuss how it's all going to be settled?

MRS YANG: Now, not a word about business today. It so lowers the tone of a party, don't you think?

The bell at the door rings. All look towards the door, but nobody comes in.

SHEN TEH: Who is your mother waiting for, Sun?

SUN: It's to be a surprise for you. By the way, where is your cousin, Shui Ta? I get on well with him. A very sensible fellow! Brainy! Why don't you say something?

SHEN TEH: I don't know. I don't want to think about him.

SUN: Why not?

SHEN TEH: Because I wish you didn't get on with him. If you like me, you can't like him.

SUN: Then I hope the gremlins got him: the engine gremlin, the petrol gremlin and the fog gremlin. Drink, you old obstinate!

He forces her.

THE SISTER-IN-LAW, *to Mrs Shin*: Something fishy here.

MRS SHIN: What else did you expect?

THE PRIEST *comes firmly up to Mrs Yang, with his watch in his hand*: I must go, Mrs Yang. I've got a second wedding, and a funeral first thing in the morning.

MRS YANG: Do you imagine I'm holding things up for pleasure? We hoped that one jug of wine would see us through. Now look how low it's getting. *Loudly, to Shen Teh*: I can't understand, my dear Shen Teh, why your cousin should let us wait for him like this!

SHEN TEH: My cousin?

MRS YANG: But my dear girl, it's him we're waiting for. I am old-fashioned enough to feel that such a close relation of the bride ought to be at the wedding.

SHEH TEH: Oh Sun, is it about the 300 dollars?

SUN, *without looking at her*: You've heard what it's about. She is old-fashioned. I've got to consider her. We'll just wait a quarter of an hour, and if he hasn't come by then it'll mean the three gremlins have got him, and we'll start without!

MRS YANG: I expect you have all heard that my son is getting a position as a mail pilot. I am delighted about it. It's important to have a well-paid job in these days.

THE SISTER-IN-LAW: In Pekin, they say: is that right?

MRS YANG: Yes, in Pekin.

SHEN TEH: Sun, hadn't you better tell your mother that Pekin is off?

SUN: Your cousin can tell her if he feels the same way as you. Between you and me, I don't.

SHEN TEH, *shocked*: Sun!

SUN: God, how I loathe Szechwan! What a town! Do you realise what they all look like when I half shut my eyes? Like horses. They look up nervously: what's that thundering over their heads? What, won't people need them any more? Have they outlived their time? They can bite each other to death in their horse town! All I want is to get out of here!

SHEN TEH: But I promised the old couple I'd pay them back.

SUN: Yes, that's what you told me. And it's a good thing your cousin's coming as you're so silly. Drink your wine and leave business to us! We'll fix it.

SHEN TEH, *horrified*: But my cousin can't come!

SUN: What do you mean?

SHEN TEH: He's not there.

SUN: And how do you picture our future: will you kindly tell me?

SHEN TEH: I thought you still had the 200 silver dollars. We can pay them back tomorrow and keep the tobacco, which is worth much more, and sell it together outside the cement works as we can't pay the rent.

SUN: Forget it! Put it right out of your mind, sister! Me stand in the street and hawk tobacco to the cement workers: me, Yang Sun the pilot? I'd sooner blow the whole 200 in a single night. I'd sooner chuck it in the river! And your cousin knows me. I fixed with him he was to bring the 300 to the wedding.

SHEN TEH: My cousin cannot come.

SUN: And I thought he couldn't possibly stay away.

SHEN TEH: It is impossible for him to be where I am.

SUN: How very mysterious!

SHEN TEH: Sun, you must realise he is no friend of yours. It is I who love you. My cousin Shui Ta loves nobody. He is a friend to me, but not to my friends. He agreed that you should have the old people's money because he was thinking of your pilot's job in Pekin. But he will not bring the 300 silver dollars to the wedding.

SUN: Any why not?

SHEN TEH, *looking him in the eyes*: He says you only bought one ticket to Pekin.

SUN: Yes, but that was yesterday, and look what I've got to show him today! *He half pulls two tickets out of his breast pocket.* There's no need for the old woman to see. That's two tickets to Pekin, for me and for you. Do you still think your cousin's against the marriage?

SHEN TEH: No. The job is a good one. And my business has gone.

SUN: It's for your sake I sold the furniture.

SHEN TEH: Don't say any more! Don't show me the tickets! It makes me too afraid that I might simply go off with you. But do you see, Sun, I can't give you the 300 silver dollars, or what is to become of the two old people?

SUN: What's to become of me? *Pause.* You'd better have a drink! Or do you believe in being careful? I can't stick a careful woman. When I drink I start flying again. And you: if you drink there's just the faintest shadow of a possibility you may understand me.

SHEN TEH: Don't think I don't understand you. You want to fly, and I can't be any help.

SUN: 'Here's your plane, beloved, but I'm afraid it's a wing short.'

SHEN TEH: Sun, there's no honourable way for us to get that job in Pekin. That's why I need you to hand back the 200 silver dollars I gave you. Give them to me now, Sun!

SUN: 'Give them to me now, Sun!' What do you think you are talking about? Are you my wife or aren't you? Because you're ratting on me, don't you realise? Luckily – and luckily for you too – it doesn't depend on you, because it's all been settled.

MRS YANG, *icily*: Sun, are you certain the bride's cousin will be coming? It almost looks as though he had something against this marriage, as he doesn't appear.

SUN: But what are you thinking of, mother! Him and me are like that. I'll open the door wide so that he spots us at once as he comes rushing up to act as best man to his old friend Sun. *He goes to the door and kicks it open. Then he comes back, swaying slightly because he has already drunk too much, and sits down again by Shen Teh.* We'll wait. Your cousin has got more sense than you. Love is an essential part of living, he wisely says. And what's more he knows what it would mean for you: no shop left and no wedding either!

They wait.

MRS YANG: At last!

Footsteps are heard, and all look towards the door. But the footsteps move on.

MRS SHIN: There's going to be a scandal. One can feel it; one can sniff it in the air. The bride is waiting for the ceremony, but the bridegroom is waiting for her honourable cousin.

SUN: The honourable cousin is taking his time.

SHEN TEH, *softly*: Oh, Sun!

SUN: Sitting here with the tickets in my pocket, and an idiot beside me who can't do arithmetic! And I see the day coming when you'll be putting the police on me to get your 200 silver dollars back.

SHEN TEH, *to the audience*: He is evil and he would like me to be evil too. Here am I who love him, and he stays waiting for a cousin. But round me sit the defenceless: the old woman with her sick husband, the poor who wait at the door every morning for rice, and an unknown man from Pekin who is worried about his job. And they all protect me because they all have faith in me.

SUN *stares at the glass jug in which the wine is near the bottom*: The wine-jug is our clock. We are poor people, and once the guests have drunk the wine the clock has run down for ever. *Mrs Yang signs to him to keep silent, and footsteps can be heard once more.*

THE WAITER *enters*: Do you wish to order another jug of wine, Mrs Yang?

MRS YANG: No, I think there will be enough. Wine only makes one too hot, don't you think?

MRS SHIN: I imagine it costs a lot too.

MRS YANG: Drinking always makes me perspire.

THE WAITER: Would you mind settling the bill now, madam?

MRS YANG *ignores him*: Ladies and gentlemen, I hope you can be patient a little longer: our relative must be on his way by now. *To the waiter*: Don't interrupt the party.

THE WAITER: My orders are not to let you leave until the bill is settled.

MRS YANG: But I am well known here!

THE WAITER: Exactly!

MRS YANG: The service nowadays is really outrageous! Don't you think so, Sun?

THE PRIEST: I fear that I must leave. *Exit weightily.*

MRS YANG, *desperate*: Please all of you remain seated! The priest will be back in a few minutes.

SUN: Drop it, mother. Ladies and gentlemen, now that the priest has left we cannot detain you any longer.

THE SISTER-IN-LAW: Come on, Grandpa!

THE GRANDFATHER *solemnly empties his glass*: The bride!

THE NIECE, *to Shen Teh*: Don't mind him. He means it friendly-like. He's fond of you.

MRS SHIN: That's what I call a flop!

All the guests leave.

SHEN TEH: Shall I leave too, Sun?

SUN: No, you wait. *He pulls at her wedding finery so that it is askew.* It's your wedding, isn't it? I'm going to wait on, and the old lady will wait on. She is anxious to see her bird in the air again anyhow. It's my opinion that the moon will be nothing but green cheese before she can step outside and see his plane thundering over the house. *To the empty chairs as if the guests were still there*: Ladies and gentlemen, can't you make conversation? Don't you like it here? The wedding has only been somewhat postponed, on account of the non-arrival of influential relations, and because the bride doesn't know what love is. To keep you amused I, the bridegroom, will sing you a song. *He sings*:

THE SONG OF GREEN CHEESE

A day will come, so the poor were informed
As they sat at their mother's knees
When a child of low birth shall inherit the earth
And the moon shall be made of green cheese.
    When the moon is green cheese
    The poor shall inherit the earth.

Then goodness will be a thing to reward
And evil a mortal offence.
'Where there's merit there's money' won't sound quite
    so funny
There will really be no difference.
    When the moon is green cheese
    There won't be this difference.

Then the grass will look down on the blue sky below
And the pebbles will roll up the stream
And man is a king. Without doing a thing
He gorges on honey and cream.
    When the moon is green cheese
    The world flows with honey and cream.

Then I shall become a pilot again
And you'll get a deputy's seat.
You, man on the loose, will find you're some use
And you, ma, can put up your feet.
    When the moon is green cheese
    The weary can put up their feet.

And as we have waited quite long enough
This new world has got to be born
Not at the last minute so there's nothing left in it
But at the first glimmer of dawn
    When the moon is green cheese
    The very first glimmer of dawn.

MRS YANG: He won't come now.
The three of them sit there and two of them look towards the door.

Interlude

Wang's Sleeping-Place

Once more the gods appear to the water-seller in a dream. He has fallen asleep over a large book. Music.

WANG: How good that you have come, Illustrious Ones! Permit me a question which disturbs me greatly. In the tumbledown hut belonging to a priest who has left to become an unskilled labourer in the cement works I discovered a book, and in it I found a remarkable passage. I should like to read it to you. It runs: *With his left hand he thumbs through an imaginary book laid over the book in his lap, and lifts this imaginary book up to read from it, leaving the real one lying where it was.* 'In Sung there is a place known as Thorn Hedge. There catalpas, cypresses and mulberries flourish. Now those trees which are nine or ten inches in circumference are chopped down by the people who need stakes for their dog kennels. Those which are three or four feet in circumference are chopped down by rich and respectable families who want planks for their coffins. Those which are seven or eight feet in circumference are chopped down by persons seeking beams for their luxurious villas. And so none reaches its full quota of years, but is brought down prematurely by saw or by axe. That is the price of utility.'

THE THIRD GOD: That would mean that the least useful is the best.

WANG: No, only the most fortunate. The least good is the most fortunate.

THE FIRST GOD: Ah, what things they write!

THE SECOND GOD: Why are you so deeply moved by this comparison, O water-seller?

WANG: On account of Shen Teh, Illustrious Ones! She has

failed in her love because she obeyed the commandment to love her neighbours. Perhaps she really is too good for this world, O Illustrious Ones!

THE FIRST GOD: Nonsense. You poor, feeble creature! It seems to me that you are half eaten away by scepticism and lice.

WANG: Certainly, O Illustrious One! I only thought you might perhaps intervene.

THE FIRST GOD: Out of the question. Our friend here – *he points to the third god, who has a black eye* – intervened in a quarrel only yesterday; you see the result.

WANG: But they had to send for her cousin yet again. He is an unusually capable man, I know from experience, but even he could not set things straight. It looks as if the shop were already lost.

THE THIRD GOD, *disturbed*: Do you think perhaps we ought to help?

THE FIRST GOD: My view is that she has got to help herself.

THE SECOND GOD, *strictly*: The worse the difficulties, the better the good man will prove to be. Suffering ennobles!

THE FIRST GOD: We are putting all our hopes in her.

THE THIRD GOD: Our search is not progressing well. Now and again we come across a good start, admirable intentions, a lot of high principles, but it hardly adds up to a good person. When we do find people who are halfway good, they are not living a decent human experience. *Confidentially*: The nights are getting worse and worse. You can tell where we have been spending them from the straws sticking to our clothes.

WANG: Just one request. Could you not at least . . .

THE GODS: Nothing. We are but observers. We firmly believe that our good person will find her own feet on this sombre earth. Her powers will wax with her burden. Only wait a little, O water-seller, and you will find all's well that ends . . .

The gods' figures have been growing steadily paler, their

voices steadily fainter. Now they disappear, and their voices cease.

7

Yard behind Shen Teh's Shop

A few household goods on a cart. Shen Teh and Mrs Shin are taking washing down from the line.

MRS SHIN: I can't think why you don't put up a better fight for your business.

SHEN TEH: How? I can't even pay the rent. I have got to pay the old people their 200 silver dollars back today, and because I've given them to someone else I shall have to sell my stock to Mrs Mi Tzu.

MRS SHIN: All gone, eh? No man, no stock, no home! That comes of trying to set oneself up as a cut above our lot. How do you propose to live now?

SHEN TEH: I don't know. I might earn a bit as a tobacco sorter.

MRS SHIN: What are Mr Shui Ta's trousers doing here? He must have gone off in his shirt.

SHEN TEH: He's got another pair.

MRS SHIN: I thought you said he had gone away for good. What does he want to leave his trousers behind for?

SHEN TEH: Perhaps he's finished with them.

MRS SHIN: Oughtn't you to make a parcel of them?

SHEN TEH: No.

Mr Shu Fu bursts in.

MR SHU FU: Don't tell me. I know it all. You have sacrificed your young love so that two old people who trusted you should not be ruined. It was not for nothing that this malicious and mistrustful district christened you 'The Angel of the Slums'. The gentleman to whom you were engaged proved unable to raise himself to your moral stature; you threw him over. And now you are closing your shop, that little haven of refuge for so many! I cannot stand by and see it. Day after day I have stood at the door of my shop and seen the knot of down-and-outs before your window, and you yourself doling out rice. Must all that vanish for ever? Must goodness be defeated? Ah, if only you will allow me to assist you in your good works! No, don't say a thing! I wish for no assurances. No promises that you will accept my help! But herewith – *he takes out a cheque-book and writes a cheque, which he lays on the cart* – I make you out a blank cheque, which you can fill in for any sum you like; and now I shall go, quietly and modestly, demanding nothing in return, on tiptoe, full of respectful admiration, not a thought for myself.

Exit.

MRS SHIN *examines the cheque*: This'll save you! People like you have some luck! You can always find a mug. Now hurry up. Write in 1,000 silver dollars and I'll run to the bank with it before he comes to his senses.

SHEN TEH: Put the laundry basket on the cart. I can pay for the washing without the cheque.

MRS SHIN: What do you mean? You're not going to take the cheque? That's criminal! Is it just because you feel you would have to marry him? That would be plain crazy. A fellow like that just asks to be led by the nose! That sort really likes it. Are you still wanting to hang on to that pilot of yours, when everyone here and in Yellow Alley knows how badly he's treated you?

SHEN TEH: It all comes from poverty. *To the audience*:

> At night I watched him blow out his cheeks in his sleep: they were evil
>
> And at dawn I held his coat up to the light, and saw the wall through it.
>
> When I saw his sly smile I was afraid, but

When I saw the holes in his shoes I loved him dearly.

MRS SHIN: So you're still sticking up for him? I never heard anything so idiotic. *Angry*: I shall be relieved when we have got you out of the district.

SHEN TEH *staggers as she takes down the washing*: I'm feeling a bit giddy.

MRS SHIN *takes the washing from her*: Do you often feel giddy when you bend or stretch? Let's only hope it isn't a little one! *Laughs*. He has fixed you good and proper! If that's it then the big cheque will turn sour. It wasn't meant for that sort of situation. *She goes to the rear with a basket.*

Shen Teh looks after her without moving. Then she examines her body, feels it, and a great joy appears in her face.

SHEN TEH, *softly*: Oh joy! A small being is coming to life in my body. There is nothing to see yet. But he is already there. The world awaits him in secret. In the cities they have heard the rumour: someone is coming now with whom we must reckon. *She presents her small son to the audience*: An airman!

Salute a new conqueror

Of unknown mountains, inaccessible countries! One

Carrying letters from man to man

Across the wastes where no man yet has trod!

She begins to walk up and down, leading her small son by the hand. Come my son, inspect your world. Here, that is a tree. Bow politely, greet him. *She performs a bow.* There, now you know one another. Listen, that is the water-seller coming. A friend, shake hands with him. Don't be nervous. 'A glass of cool water for my son, please. It's a hot day.' *She hands him the glass.* Ah, the policeman! I think we will avoid him. Perhaps we might collect one or two cherries over there, from rich old Mr Feh Pung's orchard. This is a moment not to be seen. Come, poor little bastard! You too like cherries! Soft, soft, my son! *They walk cautiously, looking around them.* No, round this way, where the bushes will shield us. No, no going straight to the point in this case.

He seems to be dragging away; she resists. We've got to be sensible. *Suddenly she gives in.* Very well, if you can't do it any other way. . . . *She lifts him up.* Can you reach the cherries? Shove them in your mouth, that's the best place for them. *She eats one herself, which he puts into her mouth.* Tastes fine. O god, the police. This is where we run. *They flee.* Here's the road. Now gently, walk slowly so we don't attract attention. As if nothing whatever had happened. . . . *She sings as she walks along with the child*:

> A plum off my tree
> Bit a man on the knee
> The man had a thirst
> Got his own bite in first.

Wang the water-seller has entered, leading a child by the hand. He watches Shen Teh in astonishment.

SHEN TEH, *as Wang coughs*: Oh, Wang! Good day.

WANG: Shen Teh, I have heard you are in difficulties, that you must even sell your business to pay debts. But here's this child without any home. It was playing about in the slaughterhouse. They say it belongs to Lin To the carpenter, who had to give up his workshop a few weeks ago and is now on the drink. His children are wandering around starving. What can be done with them?

SHEN TEH *takes the child from him*: Come on, little man! *To the audience*:

> Here, you! Someone begging for shelter.
> A chip of tomorrow begging you for a today.
> His friend, the conqueror, whom you know
> Can answer for him

To Wang: He can quite well live in Mr Shu Fu's sheds, where I may be going too. I myself am expecting a child. But do not repeat that, or Yang Sun may hear of it, and we can only hamper him. See if you can find Lin To in the lower town, and tell him to come here.

WANG: Many thanks, Shen Teh. I knew you would find an answer. *To the child*: See? A good person always knows a way. I'll go off quickly and fetch your father. *He starts to go.*

SHEN TEH: Oh, Wang, I have just remembered. What happened about your hand? I did want to give evidence for you, but my cousin . . .

WANG: Don't bother about my hand. Look, I've already learnt to do without my right hand. I hardly need it at all. *He shows her how he can manage his carrying pole without his right hand*: See how I manage?

SHEN TEH: But you mustn't let it get stiff! Take that cart, sell the lot, and use the money to go to the doctor. I am ashamed of having let you down like that. And what must you think of me for accepting the barber's offer of the sheds!

WANG: The homeless can live there now, and you yourself. After all, that matters more than my hand. I'll go and fetch the carpenter. *Exit.*

SHEN TEH *calls after him*: Promise me you'll let me take you to the doctor!

Mrs Shin has come back and has been making repeated signs.

SHEN TEH: What is it?

MRS SHIN: Are you mad? Giving away the cart with all you've got left? What's his hand to do with you? If the barber gets to know he'll throw you out of the last lodging you're likely to find. You haven't paid me for the washing yet!

SHEN TEH: Why are you so unpleasant?

    To trample on one's fellows
    Is surely exhausting? Veins in your temples
    Stick out with the strenuousness of greed.
    Loosely held forth
    A hand gives and receives with the same suppleness. Yet
    Greedily snatching it has got to strain. Oh
    How tempting it is to be generous. How welcome
    Friendliness can somehow feel. A kindly word
    Escapes like a sign of contentment.

Mrs Shin goes off angrily.

SHEN TEH, *to the child*: Sit here and wait till your father comes. *The child sits on the ground. Enter the elderly couple who visited Shen Teh on the day of the opening of her shop. Man and wife are dragging big sacks.*

THE WOMAN: Are you by yourself, Shen Teh? *When Shen Teh nods she calls in her nephew, who is also carrying a sack.* Where's your cousin?

SHEN TEH: He went away.

THE WOMAN: Is he coming back?

SHEN TEH: No. I'm giving up the shop.

THE WOMAN: So we heard. That's why we've come. These are a few sacks of leaf tobacco which somebody owed us, and we'd be ever so grateful if you could move them to your new home with your own things. We've no place to put them yet, and if we have them in the street people are bound to notice. I don't see how you can refuse to do us this little favour after the bad luck we had in your shop.

SHEN TEH: I will do it for you gladly.

THE MAN: And if anyone happens to ask you whose sacks these are you can say they're yours.

SHEN TEH: Who would want to know?

THE WOMAN, *giving her a sharp look*: The police for one. They've got it in for us, and they're out to ruin us. Where do we put the sacks?

SHEN TEH: I don't know; just as this moment I'd sooner not do anything that might get me into gaol.

THE WOMAN: Isn't that like you? All we've been able to save of our things is a few rotten old sacks of tobacco, and a lot you care if we lose them!
Shen Teh is stubbornly silent.

THE MAN: Don't you see that this stock of tobacco might allow us to start manufacturing in a small way? Then we could work our way up.

SHEN TEH: All right, I'll keep your sacks for you. They can go in the back room for the present.
She goes in with them. The child has been watching her. Now

it looks round timidly, goes to the dustbin and starts fishing in it. It begins to eat something that it has found. Shen Teh and the others return.

THE WOMAN: You realise we're completely in your hands?

SHEN TEH: Yes. *She notices the child and stiffens.*

THE MAN: We'll call on you the day after tomorrow in Mr Shu Fu's buildings.

SHEN TEH: Please leave at once; I'm not well. *She pushes them out. Exeunt the three.* He's hungry. Fishing in the dustbin. *She lifts up the child and expresses her horror at the fate of poor children in a speech, showing the audience his dirty mouth. She proclaims her determination never to treat her own child in such a heartless way.*

> O son, O airman! What sort of a world
> Awaits you? Will you too
> Be left to fish in the garbage? Observe
> The greyness round his mouth! *She exhibits the child.* Is that
> How you treat your fellow-creatures? Have you
> Not the least compassion for the fruit
> Of your bodies? No pity
> For yourselves, you unfortunates? Henceforth I
> Shall fight at least for my own, if I have to be
> Sharp as a tiger. Yes, from the hour
> When I saw this thing I shall cut myself off
> From them all, never resting
> Till I have at least saved my son, if only him.
> What I learnt from my schooling, the gutter
> By violence and trickery now
> Shall serve you, my son: to you
> I would be kind; a tiger, a savage beast
> To all others if need be. And
> It need be.

She goes off to change herself into her cousin.

SHEN TEH, *walking off*: Once more it must be done, for the last time I hope.

She has taken Shui Ta's trousers with her. Mrs Shin returns and stares inquisitively after her. Enter the sister-in-law and the grandfather.

THE SISTER-IN-LAW: Shop shut, all her stuff in the yard! It's the finish!

MRS SHIN: That's what comes of selfishness, irresponsibility and the lusts of the flesh! And where is she heading? Downwards! To Mr Shu Fu's sheds, along with the rest of you!

THE SISTER-IN-LAW: She'll be surprised at what she finds there! We've come to complain! A damp rabbit-warren with half rotten floors! The barber only let us have them because his stock of soap was going bad there. 'I can give you shelter, what do you say to that?' We say, it's a scandal!

Enter the unemployed man.

THE UNEMPLOYED MAN: Is it true Shen Teh's clearing out?

THE SISTER-IN-LAW: Yes. She meant to sneak away so we shouldn't know.

MRS SHIN: She's ashamed because she's broke.

THE UNEMPLOYED MAN, *excited*: She must send for her cousin! All of you, advise her to send for her cousin! He's the only one can do anything.

THE SISTER-IN-LAW: That's right! He's mean enough, but at least he'll save her business, and then she'll be generous.

THE UNEMPLOYED MAN: I wasn't thinking of us, I was thinking of her. But it's a fact: he must be sent for for our sakes too.

Enter Wang with the carpenter. He is leading two children by the hand.

THE CARPENTER: Truly, I can't thank you enough. *To the others*: We're to get a lodging.

MRS SHIN: Where?

THE CARPENTER: In Mr Shu Fu's buildings. And it was little Feng who managed it! Ah, there you are! 'Here's someone begging for shelter', Miss Shen Teh's supposed to have said, and she finds us lodgings there and then. Say thank you to

your brother, all of you!
The carpenter and his children make pretence of bowing to the child.

THE CARPENTER: Our thanks, shelter-beggar!
Shui Ta has entered.

SHUI TA: May I ask what you are all doing here?

THE UNEMPLOYED MAN: Mr Shui Ta!

WANG: Good day, Mr Shui Ta. I didn't realise you were back. You know Lin To the carpenter. Miss Shen Teh promised to find him a corner in one of Mr Shu Fu's buildings.

SHUI TA: Mr Shu Fu's buildings are booked.

THE CARPENTER: Does that mean we can't lodge there?

SHUI TA: No. These premises are reserved for another purpose.

THE SISTER-IN-LAW: Have we got to move out too then?

SHUI TA: Unfortunately.

THE SISTER-IN-LAW: But where can we all go?

SHUI TA, *shrugging his shoulders*: Miss Shen Teh, who has left town, gave me to understand that she had no intention of neglecting you. In future however it must all be rather more sensibly arranged. No more free meals without working for it. Instead every man shall have the opportunity to improve his condition honourably by his labour. Miss Shen Teh has decided to find work for you all. Those of you who now choose to follow me into Mr Shu Fu's buildings will not be led into the blue.

THE SISTER-IN-LAW: Do you mean we've all got to start working for Shen Teh?

SHUI TA: Yes. You will shred tobacco. There are three full bales in the back room there. Get them!

THE SISTER-IN-LAW: Don't forget we used to have a shop of our own. We'd rather work for ourselves. We've got our own tobacco.

SHUI TA, *to the unemployed man and the carpenter*: Perhaps you would like to work for Shen Teh, as you have no tobacco of your own?

The carpenter and the unemployed man comply reluctantly, and exeunt. Mrs Mi Tzu enters.

MRS MI TZU: Now then, Mr Shui Ta, how about the sale of the stock? I have your 300 silver dollars here with me.

SHUI TA: Mrs Mi Tzu, I have decided not to sell, but to sign the lease.

MRS MI TZU: What? Don't you want the money for the pilot any more?

SHUI TA: No.

MRS MI TZU: And can you find the rent?

SHUI TA *takes the barber's cheque off the cart and fills it in.* I have here a cheque for 10,000 silver dollars, signed by Mr Shu Fu, who is taking an interest in my cousin. Look for yourself, Mrs Mi Tzu! You will get your 200 silver dollars for the next half-year's rent before six this evening. And now, Mrs Mi Tzu, you will allow me to go on with my own work. I am extremely busy today and must ask you to excuse me.

MRS MI TZU: So Mr Shu Fu is in the pilot's shoes now! 10,000 silver dollars! All the same I am astounded that young girls nowadays should be so frivolous and unstable, Mr Shui Ta. *Exit.*

The carpenter and the unemployed man bring in the sacks.

THE CARPENTER: I can't think why I should have to cart your sacks for you.

SHUI TA: The point is that I can. Your son has a healthy appetite. He wants to eat, Mr Lin To.

THE SISTER-IN-LAW *sees the sacks*: Has my brother-in-law been here?

MRS SHIN: Yes.

THE SISTER-IN-LAW: I thought so. I know those sacks. That's our tobacco.

SHUI TA: I advise you not to say that so loudly. That is my tobacco, as you can see from the fact that it was in my room. But if you have any doubts about it we can go to the police and clear them up. Do you wish to?

THE SISTER-IN-LAW, *crossly*: No.

SHUI TA: Evidently you haven't got your own stock of tobacco after all. Perhaps under those circumstances you will accept the helping hand which Miss Shen Teh is offering you? Be so good now as to show me the way to Mr Shu Fu's buildings. *Taking the hand of the carpenter's youngest child, Shui Ta walks off, followed by the carpenter, his remaining children, the sister-in-law, the grandfather, the unemployed man. Sister-in-law, carpenter and unemployed man drag out the sacks.*

WANG: He is not a wicked man, but Shen Teh is good.

MRS SHIN: I'm not sure. There's a pair of trousers missing from the clothes line, and her cousin is wearing them. That must mean something. I'd like to know what.
Enter the two old people.

THE OLD WOMAN: Is Miss Shen Teh not here?

MRS SHIN, *absently*: Left town.

THE OLD WOMAN: That's strange. She was going to bring us something.

WANG, *looking painfully at his hand*: And she was going to help me. My hand's going stiff. She's sure to be back soon. Her cousin never stays long.

MRS SHIN: He doesn't, does he?

Interlude

Wang's Sleeping-Place

Music. In a dream the water-seller informs the gods of his fears. The gods are still engaged on their long pilgrimage. They seem tired. Unresponsive at first, they turn and look back at the water-seller.

WANG: Before you appeared and awoke me, O Illustrious

Ones, I was dreaming and saw my dear sister Shen Teh in great distress among the reeds by the river, at the spot where the suicides are found. She was staggering in a strange way and held her head bent as if she were carrying something soft and heavy that was pressing her into the mud. When I called to her she called back that she must carry the whole bundle of precepts across to the other bank, keeping it dry so that the ink should not run. In fact I could see nothing on her shoulder. But I was sharply reminded that you gods had lectured her about the major virtues as a reward for her taking you in when you were stuck for a night's lodging, the more shame to us! I am certain you understand my worries for her.

THE THIRD GOD: What do you suggest?

WANG: A slight reduction of the precepts, Illustrious Ones. A slight alleviation of the bundle of precepts, O gracious ones, in view of the difficulty of the times.

THE THIRD GOD: For instance, Wang, for instance?

WANG: For instance, that only good will should be required instead of love, or . . .

THE THIRD GOD: But that is far harder, you unhappy man!

WANG: Or fairness instead of justice.

THE THIRD GOD: But that means more work!

WANG: Then plain decency instead of honour!

THE THIRD GOD: But that is far more, you man of doubts!

They wander wearily on.

8

Shui Ta's Tobacco Factory

Shui Ta has set up a small tobacco factory in Mr Shu Fu's huts. Horribly constricted, a number of families huddle behind bars.

Women and children predominate, among them the sister-in-law, the grandfather, the carpenter and his children. In front of them enter Mrs Yang, followed by her son, Sun.

MRS YANG, *to the audience*: I must describe to you how the wisdom and discipline of our universally respected Mr Shui Ta turned my son Sun from a broken wreck into a useful citizen. Near the cattle-yard, as the whole neighbourhood quickly came to hear, Mr Shui Ta started a small but rapidly prospering tobacco factory. Three months ago I found it advisable to call on him there with my son. He received me after a brief wait.
Shui Ta comes up to Mrs Yang from the factory.
SHUI TA: What can I do for you, Mrs Yang?
MRS YANG: Mr Shui Ta, I should like to put in a word for my son. The police came round this morning, and we heard that you were suing in Miss Shen Teh's name for breach of promise and fraudulent conversion of 200 silver dollars.
SHUI TA: Quite correct, Mrs Yang.
MRS YANG: Mr Shui Ta, in the gods' name can you not temper justice with mercy once more? The money has gone. He ran through it in a couple of days as soon as the idea of the pilot's job fell through. I know he is a bad lot. He had already sold my furniture and was going to set off to Pekin without his poor old mother. *She weeps.* There was a time when Miss Shen Teh thought very highly of him.
SHUI TA: Have you got anything to say to me, Mr Yang Sun?
SUN, *sombrely*: The money's gone.
SHUI TA: Mrs Yang, in view of the weakness which my cousin for some inexplicable reason felt for your broken-down son, I am prepared to give him another chance. She told me she thought honest work might bring an improvement. I can find him a place in my factory. The 200 silver dollars will be deducted in instalments from his wages.
SUN: So it's to be factory or clink?
SHUI TA: It's your own choice.

SUN: And no chance of talking to Shen Teh, I suppose.

SHUI TA: No.

SUN: Show me where I work.

MRS YANG: A thousand thanks, Mr Shui Ta. Your kindness is overwhelming, and the gods will repay you. *To Sun*: You have strayed from the narrow path. See if honest work will make you fit to look your mother in the face again.

Sun follows Shui Ta into the factory. Mrs Yang returns to the front of the stage.

MRS YANG: The first weeks were difficult for Sun. The work was not what he was used to. He had little chance to show what he could do. It was only in the third week that a small incident brought him luck. He and Lin To who used to be a carpenter were shifting bales of tobacco.

Sun and the former carpenter Lin To are each shifting two bales of tobacco.

THE FORMER CARPENTER *comes to a halt groaning, and lowers himself on to one of the bales*: I'm about done in. I'm too old for this sort of work.

SUN *likewise sits down*: Why don't you tell them they can stuff their bales?

THE FORMER CARPENTER: How would we live then? To get the barest necessities I must even set the kids to work. A pity Miss Shen Teh can't see it! She was good.

SUN: I've known worse. If things had been a bit less miserable we'd have hit it off quite well together. I'd like to know where she is. We had better get on. He usually comes about now.

They get up.

SUN *sees Shui Ta coming*: Give us one of your sacks, you old cripple! *Sun adds one of Lin To's bales to his own load.*

THE FORMER CARPENTER: Thanks a lot! Yes, if she were there you'd certainly go up a peg when she saw how helpful you were to an old man. Ah yes!

Enter Shui Ta.

MRS YANG: And a glance is enough for Mr Shui Ta to spot a

good worker who will tackle anything. And he takes a hand.

SHUI TA: Hey, you two! What's happening here? Why are you only carrying one sack?

THE FORMER CARPENTER: I feel a bit run down today, Mr Shui Ta, and Yang Sun was so kind . . .

SHUI TA: You go back and pick up three bales, my friend. If Yang Sun can do it, so can you. Yang Sun puts his heart in it, and you don't.

MRS YANG, *while the former carpenter fetches two more bales*: Not a word to Sun, of course, but Mr Shui Ta had noticed. And next Saturday, at the pay desk . . .

A table is set up and Shui Ta comes with a small bag of money. Standing next the overseer – the former unemployed man – he pays out the wages. Sun steps up to the table.

THE OVERSEER: Yang Sun – 6 silver dollars.

SUN: Sorry, but it can't be more than five. Not more than 5 silver dollars. *He takes the list which the overseer is holding.* Look, here you are, you've got me down for six full days, but I was off one day, as I had to go to court. *Ingratiatingly*: I wouldn't like to be paid money I hadn't earned, however lousy the pay is.

THE OVERSEER: 5 silver dollars, then! *To Shui Ta*: Very unusual that, Mr Shui Ta!

SHUI TA: How do you come to have six days down here when it was only five?

THE OVERSEER: Quite correct, Mr Shui Ta, I must have made a mistake. *To Sun, coldly*: It won't occur again.

SHIU TA *calls Sun aside*: I have noticed lately that you have plenty of strength and don't grudge it to the firm. Now I see that you are to be trusted too. Does it often happen that the overseer makes mistakes to the firm's loss?

SUN: He's friends with some of the workers, and they count him as one of them.

SHUI TA: I see. One good turn deserves another. Would you like a bonus?

SUN: No. But perhaps I might point out that I have also got a brain. I have had a fair education, you know. The overseer has the right ideas about the men, but being uneducated he can't see what's good for the firm. Give me a week's trial, Mr Shui Ta, and I think I can prove to you that my brains are worth more to the firm than the mere strength of my muscles.

MRS YANG: They were bold words, but that evening I told my Sun: 'You are a flying man. Show that you can get to the top where you are now! Fly, my eagle!' And indeed it is remarkable what brains and education will achieve! How can a man hope to better himself without them? Absolute miracles were performed by my son in the factory directed by Mr Shui Ta!

Sun stands behind the workers, his legs apart. They are passing a basket of raw tobacco above their heads.

SUN: Here you, that's not proper work! The basket has got to be kept moving! *To a child:* Sit on the ground, can't you? It takes up less room! And you might as well get on with a bit of pressing: yes, it's you I'm talking to! You idle loafers, what do you think you're paid for? Come on with that basket! O hell and damnation! Put grandpa over there and let him shred with the kids! There's been enough dodging here! Now take your time from me! *He claps time with his hands and the basket moves faster.*

MRS YANG: And no enmities, no slanderous allegations by the uneducated – for he was not spared that – could hold my son back from the fulfilment of his duty.

One of the workers begins singing the song of the eighth elephant. The others join in the chorus.

WORKERS' CHORUS:

SONG OF THE EIGHTH ELEPHANT

I

Seven elephants worked for Major Chung
And an eighth one followed the others.

Seven were wild and the eighth was tame
And the eighth had to spy on his brothers.

    Keep moving!
    Major Chung owns a wood
    See it's cleared before tonight.
    That's orders. Understood?

2

Seven elephants were clearing the wood
The eighth bore the Major in person
Number eight merely checked that the work was correct
And spared himself any exertion.

    Dig harder!
    Major Chung owns a wood
    See it's cleared before tonight.
    That's orders. Understood?

3

Seven elephants got tired of their work
Of shoving and digging and felling.
The Major was annoyed with the seven he employed
But rewarded the eighth one for telling.

    What's up now?
    Major Chung owns a wood
    See it's cleared before tonight.
    That's orders. Understood?

4

Seven elephants, not a tusk in their heads
The eighth's were in excellent order.
So eight used his wits, slashed the seven to bits
And the Major had never laughed harder.

    Dig away!
    Major Chung owns a wood
    See it's cleared before tonight.
    That's orders. Understood?

Shui Ta has lounged forward, smoking a cigar. Yang Sun has laughingly joined in the chorus of the third verse and quickened the tempo in the fourth verse by clapping his hands.

MRS YANG: We really owe everything to Mr Shui Ta. With wisdom and discipline, but with hardly a word of interference, he has brought out all the good that lay in Sun! He made no fantastic promises like his much overrated cousin, but forced him to do good honest work. Today Sun is a different person from what he was three months ago. I think you will admit it! 'The noble soul is like a bell, strike it and it rings, strike it not and it rings not', as our forebears used to say.

9

Shen Teh's Shop

The shop has been turned into an office, with easy chairs and fine carpets. It is raining. Shui Ta, now become fat, is showing out the old couple of carpet-dealers. Mrs Shin watches with amusement. It is plain that she is wearing new clothes.

SHUI TA: I regret that I cannot say when she will be back.

THE OLD WOMAN: We had a letter today enclosing the 200 silver dollars we once lent her. It didn't say who from. But it can only be Shen Teh who sent it. We'd like to write to her: what's her address?

SHUI TA: I'm afraid I don't know that either.

THE OLD MAN: We'd better go.

THE OLD WOMAN: Sooner or later she is bound to come back.
  Shui Ta bows. The two old people go off uncertain and upset.

MRS SHIN: It was too late when they got their money back. Now they've lost their shop because they couldn't pay their taxes.

SHUI TA: Why didn't they come to me?

MRS SHIN: People don't like coming to you. I expect they started by waiting for Shen Teh to come back as they'd got nothing in writing. Then the old man got ill at the critical moment, and his wife had to nurse him night and day.

SHUI TA *has to sit down because he feels sick*: I feel giddy again.

MRS SHIN *fusses around him*: You're six months gone! You mustn't let yourself get worked up. Lucky for you you've got me. Everyone can do with a helping hand. Yes, when your time comes I shall be at your side. *She laughs.*

SHUI TA, *feebly*: Can I count on that, Mrs Shin?

MRS SHIN: You bet! It'll cost money of course. Undo your collar, and you'll feel better.

SHUI TA, *pitifully*: It's all for the baby's sake, Mrs Shin.

MRS SHIN: All for the baby's sake.

SHUI TA: I'm getting fat so quickly, though. People are bound to notice.

MRS SHIN: They think it's because you're doing so well.

SHUI TA: And what will happen to him?

MRS SHIN: You're always asking that. He will be looked after. The best that money can buy.

SHUI TA: Yes. *Anxiously*: And he must never see Shui Ta.

MRS SHIN: Never. Only Shen Teh.

SHUI TA: But all the gossip round here! The water-seller and his rumours! They're watching the shop!

MRS SHIN: As long as the barber doesn't hear there's no harm done. Come on dear, have a drop of water.

Enter Sun in a smart suit carrying a business man's brief-case. He is amazed to see Shui Ta in Mrs Shin's arms.

SUN: Am I disturbing you?

SHUI TA *gets up with difficulty and goes unsteadily to the door*: Till tomorrow, then, Mrs Shin!

Mrs Shin puts on her gloves and goes off smiling.

SUN: Gloves! How, why, what for? Is she milking you? *On Shui Ta not replying*: Don't tell me even you have your softer moments. Curious. *He takes a document from his*

—

brief-case. Anyway, you haven't been on form lately, not on your old form. Moody. Hesitant. Are you ill? It's doing no good to the business. Here's another notice from the police. They want to shut the factory. They say they can't possibly allow more than twice the legal number of people to a room. It's about time you took some action, Mr Shui Ta!
Shui Ta looks at him distractedly for a moment. Then he goes into the back room and returns with a box. He takes out a new bowler and throws it on the table.

SHUI TA: The firm wishes its representatives to dress according to their position.

SUN: Did you get that for me?

SHUI TA, *indifferently:* See if it fits.
Sun looks astonished, then puts it on. Shui Ta tries adjusting it at the right angle.

SUN: At your service, sir. But don't try and dodge the question. You must see the barber today and talk about the new scheme.

SHUI TA: The barber makes impossible conditions.

SUN: I wish you'd tell me what conditions.

SHUI TA, *evasively:* The sheds are quite good enough.

SUN: Good enough for the riffraff who work there, but not good enough for the tobacco. The damp's getting in it. Before we have another meeting I'll see Mrs Mi Tzu again about her premises. If we can get them we can chuck out this rag, tag and bobtail. They're not good enough. I'll tickle Mrs Mi Tzu's fat knees over a cup of tea, and we'll get the place for half the money.

SHUI TA, *sharply:* That is out of the question. For the sake of the firm's reputation I wish you always to be coolly business-like, and to be reserved in personal matters.

SUN: What are you so irritable for? Is it the unpleasant local gossip?

SHUI TA: I am not concerned with gossip.

SUN: Then it must be the weather again. Rain always makes you so touchy and melancholic. I'd like to know why.

WANG'S VOICE, *from without*:
    I sell water. Who would taste it?
    – Who would want to in this weather?
    All my labour has been wasted
    Fetching these few pints together.
    I stand shouting Buy my Water!
    And nobody thinks it
    Worth stopping and buying
    Or greedily drinks it.

SUN: There's that bloody water-seller. Now he'll be nagging us again.

WANG'S VOICE, *from without*: Isn't there a good person left in this town? Not even on the square where the good Shen Teh used to live? Where is the woman who once bought a mug of water from me in the rain, months ago, in the joy of her heart? Where is she now? Has nobody seen her? Has none of you heard from her? This is the house which she entered one evening and never left!

SUN: Hadn't I better shut his mouth for good? What's it got to do with him, where she is? Incidentally, I believe the only reason why you don't say is so that I shouldn't know.

WANG *enters*: Mr Shui Ta, I ask you once more: when is Shen Teh coming back? It's now six months since she went off on her travels. *On Shui Ta remaining silent*: Since then a lot has happened which could never have taken place if she'd been here. *On Shui Ta still remaining silent*: Mr Shui Ta, the rumour round here is that something must have happened to Shen Teh. Her friends are very worried. Would you please be so good as to let us know her address?

SHUI TA: I fear I have no time at the moment, Mr Wang. Come again next week.

WANG, *worked up*: People have also begun to notice that the rice she used to give the needy is being put out at the door again.

SHUI TA: What do they conclude from that?

WANG: That Shen Teh hasn't gone away at all.

SHUI TA: But? *On Wang's remaining silent*: In that case I will give you my answer. It is final. If you consider yourself a friend of Shen Teh's, Mr Wang, then you will refrain from enquiring as to her whereabouts. That is my advice.

WANG: Marvellous advice! Mr Shui Ta, Shen Teh told me before she disappeared that she was pregnant!

SUN: What?

SHUI TA, *quickly*: A lie!

WANG, *most seriously, to Shui Ta*: Mr Shui Ta, please don't think Shen Teh's friends will ever give up the search for her. A good person is not easily forgotten. There are not many. *Exit.*

Shui Ta stares after him. Then he goes quickly into the back room.

SUN, *to the audience*: Shen Teh pregnant! That makes me livid! I've been done! She must have told her cousin, and of course that swine hurried her off at once. 'Pack your bags and clear out, before the child's father gets wind of it!' It's utterly against nature. Inhuman, in fact. I've got a son. A Yang is about to appear on the scene! And what happens? The girl vanishes, and I'm left here to work like a slave. *He is losing his temper.* They buy me off with a hat! *He tramples on it.* Crooks! Thieves, kidnappers! And the girl has nobody to look after her! *Sobbing is heard from the back room. He stops still.* Wasn't that someone crying? Who's there? It's stopped. What's that crying in the back room? I bet that half-baked swine Shui Ta doesn't cry. So who's crying? And what's the meaning of the rice being put outside the door every morning? Is the girl there after all? Is he simply hiding her? Who else could be crying in there? That would be a fine kettle of fish! I've absolutely got to find her if she's pregnant! *Shui Ta returns from the back room. He goes to the door and peers out into the rain.*

SUN: Well, where is she?

SHUI TA *raises his hand and listens*: Just a moment! Nine o'clock. But one can't hear today. The rain is too heavy.

SUN, *ironically*: What do you hope to hear?

SHUI TA: The mail plane.

SUN: Don't be funny.

SHUI TA: I thought they told me you were interested in flying? Have you dropped that?

SUN: I have no complaints about my present job, if that's what you mean. I'd sooner not do night work, you know. The mail service means flying at night. I've begun to get a sort of soft spot for the firm. After all, it is my former fiancée's firm, even if she is away. She did go away, didn't she?

SHUI TA: Why do you ask?

SUN: Maybe because her affairs don't leave me entirely cold.

SHUI TA: My cousin might like to hear that.

SUN: Anyway I'm concerned enough to be unable to shut my eyes if I find, for instance, that she is being deprived of her freedom.

SHUI TA: By whom?

SUN: By you!

Pause.

SHUI TA: What would you do in such an eventuality?

SUN: I might start by wanting to reconsider my position in the firm.

SHUI TA: Indeed. And supposing the firm – that is to say I – found a suitable position for you, would it be able to count on your giving up all further enquiries about your former fiancée?

SUN: Possibly.

SHUI TA: And how do you picture your new position in the firm?

SUN: Full control. For instance, I picture chucking you out.

SHUI TA: And suppose the firm chucked you out instead?

SUN: Then I should probably return, but not on my own.

SHUI TA: But?

SUN: With the police.

SHUI TA: With the police. Let us suppose the police found no one here.

SUN: Then I presume they would look in that room! Mr Shui Ta, my longing for the lady of my heart cannot be suppressed. I feel I shall have to take steps if I am to enfold her in my arms once more. *Quietly*: She's pregnant, and needs a man beside her. I must talk it over with the water-seller. *He leaves.*

Shui Ta looks after him without moving. Then he goes quickly into the back room once more. He fetches all kinds of everyday articles of Shen Teh's: underwear, dresses, toilet things. He looks lengthily at the shawl which Shen Teh bought from the old carpet-dealers. Then he packs it all into a bundle and hides it under the table, as he hears sounds. Enter Mrs Mi Tzu and Mr Shu Fu. They greet Shui Ta and dispose of their umbrellas and galoshes.

MRS MI TZU: Autumn's on the way, Mr Shui Ta.

MR SHU FU: A melancholy time of year!

MRS MI TZU: And where is that charming manager of yours? A shocking lady-killer! But of course you don't know that side of him. Still, he knows how to reconcile his charm with his business obligations, so you only profit from it.

SHUI TA *bows*: Will you please sit down?

They sit and start smoking.

SHUI TA: My friends, an unpredictable eventuality, which may have certain consequences, compels me to speed up the negotiations which I have recently initiated as to the future of my business. Mr Shu Fu, my factory is in difficulties.

MR SHU FU: It always is.

SHUI TA: But now the police are frankly threatening to shut it down if I cannot show that I am negotiating for a new arrangement. Mr Shu Fu, what is at stake is nothing less than the sole remaining property of my cousin, in whom you have always shown such interest.

MR SHU FU: Mr Shui Ta, it is deeply repugnant to me to discuss your ever-expanding projects. I suggest a small supper with your cousin, you indicate financial difficulties. I offer your cousin buildings for the homeless, you use them to set up a factory. I hand her a cheque, you cash it. Your cousin vanishes, you ask for 100,000 silver dollars and tell me my buildings are not big enough. Sir, where is your cousin?

SHUI TA: Mr Shu Fu, please be calm. I can now inform you that she will very shortly be back.

MR SHU FU: 'Shortly.' When? You have been saying 'shortly' for weeks.

SHUI TA: I have not asked you to sign anything further. I have simply asked whether you would be more closely associated with my project supposing my cousin came back.

MR SHU FU: I have told you a thousand times that I am not prepared to go on discussing with you, but will discuss anything with your cousin. However, you seem to want to put obstacles in the way of such a discussion.

SHUI TA: Not now.

MR SHU FU: Can we fix a date?

SHUI TA, *uncertainly*: In three months.

MR SHU FU, *irritably*: Then you can have my signature in three months too.

SHUI TA: But it must all be prepared.

MR SHU FU: You can prepare everything yourself, Shui Ta, if you are sure this time your cousin really is coming.

SHUI TA: Mrs Mi Tzu, are you for your part ready to certify to the police that I can have your workshops?

MRS MI TZU: Certainly, if you will let me take over your manager. I told you weeks ago that that was my condition. *To Mr Shu Fu*: The young man is so conscientious, and I must have someone to run things.

SHUI TA: Please understand that I cannot let Mr Yang Sun go at this moment: there are all these problems, and my health has been so uncertain lately. I was always prepared to let you have him but . . .

MRS MI TZU: Ha! But!

Pause.

SHUI TA: Very well, he shall report at your office tomorrow.

MR SHU FU: I am glad you could arrive at this decision, Mr

Shiu Ta. If Miss Shen Teh really comes back it will be most
undesirable that this young man should be here. We all
know that in his time he has had a most pernicious influence
on her.

SHUI TA, *bowing*: No doubt. Forgive my undue hesitation in
these questions relating to my cousin Shen Teh and Mr Yang
Sun: it was quite unworthy of a business man. These two
were once very close to each other.

MRS MI TZU: We forgive you.

SHUI TA, *looking towards the door*: My friends, it is time for us
to come to a decision. At this spot, in what used to be the
drab little shop where the poor of the district bought the
good Shen Teh's tobacco, we, her friends, herewith resolve
to establish twelve fine new branches, which from now on
shall retail Shen Teh's good tobacco. I am told that people
have begun calling me the Tobacco King of Szechwan. But
the fact is that I have conducted this enterprise solely and
exclusively in my cousin's interest. It will belong to her, and
to her children, and to her children's children.

*From without come sounds of a crowd of people. Enter Wang,
Sun and the policeman.*

THE POLICEMAN: Mr Shui Ta, I am extremely sorry, but in
view of the disturbed state of the district I have to follow up
certain information received from your own firm, according
to which you are alleged to be keeping your cousin Miss
Shen Teh under illegal restraint.

SHUI TA: That is not true.

THE POLICEMAN: Mr Yang Sun here states that he heard
crying from the room behind your office, and that it can
only have proceeded from a female person.

MRS MI TZU: That is absurd. Mr Shu Fu and I, two respected
citizens of this town whose word the police can hardly
doubt, will witness that there has been no crying here. We
have been smoking our cigars perfectly quietly.

THE POLICEMAN: I'm afraid I have an order to search the
aforementioned room.

Shui Ta opens the door. The policeman bows and crosses the threshold. He looks in, then turns round and smiles.

THE POLICEMAN: Perfectly true, there's no one there.

SUN, *who has accompanied him*: But someone was crying! *His eye falls on the table under which Shui Ta shoved the bundle. He pounces on it.* That wasn't there before!

He opens it and reveals Shen Teh's clothes, etc.

WANG: Those are Shen Teh's things! *He runs to the door and calls out*: They've found her clothes!

THE POLICEMAN, *taking charge of things*: You state that your cousin is away. A bundle containing her property is found concealed beneath your desk. Where can the young lady be contacted, Mr Shui Ta?

SHUI TA: I don't know her address.

THE POLICEMAN: That is a great pity.

SHOUTS FROM THE CROWD: Shen Teh's things have been found! The Tobacco King did the girl in and got rid of her!

THE POLICEMAN: Mr Shui Ta, I must ask you to come to the station with me.

SHUI TA, *bowing to Mrs Mi Tzu and to Mr Shu Fu*: Please forgive this disturbance, my dear colleagues. But we still have magistrates in Szechwan. I am sure it will all be cleared up quickly.

He precedes the policeman out.

WANG: There has been a most frightful crime!

SUN, *overcome*: But I did hear somebody crying!

Interlude

Wang's Sleeping-Place

Music. For the last time the gods appear to the water-seller in a dream. They are greatly changed. It is impossible to mistake the symptoms of prolonged travel, utter exhaustion and unhappy experiences of every kind. One of them has had his hat knocked off his head, one has lost a leg in a fox-trap, and all three are going barefoot.

WANG: At last you have appeared! Fearful things are happening in Shen Teh's shop, Illustrious Ones! Shen Teh has again been away, this time for months! Her cousin has been grabbing everything! Today they arrested him. He is supposed to have murdered her in order to get hold of her shop. But I cannot believe that, for I had a dream in which she appeared to me and said that her cousin was keeping her a prisoner. Oh, Illustrious Ones, you must come back at once and find her.

THE FIRST GOD: That is terrible. Our whole search has been in vain. We found few good people, and those we found were not living a decent human existence. We had already decided to settle on Shen Teh.

THE SECOND GOD: If only she is still good!

WANG: That she surely is, but she has vanished!

THE FIRST GOD: Then all is lost!

THE SECOND GOD: You forget yourself.

THE FIRST GOD: What's wrong with forgetting oneself? We shall have to give up if she cannot be found! What a world we have found here: nothing but poverty, debasement and dilapidation! Even the landscape crumbles away before our eyes. Beautiful trees are lopped off by cables, and over the mountains we see great clouds of smoke and hear the thunder of guns, and nowhere a good person who survives it!

THE THIRD GOD: Alas, water-seller, our commandments seem to be fatal! I fear that all the moral principles that we have evolved will have to be cancelled. People have enough to do to save their bare lives. Good precepts bring them to the edge of the precipice; good deeds drag them over. *To the other gods:* The world is unfit to live in, you have got to admit it!

THE FIRST GOD, *emphatically*: No, mankind is worthless!

THE THIRD GOD: Because the world is too chilling!

THE SECOND GOD: Because men are too feeble!

THE FIRST GOD: Remember your dignity, my friends! Brothers, we cannot afford to despair. We did discover one who was good and has not become evil, and she has only disappeared. Let us hasten to find her. One is enough. Did we not say that all could still be redeemed if just one can be found who stands up to this world, just one?

They swiftly disappear.

10

Courtroom

In groups: Mr Shu Fu and Mrs Mi Tzu. Sun and his mother. Wang, the carpenter, the grandfather, the young prostitute, the two old people. Mrs Shin. The policeman. The sister-in-law.

THE OLD WOMAN: He is too powerful.

WANG: He means to open twelve new branches.

THE CARPENTER: How can the magistrate give a fair verdict when the defendant's friends, Shu Fu the barber and Mrs Mi Tzu the property owner, are his friends too?

THE SISTER-IN-LAW: Last night old Shin was seen carrying a fat goose into the judge's kitchen on Mr Shui Ta's orders. The grease was oozing through the basket.

THE OLD WOMAN, *to Wang*: Our poor Shen Teh will never be found again.

WANG: Yes, it will take the gods to get at the truth.

THE POLICEMAN: Silence! The court is assembling.

The three gods appear in magistrates' robes. As they pass

along the front of the stage to go to their places they can be heard whispering.

THE THIRD GOD: There will be trouble. The certificates were most incompetently forged.

THE SECOND GOD: And people will be curious about the magistrate's sudden indisposition.

THE FIRST GOD: It is natural enough after eating half a goose.

MRS SHIN: We've got new magistrates!

WANG: And very good ones!

The third god, last of the three, hears him, turns and smiles at him. The gods take their seats. The first god taps on the table with a hammer. The policeman brings in Shui Ta, who is received with catcalls but maintains an air of arrogance as he enters.

THE POLICEMAN: This may be a shock to you. Fu Yi Cheng is not on the bench. But the new magistrates look pretty soft too.

Shui Ta catches sight of the gods and faints.

THE YOUNG PROSTITUTE: What's happened? The Tobacco King has fainted.

THE SISTER-IN-LAW: As soon as he saw the new magistrates!

WANG: He seems to know them! That's beyond me.

THE FIRST GOD: Are you Shui Ta, tobacco merchant?

SHUI TA, *very faintly*: Yes.

THE FIRST GOD: You are charged with having made away with your cousin Miss Shen Teh, in order to gain control of her business. Do you plead guilty?

SHUI TA: No.

THE FIRST GOD, *thumbing through the papers*: The court will begin with the local constable's evidence as to the characters of the accused and his cousin.

THE POLICEMAN *steps forward*: Miss Shen Teh was a girl who made herself pleasant to everyone – live and let live, as they say. Mr Shui Ta, on the other hand, is a man of principle. The young lady's warm-hearted nature sometimes drove him to strict measures. But unlike the girl he was always on the side of the law, your worships. There were some people whom his cousin had trusted and taken in, and he was able to show them up as a gang of thieves, and another time he barely managed to save Shen Teh from straight perjury. Mr Shui Ta is known to me as a respectable citizen who respects the law.

THE FIRST GOD: Are there other witnesses in court who wish to testify that the accused is incapable of a crime of the sort attributed to him?

Mr Shu Fu and Mrs Mi Tzu step forward.

THE POLICEMAN *whispers to the gods*: Mr Shu Fu, one of our more prominent citizens!

MR SHU FU: The town looks up to Mr Shui Ta as an able businessman. He is vice-chairman of the chamber of commerce and has been proposed as a justice of the peace.

WANG, *interrupting*: By you! You two are hand in glove with him.

THE POLICEMAN, *whispering*: An undesirable character!

MRS MI TZU: In my capacity as Chairman of the Charitable Welfare Association I should like to point out to the court that Mr Shui Ta is not only turning over the best possible rooms in his tobacco works – all light and healthy – to a considerable number of the homeless, but also makes regular subscriptions to our Disabled Persons' Institution.

THE POLICEMAN, *whispering*: Mrs Mi Tzu, a close friend of our magistrate Fu Yi Cheng!

THE FIRST GOD: Yes, yes, but now we must also hear whether anyone has a less favourable report to make on the accused. *There step forward: Wang, the carpenter, the old couple, the unemployed man, the sister-in-law, the young prostitute.*

THE POLICEMAN: The scum of the district.

THE FIRST GOD: Tell us, what do you know of Shui Ta's general conduct?

CRIES, *confusedly*: He ruined us! He bled me white! Led us into bad ways! Exploited the helpless! Lied! Swindled! Murdered!

THE FIRST GOD: Accused, what have you to say for yourself?

SHUI TA: All I did was to save my cousin's bare means of existence, your worships. I only came when she was in danger of losing her small business. Three times I had to come. I never meant to stay. Circumstances were such that last time I was forced to remain. All the time I have had nothing but trouble. They loved my cousin, and I had to do the dirty work. That is why they hate me.

THE SISTER-IN-LAW: You bet we do. Look at our boy, your worships. *To Shui Ta*: Not to mention the sacks.

SHUI TA: Why not? Why not?

THE SISTER-IN-LAW, *to the gods*: Shen Teh put us up, and he had us arrested.

SHUI TA: You were stealing cakes!

THE SISTER-IN-LAW: Now he's pretending he cared about the baker and his cakes! He wanted the shop for himself!

SHUI TA: The shop wasn't a dosshouse, you selfish brutes!

THE SISTER-IN-LAW: But we had nowhere to go!

SHUI TA: There were too many of you!

WANG: And these two! *He points to the old couple.* Are they also too selfish?

THE OLD WOMAN: We put our savings into Shen Teh's business. Why did you do us out of our own?

SHUI TA: Because my cousin was helping an airman to get back into the air again. I was supposed to find the money!

WANG: She may have wanted that, but you had your eye on that good job in Pekin. The shop wasn't good enough for you.

SHUI TA: The rent was too high!

MRS SHIN: I can confirm that.

SHUI TA: And my cousin had no idea of business.

MRS SHIN: That too! Besides, she was in love with the airman.

SHUI TA: Hadn't she the right to love?

WANG: Of course she had! So why did you try to make her marry a man she didn't love: the barber there?

SHUI TA: The man she loved was a crook.

WANG: Him?

He indicates Sun.

SUN *leaps up*: Was it because he was a crook you took him into your office?

SHUI TA: To help you! To help you improve!

THE SISTER-IN-LAW: To turn him into a slave-driver!

WANG: And when you had finished improving him, didn't you sell him to her? *He indicates Mrs Mi Tzu.* She was crowing all over the place about it!

SHUI TA: Because she wouldn't let me have her workshops unless he tickled her knees!

MRS MI TZU: Lies! Don't ever mention my workshops again! I'll have nothing more to do with you. Murderer!

She rushes off in a dudgeon.

SUN, *firmly*: Your worships, I must put in a word for him!

THE SISTER-IN-LAW: You've got to; he's your boss.

THE UNEMPLOYED MAN: He's the worst slave-driver there ever was. They completely broke him.

SUN: Your worships, whatever the accused made of me he is not a murderer. A few minutes before his arrest I heard Shen Teh's voice from the room behind the shop!

THE FIRST GOD, *intrigued*: She was alive, was she? Describe exactly what you heard.

SUN, *triumphantly*: Crying, your worships, crying!

THE THIRD GOD: You could recognise it?

SUN: Absolutely certain. Don't I know her voice?

MR SHU FU: Yes, you've made her cry often enough!

SUN: But I've also made her happy. And then he wanted – *pointing to Shui Ta* – to sell her to you.

SHUI TA, *to Sun*: Because you didn't love her!

WANG: No: for the money!

SHUI TA: But what was the money needed for, your worships? *To Sun:* You would have liked her to give up all her friends, but the barber offered his buildings and his money so that she could help the poor. I had to promise her to the barber even to allow her to do good.

WANG: Why didn't you allow her to do good when the big cheque was filled in? Why did you shove Shen Teh's friends in your stinking sweat-shops, your tobacco factory, you tobacco king?

SHUI TA: It was for the child's sake!

THE CARPENTER: And what about my children? What did you do to them?

Shui Ta remains silent.

WANG: That has made you think! The gods gave Shen Teh her shop to be a little source of goodness. And she always tried to do good, and you always came and brought it to nothing.

SHUI TA, *beside himself*: Because they'd have stifled the source, you fool.

MRS SHIN: That's quite true, your worships!

WANG: What's the good of a source that can't be drawn on?

SHUI TA: Good deeds are the road to ruin!

WANG, *wildly*: And evil deeds are the road to the good life, I suppose? What have you done with the good Shen Teh, you evil man? How many good people are there left, Illustrious Ones? She was certainly good! When that barber broke my hand she wanted to give evidence for me. And now I'm giving evidence for her. She was good, I swear it.

He raises his hand to swear.

THE THIRD GOD: What is wrong with your hand, water-seller? It seems stiff.

WANG *points to Shui Ta*: He's to blame, no one else! She was going to give me the money for the doctor, then he came along. You were her mortal enemy!

SHUI TA: I was her only friend!

ALL: Where is she?

SHUI TA: Gone away.

WANG: Where to?

SHUI TA: I shan't tell!

ALL: What made her go?

SHUI TA, *screaming*: You were tearing her to bits!

There is a sudden silence.

SHUI TA *has collapsed on to his chair*: I can't go on. If the court can be cleared so that only the magistrates are present I will make a confession.

ALL: Confession! We've won!

THE FIRST GOD *taps on the table with his hammer*: Clear the court.

The policeman clears the court.

MRS SHIN, *as she goes out, laughing*: They've got a surprise coming!

SHUI TA: Have they gone? All of them? I cannot hold out any longer. Illustrious Ones, I have recognised you!

THE SECOND GOD: What have you done with our good person of Szechwan?

SHUI TA: Let me confess the frightful truth. I am your good person!

He takes off his mask and rips away his costume. Shen Teh stands there.

THE SECOND GOD: Shen Teh!

SHEN TEH:
       Yes, it is me. Shui Ta and Shen Teh, I am both of them.
       Your original order
       To be good while yet surviving
       Split me like lightning into two people. I
       Cannot tell what occurred: goodness to others
       And to myself could not both be achieved.
       To serve both self and others I found too hard.
       Oh, your world is arduous! Such need, such desperation!
       The hand which is held out to the starving
       Is quickly wrenched off! He who gives help to the lost
       Is lost for his own part! For who would
       Hold himself back from anger when the hungry are dying?
       Where could I find so much that was needed, if not
       In myself? But that was my downfall! The load of commandments

Forced me into the sludge. Yet if I broke the rules
I strode proudly around, and could eat myself full!
Something is wrong with this world of yours. Why
Is wickedness so rewarded, and why is so much suf-
    fering
Reserved for the good? Oh, I felt such
Temptation to treat myself kindly! I felt too
A secret awareness inside me, for my foster-mother
Washed me with slops from the gutter! So I acquired
A sharp eye. And yet pity
Brought me such pain that I at once felt wolfish anger
At the sight of misery. Then
I could feel how I gradually altered and
My lips grew tight and hard. Bitter as ashes
The kind word felt in my mouth. And yet
I should gladly have been an Angel to the slums. For
    giving
Was still my delight. A smiling face
And I walked in the clouds.
Condemn me: each of my crimes
Was committed to help out my neighbour
To love my beloved or
To save my young son from going without.
O gods, for your vast projects
I, poor human, was too small.

THE FIRST GOD, *with every indication of horror*: Speak no
further, you unhappy creature! What are we to think, who
so rejoice to have found you again?

SHEN TEH: But do you not understand that I am the wicked
person whose many crimes you have heard described?

THE FIRST GOD: The good person, of whom no one speaks
anything but good!

SHEN TEH: No, the wicked person as well!

THE FIRST GOD: A misunderstanding! A few unfortunate
incidents. One or two hard-hearted neighbours! A little too
much zeal!

THE SECOND GOD: But how is she to go on living?

THE FIRST GOD: She can manage! She is strong, healthy and well-built, and can endure much.

THE SECOND GOD: But didn't you hear what she said?

THE FIRST GOD, *emphatically*: Muddled, completely muddled! Hard to accept, extremely hard to accept! Are we to admit that our commandments are fatal? Are we to sacrifice them? *Grimly*: Never! Is the world to be altered? How? By whom? No, everything is as it should be.

He taps rapidly on the table with his hammer. And now – at a sign from him – music is heard. A rosy glow is seen.

    Now we return to heaven. This little world
    Still fascinates us. All its joys and hurts
    Encouraged us or caused us pain. And still
    We'll gladly think, away beyond the planets
    Of you, Shen Teh, the good person we sought
    Who makes our spirit manifest down here
    And through this bitter darkness bears the tiny lamp.
    Farewell, good luck!

At a sign from him the ceiling opens. A pink cloud descends. On it the three gods mount slowly upwards.

SHEN TEH: Oh no, Illustrious Ones! Do not go away! Don't leave me! How am I to face the two good old people who lost their shop, or the water-seller with his stiff hand? And how can I protect myself against the barber, whom I don't love, and how against Sun, whom I do? And my body has been blessed; soon my little son will be there and wanting to eat. I cannot remain here!

She looks frantically towards the door through which her tormentors will come.

THE FIRST GOD: You can manage. Only be good, and all will be well!

Enter the witnesses. They are amazed to see the magistrates floating on their pink cloud.

WANG: Show your respect! The gods have appeared among us! Three of the mightiest gods have come to Szechwan in search of a good person. They thought they had found one, but . . .

THE FIRST GOD: No but! Here she is!

ALL: Shen Teh!

THE FIRST GOD: She was not dead, she lay but hidden. She will remain among you, a good person!

SHEN TEH: But I must have my cousin!

THE FIRST GOD: Not too often!

SHEN TEH: Once a week anyway!

THE FIRST GOD: Once a month: that will be enough!

SHEN TEH: Oh, do not go away, Illustrious Ones! I haven't told you all! I need you terribly!

THE GODS *sing*:

TRIO OF THE VANISHING GODS ON THEIR CLOUD

All too long on earth we lingered.
Swiftly droops the lovely day:
Shrewdly studied, closely fingered
Precious treasures melt away.
Now the golden flood is dying
While your shadows onward press
Time that we too started flying
Homeward to our nothingness.

SHEN TEH: Help!

THE GODS:

Now let us go: the search at last is o'er
We have to hurry on!
Then give three cheers, and one cheer more
For the good person of Szechwan!

As Shen Teh stretches desperately towards them they disappear upwards, waving and smiling.

Epilogue

A player appears before the curtain and addresses the audience apologetically in an epilogue:

THE PLAYER:
 Ladies and gentlemen, don't feel let down:
 We know this ending makes some people frown.
 We had in mind a sort of golden myth
 Then found the finish had been tampered with.
 Indeed it is a curious way of coping:
 To close the play, leaving the issue open.
 Especially since we live by your enjoyment.
 Frustrated audiences mean unemployment.
 Whatever optimists may have pretended
 Our play will fail if you can't recommend it.
 Was it stage fright made us forget the rest?
 Such things occur. But what would you suggest?
 What is your answer? Nothing's been arranged.
 Should men be better? Should the world be changed?
 Or just the gods? Or ought there to be none?
 We for our part feel well and truly done.
 There's only one solution that we know:
 That you should now consider as you go
 What sort of measures you would recommend
 To help good people to a happy end.
 Ladies and gentlemen, in you we trust:
 There must be happy endings, must, must, must!

The Resistible Rise of Arturo Ui

A parable play

Collaborator: M. STEFFIN

Translator: RALPH MANHEIM

Characters
THE ANNOUNCER
FLAKE
CARUTHER
BUTCHER   *Businessmen, directors of the*
MULBERRY   *Cauliflower Trust*
CLARK
SHEET, *shipyard owner*
OLD DOGSBOROUGH
YOUNG DOGSBOROUGH
ARTURO UI, *gang leader*
ERNESTO ROMA, *his lieutenant*
EMANUELE GIRI, *gangster*
The florist GIUSEPPE GIVOLA, *gangster*
TED RAGG, *reporter on* The Star
DOCKDAISY

BOWL, *Sheet's chief accountant*
GOODWILL *and* GAFFLES, *members of the city council*
O'CASEY, *investigator*
AN ACTOR
HOOK, *wholesale vegetable dealer*
DEFENDANT FISH
THE DEFENCE COUNSEL
THE JUDGE
THE DOCTOR
THE PROSECUTOR
A WOMAN
YOUNG INNA, *Roma's familiar*
A LITTLE MAN
IGNATIUS DULLFEET
BETTY DULLFEET, *his wife*
Dogsborough's BUTLER

Bodyguards
Gunmen
Vegetable dealers of Chicago and Cicero
Reporters

Prologue

The Announcer steps before the curtain. Large notices are attached to the curtain: 'New developments in dock subsidy scandal' . . . 'The true facts about Dogsborough's will and confession' . . . 'Sensation at warehouse fire trial' . . . 'Friends murder gangster Ernesto Roma' . . . 'Ignatius Dullfeet blackmailed and murdered' . . . 'Cicero taken over by gangsters'. Behind the curtain popular dance music.

THE ANNOUNCER:
Friends, tonight we're going to show –
Pipe down, you boys in the back row!
And, lady, your hat is in the way! –
Our great historical gangster play
Containing, for the first time, as you'll see
The truth about the scandalous dock subsidy.
Further we give you, for your betterment
Dogsborough's confession and testament.
Arturo Ui's rise while the stock market fell.
The notorious warehouse fire trial. What a sell!
The Dullfeet murder! Justice in a coma!
Gang warfare: the killing of Ernesto Roma!
All culminating in our stunning last tableau:
Gangsters take over the town of Cicero!
Brilliant performers will portray
The most eminent gangsters of our day.
You'll see some dead and some alive
Some by-gone and others that survive
Some born, some made – for instance, here we show

The good old honest Dogsborough!
Old Dogsborough steps before the curtain.
His hair is white, his heart is black.
Corrupt old man, you may step back.
Dogsborough bows and steps back.
The next exhibit on our list
Is Givola –
Givola has stepped before the curtain.
                    – the horticulturist.
His tongue's so slippery he'd know how
To sell you a billy-goat for a cow!
Short, says the proverb, are the legs of lies.
Look at his legs, just use your eyes.
Givola steps back limping.
Now to Emanuele Giri, the super-clown.
Come out, let's look you up and down!
Giri steps before the curtain and waves his hand at the audience.
One of the greatest killers ever known!
Okay, beat it!
Giri steps back with an angry look.
And lastly Public Enemy Number One
Arturo Ui. Now you'll see
The biggest gangster of all times
Whom heaven sent us for our crimes
Our weakness and stupidity!
Arturo Ui steps before the curtain and walks out along the footlights.
Doesn't he make you think of Richard the Third?
Has anybody ever heard
Of blood so ghoulishly and lavishly shed
Since wars were fought for roses white and red?
In view of this the management
Has spared no cost in its intent
To picture his spectacularly vile
Manoeuvres in the grandest style.
But everything you'll see tonight is true.

Nothing's invented, nothing's new
Or made to order just for you.
The gangster play that we present
Is known to our whole continent.
*While the music swells and the sound of a machine-gun mingles
with it, the Announcer retires with an air of bustling self-
importance.*

I

a

Financial district. Enter five businessmen, the directors of the Cauliflower Trust.

FLAKE: The times are bad.
CLARK: It looks as if Chicago
  The dear old girl, while on her way to market
  Had found her pocket torn and now she's starting
  To scrabble in the gutter for her pennies.
CARUTHER: Last Thursday Jones invited me and eighty
  More to a partridge dinner to be held
  This Monday. If we really went, we'd find
  No one to greet us but the auctioneer.
  This awful change from glut to destitution
  Has come more quickly than a maiden's blush.
  Vegetable fleets with produce for this city
  Still ply the lakes, but nowhere will you find
  A buyer.
BUTCHER: It's like darkness at high noon.
MULBERRY: Robber and Clive are being auctioned off.
CLARK: Wheeler – importing fruit since Noah's ark –
  Is bankrupt.
FLAKE: And Dick Havelock's garages
  Are liquidiating.
CARUTHER: Where is Sheet?
FLAKE: Too busy
  To come. He's dashing round from bank to bank.
CLARK: What? Sheet?
  Pause.

　　　　　　　　　　　　In other words, the cauliflower
　Trade in this town is through.
BUTCHER:　　　　　　　　　Come, gentlemen
　Chin up! We're not dead yet.
MULBERRY:　　　　　　　Call this a life?
BUTCHER: Why all the gloom? The produce business in
　This town is basically sound. Good times
　And bad, a city of four million needs
　Fresh vegetables. Don't worry. We'll pull through.
CARUTHER: How are the stores and markets doing?
MULBERRY:　　　　　　　　　　　　Badly.
　The customers buy half a head of cabbage
　And that on credit.
CLARK:　　　　　Our cauliflower's rotting.
FLAKE: Say, there's a fellow waiting in the lobby –
　I only mention it because it's odd –
　The name is Ui . . .
CLARK:　　　　The gangster?
FLAKE:　　　　　　　　Yes, in person.
　He's smelled the stink and thinks he sees an opening.
　Ernesto Roma, his lieutenant, says
　They can convince shopkeepers it's not healthy
　To handle other people's cauliflower.
　He promises our turnover will double
　Because, he says, the shopkeepers would rather
　Buy cauliflower than coffins.
　They laugh dejectedly.
CARUTHER:　　　　　　　It's an outrage.
MULBERRY, *laughing uproariously*:
　Bombs and machine guns! New conceptions of
　Salesmanship! That's the ticket. Fresh young
　Blood in the Cauliflower Trust. They heard
　We had insomnia, so Mr Ui
　Hastens to offer us his services.
　Well, fellows, we'll just have to choose. It's him

Or the Salvation Army. Which one's soup
Do you prefer?

CLARK: I tend to think that Ui's
Is hotter.

CARUTHER: Throw him out!

MULBERRY: Politely though.
How do we know what straits we'll come to yet?
They laugh.

FLAKE, *to Butcher*:
What about Dogsborough and a city loan?
To the others.
Butcher and I cooked up a little scheme
To help us through our pesent money troubles.
I'll give it to you in a nutshell. Why
Shouldn't the city that takes in our taxes
Give us a loan, let's say, for docks that we
Would undertake to build, so vegetables
Can be brought in more cheaply? Dogsborough
Is influential. He could put it through.
Have you seen Dogsborough?

BUTCHER: Yes. He refuses
To touch it.

FLAKE: He refuses? Damn it, he's
The ward boss on the waterfront, and he
Won't help us!

CARUTHER: I've contributed for years
To his campaign fund.

MULBERRY: Hell, he used to run
Sheet's lunchroom. Before he took up politics
He got his bread and butter from the Trust.
That's rank ingratitude. It's just like I've been
Telling you, Flake. All loyalty is gone!
Money is short, but loyalty is shorter.
Cursing, they scurry from the sinking ship
Friend turns to foe, employee snubs his boss
And our old lunchroom operator

Who used to be all smiles is one cold shoulder.
Morals go overboard in times of crisis.
CARUTHER: I'd never have expected that of Dogsborough.
FLAKE: What's his excuse?
BUTCHER: He says our proposition
Is fishy.
FLAKE: What's fishy about building docks?
Think of the men we'd put to work.
BUTCHER: He says
He has his doubts about our building docks.
FLAKE: Outrageous!
BUTCHER: What? Not building?
FLAKE: No. His doubts.
CLARK: Then find somebody else to push the loan.
MULBERRY: Sure, there are other people.
BUTCHER: True enough.
But none like Dogsborough. No, take it easy.
The man is good.
CLARK: For what?
BUTCHER: He's honest. And
What's more, reputed to be honest.
FLAKE: Rot!
BUTCHER: He's got to think about his reputation.
That's obvious.
FLAKE: Who gives a damn? We need
A loan from City Hall. His reputation
Is his affair.
BUTCHER: You think so? I should say
It's ours. It takes an honest man to swing
A loan like this, a man they'd be ashamed
To ask for proofs and guarantees. And such
A man is Dogsborough. Old Dogsborough's
Our loan. All right, I'll tell you why. Because they
Believe in him. They may have stopped believing
In God, but not in Dogsborough. A hard-boiled
Broker, who takes a lawyer with him to

His lawyer's, wouldn't hesitate to put his
Last cent in Dogsborough's apron for safe keeping
If he should see it lying on the bar.
Two hundred pounds of honesty. In eighty
Winters he's shown no weakness. Such a man
Is worth his weight in gold – especially
To people with a scheme for building docks
And building kind of slowly.

FLAKE: Okay, Butcher
He's worth his weight in gold. The deal he vouches
For is tied up. The only trouble is:
He doesn't vouch for ours.

CLARK: Oh no, not he!
'The city treasury is not a grab bag!'

MULBERRY: And 'All for the city, the city for itself!'

CARUTHER: Disgusting. Not an ounce of humour.

MULBERRY: Once
His mind's made up, an earthquake wouldn't change it.
To him the city's not a place of wood
And stone, where people live with people
Struggling to feed themselves and pay the rent
But words on paper, something from the Bible.
The man has always gotten on my nerves.

CLARK: His heart was never with us. What does he care
For cauliflower and the trucking business?
Let every vegetable in the city rot
You think he'd lift a finger? No, for nineteen years
Or is it twenty, we've contributed
To his campaign fund. Well, in all that time
The only cauliflower he's ever seen
Was on his plate. What's more, he's never once
Set foot in a garage.

BUTCHER: That's right.

CLARK: The devil
Take him!

BUTCHER: Oh no! We'll take him.

FLAKE: But Clark says
   It can't be done. The man has turned us down.
BUTCHER: That's so. But Clark has also told us why.
CLARK: The bastard doesn't know which way is up.
BUTCHER: Exactly. What's his trouble? Ignorance.
   He hasn't got the faintest notion what
   It's like to be in such a fix. The question
   Is therefore how to put him in our skin.
   In short, we've got to educate the man.
   I've thought it over. Listen, here's my plan.
   A sign appears, recalling certain incidents in the recent past.*

b

Outside the produce exchange. Flake and Sheet in conversation.

SHEET: I've run from pillar to post. Pillar was out
   Of town, and Post was sitting in the bathtub.
   Old friends show nothing but their backs. A brother
   Buys wilted shoes before he meets his brother
   For fear his brother will touch him for a loan.
   Old partners dread each other so they use
   False names when meeting in a public place.
   Our citizens are sewing up their pockets.
FLAKE: So what about my proposition?
SHEET: No. I
   Won't sell. You want a five-course dinner for the
   Price of the tip. And to be thanked for the tip
   At that. You wouldn't like it if
   I told you what I think of you.
FLAKE: Nobody
   Will pay you any more.

* See the Chronological Table at the end of the play.

SHEET: And friends won't be
  More generous than anybody else.
FLAKE: Money is tight these days.
SHEET: Especially
  For those in need. And who can diagnose
  A friend's need better than a friend?
FLAKE: You'll lose
  Your shipyard either way.
SHEET: And that's not all
  I'll lose. I've got a wife who's likely to
  Walk out on me.
FLAKE: But if you sell . . .
SHEET: . . . she'll last another year. But what I'm curious
  About is why you want my shipyard.
FLAKE: Hasn't
  It crossed your mind that we – I mean the Trust –
  Might want to help you?
SHEET: No, it never crossed
  My mind. How stupid of me to suspect you
  Of trying to grab my property, when you
  Were only trying to help.
FLAKE: Such bitterness
  Dear Sheet, won't save you from the hammer.
SHEET: At least, dear Flake, it doesn't help the hammer.
  *Three men saunter past: Arturo Ui, the gangster, his lieutenant
  Ernesto Roma, and a bodyguard. In passing, Ui stares at Flake
  as though expecting to be spoken to, while, in leaving, Roma turns
  his head and gives Flake an angry look.*
SHEET: Who's that?
FLAKE: Arturo Ui, the gangster . . . How
  About it? Are you selling?
SHEET: He seemed eager
  To speak to you.
FLAKE, *laughing angrily*: And so he is. He's been
  Pursuing us with offers, wants to sell
  Our cauliflower with his tommy guns.

The town is full of types like that right now
Corroding it like leprosy, devouring
A finger, then an arm and shoulder. No one
Knows where it comes from, but we all suspect
From deepest hell. Kidnapping, murder, threats
Extortion, blackmail, massacre:
'Hands up!' 'Your money or your life!' Outrageous!
It's got to be wiped out.

SHEET, *looking at him sharply*: And quickly. It's contagious.

FLAKE: Well, how about it? Are you selling?

SHEET, *stepping back and looking at him*:
No doubt about it: a resemblance to
Those three who just passed by. Not too pronounced
But somehow there, one senses more than sees it.
Under the water of a pond sometimes
You see a branch, all green and slimy. It
Could be a snake. But no, it's definitely
A branch. Or is it? That's how you resemble
Roma. Don't take offence. But when I looked
At him just now and then at you, it seemed
To me I'd noticed it before, in you
And others, without understanding. Say it
Again, Flake: 'How about it? Are you selling?'
Even your voice, I think . . . No, better say
'Hands up!' because that's what you really mean.
He puts up his hands.
All right, Flake, Take the shipyard!
Give me a kick or two in payment. Hold it!
I'll take the higher offer. Make it two.

FLAKE: You're crazy!

SHEET: I only wish that that were true.

2

Back room in Dogsborough's restaurant. Dogsborough and his son are washing glasses. Enter Butcher and Flake.

DOGSBOROUGH: You didn't need to come. The answer is
    No. Your proposition stinks of rotten fish.
YOUNG DOGSBOROUGH: My father turns it down.
BUTCHER: Forget it, then.
    We ask you. You say no. So no it is.
DOGSBOROUGH: It's fishy. I know your kind of docks.
    I wouldn't touch it.
YOUNG DOGSBOROUGH: My father wouldn't touch it.
BUTCHER: Good.
    Forget it.
DOGSBOROUGH: You're on the wrong road, fellows.
    The city treasury is not a grab bag
    For everyone to dip his fingers into.
    Anyway, damn it all, your business is
    Perfectly sound.
BUTCHER: What did I tell you, Flake?
    You fellows are too pessimistic.
DOGSBOROUGH: Pessimism
    Is treason. You're only making trouble for
    Yourselves. I see it this way: What do you
    Fellows sell? Cauliflower. That's as good
    As meat and bread. Man doesn't live by bread
    And meat alone, he needs his green goods.
    Suppose I served up sirloin without onions
    Or mutton without beans. I'd never see
    My customers again. Some people are
    A little short right now. They hesitate
    To buy a suit. But people have to eat.

They'll always have a dime for vegetables.
Chin up! If I were you, I wouldn't worry.
FLAKE: It does me good to hear you, Dogsborough.
It gives a fellow courage to go on.
BUTCHER: Dogsborough, it almost makes me laugh to find
You so staunchly confident about the future
Of cauliflower, because quite frankly we
Have come here for a purpose. No, don't worry.
Not what you think, that's dead and buried. Something
Pleasant, or so at least we hope. Old man
It's come to our attention that it's been
Exactly-twenty three years this June, since you –
Well known to us for having operated
The lunchroom in one of our establishments for
More than three decades – left us to devote
Your talents to the welfare of this city.
Yes, without you our town would not be what
It is today. Nor, like the city, would
The Trust have prospered as it has. I'm glad
To hear you call it sound, for yesterday
Moved by this festive occasion, we resolved
In token of our high esteem, as proof
That in our hearts we somehow still regard you
As one of us, to offer you the major share
Of stock in Sheet's shipyard for twenty thousand
Dollars, or less than half its value.
He lays the packet of stocks on the bar.
DOGSBOROUGH: I
Don't understand.
BUTCHER: Quite frankly, Dogsborough
The Cauliflower Trust is not reputed
For tenderness of heart, but yesterday
After we'd made our . . . well, our
Stupid request about the loan, and heard
Your answer, honest, incorruptible
Old Dogsborough to a hair, a few of us –

It's not an easy thing to say – were close
To tears. Yes, one man said – don't interrupt
Me, Flake, I won't say who – 'Good God'
He said, 'the man has saved us from ourselves.'
For some time none of us could speak. Then this
Suggestion popped up of its own accord.

DOGSBOROUGH:
I've heard you, friends. But what is there behind it?

BUTCHER: What should there be behind it? It's an offer.

FLAKE: And one that we are really pleased to make.
For here you stand behind your bar, a tower
Of strength, a sterling name, the model of
An upright citizen. We find you washing
Glasses, but you have cleansed our souls as well.
And yet you're poorer than your poorest guest.
It wrings our hearts.

DOGSBOROUGH: I don't know what to say.

BUTCHER: Don't say a word. Just take this little package.
An honest man can use it, don't you think?
By golly, it's not often that the gravy train
Travels the straight and narrow. Take your boy here:
I know a good name's better than a bank
Account, and yet I'm sure he won't despise it.
Just take the stuff and let us hope you won't
Read us the riot act for *this*!

DOGSBOROUGH: Sheet's shipyard!

FLAKE: Look, you can see it from right here.

DOGSBOROUGH, *at the window*:   I've seen it
For twenty years.

FLAKE: We thought of that.

DOGSBOROUGH: And what is
Sheet going to do?

FLAKE: He's moving into beer.

BUTCHER: Okay?

DOGSBOROUGH: I certainly appreciate

Your oldtime sentiments, but no one gives
Away a shipyard for a song.
FLAKE: There's something
In that. But now the loan has fallen through
Maybe the twenty thousand will come in handy.
BUTCHER: And possibly right now we're not too eager
To throw our stock upon the open market . . .
DOGSBOROUGH: That sounds more like it. Not a bad deal if
It's got no strings attached.
FLAKE: None whatsoever.
DOGSBOROUGH: The price you say is twenty thousand?
FLAKE: Is it
Too much?
DOGSBOROUGH: No. And imagine, it's the selfsame
Shipyard where years ago I opened my first lunchroom.
As long as there's no nigger in the woodpile . . .
You've really given up the loan?
FLAKE: Completely.
DOGSBOROUGH: I might consider it. Hey, look here, son
It's just the thing for you. I thought you fellows
Were down on me and here you make this offer.
You see, my boy, that honesty sometimes
Pays off. It's like you say: When I pass on
The youngster won't inherit much more than
My name, and these old eyes have seen what evil
Can spring from penury.
BUTCHER: We'll feel much better
If you accept. The ugly aftertaste
Left by our foolish proposition would be
Dispelled. In future we could benefit
By your advice. You'd show us how to ride
The slump by honest means, because our business
Would be your business, Dogsborough, because
You too would be a cauliflower man
And want the Cauliflower Trust to win.
Dogsborough takes his hand.

DOGSBOROUGH: Butcher and Flake, I'm in.
YOUNG DOGSBOROUGH: My father's in.
  A sign appears.

3

*Bookmaker's office on 122nd Street. Arturo Ui and his lieutenant
Ernesto Roma, accompanied by bodyguards, are listening to the
racing news on the radio. Next to Roma is Dockdaisy.*

ROMA: I wish, Arturo, you could cure yourself
  Of this black melancholy, this inactive
  Dreaming. The whole town's talking.
UI, *bitterly*:   Talking? Who's talking?
  Nobody talks about me any more.
  This city's got no memory. Short-lived
  Is fame in such a place. Two months without
  A murder, and a man's forgotten.
  He whisks through the newspapers.
                     When
  The rod falls silent, silence strikes the press.
  Even when I deliver murders by the
  Dozen, I'm never sure they'll print them.
  It's not accomplishment that counts; it's
  Influence, which in turn depends on my
  Bank balance. Things have come to such a pass
  I sometimes think of chucking the whole business.
ROMA: The boys are chafing too from lack of cash.
  Morale is low. This inactivity's
  No good for them. A man with nothing but
  The ace of spades to shoot at goes to seed.
  I feel so sorry for those boys, Arturo
  I hate to show my face at headquarters. When
  They look at me, my 'Tomorrow we'll see action'

Sticks in my throat. Your vegetables idea was
So promising. Why don't we start right in?
UI: Not now. Not from the bottom. It's too soon.
ROMA: 'Too soon' is good. For four months now–
Remember? – since the Cauliflower Trust
Gave you the brush-off, you've been idly brooding.
Plans! Plans! Half-hearted feelers! That rebuff
Frizzled your spine. And then that little mishap –
Those cops at Harper's Bank – you've never gotten
Over it.
UI: But they fired!
ROMA: Only in
The air. That was illegal.
UI: Still too close
For me. I'd be in stir if they had plugged
My only witness. And that judge! Not two
Cent's worth of sympathy.
ROMA: The cops won't shoot
For grocery stores. They shoot for banks. Look here
Arturo, we'll start on Eleventh Street
Smash a few windows, wreck the furniture
Pour kerosene on the veg. And then we work
Our way to Seventh. Two or three days later
Giri, a posy in his buttonhole
Drops in and offers our protection for
A suitable percentage on their sales.
UI: No. First I need protection for myself
From cops and judges. Then I'll start to think
About protecting other people. We've
Got to start from the top.
Gloomily:
                            Until I've put the
Judge in my pocket by slipping something
Of mine in his, the law's against me. I
Can't even rob a bank without some two-bit cop
Shooting me dead.

ROMA: You're right. Our only hope is
  Givola's plan. He's got a nose for smells
  And if he says the Cauliflower Trust
  Smells promisingly rotten, I believe
  There's something in it. And there *was* some talk
  When, as they say, on Dogsborough's commendation
  The city made that loan. Since then I've heard
  Rumours about some docks that aren't being built
  But ought to be. Yet on the other hand
  Dogsborough recommended it. Why should
  That do-good peg for fishy business? Here comes
  Ragg of the 'Star'. If anybody knows
  About such things, it's him. Hi Ted.
RAGG, *slightly drunk*:   Hi, boys!
  Hi, Roma! Hi, Arturo! How are things in
  Capua?
UI: What's he saying?
RAGG: Oh, nothing much.
  That was a one-horse town where long ago
  An army went to pot from idleness
  And easy living.
UI: Go to hell!
ROMA, *to Ragg*:   No fighting.
  Tell us about that loan the Cauliflower
  Trust wangled.
RAGG: What do you care? Say! Could you
  Be going into vegetables? I've got it!
  You're angling for a loan yourselves. See Dogsborough.
  He'll put it through.
  Imitating the old man:
                        'Can we allow a business
  Basically sound but momentarily
  Threatened with blight, to perish?' Not an eye
  At City Hall but fills with tears. Deep feeling
  For cauliflower shakes the council members
  As though it were a portion of themselves.

Too bad, Arturo, guns call forth no tears.
The other customers laugh.
ROMA: Don't bug him, Ted. He's out of sorts.
RAGG: I shouldn't
Wonder. I hear that Givola has been
To see Capone for a job.
DOCKDAISY: You liar!
You leave Giuseppe out of this!
RAGG: Hi, Dockdaisy!
Still got your place in Shorty Givola's harem?
Introducing her:
Fourth super in the harem of the third
Lieutenant of a –
Points to Ui.

                          – fast declining star
Of second magnitude! Oh, bitter fate!
DOCKDAISY: Somebody shut the rotten bastard up!
RAGG: Posterity plaits no laurels for the gangster!
New heroes captivate the fickle crowd.
Yesterday's hero has been long forgotten
His mug-shot gathers dust in ancient files.
'Don't you remember, folks, the wounds I gave you?' –
'When?' – 'Once upon a time.' – 'Those wounds have
Turned to scars long since.' Alas, the finest scars
Get lost with those who bear them. 'Can it be
That in a world where good deeds go unnoticed
No monument remains to evil ones?' –
'Yes, so it is.' – 'Oh, lousy world!'
UI, *bellows*:   Shut
Him up!
The bodyguards approach Ragg.
RAGG, *turning pale*: Be careful, Ui. Don't insult
The press.
The other customers have risen to their feet in alarm.
ROMA: You'd better beat it, Ted. You've said
Too much already.

RAGG, *backing out, now very much afraid*:
                              See you later, boys.
The room empties quickly.
ROMA: Your nerves are shot, Arturo.
UI: Those bastards
  Treat me like dirt.
ROMA: Because of your long silence.
  No other reason.
UI, *gloomily*:   Say, what's keeping Giri
  And that accountant from the Cauliflower
  Trust?
ROMA: They were due at three.
UI: And Givola?
  What's this I hear about him seeing Capone?
ROMA: Nothing at all. He's in his flower shop
  Minding his business, and Capone comes in
  To buy some wreaths.
UI: Some wreaths? For who?
ROMA: Not us.
UI: I'm not so sure.
ROMA: You're seeing things too black.
  Nobody's interested in us.
UI: Exactly.
  They've more respect for dirt. Take Givola.
  One setback and he blows. By God
  I'll settle his account when things look up.
ROMA: Giri!
Enter Emanuele Giri with a rundown individual, Bowl.
GIRI: I've got him, boss.
ROMA, *to Bowl*:   They tell me you
  Are Sheet's accountant at the Cauliflower
  Trust.
BOWL: Was. Until last week that bastard . . .
GIRI: He hates the very smell of cauliflower.
BOWL: Dogsborough . . .
UI, *quickly*:   Dogsborough! What about him?

ROMA: What have you got to do with Dogsborough?
GIRI: That's why I brought him.
BOWL: Dogsborough
   Fired me.
ROMA: He fired you? From Sheet's shipyard?
BOWL: No, from his own. He took it over on
   September first.
ROMA: What's that?
GIRI: Sheet's shipyard
   Belongs to Dogsborough. Bowl here was present
   When Butcher of the Cauliflower Trust
   Handed him fifty-one percent of the stock.
UI: So what?
BOWL: So what? It's scandalous . . .
GIRI   Don't you
   Get it, boss?
BOWL: . . . Dogsborough sponsoring that
   Loan to the Cauliflower Trust . . .
GIRI: . . . when he
   Himself was secretly a member of
   The Cauliflower Trust.
UI, *who is beginning to see the light*:
                           Say, that's corrupt.
   By God the old man hasn't kept his nose
   Too clean.
BOWL: The loan was to the Cauliflower
   Trust, but they did it through the shipyard. Through
   Me. And I signed for Dogsborough. Not for Sheet
   As people thought.
GIRI: By golly, it's a killer.
   Old Dogsborough. The trusty and reliable
   Signboard. So honest. So responsible!
   Whose handshake was an honour and a pledge!
   The staunch and incorruptible old man!
BOWL: I'll make the bastard pay. Can you imagine?
   Firing me for embezzlement when he himself . . .

ROMA: Cool it! You're not the only one whose blood
    Boils at such abject villainy. What do
    You say, Arturo?
UI, *referring to Bowl*:
                        Will he testify?
GIRI: He'll testify.
UI, *grandly getting ready to leave*:
                        Keep an eye on him, boys. Let's go
    Roma. I smell an opening.
    *He goes out quickly, followed by Ernesto Roma and the body-
    guards.*
GIRI, *slaps Bowl on the back*: Bowl, I
    Believe you've set a wheel in motion, which . . .
BOWL: I hope you'll pay me back for any loss . . .
GIRI: Don't worry about that. I know the boss.
    A sign appears.

4

Dogsborough's country house. Dogsborough and his son.

DOGSBOROUGH: I should never have accepted this estate.
    Taking that package as a kind of gift was
    Beyond reproach.
YOUNG DOGSBOROUGH: Of course it was.
DOGSBOROUGH: And sponsoring
    That loan, when I discovered to my own
    Detriment that a thriving line of business
    Was languishing for lack of funds, was hardly
    Dishonest. But when, confident the shipyard
    Would yield a handsome profit, I accepted
    This house before I moved the loan, so secretly
    Acting in my own interest – that was wrong.
YOUNG DOGSBOROUGH: Yes, father.

DOGSBOROUGH: That was faulty judgment
  Or might be so regarded. Yes, my boy
  I should never have accepted this estate.
YOUNG DOGSBOROUGH: No.
DOGSBOROUGH: We've stepped into a trap.
YOUNG DOGSBOROUGH: Yes, father.
DOGSBOROUGH: That
  Package of stocks was like the salty titbit
  They serve free gratis at the bar to make
  The customer, appeasing his cheap hunger
  Work up a raging thirst.
  Pause.
                              That inquiry
  At City Hall about the docks, has got
  Me down. The loan's used up. Clark helped
  Himself; so did Caruther, Flake and Butcher
  And so, I'm sad to say, did I. And no
  Cement's been bought yet, not a pound! The one
  Good thing is this: at Sheet's request I kept
  The deal a secret; no one knows of my
  Connection with the shipyard.
A BUTLER *enters*:   Telephone
  Sir, Mr Butcher of the Cauliflower
  Trust.
DOGSBOROUGH: Take it, son.
  *Young Dogsborough goes out with the Butler. Church bells are
  heard in the distance.*
DOGSBOROUGH   Now what can Butcher want?
  Looking out of the window.
  Those poplars are what tempted me to take
  The place. The poplars and the lake down there, like
  Silver before it's minted into dollars.
  And air that's free of beer fumes. The fir trees
  Are good to look at too, especially
  The tops. Grey-green and dusty. And the trunks –

Their colour calls to mind the leathers we used to wrap
  around
The taps when drawing beer. It was the poplars, though
That turned the trick. Ah yes, the poplars.
It's Sunday. Hm. The bells would sound so peaceful
If the world were not so full of wickedness.
But what can Butcher want on Sunday?
I never should have . . .

YOUNG DOGSBOROUGH, *returning*: Father, Butcher says
  Last night the City Council voted to
  Investigate the Cauliflower Trust's
  Projected docks. Father, what's wrong?

DOGSBOROUGH: My smelling salts!

YOUNG DOGSBOROUGH, *gives them to him*:
  Here.

DOGSBOROUGH: What does Butcher want?

YOUNG DOGSBOROUGH: He wants to come here.

DOGSBOROUGH: Here? I refuse to see him. I'm not well.
  My heart.
  He stands up. Grandly:
  I haven't anything to do
  With this affair. For sixty years I've trodden
  The narrow path, as everybody knows.
  They can't involve me in their schemes.

YOUNG DOGSBOROUGH: No, father.
  Do you feel better now?

THE BUTLER *enters*:   A Mr Ui
  Desires to see you, sir.

DOGSBOROUGH: The gangster!

THE BUTLER: Yes
  I've seen his picture in the papers. Says he
  Was sent by Mr Clark of the Cauliflower
  Trust.

DOGSBOROUGH:
  Throw him out! Who sent him? Clark? Good God!
  Is he threatening me with gangsters now? I'll . . . .

Enter Arturo Ui and Ernesto Roma.

UI: Mr
  Dogsborough.
DOGSBOROUGH: Get out!
ROMA: I wouldn't be in such
  A hurry, friend. It's Sunday. Take it easy.
DOGSBOROUGH: Get out, I said!
YOUNG DOGSBOROUGH: My father says: Get out!
ROMA: Saying it twice won't make it any smarter.
UI, *unruffled*:
  Mr Dogsborough.
DOGSBOROUGH: Where are the servants? Call the
  Police.
ROMA: I wouldn't leave the room if I
  Were you, son. In the hallway you might run
  Into some boys who wouldn't understand.
DOGSBOROUGH: Ho! Violence!
ROMA: I wouldn't call it that.
  Only a little emphasis perhaps.
UI: Mr Dogsborough. I am well aware that you
  Don't know me, or even worse, you know me but
  Only from hearsay. Mr Dogsborough
  I have been very much maligned, my image
  Blackened by envy, my intentions disfigured
  By baseness. When some fourteen years ago
  Yours truly, then a modest, unemployed
  Son of the Bronx, appeared within the gates
  Of this your city to launch a new career
  Which, I may say, has not been utterly
  Inglorious, my only followers
  Were seven youngsters, penniless like myself
  But brave and like myself determined
  To cut their chunk of meat from every cow
  The Lord created. I've got thirty now
  And will have more. But now you're wondering: What
  Does Arturo Ui want of me? Not much. Just this.

What irks me is to be misunderstood
To be regarded as a fly-by-night
Adventurer and heaven knows what else.
Clears his throat.
Especially by the police, for I
Esteem them and I'd welcome their esteem.
And so I've come to ask you – and believe me
Asking's not easy for my kind of man –
To put a word in for me with the precinct
When necessary.

DOGSBOROUGH, *incredulously*:
                        Vouch for you, you mean?
UI: If necessary. That depends on whether
   We strike a friendly understanding with
   The vegetable dealers.
DOGSBOROUGH: What is your
   Connection with the vegetable trade?
UI: That's what I'm coming to. The vegetable
   Trade needs protection. By force if necessary.
   And I'm determined to supply it.
DOGSBOROUGH: No
   One's theatening it as far as I can see.
UI: Maybe not. Not yet. But I see further. And
   I ask you: How long with our corrupt police
   Force will the vegetable dealer be allowed
   To sell his vegetables in peace? A ruthless
   Hand may destroy his little shop tomorrow
   And make off with his cash-box. Would he not
   Prefer at little cost to arm himself
   Before the trouble starts, with powerful protection?
DOGSBOROUGH: I doubt it.
UI: That would mean he doesn't know
   What's good for him. Quite possible. The small
   Vegetable dealer, honest but short-sighted
   Hard-working but too often unaware
   Of his best interest, needs strong leadership.

Moreover, toward the Cauliflower Trust
That gave him everything he has, he feels
No sense of responsibility. That's where I
Come in again. The Cauliflower Trust
Must likewise be protected. Down with the welshers!
Pay up, say I, or close your shop! The weak
Will perish. Let them, that's the law of nature.
In short, the Trust requires my services.

DOGSBOROUGH: But what's the Cauliflower Trust to me?
Why come to me with this amazing plan?

UI: We'll get to that. I'll tell you what you need.
The Cauliflower Trust needs muscle, thirty
Determined men under my leadership.

DOGSBOROUGH:
Whether the Trust would want to change its typewriters
For tommy-guns I have no way of knowing.
You see, I'm not connected with the Trust.

UI: We'll get to that. You say: With thirty men
Armed to the teeth, at home on our premises
How do we know that we ourselves are safe?
The answer's very simple. He who holds
The purse strings holds the power. And it's you
Who hand out the pay envelopes. How could
I turn against you even if I wanted
Even without the high esteem I bear you?
For what do I amount to? What
Following have I got? A handful. And some
Are dropping out. Right now it's twenty. Or less.
Without your help I'm finished. It's your duty
Your human duty to protect me from
My enemies, and (I may as well be frank)
My followers too! The work of fourteen years
Hangs in the balance! I appeal to you
As man to man.

DOGSBOROUGH: As man to man I'll tell
You what I'll do. I'm calling the police.

UI: What? The police?

DOGSBOROUGH: Exactly, the police!

UI: Am I to understand that you refuse
   To help me as a man?
   Bellows.

                        Then I demand
   It of you as a criminal. Because
   That's what you are. I'm going to expose you.
   I've got the proofs. There's going to be a scandal
   About some docks. And you're mixed up in it. Sheet's
   Shipyard – that's you. I'm warning you! Don't
   Push me too far! They've voted to investigate.

DOGSBOROUGH, *very pale*:
   They never will. They can't. My friends . . .

UI: You haven't got any. You had some yesterday.
   Today you haven't got a single friend
   Tomorrow you'll have nothing but enemies.
   If anybody can rescue you, it's me
   Arturo Ui! Me! Me!

DOGSBOROUGH: Nobody's going to
   Investigate. My hair is white.

UI: But nothing else
   Is white about you, Dogsborough.
   Tries to seize his hand.
   Think, man! It's now or never. Let me save you!
   One word from you and any bastard who
   Touches a hair of yon white head, I'll drill him.
   Dogsborough, help me now. I beg you. Once.
   Just once! Oh, say the word, or I shall never
   Be able to face my boys again.
   He weeps.

DOGSBOROUGH: Never!
   I'd sooner die than get mixed up with you.

UI: I'm washed up and I know it. Forty
   And still a nobody. You've got to help me.

DOGSBOROUGH: Never.

UI: I'm warning you. I'll crush you.
DOGSBOROUGH: Never
   Never while I draw breath will you get away with
   Your green goods racket.
UI, *with dignity*:   Mr Dogsborough
   I'm only forty. You are eighty. With God's
   Help I'll outlast you. And one thing I know:
   I'll break into the green goods business yet.
DOGSBOROUGH: Never!
UI: Come, Roma. Let's get out of here.
   He makes a formal bow and leaves the room with Ernesto Roma.
DOGSBOROUGH: Air! Give me air. Oh, what a mug!
   Oh, what a mug! I should never have accepted
   This estate. But they won't dare. I'm sunk
   If they investigate, but they won't dare.
THE BUTLER *enters*: Goodwill and Gaffles of the city
   council.
   Enter Goodwill and Gaffles.
GOODWILL: Hello, Dogsborough.
DOGSBOROUGH: Hello, Goodwill and Gaffles.
   Anything new?
GOODWILL: Plenty, and not so good, I fear.
   But wasn't that Arturo Ui who
   Just passed us in the hall?
DOGSBOROUGH, *with a forced laugh*: Himself in person.
   Hardly an ornament to a country home.
GOODWILL: No.
   Hardly an ornament. It's no good wind
   That brings us. It's that loan we made the Trust
   To build their docks with.
DOGSBOROUGH, *stiffly*:   What about the loan?
GAFFLES: Well, certain council members said – don't get
   Upset – the thing looked kind of fishy.
DOGSBOROUGH: Fishy.
GOODWILL: Don't worry The majority flew off
   The handle. Fishy! We almost came to blows.

GAFFLES: Dogsborough's contracts fishy! they shouted.
    What
  About the Bible? Is that fishy too?
  It almost turned to an ovation for you
  Dogsborough. When your friends demanded an
  Investigation, some, infected with
  Our confidence, withdrew their motion and
  Wanted to shelve the whole affair. But the
  Majority, resolved to clear your name
  Of every vestige of suspicion, shouted:
  Dogsborough's more than a name. It stands for more
    than
  A man. It's an institution! In an uproar
  They voted the investigation.
DOGSBOROUGH: The
  Investigation.
GOODWILL: O'Casey is in charge.
  The cauliflower people merely say
  The loan was made directly to Sheet's shipyard.
  The contracts with the builders were to be
  Negotiated by Sheet's shipyard.
DOGSBOROUGH: By Sheet's shipyard.
GOODWILL: The best would be for you to send a man
  Of flawless reputation and impartiality
  Someone you trust, to throw some light on this
  Unholy rat's nest.
DOGSBOROUGH: So I will.
GAFFLES: All right
  That settles it. And now suppose you show us
  This famous country house of yours. We'll want
  To tell our friends about it.
DOGSBOROUGH: Very well.
GOODWILL:
  What blessed peace! And church bells! All one can
  Wish for.

GAFFLES, *laughing*:
> No docks in sight.

DOGSBOROUGH: I'll send a man.
   They go out slowly.
   A sign appears.

5

City Hall. Butcher, Flake, Clark, Mulberry, Caruther. Across from them Dogsborough, who is as white as a sheet, O'Casey, Gaffles and Goodwill. Reporters.

BUTCHER, *in an undertone*:
   He's late.
MULBERRY: He's bringing Sheet. Quite possibly
   They haven't come to an agreement. I
   Believe they've been discussing it all night.
   Sheet *has* to say the shipyard still belongs
   To him.
CARUTHER: It's asking quite a lot of Sheet
   To come here just to tell us *he's* the scoundrel.
FLAKE: He'll never come.
CLARK: He's got to.
FLAKE: Why should he
   Ask to be sent to prison for five years?
CLARK: It's quite a pile of dough. And Mabel Sheet
   Needs luxury. He's still head over heels
   In love with Mabel. He'll play ball all right.
   And anyway he'll never serve his term.
   Old Dogsborough will see to that.
   The shouts of newsboys are heard. A reporter brings in a paper.
GAFFLES: Sheet's been found dead. In his hotel. A ticket
   To San Francisco in his pocket.

BUTCHER: Sheet
  Dead?
O'CASEY, *reading*:
      Murdered.
MULBERRY: My God!
FLAKE, *in an undertone*:   He didn't come.
GAFFLES: What is it, Dogsborough?
DOGSBOROUGH, *speaking with difficulty*:
                              Nothing. It'll pass.
O'CASEY: Sheet's death . . .
CLARK: Poor Sheet. His unexpected death
  Would seem to puncture your investigation . . .
O'CASEY: Of course the unexpected often looks
  As if it were expected. Some indeed
  Expect the unexpected. Such is life.
  This leaves me in a pretty pickle and
  I hope you won't refer me and my questions
  To Sheet; for Sheet, according to this paper
  Has been most silent since last night.
MULBERRY: Your questions?
  You know the loan was given to the shipyard
  Don't you?
O'CASEY: Correct. But there remains a question:
  Who is the shipyard?
FLAKE, *under his breath*: Funny question! He's
  Got something up his sleeve.
CLARK, *likewise*:   I wonder what.
O'CASEY:
  Something wrong, Dogsborough? Could it be the air?
  To the others.
  I only mean: some people may be thinking
  That several shovelsful of earth are not
  Enough to load on Sheet, and certain muck
  Might just as well be added. I suspect . . .
CLARK: Maybe you'd better not suspect too much

O'Casey. Ever hear of slander? We've
Got laws agaist it.
MULBERRY: What's the point of these
Insinuations? Dogsborough, they tell me
Has picked a man to clear this business up.
Let's wait until he comes.
O'CASEY: He's late. And when
He comes, I hope Sheet's not the only thing
He'll talk about.
FLAKE: We hope he'll tell the truth
No more no less.
O'CASEY: You mean the man is honest?
That suits me fine. Since Sheet was still alive
Last night, the whole thing should be clear. I only –
To Dogsborough.
– Hope that you've chosen a good man.
CLARK, *cuttingly*:   You'll have
To take him as he is. Ah, here he comes.
Enter Arturo Ui and Ernesto Roma with bodyguards.
UI: Hi, Clark! Hi, Dogsborough! Hi, everybody!
CLARK: Hi, Ui.
UI: Well, it seems you've got some questions.
O'CASEY, *to Dogsborough*:
Is this your man?
CLARK: That's right, Not good enough?
GOODWILL: Dogsborough, can you be . . . ?
Commotion among the reporters.
O'CASEY: Quiet over there!
A REPORTER: It's Ui!
*Laughter. O'Casey bangs his gavel for order. Then he musters
the bodyguards.*
O'CASEY: Who are these men?
UI: Friends.
O'CASEY, *to Roma*:   And who
Are you?
UI: Ernesto Roma, my accountant.

GAFFLES: Hold it! Can you be serious, Dogsborough?
Dogsborough is silent.
O'CASEY: Mr
   Ui, we gather from Mr Dogsborough's
   Eloquent silence that you have his confidence
   And desire ours. Well then. Where are the contracts?
UI: What contracts?
CLARK, *seeing that O'Casey is looking at Goodwill*:
                        The contracts that the shipyard no doubt
   Signed with the builders with a view to enlarging
   Its dock facilities.
UI: I never heard
   Of any contracts.
O'CASEY: Really?
CLARK: Do you mean
   There are no contracts?
O'CASEY, *quickly*:   Did you talk with Sheet?
UI, *shaking his head*:
   No.
CLARK: Oh. You didn't talk with Sheet?
UI, *angrily*:   If any-
   One says I talked with Sheet, that man's a liar.
O'CASEY: Ui, I thought that Mr Dogsborough
   Had asked you to look into this affair?
UI: I have looked into it.
O'CASEY: And have your studies
   Borne fruit?
UI: They have. It wasn't easy to
   Lay bare the truth. And it's not a pleasant truth.
   When Mr Dogsborough, in the interest of
   This city, asked me to investigate
   Where certain city funds, the hard-earned savings
   Of taxpayers like you and me, entrusted
   To a certain shipyard in this city, had gone to
   I soon discovered to my consternation
   That they had been embezzled. That's Point One.

Point Two is who embezzled them. All right
I'll answer that one too. The guilty party
Much as it pains me is . . .

O'CASEY: Well, who is it?

UI: Sheet.

O'CASEY: Oh, Sheet! The silent Sheet you didn't talk to!

UI: Why look at me like that? The guilty party
Is Sheet.

CLARK: Sheet's dead. Didn't you know?

UI: What, dead?
I was in Cicero last night. That's why
I haven't heard. And Roma here was with me.
Pause.

ROMA: That's mighty funny. Do you think it's mere
Coincidence that . . .

UI: Gentlemen, it's not
An accident. Sheet's suicide was plainly
The consequence of Sheet's embezzlement.
It's monstrous!

O'CASEY: Except it wasn't suicide.

UI: What then? Of course Ernesto here and I
Were in Cicero last night. We wouldn't know.
But this we know beyond a doubt: that Sheet
Apparently an honest businessman
Was just a gangster.

O'CASEY: Ui, I get your drift.
You can't find words too damaging for Sheet
After the damage he incurred last night.
Well, Dogsborough, let's get to you.

DOGSBOROUGH: To me?

BUTCHER, *cuttingly*:
What about Dogsborough?

O'CASEY: As I understand Mr
Ui – and I believe I understand
Him very well – there was a shipyard which
Borrowed some money which has disappeared.

But now the question rises: Who is this
Shipyard? It's Sheet, you say. But what's a name?
What interests us right now is not its name
But whom it actually belonged to. Did it
Belong to Sheet? Unquestionably Sheet
Could tell us. But Sheet has buttoned up
About his property since Ui spent
The night in Cicero. But could it be
That when this swindle was put over someone
Else was the owner? What is your opinion
Dogsborough?

DOGSBOROUGH: Me?

O'CASEY: Yes, could it be that you
  Were sitting in Sheet's office when a contract
  Was . . . well, suppose we say, not being drawn up?

GOODWILL: O'Casey!

GAFFLES, *to O'Casey*:
                Dogsborough? You're crazy!

DOGSBOROUGH: I . . .

O'CASEY: And earlier, at City Hall, when you
  Told us how hard a time the cauliflower
  People were having and how badly they
  Needed a loan – could that have been the voice
  Of personal involvement?

BUTCHER: Have you no shame?
  The man's unwell.

CARUTHER: Consider his great age!

FLAKE:
  His snow-white hair confounds your low suspicions.

ROMA: Where are your proofs?

O'CASEY: The proofs are . . .

UI   Quiet, please!
  Let's have a little quiet, friends.
  Say something, Dogsborough!

A BODYGUARD, *suddenly roars*: The chief wants quiet!
  Quiet!

Sudden silence.

UI: If I may say what moves me in
This hour and at this shameful sight – a white-
Haired man insulted while his friends look on
In silence – it is this. I trust you, Mr
Dogsborough. And I ask: Is this the face
Of guilt? Is this the eye of one who follows
Devious ways? Can you no longer
Distinguish white from black? A pretty pass
If things have come to such a pass!

CLARK: A man of
Untarnished reputation is accused
Of bribery.

O'CASEY: And more: of fraud. For I
Contend that this unholy shipyard, so
Maligned when Sheet was thought to be the owner
Belonged to Dogsborough at the time the loan
Went through.

MULBERRY: A filthy lie!

CARUTHER: I'll stake my head
For Dogsborough. Summon the population!
I challenge you to find one man to doubt him.

A REPORTER, *to another who has come in*:
Dogsborough's under suspicion.

THE OTHER REPORTER: Dogsborough?
Why not Abe Lincoln?

MULBERRY *and* FLAKE: Witnesses!

O'CASEY: Oh
It's witnesses you want? Hey, Smith, where *is*
Our witness? Is he here? I see he is.
*One of his men has stepped into the doorway and made a sign.
All look toward the door. Short pause. Then a burst of shots
and noise are heard. Tumult. The reporters run out.*

THE REPORTERS: It's outside. A machine-gun. – What's
your witness's name, O'Casey? – Bad business. – Hi, Ui!

O'CASEY, *going to the door*: Bowl! *Shouts out the door*. Come
  on in!
THE MEN OF THE CAULIFLOWER TRUST: What's going
  on? – Somebody's been shot – On the stairs – God damn it!
BUTCHER, *to Ui*:
  More monkey business? Ui, it's all over
  Between us if . . .
UI: Yes?
O'CASEY: Bring him in!
  Policemen carry in a corpse.
O'CASEY: It's Bowl. My witness, gentlemen, I fear
  Is not in a fit state for questioning.
  *He goes out quickly. The policemen have set down Bowl's body
  in a corner.*
DOGSBOROUGH:
  For God's sake, Gaffles, get me out of here!
  Without answering Gaffles goes out past him.
UI, *going toward Dogsborough with outstretched hand*:
  Congratulations, Dogsborough. Don't doubt
  One way or another, I'll get things straightened out.
  A sign appears.

6

*Hotel Mammoth. Ui's suite. Two bodyguards lead a ragged actor
  to Ui. In the background Givola.*

FIRST BODYGUARD: It's an actor, boss. Unarmed.
SECOND BODYGUARD: He can't afford a rod. He was able to
  get tight because they pay him to declaim in the saloons
  when they're tight. But I'm told that he's good. He's one
  of them classical guys.
UI: Okay. Here's the problem. I've been given to understand
  that my pronunciation leaves something to be desired. It

looks like I'm going to have to say a word or two on certain occasions, especially when I get into politics, so I've decided to take lessons. The gestures too.

THE ACTOR: Very well.

UI: Get the mirror.

A bodyguard comes front stage with a large standing mirror.

UI: First the walk. How do you guys walk in the theatre or the opera?

THE ACTOR: I see what you mean. The grand style. Julius Caesar, Hamlet, Romeo – that's Shakespeare. Mr Ui, you've come to the right man. Old Mahonney can teach you the classical manner in ten minutes. Gentlemen, you see before you a tragic figure. Ruined by Shakespeare. An English poet. If it weren't for Shakespeare, I could be on Broadway right now. The tragedy of a character. 'Don't play Shakespeare when you're playing Ibsen, Mahonney! Look at the calendar! This is 1912, sir!' – 'Art knows no calendar, sir!' say I. 'And art is my life.' Alas.

GIVOLA: I think you've got the wrong guy, boss. He's out of date.

UI: We'll see about that. Walk around like they do in this Shakespeare.

The actor walks around.

UI: Good!

GIVOLA: You can't walk like that in front of cauliflower men. It ain't natural.

UI: What do you mean it ain't natural? Nobody's natural in this day and age. When I walk I want people to know I'm walking.

He copies the actor's gait.

THE ACTOR: Head back. *Ui throws his head back.* The foot touches the ground toe first. *Ui's foot touches the ground toe first.* Good. Excellent. You have a natural gift. Only the arms. They're not quite right. Stiff. Perhaps if you joined your arms in front of your private parts. *Ui joins his arms in front of his private parts.* Not bad. Relaxed but firm. But head back. Good. Just the right gait for your purposes, I believe, Mr Ui. What else do you wish to learn?

UI: How to stand. In front of people.

GIVOLA: Have two big bruisers right behind you and you'll be standing pretty.

UI: That's bunk. When I stand I don't want people looking at the two bozos behind me. I want them looking at me. Correct me!

He takes a stance, his arms crossed over his chest.

THE ACTOR: A possible solution. But common. You don't want to look like a barber, Mr Ui. Fold your arms like this. *He folds his arms in such a way that the backs of his hands remain visible. His palms are resting on his arms not far from the shoulder.* A trifling change, but the difference is incalculable. Draw the comparison in the mirror, Mr Ui.

Ui tries out the new position before the mirror.

UI: Not bad.

GIVOLA: What's all this for, boss? Just for those Fancy-pants in the Trust?

UI: Hell, no! It's for
The little people. Why, for instance, do
You think this Clark makes such a show of grandeur?
Not for his peers. His bank account
Takes care of them, the same as my big bruisers
Lend me prestige in certain situations.
Clark makes a show of grandeur to impress
The little man. I mean to do the same.

GIVOLA: But some will say it doesn't look inborn.
Some people stick at that.

UI: I know they do.
But I'm not trying to convince professors
And smart-alecks. My object is the little
Man's image of his master.

GIVOLA: Don't overdo
The master, boss. Better the democrat
The friendly, reassuring type in shirtsleeves.

UI: I've got old Dogsborough for that.

GIVOLA: His image
  Is kind of tarnished, I should say. He's still
  An asset on the books, a venerable
  Antique. But people aren't as eager as they
  Were to exhibit him. They're not so sure
  He's genuine. It's like the family Bible
  Nobody opens any more since, piously
  Turning the yellowed pages with a group
  Of friends, they found a dried-out bedbug. But
  Maybe he's good enough for Cauliflower.

UI: I decide who's respectable.

GIVOLA: Sure thing, boss.
  There's nothing wrong with Dogsborough. We can
  Still use him. They haven't even dropped him
  At City Hall. The crash would be too loud.

UI: Sitting.

THE ACTOR: Sitting. Sitting is almost the hardest, Mr Ui.
  There are men who can walk; there are men who can
  stand; but find me a man who can sit. Take a chair with a
  back-rest, Mr Ui. But don't lean against it. Hands on thighs,
  level with the abdomen, elbows away from body. How
  long can you sit like that, Mr Ui?

UI: As long as I please.

THE ACTOR: Then everything's perfect, Mr Ui.

GIVOLA: You know, boss, when old Dogsborough passes
    on
  Giri could take his place. He's got the
  Popular touch. He plays the funny man
  And laughs so loud in season that the plaster
  Comes tumbling from the ceiling. Sometimes, though
  He does it out of season, as for instance
  When you step forward as the modest son of
  The Bronx you really were and talk about
  Those seven determined youngsters.

UI: Then he laughs?

GIVOLA: The plaster tumbles from the ceiling. Don't
  Tell him I said so or he'll think I've got
  It in for him. But maybe you could make
  Him stop collecting hats.
UI: What kind of hats?
GIVOLA: The hats of people he's rubbed out. And running
  Around with them in public. It's disgusting.
UI: Forget it. I would never think of muzzling
  The ox that treads my corn. I overlook
  The petty foibles of my underlings.
  To the actor.
  And now to speaking! Speak a speech for me!
THE ACTOR: Shakespeare. Nothing else. Julius Caesar. The
  Roman hero. *He draws a little book from his pocket.* What
  do you say to Mark Antony's speech? Over Caesar's body.
  Against Brutus. The ringleader of Caesar's assassins. A
  model of demagogy. Very famous. I played Antony in
  Zenith in 1908. Just what you need, Mr Ui. *He takes a
  stance and recites Mark Antony's speech line for line.*
  Friends, Romans, countrymen, lend me your ears!
  *Reading from the little book, Ui speaks the lines after him. Now
  and then the actor corrects him, but in the main Ui keeps his
  rough staccato delivery.*
THE ACTOR: I come to bury Caesar, not to praise him.
  The evil that men do lives after them;
  The good is oft interred with their bones;
  So let it be with Caesar. The noble Brutus
  Hath told you Caesar was ambitious.
  If it were so, it was a grievous fault,
  And grievously hath Caesar answer'd it.
UI, *continues by himself*:
  Here, under leave of Brutus and the rest –
  For Brutus is an honourable man;
  So are they all, all honourable men –
  Come I to speak in Caesar's funeral.
  He was my friend, faithful and just to me;

But Brutus says he was ambitious;
And Brutus is an honourable man.
He hath brought many captives home to Rome,
Whose ransoms did the general coffers fill;
Did this in Caesar seem ambitious?
When that the poor have cried, Caesar hath wept;
Ambition should be made of sterner stuff.
Yet Brutus says he was ambitious;
And Brutus is an honourable man.
You all did see that on the Lupercal
I thrice presented him a kingly crown,
Which he did thrice refuse. Was this ambition?
Yet Brutus says he was ambitious;
And sure he is an honourable man.
I speak not to disprove what Brutus spoke,
But here I am to speak what I do know.
You all did love him once, not without cause?
What cause withholds you then, to mourn for him?
During the last lines the curtain slowly falls.
A sign appears.

7

*Offices of the Cauliflower Trust. Arturo Ui, Ernesto Roma,
Giuseppe Givola, Emanuele Giri and bodyguards. A group of
small vegetable dealers is listening to Ui. Old Dogsborough, who is
ill, is sitting on the platform beside Ui. In the background Clark.*

UI, *bellowing*: Murder! Extortion! Highway robbery!
  Machine-guns sputtering on our city streets!
  People going about their business, law-abiding
  Citizens on their way to City Hall
  To make a statement, murdered in broad daylight!
  And what, I ask you, do our town fathers do?

Nothing! These honourable men are much
Too busy planning their shady little deals
And slandering respectable citizens
To think of law enforcement.

GIVOLA: Hear!
UI: In short
Chaos is rampant. Because if everybody
Can do exactly what he pleases, if
Dog can eat dog without a second thought
I call it chaos. Look. Suppose I'm sitting
Peacefully in my vegetable store
For instance, or driving my cauliflower truck
And someone comes barging not so peacefully
Into my store: 'Hands up!' Or with his gun
Punctures my tyres. Under such conditions
Peace is unthinkable. But once I know
The score, once I recognise that men are not
Innocent lambs, then I've got to find a way
To stop these men from smashing up my shop and
Making me, when it suits them put 'em up
And keep 'em up, when I could use my hands
For better things, for instance, counting pickles.
For such is man. He'll never put aside
His hardware of his own free will, say
For love of virtue, or to earn the praises
Of certain silver tongues at City Hall.
If I don't shoot, the other fellow will.
That's logic. Okay. And maybe now you'll ask:
What's to be done? I'll tell you. But first get
This straight: What you've been doing so far is
Disastrous: Sitting idly at your counters
Hoping that everything will be all right
And meanwhile disunited, bickering
Among yourselves, instead of mustering
A strong defence force that would shield you from
The gangsters' depredations. No, I say

This can't go on. The first thing that's needed
Is unity. The second is sacrifices.
What sacrifices? you may ask. Are we
To part with thirty cents on every dollar
For mere protection? No, nothing doing.
Our money is too precious. If protection
Were free of charge, then yes, we'd be all for it.
Well, my dear vegetable dealers, things
Are not so simple. Only death is free:
Everything else costs money. And that includes
Protection, peace and quiet. Life is like
That, and because it never will be any different
These gentlemen and I (there are more outside)
Have resolved to offer you protection.
Givola and Roma applaud.

                                             But

To show you that we mean to operate
On solid business principles, we've asked
Our partner, Mr Clark here, the wholesaler
Whom you all know, to come here and address you.
*Roma pulls Clark forward. A few of the vegetable dealers
applaud.*

GIVOLA: Mr Clark, I bid you welcome in the name
Of this assembly. Mr Ui is honoured
To see the Cauliflower Trust supporting his
Initiative. I thank you, Mr Clark.
CLARK: We of the Cauliflower Trust observe
Ladies and gentlemen, with consternation
How hard it's getting for you vegetable
Dealers to sell your wares. 'Because,' I hear
You say, 'they're too expensive.' Yes, but why
Are they expensive? It's because our packers
And teamsters, pushed by outside agitators
Want more and more. And that's what Mr Ui
And Mr Ui's friends will put an end to.

FIRST DEALER: But if the little man gets less and less
  How is he going to buy our vegetables?
UI: Your question is a good one. Here's my answer:
  Like it or not, this modern world of ours
  Is inconceivable without the working man
  If only as a customer. I've always
  Insisted that honest work is no disgrace.
  Far from it. It's constructive and conducive
  To profits. As an individual
  The working man has all my sympathy.
  It's only when he bands together, when he
  Presumes to meddle in affairs beyond
  His understanding, such as profits, wages
  Etcetera, that I say: Watch your step
  Brother, a worker is somebody who works.
  But when you strike, when you stop working, then
  You're not a worker any more. Then you're
  A menace to society. And that's
  Where I step in.
  Clark applauds.
                    However, to convince you
  That everything is open and above
  Board, let me call your attention to the presence
  Here of a man well-known, I trust, to
  Everybody here for his sterling honesty
  And incorruptible morality.
  His name is Dogsborough.
  The vegetable dealers applaud a little louder.
                              Mr Dogsborough
  I owe you an incomparable debt
  Of gratitude. Our meeting was the work
  Of Providence. I never will forget –
  Not if I live to be a hundred – how
  You took me to your arms, an unassuming
  Son of the Bronx and chose me for your friend
  Nay more, your son.

He seizes Dogsborough's limply dangling hand and shakes it.
GIVOLA, *in an undertone*: How touching! Father and Son!
GIRI, *steps forward*:
    Well, folks, the boss has spoken for us all.
    I see some questions written on your faces.
    Ask them! Don't worry. We won't eat you. You
    Play square with us and we'll play square with you.
    But get this straight: we haven't got much patience
    With idle talk, especially the kind
    That carps and cavils and finds fault
    With everything. You'll find us open, though
    To any healthy, positive suggestion
    On ways and means of doing what must be done.
    So fire away!
    The vegetable dealers don't breathe a word.
GIVOLA, *unctuously*: And no holds barred. I think
    You know me and my little flower shop.
A BODYGUARD: Hurrah for Givola!
GIVOLA: Okay, then. Do
    You want protection? Or would you rather have
    Murder, extortion and highway robbery?
FIRST DEALER: Things have been pretty quiet lately. I
    Haven't had any trouble in my store.
SECOND DEALER: Nothing's wrong in my place.
THIRD DEALER: Nor in mine.
GIVOLA: That's odd.
SECOND DEALER: We've heard that recently in bars
    Things have been happening just like Mr Ui
    Was telling us, that glasses have been smashed
    And gin poured down the drain in places that
    Refused to cough up for protection. But
    Things have been peaceful in the greengoods business.
    So far at least, thank God.
ROMA: And what about
    Sheet's murder? And Bowl's death? Is that
    What you call peaceful?

SECOND DEALER: But is that connected
With cauliflower, Mr Roma?

ROMA: No. Just a minute.

Roma goes over to Ui, who after his big speech has been sitting there exhausted and listless. After a few words he motions to Giri to join them. Givola also takes part in a hurried whispered conversation. Then Giri motions to one of the bodyguards and goes out quickly with him.

GIVOLA: Friends, I've been asked to tell you that a poor
Unhappy woman wishes to express
Her thanks to Mr Ui in your presence.

He goes to the rear and leads in a heavily made-up and flashily dressed woman – Dockdaisy – who is holding a little girl by the hand. The three stop in front of Ui, who has stood up.

GIVOLA: Speak, Mrs Bowl.

To the vegetable dealers.

It's Mrs Bowl, the young
Widow of Mr Bowl, the late accountant
Of the Cauliflower Trust, who yesterday
While on his way to City Hall to do
His duty, was struck down by hand unknown.
Mrs Bowl!

DOCKDAISY: Mr Ui, in my profound bereavement over my husband who was foully murdered while on his way to City Hall in the exercise of his civic duty, I wish to express my heartfelt thanks for the flowers you sent me and my little girl, aged six, who has been robbed of her father. *To the vegetable dealers.* Gentlemen, I'm only a poor widow and all I have to say is that without Mr Ui I'd be out in the street as I shall gladly testify at any time. My little girl, aged five, and I will never forget it, Mr Ui.

Ui gives Dockdaisy his hand and chucks the child under the chin.

GIVOLA: Bravo!

Giri wearing Bowl's hat cuts through the crowd, followed by several gangsters carrying large gasoline cans. They make their way to the exit.

UI: Mrs Bowl, my sympathies. This lawlessness
    This crime wave's got to stop because . . .
GIVOLA, *as the dealers start leaving*:   Hold it!
    The meeting isn't over. The next item
    Will be a song in memory of poor Bowl
    Sung by our friend James Greenwool, followed by
    A collection for the widow. He's a baritone.
    *One of the bodyguards steps forward and sings a sentimental song
    in which the word 'home' occurs frequently. During the perform-
    ance the gangsters sit rapt, their heads in their hands, or leaning
    back with eyes closed, etc. The meagre applause at the end is
    interrupted by the howling of police and fire sirens. A red glow
    is seen in a large window in the background.*
ROMA: Fire on the waterfront!
A VOICE: Where?
A BODYGUARD *entering*:   Is there a vegetable
    Dealer named Hook in the house?
SECOND DEALER: That's me. What's wrong?
THE BODYGUARD: Your warehouse is on fire.
    *Hook, the dealer, rushes out. A few follow him. Others go to the
    window.*
ROMA: Hold it!
    Nobody leave the room!
    To the bodyguard.
                                 Is it arson?
THE BODYGUARD: It must be. They've found some gasoline
    cans.
THIRD DEALER: Some gasoline cans were taken out of here!
ROMA, *in a rage*: What's that? Is somebody insinuating
    We did it?
A BODYGUARD, *pokes his automatic into the man's ribs*:
                                 What was being taken out
    Of here? Did you see any gasoline cans?
OTHER BODYGUARDS, *to other dealers*:
    Did you see any cans? – Did you?

THE DEALERS: Not I ...
  Me neither.
ROMA: That's better.
GIVOLA, *quickly*:   Ha. The very man
  Who just a while ago was telling us
  That all was quiet on the green goods front
  Now sees his warehouse burning, turned to ashes
  By malefactors. Don't you see? Can you
  Be blind? You've got to get together. And quick!
UI, *bellowing*: Things in this town are looking very sick!
  First murder and now arson! This should show
  You men that no one's safe from the next blow!
  A sign appears. ˙

8

*The warehouse fire trial. Press. Judge. Prosecutor. Defence counsel.
Young Dogsborough. Giri. Givola. Dockdaisy. Bodyguards.
Vegetable dealers and Fish, the accused.*

a

*Emanuele Giri stands in front of the witness's chair, pointing at
Fish, the accused, who is sitting in utter apathy.*

GIRI, *shouting*: There sits the criminal who lit the fire!
  When I challenged him he was slinking down the street
  Clutching a gasoline can to his chest.
  Stand up, you bastard, when I'm talking to you.
  Fish is pulled to his feet. He stands swaying.
THE JUDGE: Defendant, pull yourself together. This is a

court of law. You are on trial for arson. That is a very serious matter, and don't forget it!

FISH, *in a thick voice*: Arlarlarl.

THE JUDGE: Where did you get that gasoline can?

FISH: Arlarl.

At a sign from the judge an excessively well-dressed, sinister-looking doctor bends down over Fish and exchanges glances with Giri.

THE DOCTOR: Simulating.

DEFENCE COUNSEL: The defence moves that other doctors be consulted.

THE JUDGE, *smiling*: Denied.

DEFENCE COUNSEL: Mr Giri, how did you happen to be on the spot when this fire, which reduced twenty-two buildings to ashes, broke out in Mr Hook's warehouse?

GIRI: I was taking a walk for my digestion.

Some of the bodyguards laugh. Giri joins in the laughter.

DEFENCE COUNSEL: Are you aware, Mr Giri, that Mr Fish, the defendant, is an unemployed worker, that he had never been in Chicago before and arrived here on foot the day before the fire?

GIRI: What? When?

DEFENCE COUNSEL: Is the registration number of your car XXXXXX?

GIRI: Yes.

DEFENCE COUNSEL: Was this car parked outside Dogsborough's restaurant on 87th Street during the four hours preceding the fire, and was defendant Fish dragged out of that restaurant in a state of unconsciousness?

GIRI: How should I know? I spent the whole day on a little excursion to Cicero, where I met fifty-two persons who are all ready to testify that they saw me.

The bodyguards laugh.

DEFENCE COUNSEL: Your previous statement left me with the impression that you were taking a walk for your digestion in the Chicago waterfront area.

GIRI: Any objection to my eating in Cicero and digesting in Chicago?

Loud and prolonged laughter in which the judge joins. Darkness. An organ plays Chopin's Funeral March *in dance rhythm.*

b

When the lights go on, Hook, the vegetable dealer, is sitting in the witness's chair.

DEFENCE COUNSEL: Did you ever quarrel with the defendant, Mr Hook? Did you ever see him before?

HOOK: Never.

DEFENCE COUNSEL: Have you ever seen Mr Giri?

HOOK: Yes. In the office of the Cauliflower Trust on the day of the fire.

DEFENCE COUNSEL: Before the fire?

HOOK: Just before the fire. He passed through the room with four men carrying gasoline cans.

Commotion on the press bench and among the bodyguards.

THE JUDGE: Would the gentlemen of the press please be quiet.

DEFENCE COUNSEL: What premises does your warehouse adjoin, Mr Hook?

HOOK: The premises of the former Sheet shipyard. There's a passage connecting my warehouse with the shipyard.

DEFENCE COUNSEL: Are you aware, Mr Hook, that Mr Giri lives in the former Sheet shipyard and consequently has access to the premises?

HOOK: Yes. He's the stockroom superintendent.

Increased commotion on the press bench. The bodyguards boo and take a menacing attitude toward Hook, the defence and the press. Young Dogsborough rushes up to the judge and whispers something in his ear.

JUDGE: Order in the court! The defendant is unwell. The court is adjourned.
Darkness. The organ starts again to play Chopin's Funeral March *in dance rhythm.*

c

When the lights go on, Hook is sitting in the witness's chair. He is in a state of collapse, with a cane beside him and bandages over his head and eyes.

THE PROSECUTOR: Is your eyesight poor, Hook?
HOOK, *with difficulty*: Yes.
THE PROSECUTOR: Would you say you were capable of recognising anyone clearly and definitely?
HOOK: No.
THE PROSECUTOR: Do you, for instance, recognise this man?
He points at Giri.
HOOK: No.
THE PROSECUTOR: You're not prepared to say that you ever saw him before?
HOOK: No.
THE PROSECUTOR: And now, Hook, a very important question. Think well before you answer. Does your warehouse adjoin the premises of the former Sheet shipyard?
HOOK, *after a pause*: No.
THE PROSECUTOR: That is all.
Darkness. The organ starts playing again.

d

When the lights go on, Dockdaisy is sitting in the witness's chair.

DOCKDAISY, *mechanically*: I recognise the defendant
perfectly because of his guilty look and because he is
five feet eight inches tall. My sister-in-law has informed me
that he was seen outside City Hall on the afternoon my
husband was shot while entering City Hall. He was
carrying a Webster sub-machine gun and made a suspicious impression.
Darkness. The organ starts playing again.

e

*When the lights go on, Giuseppe Givola is sitting in the witness's
chair. Greenwool, the bodyguard, is standing near him.*

THE PROSECUTOR: It has been alleged that certain men
were seen carrying gasoline cans out of the offices of the
Cauliflower Trust before the fire. What do you know
about this?
GIVOLA: It couldn't be anybody but Mr Greenwool.
THE PROSECUTOR: Is Mr Greenwool in your employ?
GOVOLA: Yes.
THE PROSECUTOR: What is your profession, Mr Givola?
GIVOLA: Florist.
THE PROSECUTOR: Do florists use large quantities of
gasoline?
GIVOLA, *seriously*: No, only for plant lice.

THE PROSECUTOR: What was Mr Greenwool doing in the offices of the Cauliflower Trust?

GIVOLA: Singing a song.

THE PROSECUTOR: Then he can't very well have carried any gasoline cans to Hook's warehouse at the same time.

GIVOLA: It's out of the question. It's not in his character to start fires. He's a baritone.

THE PROSECUTOR: If it please the court, I should like witness Greenwool to sing the fine song he was singing in the offices of the Cauliflower Trust while the warehouse was being set on fire.

THE JUDGE: The court does not consider it necessary.

GIVOLA: I protest.

He rises.

The bias in this courtroom is outrageous.
Cleancut young fellows who in broadest daylight
Fire a well-meant shot or two are treated
Like shady characters. It's scandalous.

Laughter. Darkness. The organ starts playing again.

f

When the lights go on, the courtroom shows every indication of utter exhaustion.

THE JUDGE: The press has dropped hints that this court might be subject to pressure from certain quarters. The court wishes to state that it has been subjected to no pressure of any kind and is conducting this trial in perfect freedom. I believe this will suffice.

THE PROSECUTOR: Your Honour! In view of the fact that defendant Fish persists in simulating dementia, the prosecution holds that he cannot be questioned any further. We therefore move . . .

DEFENCE COUNSEL: Your honour. The defendant is coming to!
Commotion.

FISH, *seems to be waking up*: Arlarlwaratarlawatrla.

DEFENCE COUNSEL: Water! Your Honour! I ask leave to question defendant Fish.
Uproar.

THE PROSECUTOR: I object. I see no indication that Fish is in his right mind. It's all a machination on the part of the defence, cheap sensationalism, demagogy!

FISH: Watr.
Supported by the defence counsel, he stands up.

DEFENCE COUNSEL: Fish. Can you answer me?

FISH: Yarl.

DEFENCE COUNSEL: Fish, tell the court: Did you, on the 28th of last month, set fire to a vegetable warehouse on the waterfront? Yes or no?

FISH: N-n-no.

DEFENCE COUNSEL: When did you arrive in Chicago, Fish?

FISH: Water.

DEFENCE COUNSEL: Water!
Commotion. Young Dogsborough has stepped up to the judge and is talking to him emphatically.

GIRI *stands up square-shouldered and bellows*: Frame-up! Lies! Lies!

DEFENCE COUNSEL: Did you ever see this man – *He indicates Giri.* – before?

FISH: Yes. Water.

DEFENCE COUNSEL: Where? Was it in Dogsborough's restaurant on the waterfront?

FISH, *faintly*: Yes.
Uproar. The bodyguards draw their guns and boo. The doctor comes running in with a glass. He pours the contents into Fish's mouth before the defence counsel can take the glass out of his hand.

DEFENCE COUNSEL: I object. I move that this glass be examined.

THE JUDGE, *exchanging glances with the prosecutor*: Motion denied.

DOCKDAISY *screams at Fish*: Murderer!

DEFENCE COUNSEL: Your Honour!
Because the mouth of truth cannot be stopped with earth
They're trying to stop it with a piece of paper
A sentence to be handed down as though
Your Honour – that's their hope – should properly
Be titled Your Disgrace. They cry to justice:
Hands up! Is this our city, which has aged
A hundred years in seven days beneath
The onslaught of a small but bloody brood
Of monsters, now to see its justice murdered
Nay, worse than murdered, desecrated by
Submission to brute force? Your Honour!
Suspend this trial!

THE PROSECUTOR: I object!

GIRI: You dog!
You lying, peculating dog! Yourself
A poisoner! Come on! Let's step outside!
I'll rip your guts out! Gangster!

DEFENCE COUNSEL: The whole
Town knows this man.

GIRI, *fuming*: Shut up!
When the judge tries to interrupt him:
You too!
Just keep your trap shut if you want to live!
He runs short of breath and the judge manages to speak.

THE JUDGE: Order in the court. Defence counsel will incur charges of contempt of court. Mr Giri's indignation is quite understandable. *To the defence counsel*: Continue.

DEFENCE COUNSEL: Fish! Did they give you anything to drink at Dogsborough's restaurant? Fish! Fish!

GIEI, *bellowing*: Go on and shout! Looks like his tyre's gone
down.
We'll see who's running things in this here town!
Uproar. Darkness. The organ starts again to play Chopin's
Funeral March *in dance rhythm.*

g

As the lights go on for the last time, the judge stands up and in a
toneless voice delivers the sentence. The defendant is deathly pale.

THE JUDGE: Charles Fish, I find you guilty of arson and
sentence you to fifteen years at hard labour.
A sign appears.

9

a

Cicero. A woman climbs out of a shot-up truck and staggers
forward.

THE WOMAN: Help! Help! Don't run away. Who'll testify?
My husband is in that truck. They got him. Help!
My arm is smashed . . . And so's the truck. I need
A bandage for my arm. They gun us down
Like rabbits. God! Won't anybody help?
You murderers! My husband! I know who's
Behind it. Ui! *Raging*: Fiend! Monster! Shit!
You'd make an honest piece of shit cry out:
Where can I wash myself? You lousy louse!
And people stand for it. And we go under.

Hey you! It's Ui!
A burst of machine-gun fire nearby. She collapses.
Ui did this job!
Where's everybody? Help! who'll stop that mob?

b

Dogsborough's country house. Night toward morning.
Dogsborough is writing his will and confession.

DOGSBOROUGH:
And so I, honest Dogsborough acquiesced
In all the machinations of that bloody gang
After full eighty years of uprightness.
I'm told that those who've known me all along
Are saying I don't know what's going on
That if I knew I wouldn't stand for it.
Alas, I know it all. I know who set
Fire to Hook's warehouse. And I know who dragged
Poor Fish into the restaurant and doped him.
I know that when Sheet died a bloody death
His steamship ticket in his pocket, Roma
Was there. I know that Giri murdered Bowl
That afternoon outside of City Hall
Because he knew too much about myself
Honest old Dogsborough. I know that he
Shot Hook, and saw him with Hook's hat.
I know that Givola committed five
Murders, here itemised. I also know
All about Ui, and I know he knew
All this – the deaths of Sheet and Bowl, Givola's
Murderers and all about the fire. All this
Your honest Dogsborough knew. All this
He tolerated out of sordid lust
For gain, and fear of forfeiting your trust.

10

Hotel Mammoth. Ui's suite. Ui is sitting slumped in a deep chair, staring into space. Givola is writing and two bodyguards are looking over his shoulder, grinning.

GIVOLA: And so I, Dogsborough, bequeath my bar
  To good hard-working Givola. My country
  House to the brave, though somewhat hot-headed Giri.
  And I bequeath my son to honest Roma.
  I furthermore request that you appoint
  Roma police chief, Giri judge, and Givola
  Commissioner of welfare. For my own
  Position I would warmly recommend
  Arturo Ui, who, believe your honest
  Old Dogsborough, is worthy of it. – That's
  Enough, I think, let's hope he kicks in soon.
  This testament will do wonders. Now that the old
  Man's known to be dying and the hope arises
  Of laying him to rest with relative
  Dignity, in clean earth, it's well to tidy up
  His corpse. A pretty epitaph is needed.
  Ravens from olden time have battened on
  The reputation of the fabulous
  White raven that somebody saw sometime
  And somewhere. This old codger's their white raven.
  I guess they couldn't find a whiter one.
  And by the way, boss, Giri for my taste
  Is too much with him. I don't like it.
UI, *starting up*:   Giri?
  What about Giri?

GIVOLA: Only that he's spending
  A little too much time with Dogsborough.
UI: I
  Don't trust him.
  Giri comes in wearing a new hat, Hook's.
GIVOLA: I don't either. Hi, Giri
  How's Dogsborough's apoplexy?
GIRI: He refuses
  To let the doctor in.
GIVOLA: Our brilliant doctor
  Who took such loving care of Fish?
GIRI: No other
  Will do. The old man talks too much.
UI: Maybe somebody's talked too much to him . . .
GIRI: What's that? *To Givola*: You skunk, have you been
    stinking up
  The air around here again?
GIVOLA, *alarmed*:   Just read the will
  Dear Giri.
GIRI, *snatches it from him*:
              What! Police chief? Him? Roma?
  You must be crazy.
GIVOLA: He demands it. I'm
  Against it too. The bastard can't be trusted
  Across the street.
  Roma comes in followed by bodyguards.
              Hi, Roma. Take a look at
  This will.
ROMA, *grabbing it out of his hands*:
              Okay, let's see it. What do you know!
  Giri a judge! But where's the old man's scribble?
GIRI: Under his pillow. He's been trying to
  Smuggle it out. Five times I've caught his son.
ROMA *holds out his hand*:
  Let's have it, Giri.
GIRI: What? I haven't got it.

ROMA: Oh yes, you have!
They glare at each other furiously.
                                  I know what's on your mind.
There's something about Sheet. That concerns me.
GIRI: Bowl figures in it too. That concerns *me*.
ROMA: Okay, but you're both jerks, and I'm a man.
  I know you, Giri, and you too, Givola.
  I'd even say your crippled leg was phony.
  Why do I always find you bastards here?
  What are you cooking up? What lies have they
  Been telling you about me, Arturo? Watch
  Your step, you pipsqueaks. If I catch you trying
  To cross me up, I'll rub you out like blood spots.
GIRI: Roma, you'd better watch your tongue. I'm not
  One of your two-bit gunmen.
ROMA, *to his bodyguards*:   That means you!
  That's what they're calling you at headquarters.
  They hobnob with the Cauliflower Trust –
Pointing to Giri.
  That shirt was made to order by Clark's tailor –
  You two-bit gunmen do the dirty work –
  And you – *To Ui.* – put up with it.
UI, *as though waking up*:   Put up with what?
GIVOLA: His shooting up Caruther's trucks. Caruther's
  A member of the Trust.
UI: Did you shoot up
  Caruther's trucks?
ROMA: I gave no orders. Just
  Some of the boys. Spontaneous combustion.
  They don't see why it's always the small grocers
  That have to sweat and bleed. Why not the big wheels?
  Damn it, Arturo, I myself don't get it.
GIVOLA: The Trust is good and mad.
GIRI: Clark says they're only
  Waiting for it to happen one more time.
  He's put in a complaint with Dogsborough.

UI, *morosely*: Ernesto, these things mustn't happen.

GIRI: Crack down, boss!
   These guys are getting too big for their breeches.

GIVOLA: The Trust is good and mad, boss.

ROMA *pulls his gun. To Giri and Givola*:
   Okay. Hands up!
   To their bodyguards:
                         You too!
   Hands up the lot of you. No monkey business!
   Now back up to the wall.
   *Givola, his men, and Giri raise their hands and with an air of
   resignation back up to the wall.*

UI, *indifferently*:   What is all this?
   Ernesto, don't make them nervous. What are you guys
   Squabbling about? So some palooka's wasted
   Some bullets on a cauliflower truck.
   Such misunderstandings can be straightened out.
   Everything is running smooth as silk.
   The fire was a big success. The stores
   Are paying for protection. Thirty cents
   On every dollar. Almost half the city
   Has knuckled under in five days. Nobody
   Raises a hand against us. And I've got
   Bigger and better projects.

GIVOLA, *quickly*:   Projects? What
   For instance?

GIRI: Fuck your projects. Get this fool
   To let me put my hands down.

ROMA: Safety first, Arturo.
   We'd better leave them up.

GIVOLA: Won't it look sweet
   If Clark comes in and sees us here like this?

UI: Ernesto, put that rod away!

ROMA: No dice!
   Wake up, Arturo. Don't you see their game?
   They're selling you out to the Clarks and Dogsboroughs.

'If Clark comes in and sees us!' What, I ask you
Has happened to the shipyard's funds? We haven't
Seen a red cent. The boys shoot up the stores
Tote gasoline to warehouses and sigh:
We made Arturo what he is today
And he doesn't know us any more. He's playing
The shipyard owner and tycoon. Wake up
Arturo!

GIRI: Right. And speak up. Tell us where
You stand.

UI *jumps up*:   Are you boys trying to pressure me
At gunpoint? Better not, I'm warning you
You won't get anywhere with me like that.
You'll only have yourselves to blame for
The consequences. I'm a quiet man. But
I won't be threatened. Either trust me blindly
Or go your way. I owe you no accounting.
Just do your duty, and do it to the full.
The recompense is up to me, because
Duty comes first and then the recompense.
What I demand of you is trust. You lack
Faith, and where faith is lacking, all is lost.
How do you think I got this far? By faith!
Because of my fanatical, my unflinching
Faith in the cause. With faith and nothing else
I flung a challenge at this city and forced
It to its knees. With faith I made my way
To Dogsborough. With faith I climbed the steps
Of City Hall. With nothing in my naked
Hands but indomitable faith.

ROMA: And
A tommy gun.

UI: No, other men have them
But lack firm faith in their predestination
To leadership. And that is why you too
Need to have faith in me. Have faith! Believe that

I know what's best for you and that I'm
Resolved to put it through. That I will find
The road to victory. If Dogsborough
Passes away, then I decide who gets to
Be what. I say no more, but rest assured:
You'll all be satisfied.

GIVOLA *puts his hand on his heart*:

Arturo!

ROMA, *sullenly*: Scram
You guys!
Giri, Givola and Givola's bodyguard go out slowly with their hands up.

GIRI, *leaving, to Roma*: I like your hat.
GIVOLA, *leaving*: Dear Roma ...
ROMA: Scram!
Giri, you clown, don't leave your laugh behind.
And Givola, you crook, be sure to take
Your clubfoot, though I'm pretty sure you stole it.
When they are gone, Ui relapses into his brooding.

UI: I want to be alone.
ROMA, *standing still*: Arturo, if I
Hadn't the kind of faith you've just described
I'd sometimes find it hard to look my
Men in the face. We've got to act. And quickly.
Giri is cooking up some dirty work.

UI: Don't worry about Giri. I am planning
Bigger and better things. And now, Ernesto
To you, my oldest friend and trusted lieutenant
I will divulge them.

ROMA, *beaming*: Speak, Arturo. Giri
And what I had to say of him can wait.
He sits down with Ui. Roma's men stand waiting in the corner.

UI: We're finished with Chicago. I need more.
ROMA: More?
UI: Vegetables are sold in other cities.
ROMA: But how are you expecting to get in?

UI: Through
  The front door, through the back door, through the
    windows.
  Resisted, sent away, called back again.
  Booed and acclaimed. With threats and supplications
  Appeals and insults, gentle force and steel
  Embrace. In short, the same as here.
ROMA: Except
  Conditions aren't the same in other places.
UI: I have in mind a kind of dress rehearsal
  In a small town. That way we'll see
  Whether conditions are so different. I
  Doubt it.
ROMA: And where have you resolved to stage
  This dress rehearsal?
UI: In Cicero.
ROMA: But there
  They've got this Dullfeet with his Journal
  For Vegetables and Positive Thinking
  Which every Saturday accuses me
  Of murdering Sheet.
UI: That's got to stop.
ROMA: It will. These journalists have enemies.
  Their black and white makes certain people
  See red. Myself, for instance. Yes, Arturo
  I think these accusations can be silenced.
UI: I'm sure they can. The Trust is negotiating
  With Cicero right now. For the time being
  We'll just sell cauliflower peacefully.
ROMA: Who's doing this negotiating?
UI: Clark.
  But he's been having trouble. On our account.
ROMA: I see. So Clark is in it. I wouldn't trust
  That Clark around the corner.
UI: In Cicero
  They say we're following the Cauliflower

Trust like its shadow. They want cauliflower, but
They don't want us. The shopkeepers don't like us.
A feeling shared by others: Dullfeet's wife
For instance, who for years now has been running
A greengoods wholesale house. She'd like to join
The Trust, and would have joined except for us.

ROMA: You mean this plan of moving in on Cicero
Didn't start with you at all, but with the Trust?
Arturo, now I see it all. I see
Their rotten game.

UI: Whose game?

ROMA: The Trust's.
The goings-on at Dogsborough's! His will!
It's all a machination of the Trust.
They want the Cicero connection. You're in
The way. But how can they get rid of you?
You've got them by the balls, because they needed
You for their dirty business and connived at
Your methods. But now they've found a way:
Old Dogsborough confesses and repairs
In ash and sackcloth to his coffin.
The cauliflower boys with deep emotion
Retrieve this paper from his hands and sobbing
Read it to the assembled press: how he repents
And solemnly adjures them to wipe out
The plague which he – as he confesses – brought
In, and restore the cauliflower trade
To its time-honoured practices.
That's what they plan, Arturo. They're all in it:
Giri, who gets Dogsborough to scribble wills
And who is hand in glove with Clark, who's having
Trouble in Cicero because of us
And wants pure sunshine when he shovels shekels.
Givola, who smells carrion. – This Dogsborough
Honest old Dogsborough with his two-timing will
That splatters you with muck has got to be

Rubbed out, Arturo, or your best-laid plans
For Cicero are down the drain.

UI: You think
  It's all a plot? It's true. They've kept me out
  Of Cicero. I've noticed that.

ROMA: Arturo
  I beg you: let me handle this affair.
  I tell you what: my boys and I will beat
  It out to Dogsborough's tonight
  And take him with us. To the hospital
  We'll tell him – and deliver him to the morgue.

UI: But Giri's with him at the villa.

ROMA: He
  Can stay there.
  They exchange glances.
                 Two birds one stone.

UI: And Givola?

ROMA: On the way back I'll drop in at the florist's
  And order handsome wreaths for Dogsborough.
  For Giri too, the clown. And I'll pay cash.
  He pats his gun.

UI: Ernesto, this contemptible project of
  The Dogsboroughs and Clarks and Dullfeets
  To squeeze me out of Cicero's affairs
  By coldly branding me a criminal
  Must be frustrated with an iron hand.
  I put my trust in you.

ROMA: And well you may.
  But you must meet with us before we start
  And give the boys a talk to make them see
  The matter in its proper light. I'm not
  So good at talking.

UI, *shaking his hand*: It's a deal.

ROMA: I knew it
  Arturo. This was how it had to be
  Decided. Say, the two of us! Say, you

And me! Like in the good old days.
To his men.

What did
I tell you, boys? He gives us the green light.
UI: I'll be there.
ROMA: At eleven.
UI: Where?
ROMA: At the garage.
I'm a new man. At last we'll see some fight!
*He goes out quickly with his men. Pacing the floor, Ui prepares
the speech he is going to make to Roma's men.*
UI: Friends, much as I regret to say it, word
Has reached me that behind my back perfidious
Treason is being planned. Men close to me
Men whom I trusted implicitly
Have turned against me. Goaded by ambition
And crazed by lust for gain, these despicable
Fiends have conspired with the cauliflower
Moguls – no, that won't do – with who? I've got it!
With the police, to coldly liquidate you
And even, so I hear, myself. My patience
Is at an end. I therefore order you
Under Ernesto Roma who enjoys
My fullest confidence, tonight . . .
Enter Clark, Giri and Betty Dullfeet.
GIRI, *noticing that Ui looks frightened*: It's only
Us, boss.
CLARK: Ui, let me introduce
Mrs Dullfeet of Cicero. The Trust
Asks you to give her your attention, and hopes
The two of you will come to terms.
UI, *scowling*:   I'm listening.
CLARK: A merger, as you know, is being considered
Between Chicago's Cauliflower Trust
And Cicero's purveyors. In the course
Of the negotiations, Cicero

Objected to your presence on the board.
The Trust was able, after some discussion
To overcome this opposition. Mrs Dullfeet
Is here . . .

MRS DULLFEET: To clear up the misunderstanding.
Moreover, I should like to point out that
My husband, Mr Dullfeet's newspaper
Campaign was not directed against you
Mr Ui.

UI: Against who was it directed?

CLARK: I may as well speak plainly, Ui. Sheet's
'Suicide' made a very bad impression
In Cicero. Whatever else Sheet may
Have been, he was a shipyard owner
A leading citizen, and not some Tom
Dick or Harry whose death arouses no
Comment. And something else. Caruther's
Garage complains of an attack on one of
Its trucks. And one of your men, Ui, is
Involved in both these cases.

MRS DULLFEET: Every child in
Cicero knows Chicago's cauliflower
Is stained with blood.

UI: Have you come here to insult me?

MRS DULLFEET:
No, no. Not you, since Mr Clark has vouched
For you. It's this man Roma.

CLARK, *quickly*:   Cool it, Ui!

GIRI: Cicero . . .

UI: You can't talk to me like this!
What do you take me for? I've heard enough!
Ernesto Roma is my man. I don't
Let anybody tell me who to pal with.
This is an outrage.

GIRI: Boss!

MRS DULLFEET: Ignatius Dullfeet

Will fight the Romas of this world to his
Last breath.
CLARK, *coldly*: And rightly so. In that the Trust
Is solidly behind him. Think it over.
Friendship and business are two separate things.
What do you say?
UI, *likewise coldly*:   You heard me, Mr Clark.
CLARK: Mrs Dullfeet, I regret profoundly
The outcome of this interview.
On his way out, to Ui:

                              Most unwise, Ui.
Left alone, Ui and Giri do not look at each other.   .
GIRI: This and the business with Caruther's truck
Means war. That's plain.
UI: I'm not afraid of war.
GIRI: Okay, you're not afraid. You'll only have
The Trust, the papers, the whole city, plus
Dogsborough and his crowd against you.
Just between you and me, boss, I'd think twice . . .
UI: I know my duty and need no advice.
A sign appears.

11

*Garage. Night. The sound of rain. Ernesto Roma and young Inna.
In the background gunmen.*

INNA: It's one o'clock.
ROMA: He must have been delayed.
INNA: Could he be hesitating?
ROMA: He could be.
Arturo's so devoted to his henchmen
He'd rather sacrifice himself than them.
Even with rats like Givola and Giri

He can't make up his mind. And so he dawdles
And wrestles with himself. It might be two
Or even three before he gets a move on.
But never fear, he'll come. Of course he will.
I know him, Inna.
Pause.
                        When I see that Giri
Flat on the carpet, pouring out his guts
I'll feel as if I'd taken a good leak.
Oh well, it won't be long.
INNA: These rainy nights are
Hard on the nerves.
ROMA: That's what I like about them.
Of nights the blackest
Of cars the fastest
And of friends
The most resolute.
INNA: How many years have
You known him?
ROMA: Going on eighteen.
INNA: That's a long time.
A GUNMAN *comes forward*:
The boys want whisky.
ROMA: No. Tonight I need
Them sober.
A little man is brought in by the bodyguards.
THE LITTLE MAN, *out of breath*:
                    Dirty work at the crossroads!
Two armoured cars outside police H.Q.
Jam-packed with cops.
ROMA: Okay, boys, get the
Bullet-proof shutter down. Those cops have got
Nothing to do with us, but foresight's better
Than hindsight.
Slowly an iron shutter falls, blocking the garage door.
                    Is the passage clear?

INNA *nods*: It's a funny thing about tobacco. When a man
   Is smoking, he looks calm. And if you imitate
   A calm-looking man and light a cigarette, you
   Get to be calm yourself.
ROMA, *smiling*:   Hold out your hand.
INNA *does so*: It's trembling. That's no good.
ROMA: Don't worry. It's all
   Right. I don't go for bruisers. They're unfeeling.
   Nothing can hurt them and they won't hurt you.
   Not seriously. Tremble all you like.
   A compass needle is made of steel but trembles
   Before it settles on its course. Your hand
   Is looking for its pole. That's all.
A SHOUT, *from the side*:   Police car
   Coming down Church Street.
ROMA, *intently*:   Is it stopping?
THE VOICE: No.
A GUNMAN *comes in*:
   Two cars with blacked-out lights have turned the corner.
ROMA: They're waiting for Arturo. Givola and
   Giri are laying for him. He'll run straight
   Into their trap. We've got to head him off.
   Let's go!
A GUNMAN: It's suicide.
ROMA: If suicide it is
   Let it be suicide! Hell! Eighteen years
   Of friendship!
INNA, *loud and clear*: Raise the shutter!
   Machine-gun ready?
A GUNMAN: Ready.
INNA: Up she goes.
   The bullet-proof shutter rises slowly. Ui and Givola enter briskly,
   followed by bodyguards.
ROMA: Arturo!
INNA, *under his breath*: Yeah, and Givola.
ROMA: What's up?

Arturo, man, you had us worried. *Laughs loudly*. Hell!
But everything's okay.

UI, *hoarsely*:   Why wouldn't it be okay?

INNA: We thought
Something was wrong. If I were you I'd give him
The glad-hand, boss. He was going to lead
Us all through fire to save you. Weren't you, Roma?
Ui goes up to Roma, holding out his hand. Roma grasps it,
laughing. At this moment, when Roma cannot reach for his gun,
Givola shoots him from the hip.

UI: Into the corner with them!
Roma's men stand bewildered. Inna in the lead, they are driven
into the corner. Givola bends down over Roma, who is lying on the
floor.

GIVOLA: He's still breathing.

UI: Finish him off.
To the men lined up against the wall.
Your vicious plot against me is exposed.
So are your plans to rub out Dogsborough.
I caught you in the nick of time. Resistance
Is useless. I'll teach you to rebel against me!
You bastards!

GIVOLA: Not a single one unarmed!
Speaking of Roma:
He's coming to. He's going to wish he hadn't.

UI: I'll be at Dogsborough's country house tonight.
He goes out quickly.

INNA: You stinking rats! You traitors!

GIVOLA, *excitedly*:   Let 'em have it!
The men standing against the wall are mowed down by machine-
gun fire.

ROMA *comes to:*
Givola! Christ.
Turns over, his face chalky-white.
                    What happened over there?

GIVOLA: Nothing. Some traitors have been executed.

ROMA: You dog! My men! What have you done to them?
Givola does not answer.
And where's Arturo? You've murdered him. I knew it!
Looking for him on the floor.
Where is he?
GIVOLA: He's just left.
ROMA, *as he is being dragged to the wall*: You stinking dogs!
GIVOLA, *coolly*: You say my leg is short, I say your brain is
    small.
Now let your pretty legs convey you to the wall!
A sign appears.

12

*Givola's flower shop. Ignatius Dullfeet, a very small man, and
Betty Dullfeet come in.*

DULLFEET: I don't like this at all.
BETTY: Why not? They've gotten rid
    Of Roma.
DULLFEET: Yes, they've murdered him.
BETTY: That's how
    They do it. Anyway, he's gone. Clark says
    That Ui's years of storm and stress, which even
    The best of men go through, are over. Ui
    Has shown he wants to mend his uncouth ways.
    But if you persevere in your attacks
    You'll only stir his evil instincts up
    Again, and you, Ignatius, will be first
    To bear the brunt. But if you keep your mouth shut
    They'll leave you be.
DULLFEET: I'm not so sure my silence
    Will help.

BETTY: It's sure to. They're not beasts.
Giri comes in from one side, wearing Roma's hat.
GIRI: Hi. Here already? Mr Ui's inside.
  He'll be delighted. Sorry I can't stay.
  I've got to beat it quick before I'm seen.
  I've swiped a hat from Givola.
  He laughs so hard that plaster falls from the ceiling, and goes out, waving.
DULLFEET:
  Bad when they growl. No better when they laugh.
BETTY: Don't say such things, Ignatius. Not here.
DULLFEET, *bitterly*:   Nor
  Anywhere else.
BETTY: What can you do? Already
  The rumour's going around in Cicero
  That Ui's stepping into Dogsborough's shoes.
  And worse, the greengoods men of Cicero
  Are flirting with the Cauliflower Trust.
DULLFEET:
  And now they've smashed two printing presses on me.
  Betty, I've got a dark foreboding.
  Givola and Ui come in with outstretched hands.
BETTY: Hi, Ui!
UI: Welcome. Dullfeet!
DULLFEET: Mr Ui
  I tell you frankly that I hesitated
  To come, because . . .
UI: Why hesitate? A man
  Like you is welcome everywhere.
GIVOLA: So is a
  Beautiful woman.
DULLFEET: Mr Ui, I've felt
  It now and then to be my duty to
  Come out against . . .
UI: A mere misunderstanding!
  If you and I had known each other from

The start, it never would have happened. It
Has always been my fervent wish that what
Had to be done should be done peacefully.

DULLFEET: Violence . . .

UI: No one hates it more than I do.
If men were wise, there'd be no need of it.

DULLFEET: My aim . . .

UI: Is just the same as mine. We both
Want trade to thrive. The small shopkeeper whose
Life is no bed of roses nowadays
Must be permitted to sell his greens in peace.
And find protection when attacked.

DULLFEET, *firmly*:   And be
Free to determine whether he desires
Protection. I regard that as essential.

UI: And so do I. He's *got* to be free to choose.
Why? Because when he chooses his protector
Freely, and puts his trust in somebody he himself
Has chosen, then the confidence, which is
As necessary in the greengoods trade
As anywhere else, will prevail. That's always been
My stand.

DULLFEET: I'm glad to hear it from your lips.
For, no offence intended, Cicero
Will never tolerate coercion.

UI: Of course not.
No one, unless he has to, tolerates
Coercion.

DULLFEET: Frankly, if this merger with the Trust
Should mean importing the ungodly bloodbath
That plagues Chicago to our peaceful town
I never could approve it.
Pause.

UI: Frankness calls
For frankness, Mr Dullfeet. Certain things
That might not meet the highest moral standards

May have occurred in the past. Such things
Occur in battle. Among friends, however
They cannot happen. Dullfeet, what I want
Of you is only that in the future you should
Trust me and look upon me as a friend
Who never till the seas run dry will forsake
A friend – and, to be more specific, that
Your paper should stop printing these horror stories
That only make bad blood. I don't believe
I'm asking very much.

DULLFEET: It's easy not
To write about what doesn't happen, sir.

UI: Exactly. And if now and then some trifling
Incident should occur, because the earth
Is inhabited by men and not by angels
You will abstain, I hope, from printing lurid
Stories about trigger-happy criminals.
I wouldn't go so far as to maintain that
One of our drivers might not on occasion
Utter an uncouth word. That too is human.
And if some vegetable dealer stands
One of our men to a beer for punctual
Delivery of his carrots, let's not rush
Into print with stories of corruption.

BETTY: Mr
Ui, my husband's human.

GIVOLA: We don't doubt it.
And now that everything has been so amiably
Discussed and settled among friends, perhaps
You'd like to see my flowers . . .

UI, *to Dullfeet*:   After you.
*They inspect Givola's flower shop. Ui leads Betty, Givola leads
Dullfeet. In the following they keep disappearing behind the
flower displays. Givola and Dullfeet emerge.*

GIVOLA: These, my dear Dullfeet, are Malayan fronds.

DULLFEET: Growing, I see, by little oval ponds.

GIVOLA: Stocked with blue carp that stay stock-still for
  hours.
DULLFEET: The wicked are insensitive to flowers.
  They disappear. Ui and Betty emerge.
BETTY: A strong man needs no force to win his suit.
UI: Arguments carry better when they shoot.
BETTY: Sound reasoning is bound to take effect.
UI: Except when one is trying to collect.
BETTY: Intimidation, underhanded tricks . . .
UI: I prefer to speak of pragmatic politics.
  They disappear. Givola and Dullfeet emerge.
DULLFEET: Flowers are free from lust and wickedness.
GIVOLA: Exactly why I love them, I confess.
DULLFEET: They live so quietly. They never hurry.
GIVOLA, *mischievously*:
  No problems. No newspapers. No worry.
  They disappear. Ui and Betty emerge.
BETTY: They tell me you're as abstinent as a vicar.
UI: I never smoke and have no use for liquor.
BETTY: A saint perhaps when all is said and done.
UI: Of carnal inclinations I have none.
  They disappear. Givola and Dullfeet emerge.
DULLFEET: Your life with flowers must deeply satisfy.
GIVOLA: It would, had I not other fish to fry.
  They disappear. Ui and Betty emerge.
BETTY: What, Mr Ui, does religion mean to you?
UI: I am a Christian. That will have to do.
BETTY: Yes. But the Ten Commandments, where do they
  Come in?
UI: In daily life they don't, I'd say.
BETTY: Forgive me if your patience I abuse
  But what exactly are your social views?
UI: My social views are balanced, clear and healthy.
  What proves it is: I don't neglect the wealthy.
  They disappear. Givola and Dullfeet emerge.
DULLFEET: The flowers have their life, their social calls.

GIVOLA: I'll say they do. Especially funerals!

DULLFEET: Oh, I forgot that flowers were your bread.

GIVOLA: Exactly. My best clients are the dead.

DULLFEET: I hope that's not your only source of trade.

GIVOLA: Some people have the sense to be afraid.

DULLFEET: Violence, Givola, brings no lasting glory.

GIVOLA: It gets results, though.

DULLFEET: That's another story.

GIVOLA: You look so pale.

DULLFEET: The air is damp and close.

GIVOLA: The heavy scent affects you, I suppose.

They disappear. Ui and Betty emerge.

BETTY: I am so glad you two have worked things out.

UI: Once frankness showed what it was all about . . .

BETTY: Foul-weather friends will never disappoint . . .

UI, *putting his arm around her shoulder*:

    I like a woman who can get the point.

    Givola and Dullfeet, who is deathly pale, emerge. Dullfeet sees
    the hand on his wife's shoulder.

DULLFEET: Betty, we're leaving.

UI *comes up to him, holding out his hand*:

                             Mr Dullfeet, your

    Decision honours you. It will redound to

    Cicero's welfare. A meeting between such men

    As you and me can only be auspicious.

GIVOLA, *giving Betty flowers*:

    Beauty to beauty!

BETTY: Look, how nice, Ignatius!

    Oh, I'm so happy. 'Bye, 'bye.

GIVOLA: Now we can

    Start going places.

UI, *darkly*:   I don't like that man.

    A sign appears.

13

Bells. A coffin is being carried into the Cicero funeral chapel, followed by Betty Dullfeet in widow's weeds, and by Clark, Ui, Giri and Givola bearing enormous wreaths. After handing in their wreaths, Giri and Givola remain outside the chapel. The pastor's voice is heard from inside.

VOICE: And so Ignatius Dullfeet's mortal frame
  Is laid to rest. A life of meagrely
  Rewarded toil is ended, of toil devoted
  To others than the toiler who has left us.
  The angel at the gates of heaven will set
  His hand upon Ignatius Dullfeet's shoulder
  Feel that his cloak has been worn thin and say:
  This man has borne the burdens of his neighbours.
  And in the city council for some time
  To come, when everyone has finished speaking
  Silence will fall. For so accustomed are
  His fellow citizens to listen to
  Ignatius Dullfeet's voice that they will wait
  To hear him. 'Tis as though the city's conscience
  Had died. This man who met with so untimely
  An end could walk the narrow path unseeing.
  Justice was in his heart. This man of lowly
  Stature but lofty mind created in
  His newspaper a rostrum whence his voice
  Rang out beyond the confines of our city.
  Ignatius Dullfeet, rest in peace! Amen.
GIVOLA: A tactful man: no word of how he died.
GIRI, *wearing Dullfeet's hat*:
  A tactful man? A man with seven children.
  Clark and Mulberry come out of the chapel.

CLARK: God damn it! Are you mounting guard for fear
  The truth might be divulged beside his coffin?
GIVOLA: Why so uncivil, my dear Clark? I'd think
  This holy place would curb your temper. And
  Besides, the boss is out of sorts. He doesn't
  Like the surroundings here.
MULBERRY: You murderers!
  Ignatius Dullfeet kept his word – and silence.
GIVOLA: Silence is not enough. The kind of men
  We need must be prepared not only to
  Keep silent for us but to speak – and loudly.
MULBERRY: What could he say except to call you butchers?
GIVOLA: He had to go. That little Dullfeet was
  The pore through which the greengoods dealers oozed
  Cold sweat. He stank of it unbearably.
GIRI: And what about your cauliflower? Do
  You want it sold in Cicero or don't
  You?
MULBERRY: Not by slaughter.
GIRI: Hypocrite, how else?
  Who helps us eat the calf we slaughter, eh?
  You're funny bastards, clamouring for meat
  Then bawling out the cook because he uses
  A cleaver. We expect you guys to smack
  Your lips and all you do is gripe. And now
  Go home!
MULBERRY: A sorry day, Clark, when you brought
  These people in.
CLARK: You're telling me?
  The two go out, deep in gloom.
GIRI: Boss
  Don't let those stinkers keep you from enjoying
  The funeral!
GIVOLA: Pst! Betty's coming.
  Leaning on another woman, Betty comes out of the chapel.
  Ui steps up to her. Organ music from the chapel.

UI: Mrs
  Dullfeet, my sympathies.
  She passes him without a word.
GIRI, *bellowing*:   Hey, you!
  She stops still and turns around. Her face is white.
UI: ·   I said, my
  Sympathies, Mrs Dullfeet. Dullfeet – God
  Have mercy on his soul – is dead. But cauliflower –
  Your cauliflower – is still with us. Maybe you
  Can't see it, because your eyes are still
  Blinded with tears. This tragic incident
  Should not, however, blind you to the fact
  That shots are being fired from craven ambush
  On law-abiding vegetable trucks.
  And kerosene dispensed by ruthless hands
  Is spoiling sorely needed vegetables.
  My men and I stand ready to provide
  Protection. What's your answer?
BETTY, *looking heavenward*:   This
  With Dullfeet hardly settled in his grave!
UI: Believe me, I deplore the incident:
  The man by ruthless hand extinguished was
  My friend.
BETTY: The hand that felled him was the hand
  That shook his hand in friendship. Yours!
UI: Am I
  Never to hear the last of these foul rumours
  This calumny which poisons at the root
  My noblest aspirations and endeavours
  To live in harmony with my fellow men?
  Oh, why must they refuse to understand me?
  Why will they not requite my trust? What malice
  To speak of threats when I appeal to reason!
  To spurn the hand that I hold out in friendship!
BETTY: You hold it out to murder.

UI: No!
  I plead with them and they revile me.
BETTY: You
  Plead like a serpent pleading with a bird.
UI: You've heard her. That's how people talk to me.
  It was the same with Dullfeet. He mistook
  My warm, my open-hearted offer of friendship
  For calculation and my generosity
  For weakness. How, alas, did he requite
  My friendly words? With stony silence. Silence
  Was his reply when what I hoped for
  Was joyful appreciation. Oh, how I longed to
  Hear him respond to my persistent, my
  Well-nigh humiliating pleas for friendship, or
  At least for a little understanding, with
  Some sign of human warmth. I longed in vain.
  My only reward was grim contempt. And even
  The promise to keep silent that he gave me
  So sullenly and God knows grudgingly
  Was broken on the first occasion. Where
  I ask you is this silence that he promised
  So fervently? New horror stories are being
  Broadcast in all directions. But I warn you:
  Don't go too far, for even my proverbial
  Patience has got its breaking point.
BETTY: Words fail me.
UI: Unprompted by the heart, they always fail.
BETTY: You call it heart that makes you speak so glibly?
UI: I speak the way I feel.
BETTY: Can anybody feel
  The way you speak? Perhaps he can. Your murders
  Come from the heart. Your blackest crimes are
  As deeply felt as other men's good deeds.
  As we believe in faith, so you believe in
  Betrayal. No good impulse can corrupt you.
  Unwavering in your inconstancy!

True to disloyalty, staunch in deception!
Kindled to sacred fire by bestial deeds!
The sight of blood delights you. Violence
Exalts your spirit. Sordid actions move you
To tears, and good ones leave you with deep-seated
Hatred and thirst for vengeance.

UI: Mrs Dullfeet
I always – it's a principle of mine –
Hear my opponent out, even when
His words are gall. I know that in your circle
I'm not exactly loved. My origins –
Never have I denied that I'm a humble
Son of the Bronx – are held against me.
'He doesn't even know,' they say, 'which fork
To eat his fish with. How then can he hope
To be accepted in big business? When
Tariffs are being discussed, or similar
Financial matters, he's perfectly capable
Of reaching for his knife instead of his pen.
Impossible! We can't use such a man!'
My uncouth tone, my manly way of calling
A spade a spade are used as marks against me.
These barriers of prejudice compel me
To bank exclusively on my own achievement.
You're in the cauliflower business. Mrs
Dullfeet, and so am I. There lies the bridge
Between us.

BETTY: And the chasm to be bridged
Is only foul murder.

UI: Bitter experience
Teaches me not to stress the human angle
But speak to you as a man of influence
Speaks to the owner of a greengoods business.
And so I ask you: How's the cauliflower
Business? For life goes on despite our sorrows.

BETTY: Yes, it goes on – and I shall use my life

To warn the people of this pestilence.
I swear to my dead husband that in future
I'll hate my voice if it should say 'Good morning'
Or 'Pass the bread' instead of one thing only:
'Extinguish Ui!'

GIRI, *in a threatening tone*: Don't overdo it, kid!

UI: Because amid the tombs I dare not hope
For milder feelings, I'd better stick to business
Which knows no dead.

BETTY: Oh Dullfeet, Dullfeet! Now
I truly know that you are dead.

UI: Exactly.
Bear well in mind that Dullfeet's dead. With him
Has died the only voice in Cicero
That would have spoken out in opposition
To crime and terror. You cannot deplore
His loss too deeply. Now you stand defenceless
In a cold world where, sad to say, the weak
Are always trampled. You've got only one
Protector left. That's me, Arturo Ui.

BETTY: And this to me, the widow of the man
You murdered! Monster! Oh, I knew you'd be here
Because you've always gone back to the scene of
Your crimes to throw the blame on others. 'No
It wasn't me, it was somebody else.'
'I know of nothing.' 'I've been injured'
Cries injury. And murder cries: 'A murder!
Murder must be avenged!'

UI: My plan stands fast.
Protection must be given to Cicero.

BETTY, *feebly*: You won't succeed.

UI: I will. That much I know.

BETTY: From this protector God protect us!

UI: Give
Me your answer.

He holds out his hand.

Is it friendship?

BETTY:　　　　　　　　　　　　　　Never while I live!
   Cringing with horror, she runs out.
   A sign appears.

14

*Ui's bedroom at the Hotel Mammoth. Ui tossing in his bed,
plagued by a nightmare. His bodyguards are sitting in chairs, their
revolvers on their laps.*

UI, *in his sleep*: Out, bloody shades! Have pity! Get you gone!
   *The wall behind him becomes transparent. The ghost of Ernesto
   Roma appears, a bullet-hole in his forehead.*
ROMA: It will avail you nothing. All this murder
   This butchery, these threats and slaverings
   Are all in vain, Arturo, for the root of
   Your crimes is rotten. They will never flower.
   Treason is made manure. Murder, lie
   Deceive the Clarks and slay the Dullfeets, but
   Stop at your own. Conspire against the world
   But spare your fellow conspirators.
   Trample the city with a hundred feet
   But trample not the feet, you treacherous dog!
   Cozen them all, but do not hope to cozen
   The man whose face you look at in the mirror!
   In striking me, you struck yourself, Arturo!
   I cast my lot with you when you were hardly
   More than a shadow on a bar-room floor.
   And now I languish in this drafty
   Eternity, while you sit down to table
   With sleek and proud directors. Treachery
   Made you, and treachery will unmake you.

Just as you betrayed Ernesto Roma, your
Friend and lieutenant, so you will betray
Everyone else, and all, Arturo, will
Betray you in the end. The green earth covers
Ernesto Roma, but not your faithless spirit
Which hovers over tombstones in the wind
Where all can see it, even the grave-diggers.
The day will come when all whom you struck down
And all you will strike down will rise, Arturo
And, bleeding but made strong by hate, take arms
Against you. You will look around for help
As I once looked. Then promise, threaten, plead.
No one will help. Who helped me in my need?
UI, *jumping up with a start*:
   Shoot! Kill him! Traitor! Get back to the dead!
   The bodyguards shoot at the spot on the wall indicated by Ui.
ROMA, *fading away*:
   What's left of me is not afraid of lead.

15

*Financial District. Meeting of the Chicago vegetable dealers.
They are deathly pale.*

FIRST VEGETABLE DEALER:
   Murder! Extortion! Highway robbery!
SECOND VEGETABLE DEALER:
   And worse: Submissiveness and cowardice!
THIRD VEGETABLE DEALER:
   What do you mean, submissiveness? In January
   When the first two came barging into
   My store and threatened me at gunpoint, I
   Gave them, a steely look from top to toe
   And answered firmly: I incline to force.

I made it plain that I could not approve
Their conduct or have anything to do
With them. My countenance was ice.
It said: So be it, take your cut. But only
Because you've got those guns.
FOURTH VEGETABLE DEALER: Exactly!
I wash my hands in innocence! That's what
I told my missus.
FIRST VEGETABLE DEALER, *vehemently*:
                         What do you mean, cowardice?
We used our heads. If we kept quiet, gritted
Our teeth and paid, we thought those bloody fiends
Would put their guns away. But did they? No! It's
Murder! Extortion! Highway robbery!
SECOND VEGETABLE DEALER:
Nobody else would swallow it. No backbone!
FIFTH VEGETABLE DEALER:
No tommy gun, you mean. I'm not a gangster.
My trade is selling greens.
THIRD VEGETABLE DEALER: My only hope
Is that the bastard some day runs across
Some guys who show their teeth. Just let him try his
Little game somewhere else!
FOURTH VEGETABLE DEALER: In Cicero
For instance.
The Cicero vegetable dealers come in. They are deathly pale.
THE CICERONIANS: Hi, Chicago!
THE CHICAGOANS: Hi, Cicero!
What brings *you* here?
THE CICERONIANS: We were told to come.
THE CHICAGOANS: By who?
THE CICERONIANS: By him.
FIRST CHICAGOAN: Who says so? How can he command
You? Throw his weight around in Cicero?
FIRST CICERONIAN: With
His gun.

SECOND CICERONIAN: Brute force. We're helpless.

FIRST CHICAGOAN: Stinking
    cowards!
    Can't you be men? Is there no law in Cicero?

FIRST CICERONIAN: No.

SECOND CICERONIAN: No longer.

THIRD CHICAGOAN: Listen, friends. You've got
    To fight. This plague will sweep the country
    If you don't stop it.

FIRST CHICAGOAN: First one city, then another.
    Fight to the death! You owe it to your country.

SECOND CICERONIAN:
    Why us? We wash our hands in innocence.

FOURTH CHICAGOAN:
    We only hope with God's help that the bastard
    Some day comes across some guys that show
    Their teeth.
    *Fanfares. Enter Arturo Ui and Betty Dullfeet – in mourning –
    followed by Clark, Giri, Givola and bodyguards. Flanked by
    the others, Ui passes through. The bodyguards line up in the
    background.*

GIRI: Hi, friends! Is everybody here
    From Cicero?

FIRST CICERONIAN: All present.

GIRI: And Chicago?

FIRST CHICAGOAN: All present.

GIRI, *to Ui*:   Everybody's here.

GIVOLA: Greetings, my friends. The Cauliflower Trust
    Wishes you all a hearty welcome. Our
    First speaker will be Mr Clark. *To Clark*: Mr Clark.

CLARK: Gentlemen, I bring news. Negotiations
    Begun some weeks ago and patiently
    Though sometimes stormily pursued – I'm telling
    Tales out of school – have yielded fruit. The wholesale
    House of I. Dullfeet, Cicero, has joined
    The Cauliflower Trust. In consequence

The Cauliflower Trust will now supply
Your greens. The gain for you is obvious:
Secure delivery. The new prices, slightly
Increased, have already been set. It is
With pleasure, Mrs Dullfeet, that the Trust
Welcomes you as its newest member.
Clark and Betty Dullfeet shake hands.

GIVOLA: And now: Arturo Ui.
Ui steps up to the microphone.

UI: Friends, countrymen!
Chicagoans and Ciceronians! When
A year ago old Dogsborough, God rest
His honest soul, with tearful eyes
Appealed to me to protect Chicago's green-
Goods trade, though moved, I doubted whether
My powers would be able to justify
His smiling confidence. Now Dogsborough
Is dead. He left a will which you're all free
To read. In simple words therein he calls me
His son. And thanks me fervently for all
I've done since I responded to his appeal.
Today the trade in vegetables –
Be they kohlrabi, onions, carrots or what
Have you – is amply protected in Chicago.
Thanks, I make bold to say, to resolute
Action on my part. When another civic
Leader, Ignatius Dullfeet, to my surprise
Approached me with the same request, this time
Concerning Cicero, I consented
To take that city under my protection.
But one condition I stipulated, namely:
The dealers had to want me. I would come
Only pursuant to their free decision
Freely arrived at. Cicero, I told
My men, in no uncertain terms, must not be
Subjected to coercion or constraint.

The city has to elect me in full freedom.
I want no grudging 'Why not?', no teeth-gnashing
'We might as well'. Half-hearted acquiescence
Is poison in my books. What I demand
Is one unanimous and joyful 'Yes'
Succinct and, men of Cicero, expressive.
And since I want this and everything else I want
To be complete, I turn again to you
Men of Chicago, who, because you know
Me better, hold me, I have reason to believe
In true esteem, and ask you: Who is for me?
And just in passing let me add: If anyone's
Not for me he's against me and has only
Himself to blame for anything that happens.
Now you may vote.

GIVOLA: But first a word from Mrs
   Dullfeet, the widow, known to all of you, of
   A man beloved by all.

BETTY: Dear friends
   Your faithful friend and my beloved husband
   Ignatius Dullfeet is no longer with us to . . .

GIVOLA: God rest his soul!

BETTY: . . . sustain and help you. I
   Advise you all to put your trust in Mr
   Ui, as I do now that in these grievous days
   I've come to know him better.

GIVOLA: Time to vote!

GIRI: All those in favour of Arturo Ui
   Raise your right hands!
   Some raise their hands.

A CICERONIAN: Is it permissible to leave?

GIVOLA: Each man
   Is free to do exactly as he pleases.
   Hesitantly the Ciceronian goes out. Two bodyguards follow him.
   A shot is heard.

GIRI: All right, friends, Let's have your free decision!
All raise both hands.

GIVOLA: They've finished voting, boss. With deep
  emotion
  Teeth chattering for joy, the greengoods dealers
  Of Cicero and Chicago thank you
  For your benevolent protection.

UI: With
  Pride I accept your thanks. Some fifteen years
  Ago, when I was only a humble, unemployed
  Son of the Bronx; when following the call
  Of destiny I sallied forth with only
  Seven staunch men to brave the Windy City
  I was inspired by an iron will
  To create peace in the vegetable trade.
  We were a handful then, who humbly but
  Fanatically strove for this ideal
  Of peace! Today we are a multitude.
  Peace in Chicago's vegetable trade
  Has ceased to be a dream. Today it is
  Unvarnished reality. And to secure
  This peace I have put in an order
  For more machine-guns, rubber truncheons
  Etcetera. For Chicago and Cicero
  Are not alone in clamouring for protection.
  There are other cities: Washington and Milwaukee!
  Detroit! Toledo! Pittsburgh! Cincinnati!
  And other towns where vegetables are traded!
  Philadelphia! Columbus! Charleston! And New York!
  They all demand protection! And no 'Phooey!'
  No 'That's not nice!' will stop Arturo Ui!
  Amid drums and fanfares the curtain falls.
  A sign appears.

Epilogue

Therefore learn how to see and not to gape.
To act instead of talking all day long.
The world was almost won by such an ape!
The nations put him where his kind belong.
But don't rejoice too soon at your escape –
The womb he crawled from still is going strong.

Chronological Table

1. 1929–1932. Germany is hard hit by the world crisis. At the height of the crisis a number of Prussian Junkers try to obtain government loans, for a long time without success. The big industrialists in the Ruhr dream of expansion.

2. By way of winning President Hindenburg's sympathy for their cause, the Junkers make him a present of a landed estate.

3. In the autumn of 1932, Adolf Hitler's party and private army are threatened with bankruptcy and disintegration. To save the situation Hitler tries desperately to have himself appointed Chancellor, but for a long time Hindenburg refuses to see him.

4. In January 1933 Hindenburg appoints Hitler Chancellor in return for a promise to prevent the exposure of the *Osthilfe* (East Aid) scandal, in which Hindenburg himself is implicated.

5. After coming to power legally, Hitler surprises his high patrons by extremely violent measures, but keeps his promises.

6. The gang leader quickly transforms himself into a statesman. He is believed to have taken lessons in declamation and bearing from one, Basil, a provincial actor.

7. February 1933, the Reichstag fire. Hitler accuses his enemies of instigating the fire and gives the signal for the Night of the Long Knives.

8. The Supreme Court in Leipzig condemns an unemployed worker to death for causing the fire. The real incendiaries get off scot-free.

9. and 10. The impending death of the aged Hindenburg provokes bitter struggles in the Nazi camp. The Junkers

and industrialists demand Röhm's removal. The occupation of Austria is planned.

11.   On the night of 30 June 1934 Hitler overpowers his friend Röhm at an inn where Röhm has been waiting for him. Up to the last moment Röhm thinks that Hitler is coming to arrange for a joint strike against Hindenburg and Göring.

12.   Under compulsion the Austrian Chancellor Engelbert Dollfuss agrees to stop the attacks on Hitler that have been appearing in the Austrian press.

13.   Dollfuss is murdered at Hitler's instigation, but Hitler goes on negotiating with Austrian rightist circles.

15.   On 11 March 1938 Hitler marches into Austria. An election under the Nazi terror results in a 98% vote for Hitler.

Mr Puntila and his Man Matti
A people's play

After stories and
a draft play
by Hella Wuolijoki

Translator: JOHN WILLETT

Characters
PUNTILA, *landowner*
EVA PUNTILA, *his daughter*
MATTI, *his chauffeur*
THE WAITER
THE JUDGE
THE ATTACHÉ
THE VET
SLY-GROG EMMA
THE CHEMIST'S ASSISTANT
THE MILKMAID
THE TELEPHONIST
A FAT MAN
A LABOURER
THE RED-HEADED MAN
THE WEEDY MAN
RED SURKKALA
HIS FOUR CHILDREN
LAINA, *the cook*
FINA, *the parlourmaid*
THE LAYWER
THE PARSON
THE PARSON'S WIFE
WOODCUTTERS

Music by PAUL DESSAU

Red Surkkala's song at the end of Scene 9 was translated by
NAOMI REPLANSKY

*Proper names of three syllables are accented on the first syllable,
e.g. Púntila, Kúrgela, etc.*

Prologue

Spoken by the actress playing the milkmaid

Ladies and gentleman, the times are tough.
Let's hope the future's made of better stuff.
But gloomy faces cannot set things right
So we present a comedy tonight
In which you'll find the elements of fun
Will not be doled out meanly, one by one
But thunderingly in hundredweights, like spuds
That tumble from the sack with earthy thuds.
Though we shan't hesitate to use the chopper
If characters get larger than is proper.
You'll see us re-creating on this stage
A monster from a prehistoric age –
Estatium possessor, owner of big estates –
A useless beast who idly ruminates
And still clings to dear life for all he's worth
A stubborn blot disfiguring our good earth.
Here you may watch him graze without restraint
Across the loveliest landscapes we can paint.
And if our settings leave you unimpressed
We think the words ought to supply the rest:
Convey the clank of churns beneath birch trees
A midnight sun above quiet inland seas
Red-tinted villages awake before cockcrow
Smoke rising up from shingle roofs below.
Such are the pleasures which we hope now are
Awaiting you in our play *Puntila*.

1

Puntila discovers a human being

Back room in the Park Hotel, Tavasthus. Landowner Puntila, Judge, Waiter. Judge slips drunkenly off his chair.

PUNTILA: Waiter, how long we been here?

WAITER: Two days, Mr Puntila.

PUNTILA, *reproachfully, to judge*: Mere couple of days, you hear what the man said? And there you are already packing up and acting tired. Just as I was looking forward to an aquavit and a bit of a chat about me and how lonely I get and what I think of our government. But you lot crumple at the least little effort, for the spirit is willing but the flesh is weak. Where's that doctor who was ready to take on all comers only yesterday? The stationmaster watched them cart him out; must have been around seven when he too went down after an heroic struggle, very incoherent he was; the chemist was still on his feet then, as I recollect; where is he now? And these claim to be the leading personalities round here; people are going to feel let down and turn their backs on them, and [*addressing the slumbering Judge*] what kind of a bad example to the locals is that, when a judge can't even stand up to a casual call at a wayside inn; didn't that ever occur to you? If one of my men was as slack ploughing as you are drinking, I'd sack him out of hand. 'I'll teach you to scamp your duties, you bugger', I'd say. Don't you realise, Fredrik, how much all of us expect of you: an educated man whom everyone looks to to set an example and have some stamina and show a sense of responsibility? Why can't you pull yourself together and sit up properly and talk to me, you weakling? *To the Waiter*: What day's today then?

WAITER: Saturday, Mr Puntila.

PUNTILA: You amaze me. In my book it says Friday.

WAITER: I'm sorry, but it's Saturday.

PUNTILA: That's not what you said just now. Fine waiter, I don't think. Trying to drive away the customers by acting surly to them. Now, waiter, I'm ordering another aquavit; listen carefully and don't muddle it up this time, one aquavit and one Friday. Got it?

WAITER: Right, Mr Puntila. *He hurries off.*

PUNTILA, *to Judge*: Wake up, weakling! You can't abandon me like this. Knuckling under to a few bottles of aquavit! Why, you've barely had a sniff of them. There you were, skulking under the thwarts as I rowed you across the aquavit, I hadn't the gumption to look over the gunwale even; ought to be ashamed of yourself. Now watch, I step out on to the calm surface [*he acts it*] sauntering over the aquavit, and do I go under? *He sees Matti, his chauffeur, who has been standing in the doorway for some moments.* Who are you?

MATTI: I'm your chauffeur, Mr Puntila.

PUNTILA, *suspiciously*: What did you say you were?

MATTI: I'm your driver.

PUNTILA: Anyone can say that. I don't know you.

MATTI: Maybe you never had a proper look at me; I only been with you five weeks.

PUNTILA: And where have you sprung from?

MATTI: Outside. Been waiting in the car two days.

PUNTILA: What car?

MATTI: Yours. The Studebaker.

PUNTILA: Sounds fishy to me. Can you prove it?

MATTI: And I've had just about enough of waiting for you out there, let me tell you. I'm fed up to the bloody teeth. You can't treat human beings like that.

PUNTILA: **What d'you mean human beings? You a human being? Moment ago you said you were a driver. Caught you contradicting yourself, haven't I?**

MATTI: You'll see I'm a human being all right, Mr Puntila. 'Cause I'm not going to be treated like one of your cattle and left sitting in the road waiting till you are so good as to graciously condescend to come out.

PUNTILA: Moment ago you said you *wouldn't* stand for it.

MATTI: Too right. Pay me up to date, 175 marks, and I'll call for my reference back at Puntila's.

PUNTILA: I recognise that voice of yours. *He walks round him, observing his points like an animal's.* Sounds almost human, it does. Sit down, have an aquavit, we ought to get to know each other.

WAITER, *entering with a bottle*: Your aquavit, Mr Puntila, and today is Friday.

PUNTILA: Good. *Indicating Matti*: This is a friend of mine.

WAITER: Yes, your driver, Mr Puntila.

PUNTILA: So you're a driver, are you? I always say what interesting people one meets on the road. Help yourself.

MATTI: I'd like to know what you're after. I'm not sure I care to drink your grog.

PUNTILA: You're a suspicious fellow, I see. I get the point. Never sit at table with people one doesn't know. And for why? Because when you nod off they might rob you. I'm Puntila the landowner from Lammi and a man of honour, I got ninety cows. You're all right drinking with me, brother.

MATTI: Good. I'm Matti Altonen and pleased to meet you. *He drinks to him.*

PUNTILA: I've got a kind heart and I'm not ashamed of it. Once I picked up a stagbeetle in the road and put it in the bushes so it wouldn't get run over, that's how far I'd go. I let it clamber up a twig. You've a kind heart too, I can see. I hate it when people keep talking about 'I, I' all the time. Should have it flogged out of them with a horsewhip. There are farmers round here'd snatch the food from their men's mouths. I'd sooner give my hands nothing but a good roast. After all they're human beings and want a decent bit of meat just like me, so why not? Eh?

MATTI: Absolutely.

PUNTILA: Did I really leave you sitting out in the road? I don't think much of that, it's very bad of me, and I'll ask you next time I do it to take the jack handle and belt me one. Matti, you my friend?

MATTI: No.

PUNTILA: Thank you. I knew you were. Matti, look at me. What do you see?

MATTI: I'd say a fat slob, pissed as arseholes.

PUNTILA: That shows the deceptiveness of appearances. I'm not like that at all. Matti, I'm a sick man.

MATTI: Very sick.

PUNTILA: I'm glad to hear you say so. Not everybody realises. You'd never think it to look at me. *Tragically, with a sharp glance at Matti*: I get attacks.

MATTI: You don't say.

PUNTILA: It's no laughing matter, my friend. It comes over me every three months or so. I wake up, and all of a sudden I'm stone cold sober. How about that?

MATTI: And these fits of sobriety, do they attack you regularly?

PUNTILA: Absolutely. It's this way: all the rest of the time I'm perfectly normal, just as you see me now. In full possession of my faculties, master of my feelings. Then comes the attack. It starts with something going wrong with my eyesight. Instead of seeing two forks [*he raises a fork*] I only see one.

MATTI, *appalled*: Mean to say you're half blind?

PUNTILA: I only see one half of the entire world. Worse still, when I get these attacks of total senseless sobriety I sink to the level of the beasts. I have absolutely no inhibitions. Brother, you'd never believe the sort of things I get up to in that state. Not even if you're full of compassion and realise I'm a sick man. *With horror in his voice*: I become fully responsible for my actions. D'you realise what that means, brother, fully responsible for one's actions? A fully responsible person can be expected to do absolutely anything. He's no longer competent to look after his children's interests, he's lost all feelings of friendship; trample over his own dead body, he would. That's because he's fully responsible for his actions, as the law puts it.

MATTI: Can't you do anything to stop these attacks?

PUNTILA: I do all that's humanly possible, brother. *He grips his glass.* Here you are, my one medicine. I knock it back unflinching, and not just a baby's dose, believe you me. If there's one thing I can say for myself it's that I tackle these bouts of senseless sobriety like a man. But what's the use? Sobriety keeps getting the upper hand. Look at the lack of consideration I've shown you, such a splendid fellow. Here, have some of this beef. I'd like to know what good wind brought you my way. What made you come to me?

MATTI: Losing my last job by no fault of my own.

PUNTILA: How was that?

MATTI: I kept seeing ghosts.

PUNTILA: Real ones?

MATTI, *shrugging his shoulders*: They couldn't understand. There hadn't been any ghosts on Mr Pappmann's estate before I came. If you ask me I think it was the food. You see, when people have a lot of heavy dough lying on their stomachs they're apt to have heavy dreams, nightmares quite often. Bad cooking disagrees with me particularly. I thought about packing it in, but I hadn't any other job to go to and felt a bit depressed, so I made a few scary remarks in the kitchen and it wasn't long before the girls started seeing babies' heads on the fences at night and giving their notice. Or there was a grey ball which came rolling out of the cowshed like a head, so as soon as the stable girl heard my description she was took queer. And the parlourmaid left after I'd seen a dark man one night around eleven walking past the bath hut with his head tucked under his arm asking me for a light. Mr Pappmann started bawling me out, saying it was all my fault and I was scaring the staff into leaving and

there were no ghosts on his place. But when I told him how
I twice saw a ghost climbing out of the maid's window and
into his own when the missis was in hospital having her baby
there wasn't much he could say. Still, he sacked me all the
same. Last thing before going I told him I thought if he could
get the cooking improved the ghosts on the estate might lay
off, 'cause they're supposed not to abide the smell of meat.

PUNTILA: So the only reason you lost your job was that they
were scamping on the staff's food. I shan't hold it against you
if you like eating well, so long as you drive my tractor
properly and know your place and render unto Puntila the
things that are Puntila's. There's plenty for all, nobody goes
short of wood in a forest, do they? We can all get along
together, everyone can get along with Puntila. *He sings*:

> 'Dear child, why sue me when you said
> We always felt so close in bed?'

Ah, how Puntila would love to be chopping down the birch
trees with you, and digging the stones out of the fields and
driving the tractor. But will they let him? Right at the start
they stuck me in a stiff collar, and so far it's worn down two
of my chins. It's not done for daddy to plough; it's not done
for daddy to goose the maids; it's not done for daddy to have
his coffee with the men. But now I'm doing away with 'not
done', and I'm driving over to Kurgela to get my daughter
hitched to the Attaché, and after that I'll take my meals in
my shirtsleeves with nobody to watch over me, because old
Klinckmann will shut up, I'll fuck her and that'll be an end
of it. And I'll raise wages all round, for the world is a big
place and I shan't give up my forest and there'll be enough
for you all and enough for the master of Puntila Hall too.

MATTI, *after laughing long and loud*: Right you are, just you
calm down and we'll wake his honour the judge. Careful
though, or he'll get such a fright he'll sentence us to a
hundred years.

PUNTILA: I want to be sure there's no gulf between us any longer. Tell me there's no gulf.

MATTI: I take that as an order, Mr Puntila: there's no gulf.

PUNTILA: We have to talk about money, brother.

MATTI: Absolutely.

PUNTILA: But talking about money is sordid.

MATTI: Then we won't talk about money.

PUNTILA: Wrong. For why shouldn't we talk about money, I ask you. Aren't we free individuals?

MATTI: No.

PUNTILA: There you are. And as free individuals we're free to do what we want, and what we want at the moment is to be sordid. Because what we got to do is drum up a dowry for my only child; and that's a problem to be looked at without flinching – cool, calm, and drunk. I see two choices: sell my forest or sell myself. Which would you say?

MATTI: I'd never dream of selling myself if I could sell a forest.

PUNTILA: What, sell that forest? You're a profound disappointment to me, brother. Don't you know what a forest is? Is a forest simply ten thousand cords of wood? Or is it a verdant delight for all mankind? And here you are, proposing to sell a verdant delight for all mankind. Shame on you.

MATTI: Then do the other thing.

PUNTILA: *Et tu, Brute?* Do you really want me to sell myself?

MATTI: What kind of selling have you in mind?

PUNTILA: Mrs Klinckmann.

MATTI: Out at Kurgela, where we're going? The Attaché's aunty?

PUNTILA: She fancies me.

MATTI: So you're thinking of selling your body to her? That's hair-raising.

PUNTILA: Not a bit. But what price freedom, brother? I think I'd better sacrifice myself all the same. After all, what do I amount to?

MATTI: Too right.

The Judge wakes up, gropes for a non-existent bell and rings it.

THE JUDGE: Silence in court!

PUNTILA: He's asleep, so he thinks he must be in court. Brother, you've just settled the problem which is the more valuable, a forest like my forest or a human being like myself. You're a wonderful fellow. Here, take my wallet and pay for the drinks, and put it in your pocket, I'd only lose it. *Indicating the Judge*: Pick him up, get him out of here. I'm always losing things. I wish I had nothing, that's what I'd like best. Money stinks, remember. That's my ideal, to have nothing, just you and me hiking across Finland on foot or maybe in a little two-seater, nobody would grudge us the drop of petrol we'd need, and every so often when we felt tired we'd turn into a pub like this one and have one for the road, that's something you could do blindfold, brother.

They leave, Matti carrying the Judge.

2

Eva

Entrance hall of the Kurgela manor house. Eva Puntila is waiting for her father and eating chocolates. Eino Silakka, the Attaché, appears at the head of the stairs. He is very sleepy.

EVA: No wonder Mrs Klinckmann got fed up waiting.

THE ATTACHÉ: My aunt is never fed up for long. I have telephoned again for news of them. A car passed through Kirchendorf with two rowdy men in it.

EVA: That'll be them. One good thing, I can always pick out my father anywhere. Whenever there's been someone chasing a farmhand with a pitchfork or giving a cottager's widow a Cadillac it's got to be father.

THE ATTACHÉ: *Enfin*, he's not at Puntila Hall. I just don't like scandal. I may not have much head for figures or how many gallons of milk we export to Lithuania – I don't drink the stuff myself – but I am exceedingly sensitive to any breath of scandal. When the First Secretary at the French embassy in London leant across the table after his eighth cognac and called the Duchess of Catrumple an old whore I instantly foresaw a scandal. And I was proved right. I think that's them arriving now. I'm a little tired, dear. Would you excuse me if I went up to my room? *Exit rapidly.*

Great commotion. Enter Puntila, Judge and Matti.

PUNTILA: Here we are. But don't you bother about us, no need to wake anyone, we'll just have a quiet bottle together and go to bed. Happy?

EVA: We expected you three days ago.

PUNTILA: Got held up, but we've brought everything with us. Matti, unload the bag. I hope you kept it on your knee the whole time so nothing got broken, or we'll thirst to death in this place. We knew you'd be waiting, so we didn't dawdle.

THE JUDGE: May I offer my congratulations, Eva?

EVA: Daddy, it's too bad of you. Here I am, been sitting around for a week now in a strange house with nothing but an old book and the Attaché and his aunt, and I'm bored to tears.

PUNTILA: We didn't dawdle. I kept pressing on, saying we mustn't sit on our bottoms, the Attaché and I still have one or two points to settle about the engagement, and I was glad you were with the Attaché so you had company while we got held up. Look out for that suitcase, Matti, we don't want accidents. *With infinite care he helps Matti to set down the case.*

THE JUDGE: I hope the way you grumble about being left alone with the Attaché doesn't mean you've been quarrelling with him.

EVA: Oh, I don't know. He's not the sort of person you can quarrel with.

THE JUDGE: Puntila, your daughter doesn't strike me as being all that enthusiastic. Here she is, saying the Attaché's not a man you can quarrel with. I tried a divorce case once where the wife complained that her husband never belted her when she threw the lamp at him. She felt neglected.

PUNTILA: There we are. Another successful operation. Anything Puntila puts his hand to is a success. Not happy, eh? If you ask me I'd say dump the Attaché. He's not a man.

EVA, *as Matti is standing there grinning*: I merely said I wasn't certain if the Attaché was all that amusing on his own.

PUNTILA: Just what I was saying. Take Matti. Any woman'd find him amusing.

EVA: You're impossible, Daddy. All I said was that I wasn't certain. *To Matti*: Take that suitcase upstairs.

PUNTILA: Just a minute. Not till you've unpacked a bottle or two. You and me have got to get together over a bottle and discuss if the Attaché suits me. At least he'll have had time to propose to you by now.

EVA: No, he has not proposed, we didn't talk about that kind of thing. *To Matti*: That case stays shut.

PUNTILA: Good God, not proposed! After three days? What on earth were the pair of you up to? That doesn't say much for the fellow. I get engaged in three minutes flat. Wake him up and I'll fetch the cook and show him how to get engaged in two shakes of a lamb's tail. Fish out those bottles, the Burgundy; no, let's have the liqueur.

EVA: No, no more drinking for you. *To Matti*: Take it to my bedroom, second door on the right.

PUNTILA, *in alarm, as Matti picks up the case*: Really, Eva, that's not very nice of you. You can't deny your father his right to a thirst. I swear all I want to do is empty a bottle peacefully with the cook or the parlourmaid and Fredrik here too, he's still thirsty, have a heart.

EVA: That's why I stayed up: to stop you waking the domestic staff.

PUNTILA: I bet old Klinckmann would be happy to sit up with me a bit – come to think of it, where is she? – Freddie's tired anyway, he can go to bed and I'll talk things over with old Ma Klinckmann, that's something I meant to do anyway, we've always fancied each other.

EVA: I wish you'd try to pull yourself together. Mrs Klinckmann's angry enough already at your getting here three days late; I don't suppose you'll see her tomorrow at all.

PUNTILA: I'll give her a knock on her door and straighten matters out. I know how to handle her; you don't understand that sort of thing yet, Eva.

EVA: What I do understand is that no woman is going to want to sit with you in that condition. *To Matti*: You're to take that case upstairs. Those three days were the end.

PUNTILA: Eva, do be reasonable. If you don't want me to go up to her room, then get hold of that little buxom thing, housekeeper isn't she? and I'll have a talk with her.

EVA: Don't push things too far, Daddy, unless you want me to carry the case upstairs myself and accidentally drop it.
Puntila stands there appalled. Matti carries the suitcase off. Eva follows him.

PUNTILA, *quietly*: So that's how children treat their fathers. *Shaken, he turns to walk off.* Come along, Freddie.

THE JUDGE: What are you up to, Jack?

PUNTILA: I'm clearing out, I don't like it here. Here am I, hurrying all I'm worth and arriving late at night, and what kind of a loving welcome do I get? Remember the Prodigal Son, Freddie, but what if there'd been no fatted calf, just cold reproaches? I'm clearing out.

THE JUDGE: Where to?

PUNTILA: It beats me how you can ask that. Didn't you see my own daughter deny me a drink? Forcing me out into the night to see who will let me have a bottle or two?

THE JUDGE: Be sensible, Puntila, you won't get alcohol anywhere at half past two in the morning. Serving or selling liquor without a licence is not legal.

PUNTILA: So you're deserting me too? So I can't get legal liquor? I'll show you how I can get legal liquor, day or night.

EVA, *reappearing at the top of the stairs*: Take that coat off at once, Daddy.

PUNTILA: Shut up, Eva, and honour thy father and thy mother that thy days may be long upon the land. A nice house this, I don't think, where they hang up the visitor's guts to dry like underwear. And not getting a woman! I'll show you if I get a woman or not! You tell old Klinckmann I can do without her. I say she's the foolish virgin who's got no oil in her lamp. And now I shall drive off so that the earth resoundeth and all the curves straighten out in terror. *Exit.*

EVA, *coming downstairs*: Stop your master, do you hear?

MATTI, *appearing behind her*: Too late. He's too nippy for me.

THE JUDGE: I don't think I shall wait up for him. I'm not as young as I was, Eva. I don't suppose he'll come to any harm. He has the devil's own luck. Where's my room? *He goes upstairs.*

EVA: Third door at the top. *To Matti*: Now we'll have to sit up in case he starts drinking with the servants and getting familiar with them.

MATTI: That kind of intimacy's always disagreeable. I once worked in a paper mill where the porter gave notice because the director asked him how his son was getting on.

EVA: They all take advantage of my father because of this weakness of his. He's too good.

MATTI: Yes, it's just as well for everyone that he goes on the booze now and again. Then he turns into a good fellow and sees pink rats and wants to stroke them what with being so good.

EVA: I won't have you speaking about your master like that. And I would prefer you not to take the sort of thing he says about the Attaché literally. I would be sorry if you went around repeating what he said in jest.

MATTI: That the Attaché's not a man? What makes a man is a subject about which opinions differ. I used to work for a brewer's wife had a daughter wanted me to come to the bath hut and bring her a dressing-gown because she was so modest. 'Bring my dressing-gown,' she'd say as she stood there stark bollock naked. 'The men keep looking at me as I'm getting into my bath.'

EVA: I don't understand what you are implying.

MATTI: I'm not implying anything. I'm just chatting to help pass the time and keep you amused. When I talk to the gentry I imply nothing and have absolutely no opinions, as those are something they can't abide in servants.

EVA, *after a short pause*: The Attaché is very well thought of in the diplomatic service and set to have an outstanding career; I'd like everyone to be aware of that. He is one of the most promising of its younger members.

MATTI: I see.

EVA: What I was trying to say, when you were standing there just now, was that I didn't find him quite as amusing as my father expected. Naturally what counts isn't whether a man is amusing or not.

MATTI: I knew a gentleman wasn't at all amusing, but it didn't stop him making a million in margarine and fats.

EVA: My engagement was arranged a long time ago. We knew each other as children. It's just that I'm a rather vivacious sort of person and get easily bored.

MATTI: So you're not certain.

EVA: That's not what I said. Look, I don't see why you won't grasp what I am trying to say. Why don't you go to bed?

MATTI: I'm keeping you company.

EVA: There's no need for you to do that. I just wanted to point out that the Attaché is an intelligent and kind-hearted person who ought not to be judged by appearances or by what he says or what he does. He is extremely attentive and anticipates my every wish. He would never perform a vulgar

action or become familiar or try to parade his masculinity.
I have the highest regard for him. Are you feeling sleepy?
MATTI: Just go on talking. I'm only shutting my eyes so's to
concentrate better.

3

Puntila proposes to the early risers

Early morning in the village. Small wooden houses. One of them is marked 'Post Office', another 'Veterinary Surgeon', a third 'Chemist'. In the middle of the square stands a telegraph pole. Puntila, having run his Studebaker into the pole, is cursing it.

PUNTILA: What's happened to the Finnish highway system?
Get out of my way, you rat-shit pole, who are you to block
Puntila's access? Own a forest, got any cows? There, what
did I tell you? Back! If I ring the police and have them arrest
you as a Red I suppose you'll say sorry, but it wasn't you.
He gets out. So you've backed down, and about time too.
*He goes to one of the houses and raps on the window. Sly-
Grog Emma looks out.*
PUNTILA: Good morrow, your ladyship. I trust your ladyship
slept well? I have a trivial request to put to your ladyship.
I am Puntila who farms the manor at Lammi, and I am
severely perturbed because I must somehow obtain legal
alcohol for my seventy fever-ridden cows. Where does the
veterinary surgeon of your village deign to reside? I shall feel
myself regretfully compelled to smash up your dirty little
hovel if you don't show me the way to the vet's.
SLY-GROG EMMA: Heavens, what a state you're in. There's
our vet's house, right there. But did I hear you say you want

alcohol, sir? I have alcohol, good and strong, all my own make.

PUNTILA: Get thee behind me, thou Jezebel! How dare you offer me your illegal liquor? I drink legitimate only, anything else would choke me. Sooner die than fail to respect our law and order, I would. Because everything I do is according to the law. If I want to clobber a man to death I do it within the law or not at all.

SLY-GROG EMMA: Then I hope your legal alcohol makes you sick, sir. *She disappears inside her house. Puntila goes over to the vet's house and rings the bell. The vet looks out.*

PUNTILA: Vet, vet, found you at last. I am Puntila who farms the manor at Lammi, and I've got ninety cows and all ninety have scarlet fever. So I need legal alcohol right away.

THE VET: I fancy you've come to the wrong address; you'd better be on your way, my man.

PUNTILA: Vet, vet, don't disappoint me. You're no true vet or you'd know what they give Puntila throughout the province every time his cows have the scarlet fever. Because I'm not lying to you. If I said they'd got glanders that'd be a lie, but when I tell you they've got scarlet fever that's a delicate hint from one gentleman to another.

THE VET: What happens if I fail to take your hint?

PUNTILA: Then I might tell you that Puntila is the biggest bruiser in the whole of Tavastland province. There's even a folk song about him. He's got three vets on his conscience already. You see what I mean, doctor?

THE VET, *laughing*: Yes, I see all right. If only I could be sure it was scarlet fever . . .

PUNTILA: Look, doctor, if they have red patches – and two of them even have black patches – isn't that scarlet fever in its most virulent form? And what about the headaches they must have when they can't get to sleep, and toss and turn all night long thinking of their sins?

THE VET: Then clearly it is my duty to relieve them.

He throws the prescription down to him.

PUNTILA: And you can send your account to Puntila Hall at Lammi.

Puntila goes to the chemist's and rings the bell hard. While he is waiting there, Sly-Grog Emma comes out of her house.

SLY-GROG EMMA *cleans bottles and sings*:

> In our village one fine morning
> When the plums were ripe and blue
> Came a gig as day was dawning
> Bore a young man passing through.

She goes back into her house. The chemist's assistant looks out of the chemist's shop window.

CHEMIST'S ASSISTANT: You're busting our bell.

PUNTILA: Better bust the bell than wait for ever. Kittikittikittiticktickticktick! What I need is alcohol for ninety cows, my fine plump friend.

CHEMIST'S ASSISTANT: I think what you need is for me to call a policeman.

PUNTILA: Come on, my little sweetheart. Policemen for somebody like Puntila Esquire from Lammi! What good would a single policeman be for him, you'd need at least two. And why policemen anyway, I love the police, they've got bigger feet than anybody else and five toes on each foot because they stand for order and order's what I love. *He gives her the prescription.* Here, my dove, there's law and order for you.

The chemist's assistant goes to get the alcohol. While Puntila is waiting, Sly-Grog Emma again comes out of her house.

SLY-GROG EMMA *sings*:

> As we loaded up our baskets
> Down he lay beneath a tree.
> Fair his head, and if you ask it's
> Not much that he didn't see.

234 Mr Puntila and his Man Matti

She goes inside her house again. The chemist's assistant brings the alcohol.

CHEMIST'S ASSISTANT, *laughing*: That's a good-sized bottle. I hope you've plenty of herrings for your cows for the morning after. *She hands him the bottle.*

PUNTILA: Glug, glugglug, O music of Finland, loveliest music in the world! My God, I almost forgot. Here am I with alcohol but no girl. And you've no alcohol and no man. Lovely pharmacist, I'd like to get engaged to you.

CHEMIST'S ASSISTANT: Thanks for the honour, Mr Puntila Esquire from Lammi, but I can only get engaged as laid down by law with a ring and a sip of wine.

PUNTILA: Right, so long as you get engaged to me. But get engaged you must, it's high time, for what sort of life do you lead? Tell me what kind of person you are, that's something I should know if I'm going to be engaged to you.

CHEMIST'S ASSISTANT: Me? Here's the sort of life I lead. I did four years at college and now the chemist's charging me for lodging, and paying me less than he pays his cook. Half my wages go to my mother in Tavasthus, she's got a weak heart, passed it on to me. One night in two I can't sleep. The chemist's wife is jealous 'cause the chemist keeps pestering me. The doctor's handwriting's bad, once I got his prescriptions muddled, then I'm always getting stains on my dress from the drugs, and cleaning's so expensive. I've not found a boy friend, the police sergeant and the director of the co-op and the bookseller are all married already. I think I have a very sad life.

PUNTILA: There you are. So – stick to Puntila. Here, have a sip.

CHEMIST'S ASSISTANT: But what about the ring? A ring and a sip of wine, that's what's laid down.

PUNTILA: Haven't you got some curtain rings?

CHEMIST'S ASSISTANT: Do you want one or several?

PUNTILA: Lots, not just one, my girl. Puntila has to have lots of everything. One girl on her own would hardly make any

impression on him. You get me?
While the chemist's assistant is fetching a curtain rod, Sly-Grog Emma again comes out of her house.
SLY-GROG EMMA *sings*:

> Once the plums were stoned and boiling
> He joked condescendingwise
> And thereafter, blandly smiling
> Stuck his thumb in sundry pies.

The chemist's assistant hands Puntila the rings off the curtain rod.
PUNTILA, *sliding a ring on her finger*: Come up to Puntila Hall on Sunday week. There's to be a big engagement party. *He walks on. Lisu the milkmaid arrives with her pail.* Whoa, my little pigeon, you're the girl I want. Where you off to at this hour?
MILKMAID: Milk the cows.
PUNTILA: What, sitting there with nowt but a bucket between your legs? What sort of life is that? Tell me what sort of life you lead, I'm interested in you.
MILKMAID: Here's the sort of life I lead. Half past three I have to get up, muck out the cowshed and brush down the cows. Then there's the milking to do and after that I wash out the pails with soda and strong stuff that burns your hands. Then more mucking out, and after that I have my coffee but it stinks, it's cheap. I eat my slice of bread and butter and have a bit of shut-eye. In the afternoon I do myself some potatoes and put gravy on them, meat's a thing I never see, with luck the housekeeper'll give me an egg now and again or I might pick one up. Then another lot of mucking out, brushing down, milking and washing out churns. Every day I have to milk twenty-five gallons. Evenings I have bread and milk, they allow me three pints a day for free, but anything else I need to cook I have to buy from the farm. I get one Sunday off in five, but sometimes I go dancing at night and if I make

a mistake I'll have a baby. I've got two dresses and I've a bicycle too.

PUNTILA: And I've got a farm and my own flour mill and my own sawmill and no woman. What about it, my little pigeon? Here's the ring and you take a sip from the bottle and it's all according to law. Come up to Puntila Hall on Sunday week, is that a deal?

MILKMAID: It's a deal.

Puntila goes on.

PUNTILA: On, on, let's follow the village street. Fascinating how many of them are already up. They're irresistible at this hour when they've just crept out from under the feathers, when their eyes are still bright and sinful and the world's still young. *He arrives at the telephone exchange. Sandra the telephonist is standing there.*

PUNTILA: Good morning, early bird. Aren't you the well-informed lady who gets all the news from the telephone? Good morning, my dear.

TELEPHONIST: Good morning, Mr Puntila. What are you doing up so early?

PUNTILA: I'm looking for a bride.

TELEPHONIST: Isn't it you I was up half the night ringing around for?

PUNTILA: Yes, there's nothing you don't know. And up half the night all by yourself! I'd like to know what sort of life you lead.

TELEPHONIST: I can tell you that. Here's the sort of life I lead. My pay is fifty marks, but then I haven't been able to leave the switchboard for thirty years. At the back of my house I've got a little potato patch and that's where I get my potatoes from; then I have to pay for fish, and coffee keeps getting dearer. There's nothing goes on in the village or outside it that I don't know; you'd be amazed how much I do. That's why I never got married. I'm secretary of the working men's club, my father was a cobbler. Putting through phone calls, cooking potatoes and knowing everything, that's my life.

PUNTILA: Then it's high time you had a new one. And the quicker the better. Send a wire to the area manager right away to say you're marrying Puntila from Lammi. Here's a ring for you and here's the drink, it's all legal, and you're to come up to Puntila Hall on Sunday week.

TELEPHONIST, *laughing*: I'll be there. I know you're celebrating your daughter's engagement.

PUNTILA, *to Sly-Grog Emma*: And you'll have heard by now, Missis, how I'm getting engaged all round, and I hope you'll be there too.

SLY-GROG EMMA *and the* CHEMIST'S ASSISTANT *sing*:

> Ere the plums were on the table
> Up he jumped and off he ran.
> Ever since we've been unable
> To forget that fair young man.

PUNTILA: And now I shall drive on round the duckpond and through the fir trees and reach the Hiring Fair in good time. Kittikittikittiticktickick! O all you girls of the Tavast country, you who've been getting up so early year after year for nothing, till along comes Puntila and makes it all worth while! Come all of you, come all you dawn stove-lighters and smoke-makers, come barefoot, the fresh grass knows your footsteps and Puntila can hear them!

4

The Hiring Fair

Hiring Fair on the village square at Lammi. Puntila and Matti are looking for farmhands. Fairground music and noise of voices.

PUNTILA: I didn't like the way you let me drive off last night
on my own. But as for not sitting up for me, then making
me have to drag you out of bed to come here, I call that the
bloody limit. It's no better than the disciples on the Mount
of Olives, shut up, you've shown me you need watching.
You took advantage of my having had a drop too much and
thought you could do as you liked.

MATTI: Yes, Mr Puntila.

PUNTILA: I'm not prepared to argue with you, you've hurt me
too badly, what I'm telling you's for your own good: be
unassuming, that's the way to get on. Start with
covetousness and you end in gaol. A servant whose eyes pop
out of his head with covetousness at the sight of the gentry
eating, for instance, that's something no employer is going
to stand for. An unassuming fellow can keep his job, no
trouble at all. One knows he's working his arse off, so one
winks an eye. But if he's always wanting time off and steaks
the size of shithouse seats, then it turns your stomach and
you have to get rid of him. I suppose you'd sooner it was the
other way round.

MATTI: Yes, Mr Puntila. It said in the 'Helsinki Sanomat'
Sunday supplement that being unassuming is a mark of
education. Anyone who keeps quiet and controls his
passions can go a long way. That fellow Kotilainen who
owns the three paper mills outside Viborg is said to be a very
unassuming man. Shall we start choosing before all the best
ones get snapped up?

PUNTILA: They have to be strong for me. *Looking at a big
man.* He's not bad, got the right kind of build. Don't care
for his feet, though. Sooner stay sitting on your backside,
wouldn't you? *Addressing the shorter man:* How are you at
cutting peat?

A FAT MAN: Look, I'm discussing terms with this man.

PUNTILA: So am I. I'd be glad if you didn't interfere.

THE FAT MAN: Who's interfering?

PUNTILA: Don't put impertinent questions to me, I won't

have it. *To a labourer*: At Puntila Hall I pay half a mark per metre. You can report on Monday. What's your name?

THE FAT MAN: It's an outrage. Here am I, working out how to house this man and his family, and you stick your oar in. Some people should be barred from the fair.

PUNTILA: So you've got a family, have you? I can use them all, the woman can work in the fields, is she strong? How many children are there? What ages?

THE LABOURER: Three of them. Eight, eleven and twelve. The eldest's a girl.

PUNTILA: She'll do for the kitchen. You're made to order for me. *To Matti, so that the fat man can hear*: What do you say to some people's manners nowadays?

MATTI: I'm speechless.

THE LABOURER: What about lodging?

PUNTILA: You'll lodge like princes, I'll check your references in the café, get lined up against the wall there. *To Matti*: I'd take that fellow over there if I went by his build, but his trousers are too posh for me, he's not going to strain himself. Clothes are the thing to look out for: too good means he thinks he's too good to work, too torn means he's got a bad character. I only need one look to see what he's made of, his age doesn't matter, if he's old he'll carry as much or more because he's afraid of being turned off, what I go by is the man himself. I don't exactly want cripples, but intelligence is no use to me, that lot spend all day totting up their hours of work. I don't like that, I'd sooner be on friendly terms with my men. Must look out for a milkmaid too, don't let me forget. You find me one or two more hands to choose from, I got a phone call to make. *Exit to the café.*

MATTI, *addressing a red-headed labourer*: We're looking for a labourer up at Puntila Hall, for cutting peat. I'm just the driver, though, 'tain't up to me, the old man's gone to phone.

THE RED-HEADED MAN: What's it like up at Puntila Hall?

MATTI: So-so. Five pints of milk. Milk's good. You get

potatoes too, I'm told. Room's on the small side.

THE RED-HEADED MAN: How far's school? I've got a little girl.

MATTI: Hour and a quarter.

THE RED-HEADED MAN: That's nothing in fine weather.

MATTI: In summer, you mean.

THE RED-HEADED MAN, *after a pause*: I'd like the job. I've not found anything much, and fair's nearly over.

MATTI: I'll have a word with him. I'll tell him you're unassuming, he's hot on that. That's him now.

PUNTILA, *emerging from the café in a good mood*: Found anything? I got a piglet to take home, cost about twelve marks, mind I don't forget.

MATTI: This one might do. I remembered what you taught me and asked the right questions. He'll darn his trousers, only he hasn't been able to get thread.

PUNTILA: He's good, full of fire. Come to the café, we'll talk it over.

MATTI: It mustn't go wrong, Mr Puntila sir, because the fair will be closing any minute, and he won't find anything else.

PUNTILA: Why should anything go wrong between friends? I rely on your judgement, Matti, that's all right. I know you, think a lot of you. *Indicating a weedy-looking man*: That fellow wouldn't be bad either. I like the look in his eye. I need men for cutting peat, but there's plenty to do in the fields too. Come and talk it over.

MATTI: Mr Puntila, I don't want to speak out of turn, but that man's no use to you, he'll never be able to stand it.

THE WEEDY MAN: Here, I like that. What tells you I'll never be able to stand it?

MATTI: An eleven-hour day in summer. It's just that I don't want to see you let down, Mr Puntila. You'll only have to throw him out when he cracks up or when you see him tomorrow.

PUNTILA: Let's go to the café.

The first labourer, the red-headed one and the weedy man

follow him and Matti to the café, where they all sit down on the bench outside.

PUNTILA: Hey! Coffee! Before we start, there's something I've got to clear up with my friend here. Matti, you must have noticed just now that I was on the verge of one of those attacks of mine I told you about, and I wouldn't have been a bit surprised if you'd clouted me one for speaking to you as I did. Can you forgive me, Matt? I couldn't think of getting down to business if I felt we were on bad terms.

MATTI: That's all under the bridge. Just let it be. These people want their contracts, if you could settle that first.

PUNTILA, *writing something on a slip of paper for the first labourer*: I see, Matti, you're rejecting me. You want to get your own back by being cold and businesslike. *To the labourer*: I've written down what we agreed, including your woman. You'll get milk and flour, and beans in winter.

MATTI: Now give him his earnest-money, or the deal's not valid.

PUNTILA: Don't you rush me. Let me drink my coffee in peace. *To the waitress*: Same again, or why not bring us a big pot and let us serve ourselves? What d'you think of that for a fine strapping girl? I can't stand these hiring fairs. If I want to buy a horse or a cow I'll go to a fair without thinking twice about it. But you're human beings, and it's not right for human beings to be bargained over in a market. Am I right?

THE WEEDY MAN: Absolutely.

MATTI: Excuse me, Mr Puntila, but you're not right. They want work and you've got work, and that's something that has to be bargained over, and whether it's done at a fair or in church it's still buying and selling. And I wish you'd get on with it.

PUNTILA: You're annoyed with me today. That's why you won't admit I'm right when I obviously am. Would you inspect me to see if my feet are crooked, the way you inspect a horse's teeth?

MATTI, *laughs*: No, I'd take you on trust. *Referring to the red-*

headed man: He's got a missus, but his little girl's still at school.

PUNTILA: Is she nice? There's the fat man again. It's fellows like him behaving that way that makes bad blood among the workers, acting the boss and all. I bet he's in the National Guard and has his men out on Sundays training to beat the Russians. What do you people say?

THE RED-HEADED MAN: My wife could do washing. She gets through more in five hours than most women in ten.

PUNTILA: Matt, I can see it isn't all forgiven and forgotten between us. Tell them your story about the ghosts, that'll give them something to laugh about.

MATTI: Later. Do get on and pay them their earnest-money. It's getting late, I tell you. You're holding everyone up.

PUNTILA, *drinking*: I'm not going to. I won't be jockeyed into being so inhuman. I want to get on terms with my men first, before we all commit ourselves. I must start by telling them what kind of fellow I am so they can see if they're going to get on with me or not. That's the question: what kind of fellow am I?

MATTI: Mr Puntila, none of them's interested in that; they're interested in their contract. I'm recommending that one [*pointing to the red-headed man*] he may do all right for you, at any rate you can find out. And *you*'d do better to look for a different job, I'd say. You'll never earn your keep on the land.

PUNTILA: Isn't that Surkkala over there? What's Surkkala doing at a hiring fair?

MATTI: He's looking for a job. Don't you remember you promised the parson you'd get rid of him because they say he's a Red?

PUNTILA: What, Surkkala? The one intelligent worker on the whole estate? Give him ten marks at once, tell him to come along and we'll take him back in the Studebaker, we can strap his bicycle on the luggage carrier and no nonsense about going anywhere else. Four children he's got too, what must he think of me? Parson be buggered, I'll forbid him the house for his inhumanity. Surkkala's a first-class worker.

MATTI: There's no hurry, he won't find jobs easy to get with his reputation. I'd just like to settle this lot first. I don't believe you're serious about it, you're simply having a lark.

PUNTILA, *with a pained smile*: So that's what you think of me, Matti. You don't understand me, do you, though I've given you every chance to.

THE RED-HEADED MAN: Do you mind writing out my contract now. Or I'll have to look for something else.

PUNTILA: You're frightening them away, Matt. Your high-handed behaviour forces me to deny my real self. But that's not me, let me show you. I don't go buying people up, I give them a home on the Puntila estate. Don't I?

THE RED-HEADED MAN: Then I'm off. I need a job. *He goes.*

PUNTILA: Stop! He's gone. I could have used him. His trousers wouldn't matter. I look deeper than that. I don't like fixing a deal after drinking just one glass, how can you do business when you'd rather be singing because life's so beautiful? When I start thinking about that drive home – I find the Hall looks its best in the evenings, on account of the birch trees – we must have another drink. Here, buy yourselves a round, have a good time with Puntila, I like to see it and I don't count the cost when it's with people I like. *He quickly gives a mark to each of them. To the weedy man*: Don't be put off by him, he's got something against me, you'll be able to stand it all right. I'll put you in the mill, in a cushy job.

MATTI: Why not make him out a contract?

PUNTILA: What for, now we know each other? I give you people my word it'll be all right. You understand what that means, the word of a Tavastland farmer? Mount Hatelma can crumble, it's not very likely but it can, Tavasthus Castle can collapse, why not, but the word of a Tavastland farmer stands for ever, everyone knows that. You can come along.

THE WEEDY MAN: Thank you very much, Mr Puntila, I'll

certainly come.

MATTI: You'd do better to get the hell out of here. I'm not blaming you, Mr Puntila, I'm only worried for the men's sake.

PUNTILA, *warmly*: That's what I wanted to hear, Matti. I knew you weren't the sort to bear a grudge. And I admire your integrity, and how you always have my best interests at heart. But it is Puntila's privilege to have his own worst interests at heart, that's something you haven't yet learnt. All the same, Matt, you mustn't stop saying what you think. Promise me you won't. *To the others*: At Tammerfors he lost his job with a company director because when the man drove he so crashed the gears that Matt told him he ought to have been a public hangman.

MATTI: That was a stupid thing to do.

PUNTILA, *seriously*: It's those stupid things that make me respect you.

MATTI, *getting up*: Then let's go. And what about Surkkala?

PUNTILA: Matti, Matti, O thou of little faith! Didn't I tell you we'd take him back with us because he's a first-rate worker and a man who thinks for himself? And that reminds me, the fat man just now who wanted to get my men away from me. I've one or two things to say to him, he's a typical capitalist.

5

Scandal at Puntila Hall

Yard at Puntila Hall, with a bath hut into which we can see. Morning. Above the main entrance to the house Laina the cook and Fina the parlourmaid are nailing a sign saying 'Welcome to the engagement party'. Through the gateway come Puntila and Matti with a number of woodcutters including Red Surkkala.

LAINA: Welcome back to Puntila Hall. Miss Eva's here with the Attaché and his honour the Judge, and they're all having breakfast.

PUNTILA: First thing I want to do is apologise to you and your family, Surkkala. May I ask you to go and get your children, all four of them, so I can express my personal regret for the fear and insecurity they must have been through?

SURKKALA: No call for that, Mr Puntila.

PUNTILA, *seriously*: Oh yes there is.

Surkkala goes.

PUNTILA: These gentlemen are staying. Get them all an aquavit, Laina. I'm taking them on to work in the forest.

LAINA: I thought you were selling the forest.

PUNTILA: Me? I'm not selling any forest. My daughter's got her dowry between her legs, right?

MATTI: So maybe we could settle their contracts, Mr Puntila, and then you'll have it off your chest.

PUNTILA: I'm going into the sauna, Fina; bring aquavits for the gentlemen and a coffee for me.

He goes into the sauna.

THE WEEDY MAN: Think he'll take me on?

MATTI: Not when he's sober and has a look at you.

THE WEEDY MAN: But when he's drunk he won't settle any contracts.

MATTI: I told you people it was a mistake coming up here till you had your contracts in your hands.

Fina brings out aquavit, and each of the labourers takes a glass.

THE LABOURER: What's he like otherwise?

MATTI: Too familiar. It won't matter to you, you'll be in the forest, but I'm with him in the car, I can't get away from him and before I know where I am he's turning all human on me. I'll have to give notice.

Surkkala comes back with his four children. The eldest girl is holding the baby.

MATTI, *quietly*: For God's sake clear off right away. Once he's

had his bath and knocked back his coffee he'll be stone cold
sober and better look out if he catches you around the yard.
Take my advice, you'll keep out of his sight the next day or
two.

Surkkala nods and is about to hasten away with the children.

PUNTILA, *who has undressed and listened but failed to hear the
end of this, peers out of the bath hut and observes Surkkala
and the children*: I'll be with you in a moment. Matti, come
inside, I need you to pour the water over me. *To the weedy
man*: You can come in too, I want to get to know you better.
*Matti and the weedy man follow Puntila into the bath hut.
Matti sloshes water over Puntila. Surkkala quickly goes off
with the children.*

PUNTILA: One bucket's enough. I loathe water.

MATTI: You'll have to bear with a few buckets more, then you
can have a coffee and be the perfect host.

PUNTILA: I can be the perfect host as I am. You're just wanting
to bully me.

THE WEEDY MAN: I say that's enough too. Mr Puntila can't
stand water, it's obvious.

PUNTILA: There you are, Matti, there speaks somebody who
feels for me. I'd like you to tell him how I saw off the fat man
at the hiring fair.

Enter Fina.

PUNTILA: Here's that golden creature with my coffee. Is it
strong? I'd like a liqueur with it.

MATTI: Then what's the point of the coffee? No liqueur for
you.

PUNTILA: I know, you're cross with me for keeping these
people waiting, and quite right too. But tell them about the
fat man. Fina must hear this. *Starts telling*: One of those
nasty fat individuals with a blotchy face, a proper capitalist,
who was trying to sneak a worker away from me. I grabbed
hold of him, but when we reached my car he'd got his gig
parked alongside it. You go on, Matt, I must drink my
coffee.

MATTI: He was livid when he saw Mr Puntila, and took his whip and lashed his pony till it reared.

PUNTILA: I can't abide cruelty to animals.

MATTI: Mr Puntila took the pony by the reins and calmed it down and told the fat man what he thought of him, and I thought he was going to get a crack with the whip, only the fat man didn't dare since we outnumbered him. So he muttered something about uneducated people, thinking we wouldn't hear it perhaps, but Mr Puntila's got a sharp ear when he dislikes someone and answered back at once: had he been educated well enough to know that being too fat can give you a stroke?

PUNTILA: Tell him how he went red as a turkeycock and got so angry he couldn't make a witty comeback in front of them all.

MATTI: He went as red as a turkeycock and Mr Puntila told him he shouldn't get excited, it was bad for him on account of his unhealthy corpulence. He ought never to go red in the face, it was a sign the blood was going to his brain, and for the sake of his loved ones he should avoid that.

PUNTILA: You're forgetting I addressed most of my remarks to you, saying we shouldn't be exciting him and ought to treat him gently. That got under his skin, did you notice?

MATTI: We spoke about him as if he wasn't there, everybody laughed more and more and he kept getting redder and redder. That was when he really started looking like a turkeycock, before that he was more a sort of faded brick. He asked for it; what did he have to lash his horse for? I remember a fellow once got so cross when a ticket fell out of his hatband where he'd stuck it for safekeeping that he trampled his hat flat underfoot in a chock-full third class compartment.

PUNTILA: You're losing the thread. I went on and told him that any violent physical exercise like lashing ponies with a whip could easily kill him. That in itself was good enough reason why he shouldn't maltreat his beast, not in his condition.

FINA: Nobody should.

PUNTILA: That earns you a liqueur, Fina. Go and help yourself.

MATTI: She's holding the coffee tray. I hope you're starting to feel better now, Mr Puntila?

PUNTILA: I feel worse.

MATTI: I thought it was really fine of Mr Puntila to tell that fellow where he got off. Because he could easily have said 'What business is it of mine? I'm not making enemies among the neighbours.'

PUNTILA, *who is gradually sobering up*: I'm not afraid of enemies.

MATTI: That's true. But there aren't many people who can say that. You can. And you can always send your mares somewhere else.

PUNTILA: Why should we send the mares somewhere else?

MATTI: They were saying afterwards that that fat bloke is the one who has bought Summala, which has the only stallion within five hundred miles who's any good for our mares.

FINA: Gosh, it was the new owner of Summala. And you only found that out afterwards?

Puntila gets up and goes behind to pour a further bucket of water over his head.

MATTI: Not afterwards, actually. Mr Puntila already knew. He yelled after the fat man that his stallion was too beaten up for our mares. How did you put it?

PUNTILA, *curtly*: Somehow.

MATTI: Not somehow. It was witty.

FINA: But what a job it will be if we have to send the mares all that distance to be served.

PUNTILA, *brooding*: More coffee. *He is given it.*

MATTI: Kindness to animals is supposed to be a great thing with the Tavast people. That's what so surprised me about the fat man. Another thing I heard later was that he was Mrs Klinckmann's brother-in-law. I bet if Mr Puntila had known that he'd have given him an even worse going-over.

Puntila gives him a look.

FINA: Coffeee strong enough, was it?

PUNTILA: Don't ask stupid questions. You can see I've drunk it, can't you? *To Matti:* You, don't just sit on your bottom, stop loafing, clean some boots, wash the car. Don't contradict, and if I catch you spreading malicious rumours I'll put it down in your reference, so watch out.

Exit in his bathrobe, brooding.

FINA: What did you want to let him make that scene with the fat owner of Summala for?

MATTI: Am I his guardian angel? Look, if I see him doing a dangerous and kindly action, stupidly because it's against his own interests, am I supposed to stop him? Anyhow I couldn't. When he's pissed as that he's got real fire in him. He'd just despise me, and I don't want him to despise me when he's pissed.

PUNTILA *off, calls:* Fina!

Fina follows with his clothes.

PUNTILA, *to Fina:* Now this is what I've decided, and I want you to listen so what I say doesn't get twisted around later as it usually does. *Indicating one of the labourers:* I'd have taken that one, he isn't out to curry favour, he wants to work, but I've thought it over and I'm taking nobody at all. I'm going to sell the forest in any case, and you can blame it on him there for deliberately leaving me in the dark about something I needed to know, the bastard. And that reminds me. *Calls:* Here, you! *Matti emerges from the bath hut.* Yes, you. Give me your jacket. You're to hand over your jacket, d'you hear? *He is handed Matti's jacket.* Got you, boyo. *Shows him the wallet.* That's what I found in your pocket. Had a feeling about you, spotted you for an old lag first go off. Is that my wallet or isn't it?

MATTI: Yes, Mr Puntila.

PUNTILA: Now you're for it, ten years' gaol, all I have to do is ring the police.

MATTI: Yes, Mr Puntila.

PUNTILA: But that's a favour I'm not doing you. So you can lead the life of Riley in a cell, lying around and eating the taxpayer's bread, what? That'd suit you down to the ground. At harvest time too. So you'd get out of driving the tractor. But I'm putting it all down in your reference, you get me?

MATTI: Yes, Mr Puntila.

Puntila walks angrily towards the house. On the threshold stands Eva, carrying her straw hat. She has been listening.

THE WEEDY MAN: Should I come along then, Mr Puntila?

PUNTILA: You're no use to me whatever, you'll never stand it.

THE WEEDY MAN: But the hiring fair's over now.

PUNTILA: You should have thought of that sooner instead of trying to take advantage of my friendly mood. I remember exactly who takes advantage of it. *He goes brooding into the house.*

THE LABOURER: That's them. Bring you here in their car, and now we have to walk the six miles back on our flat feet. And no job. That's what comes of letting yourself get taken in by their acting friendly.

THE WEEDY MAN: I'll report him.

MATTI: Who to?

Embittered, the labourers leave the yard.

EVA: But why don't you stick up for yourself? We all know he hands his wallet to somebody else to pay for him when he's been drinking.

MATTI: If I stuck up for myself he wouldn't understand. I've noticed that the gentry don't much like it when you stick up for yourself.

EVA: Don't act so innocent and humble. I'm not in the mood for jokes today.

MATTI: Yes, they're hitching you to the Attaché.

EVA: Don't be crude. The Attaché is a very sweet person, only not to get married to.

MATTI: That's normal enough. No girl's going to be able to marry all the sweet people or all the Attachés, she has to settle for a particular one.

EVA: My father's leaving it entirely up to me, you heard him say so, that's why he said I could marry you if I liked. Only he has promised my hand to the Attaché and doesn't want anyone to say he doesn't keep his word. That's the only reason why I'm taking so long to make up my mind and might accept him after all.

MATTI: Got yourself in a nice jam, you have.

EVA: I am not in any jam, as you so vulgarly put it. In fact I can't think why I'm discussing such intimate matters with you.

MATTI: It's a very human habit, discussing. It's one great advantage we have over the animals. If cows could discuss, for instance, there'd soon be no more slaughterhouses.

EVA: What has that to do with my saying I don't think I shall be happy with the Attaché? And that he must be the one to back out, only how's one to suggest it to him?

MATTI: That's not the sort of thing you can do with a pinprick, it needs a sledgehammer.

EVA: What d'you mean?

MATTI: I mean that it's a job for me. I'm crude.

EVA: How might you picture helping me in such a delicate situation?

MATTI: Well, suppose I'd felt encouraged by Mr Puntila's kind suggestion that you should take me, like he let slip when plastered. And you felt the lure of my crude strength, just think of Tarzan, and the Attaché caught us and said to himself, she's unworthy of me, messing around with the chauffeur.

EVA: That'd be too much to ask of you.

MATTI: It'd be part of the job, like cleaning the car. It needn't take above a quarter of an hour. All we need do is show him we are on terms of intimacy.

EVA: And how do you propose to show him that?

MATTI: I could call you by your Christian name in his presence.

EVA: For instance?

MATTI: Your blouse has a button undone, Eva.

EVA *feels behind her*: No, it hasn't; oh, I see, you'd started acting. But he wouldn't mind. He's not all that easily offended, he's too much in debt for that.

MATTI: Or I could accidentally pull one of your stockings out of my pocket when I blow my nose, and make sure that he sees.

EVA: That's a bit better, but then he'll only say you pinched it in my absence because you have a secret crush on me. *Pause*. You've not got a bad imagination for that sort of thing, it seems.

MATTI: I do what I can, Miss Eva. I'm trying to picture every conceivable situation and awkward occasion that might involve us both, and hoping to come up with the right answer.

EVA: You can stop that.

MATTI: All right, I'll stop it.

EVA: For instance, what?

MATTI: If his debts are all that enormous then we'll simply have to come out of the bath hut together, nothing less will do the trick, he'll always manage to find some sort of innocent explanation. For instance if I merely kiss you he'd say I was forcing myself on you 'cause your beauty overcame me. And so on.

EVA: I never can tell when you're just laughing at me behind my back. One can't be sure with you.

MATTI: What do you want to be sure for? You're not making an investment, are you? Being unsure is much more human, as your daddy would say. I like women to be unsure.

EVA: Yes, I can imagine that.

MATTI: There you are, your imagination's not so bad either.

EVA: I was only saying how difficult it is to tell what you're really up to.

MATTI: That's something you can't tell with a dentist either, what he'll be up to once you're sitting in his chair.

EVA: Look, when you talk that way I realise the bath hut business wouldn't work, because you'd be sure to take advantage of the situation.

MATTI: At least something's sure now. If you're going to hesitate much longer I shall lose all desire to compromise you, Miss Eva.

EVA: Much better if you do it with no particular desire. Now listen to me. I accept the bath hut idea, I trust you. They'll be through with breakfast any minute, after which they're bound to walk up and down the verandah to discuss the engagement. We'd better go in there right away.

MATTI: You go ahead, I'll just fetch a pack of cards.

EVA: What d'you want cards for?

MATTI: How d'you think we're going to pass the time?

He goes into the house; she slowly walks towards the bath hut. Laina the cook arrives with a basket.

LAINA: Good morning, Miss Eva, I'm off to pick cucumbers. Would you like to come too?

EVA: No, I've a slight headache and I feel like a bath.

She goes in. Laina stands shaking her head. Puntila and the Attaché come out of the house smoking cigars.

THE ATTACHÉ: Puntila, old man, I think I'll drive Eva down to Monte and see if I can borrow Baron Vaurien's Rolls. It would be a good advertisement for Finland and her foreign service. You've no idea how few presentable ladies we have in our diplomatic corps.

PUNTILA *to Laina*: Where's my daughter? She went out.

LAINA: She's in the bath hut, Mr Puntila, she had such a headache and felt she needed a bath. *Exit.*

PUNTILA: She often gets these moods. First time I ever heard of anyone bathing with a headache.

THE ATTACHÉ: What an original idea; but you know, my dear fellow, we don't make nearly enough of the Finnish sauna. That's what I told the permanent secretary when there was some question of our raising a loan. Finnish culture is being put over all wrong. Why is there no sauna in Whitehall?

PUNTILA: What I want to know from you is if your minister's really coming to Puntila Hall for the engagement party.

THE ATTACHÉ: He definitely accepted. He owes me that, because I introduced him to the Lehtinens, the Commercial Bank chappie, he's interested in nickel.

PUNTILA: I want a word with him.

THE ATTACHÉ: He's got a soft spot for me, so they all say at the Ministry. He told me, 'We could post you anywhere, you'll never do anything indiscreet, politics don't interest you.' He thinks I'm a good advertisement for the service.

PUNTILA: You're a bright fellow, Eino. It'll be amazing if you don't do well in your career; but mind you take that seriously about the minister coming. I insist on that, it'll give me an idea what they think of you.

THE ATTACHÉ: Puntila, I'm sure as eggs is eggs. I'm always lucky. In our ministry it's become proverbial. If I lose something it comes back to me, dead sure.

Matti arrives with a towel over his shoulder and goes to the bath hut.

PUNTILA, *to Matti*: What are you hanging around for, my man? I'd be ashamed to loaf about like that. I'd ask myself what I was doing to earn my pay. You'll get no reference from me. You can rot like a putrid oyster nobody will eat.

MATTI: Yes, Mr Puntila, sir.

Puntila turns back to the Attaché. Matti calmly walks into the bath hut. At first Puntila thinks nothing of it, then it suddenly strikes him that Eva must be in there too, and he gazes after Matti in astonishment.

PUNTILA, *to the Attaché*: What kind of terms are you on with Eva?

THE ATTACHÉ: Good terms. She is a little chilly to me, but then that is her nature. It is not unlike our position with regard to Russia. In diplomatic parlance we'd say relations are correct. Come along, I think I'll pick Eva a bunch of white roses, don't you know.

PUNTILA *walks off with him, glancing at the bath hut*: A very sensible thing to do, I'd say.

MATTI, *inside the hut*: They saw me come in. All according to plan.

EVA: I'm amazed my father didn't stop you. The cook told him I was in here.

MATTI: He didn't catch on till too late, he must have a terrible hangover today. And it would have been bad timing, too early, because it's not enough to want to compromise someone, something has got to have happened.

EVA: I don't think they're going to get dirty thoughts at all. In the middle of the morning it means nothing.

MATTI: That's what you think. It's a sign of exceptional passion. Five hundred rummy? *He deals.* I had a boss once in Viborg could eat any time day or night. In the middle of the afternoon, just before tea, he made them roast him a chicken. Eating was a passion with him. He was in the government.

EVA: How can you compare the two things?

MATTI: Why not? Like with love, you get people are dead set on it. You to play. D'you imagine the cows always wait till night-time? It's summer now, you feel in the mood. So in you pop to the bath hut. Phew, it's hot. *Takes off his jacket.* Why don't you take something off? My seeing won't hurt. Half a pfennig a point, I'd suggest.

EVA: I've an idea what you're saying is rather vulgar. Kindly don't treat me as if I were a milkmaid.

MATTI: I've nothing against milkmaids.

EVA: You've no sense of respect.

MATTI: I'm always being told that. Drivers are known to be particularly awkward individuals without any esteem for the upper crust. That's because we hear what the upper crust are saying to one another on the back seat. I've got a hundred and forty, what about you?

EVA: When I was at my convent in Brussels I never heard anything but decent talk.

MATTI: I'm not talking about decent or indecent, I'm talking

about stupid. Your deal, but cut first to be on the safe side.
Puntila and the Attaché return. The latter is carrying a bunch of roses.

THE ATTACHÉ: She's so witty. I said to her 'You know, you'd be perfect if you weren't so rich'; and she said after barely a moment's thought, 'But I rather like being rich.' Hahaha! And d'you know, Puntila old man, that's exactly the answer I had from Mademoiselle Rothschild when Baroness Vaurien introduced us. She's very witty too.

MATTI: You must giggle as if I'm tickling you, or else they'll walk brazenly past. *Eva giggles a bit over her cards.* Try to sound more as if it was fun.

THE ATTACHÉ, *stopping*: Wasn't that Eva?

PUNTILA: Certainly not, it must be somebody else.

MATTI, *loudly, over the cards*: Ee, aren't you ticklish!

THE ATTACHÉ: What's that?

MATTI, *quietly*: Put up a bit of a fight.

PUNTILA: That's my chauffeur in the bath hut. Why don't you take your bouquet into the house?

EVA, *acting, loudly*: No! Don't!

MATTI: Oh yes, I will!

THE ATTACHÉ: You know, Puntila, that did sound awfully like Eva.

PUNTILA: Do you mind not being offensive?

MATTI: Now for some endearments and abandon your vain resistance!

EVA: No! No! No! *Softly*: What do I say now?

MATTI: Tell me I mustn't. Can't you get into the spirit of it? Bags of lust.

EVA: Sweetheart, you mustn't.

PUNTILA *thunders*: Eva!

MATTI: Go on, go on, unbridled passion! *He clears away the cards while they continue to suggest the love scene.* If he comes in we'll have to get down to it, like it or not.

EVA: That's out of the question.

MATTI, *kicking over a bench*: Then out you go, but like a

drowned spaniel!

PUNTILA: Eva!

Matti carefully runs his hand through Eva's hair to disarrange it, while she undoes one of her top blouse buttons. Then she steps out.

EVA: Did you call, Daddy? I was just going to change and have a swim.

PUNTILA: What the devil are you up to, messing about in the bath hut? D'you imagine we're stone deaf?

THE ATTACHÉ: No need to fly off the handle, Puntila. Why shouldn't Eva use the bath hut?

Out comes Matti and stands behind Eva.

EVA, *slightly cowed, without noticing Matti*: What do you imagine you heard, daddy? It was nothing.

PUNTILA: Is that what you call nothing, then? Perhaps you'll turn round and look.

MATTI, *pretending to be embarrassed*: Mr Puntila, Miss Eva and I were just having a game of five hundred rummy. Look at the cards if you don't believe me. You're putting a wrong interpretation on it.

PUNTILA: Shut up, you. You're fired. *To Eva*: What's Eino supposed to think?

THE ATTACHÉ: Y'know, old boy, if they were playing five hundred rummy you must have got it wrong. Princess Bibesco once got so excited over baccarat her pearl necklace broke. I've brought you some white roses, Eva. *He gives her the roses.* Come on, Puntila, what about a game of billiards? *He tugs him away by the sleeve.*

PUNTILA *growls*: I'll be talking to you later, Eva. As for you, trash, if I once hear you so much as say bo to my daughter instead of snatching your filthy cap off your head and standing to attention and feeling embarrassed because you haven't washed behind your ears – shut up, will you? – then you can pack your stinking socks and go. You should look up to your employer's daughter as to a higher being that has graciously condescended to come down amongst us. Leave

me alone, Eino, d'you think I can tolerate this sort of thing?
To Matti: Repeat that: what should you do?

MATTI: Look up to her as to a higher being that has graciously
condescended to come down amongst us, Mr Puntila.

PUNTILA: You open your eyes wide in incredulous
amazement at such a rare sight, you trash.

MATTI: I open my eyes wide in incredulous amazement, Mr
Puntila.

PUNTILA: Blushing like a lobster because well before your
confirmation you were having impure thoughts about
women, at the sight of such a model of innocence, and
wishing the earth would come and swallow you up, get me?

MATTI: I get you.

The Attaché drags Puntila off into the house.

EVA: Washout.

MATTI: His debts are even bigger than we thought.

6

A conversation about crayfish

*Farm kitchen at Puntila Hall. Evening. Intermittent dance
music from outside. Matti is reading the paper.*

FINA, *entering*: Miss Eva'd like a word with you.

MATTI: All right. I'll just finish my coffee.

FINA: No need to impress me by drinking it in such a languid
way. I bet you're getting ideas on account of Miss Eva taking
a bit of notice of you now and then whenever there's no
society for her on the estate and she needs to see someone.

MATTI: Evenings like this I quite enjoy getting ideas. Like
supposing you, Fina, felt like having a look at the river with

me, then I won't have heard Miss Eva wants me and I'll come with you.

FINA: Don't really feel like it.

MATTI, *picking up a paper*: Thinking about the school-teacher?

FINA: There's been nothing between me and the schoolteacher. He was friendly and wanted to educate me by lending me a book.

MATTI: Too bad he gets such rotten pay for his education. I get 300 marks and a schoolteacher gets 200, but then I have to be better at my job. You see, if a schoolteacher's no good then it only means the local people never learn to read the newspapers. In the old days that would have been a retrograde step, but what's the use of reading the papers now, when the censorship leaves nothing in them? I'd go so far as to say that if they did away with schoolteachers altogether then they wouldn't need censorship either, which'd save the state what it pays the censors. But if I have a breakdown on a class 3 road then the gentry are forced to plod through the mud and fall in the ditch 'cause they're all pissed.

Matti beckons to Fina and she sits on his knee. Judge and Lawyer appear with towels over their shoulders, returning from their steam bath.

THE JUDGE: Haven't you anything to drink, some of that marvellous buttermilk you used to have here?

MATTI: Would you like the parlourmaid to bring it?

THE JUDGE: No, just show us where it's kept.

Matti serves them with a ladle. Exit Fina.

THE LAWYER: That's great stuff.

THE JUDGE: I always have that after my shower at Puntila's.

THE LAWYER: These Finnish summer nights!

THE JUDGE: They make a lot of work for me. All those paternity cases are a great tribute to the Finnish summer night. The courthouse brings it home to you what a nice place a birch wood is, as for the river they can't go near it without going weak all over. One woman up before me blamed the hay, said it smelt so strong. Picking berries is a bad mistake and milking the cows brings its penalties. Each bush by the roadside needs to be surrounded with barbed wire. In the baths they separate the sexes, or else the temptation would be too great, then afterwards they go strolling across the meadows together. It's just impossible to stop them in summer. If they're on bicycles they jump off them, if there's a hayloft they climb in it; in the kitchen it happens because of the heat, and in the open because there's a cool wind. Half the time they're making babies 'cause the summer's so short, and the other half 'cause the winter's so long.

THE LAWYER: What I like is the way the old people are allowed to take part too. I'm thinking of the witnesses that come along. They see it. They see the couple disappearing into the coppice, they see the clogs on the barn floor and how hot the girl looks when she gets back from picking bilberries, which is something nobody gets all that hot over 'cause nobody works all that hard at it. And they don't just see, they hear. Milk churns rattle, bedsteads creak. That way they join in with their eyes and ears and get something out of the summer.

THE JUDGE, *since there is a ring on the bell, to Matti*: Perhaps you'd go and see what it is they want? Or we could always tell them that the eight-hour day is being taken seriously out here.

Exit with the lawyer. Matti has sat down to read his paper once more.

EVA *enters with an ultra-long cigarette holder and a seductive walk picked up from the films*: I rang for you. Is there anything more you have to do here?

MATTI: No, I'm not on again till six a.m.

EVA: I wondered if you'd like to row over to the island with me and catch a few crayfish for my engagement party tomorrow.

MATTI: Isn't it about time for bed?

EVA: I'm not a bit tired. I don't seem to sleep very well in the summer, I don't know why. Could you go off to sleep if you went to bed right now?

MATTI: Yes.

EVA: I envy you. Will you get out the nets, then? My father has expressed a desire for crayfish. *She turns on her heel and starts to leave, again showing off the walk picked up from the cinema.*

MATTI, *changing his mind*: I think I'll come after all. I'll row you.

EVA: Aren't you too tired?

MATTI: I've woken up and feel fine now. Only you'd better get changed into something you can go wading in.

EVA: The nets are in the pantry. *Exit.*
Matti puts on his jacket.

EVA, *reappearing in very short shorts*: But you haven't got the nets out.

MATTI: We'll catch them in our hands. It's much nicer. I'll show you how.

EVA: But it's easier with nets.

MATTI: The other day Cook and I and the parlourmaid were over on the island and we did it with our hands and it was very nice, you ask them. I'm pretty nippy. How about you? Lots of folk are all thumbs. Of course the crayfish move quick and it's slippery on the rocks, but it's quite light out, just a few clouds, I had a look.

EVA, *hesitating*: I'd sooner we used the nets. We'll catch more.

MATTI: Have we got to have such a lot?

EVA: Father won't eat anything unless there's lots of it.

MATTI: That's bad. I thought we could catch one or two, then have a bit of a talk. It's a nice night.

EVA: Don't keep saying everything's nice. You'd do better to get out the nets.

MATTI: Why d'you have to be so serious and bloodthirsty about the poor old crayfish? If we fill a couple of bags it ought to do. I know a place where there are lots of them; five minutes' work and we'd have enough to convince anybody.

EVA: What do you mean by that? Are you in the least interested in catching crayfish?

MATTI *after a pause*: Perhaps it is a bit late. I got to be up at six and take the Studebaker down to the station to collect the Attaché. If we're mucking about on the island till three or four there won't be much time left for sleep. Of course I could row you over if you're dead set on it.

Eva turns without a word and goes out. Matti takes off his jacket and sits down with his paper. Enter Laina from the bath.

LAINA: Fina and the milkmaid are asking if you don't feel like coming down to the lake. They're having some fun there.

MATTI: I'm tired. I was over at the hiring fair, then before that I had to take the tractor out on the heath and both the tow-ropes broke.

LAINA: Same here. All this baking's fair killed me. I've no use for engagements. But I had to tear myself away to come to bed, I really did, it's so light still and a shame to waste time sleeping. *Looks out of the window as she leaves.* I might just go back for a bit, the groom's got his harmonica out and I like that. *Exit dead tired but still dogged.*

EVA *enters*: I want you to take me to the station.

MATTI: It'll take me five minutes to bring the car round. I'll wait at the front door.

EVA: Good. I notice you don't ask me what I'm going for.

MATTI: I'd say you were thinking of catching the 11.10 to Helsinki.

EVA: Anyway that doesn't surprise you, I see.

MATTI: What d'you mean, surprise? It changes nothing and leads to very little when chauffeurs are surprised. It's seldom noticed and has no significance.

EVA: I'm going to Brussels for a few weeks to stay with a girlfriend, and I don't want to bother my father about it. You'll have to lend me 200 marks for my ticket. My father will pay it back as soon as I write.

MATTI *unenthusiastic*: I see.

EVA: I hope you aren't anxious about the money. Even if my father doesn't care who I get engaged to he wouldn't particularly want to be indebted to you.

MATTI *cautiously*: Suppose I let you have it, I'm not sure he would feel all that indebted.

EVA *after a pause*: Please forgive me for having asked you.

MATTI: I'd have thought your father would care all right if you go off in the middle of the night just before your engagement party, when the dinner's in the oven, so to speak. He may have said unthinking-like that you could make do with me, but you mustn't hold that against him. Your father's acting all for your best, Miss Eva. He told me as much. When he's pissed – I mean when he's had a glass or two more than he should – then he's not clear what your best is, he just goes by instinct. But once he's sobered up he's a very intelligent man again and buys you an Attaché who's value for money, and you become Ambassadress in Paris or Estonia or somewhere and can do as you please if you feel like something on a fine evening, and if you don't you won't have to.

EVA: So now you're saying I ought to take Mr Silakka?

MATTI: Miss Eva, you're not in a financial position to upset your father.

EVA: I see, you've changed your mind, you're just a weathercock.

MATTI: That's right. Except that it's not fair to talk about weathercocks; it's thoughtless. They're made of iron, solid as can be, only they haven't got the firm base would let them take a proper stand. Me too, I haven't got the base.

He rubs thumb and forefinger together.

EVA: That means I'll have to be careful about taking your advice, if I can't have honest advice because your base is lacking. Your beautiful speech about my father having my best interests at heart boils down to the fact that you don't care to risk the money for my ticket.

MATTI: And my job too, it's not a bad one.

EVA: You're quite a materialist, aren't you, Mr Altonen? Or as they might say in your world, you know which side your bread's buttered. Anyway I've never heard anybody admit so openly how much he minds about his money and his own welfare in general. It's not only the rich who spend their time thinking about money, I see.

MATTI: I'm sorry to have disappointed you. Can't be helped, though, since you asked me straight out. If you'd just given a hint or two and left it hanging in the air, between the lines, so to speak, then we wouldn't have had to mention money at all. It always strikes a discordant note.

EVA *sitting down*: I am not marrying the Attaché.

MATTI: I been thinking, and it puzzles me why you pick on him not to get married to. The whole lot of them seem alike to me, and I've had to handle plenty in my time. They been to posh schools and they don't throw their boots at you, not even when they're drunk, and they're not tight with their money, specially when it isn't theirs, and they appreciate you just the same way they tell one bottle of wine from another, because they been taught.

EVA: I'm not having the Attaché. I think I'll have you.

MATTI: How come?

EVA: My father could give us a sawmill.

MATTI: Give you, you mean.

EVA: Us, if we get married.

MATTI: I once worked on an estate in Karelia where the boss had been a farmhand. The lady of the house used to pack him off fishing whenever parson called. Other times when there was company he would sit in the corner by the stove playing patience by himself; soon as he'd opened the bottles, that is. The kids were quite big by then. They called him by his Christian name: 'Victor, fetch my gumboots, get a move on, will you?' I wouldn't care for that sort of thing, Miss Eva.

EVA: No, you'd want to be the master. I can picture how you'd treat a woman.

MATTI: Been thinking about it?

EVA: Of course not. I suppose you imagine I've got nothing to do all day but think about you. I don't know where you get such ideas from. Anyway I'm sick of hearing you talk about nothing but yourself the whole time, and what you'd care for and what you've heard, and don't think I don't see through all your innocent stories and your impertinences. I just can't stand the sight of you any longer, and I hate egoists, I hate them! *Exit. Matti once more sits down with his paper.*

7

The confederation of Mr Puntila's fiancées

Yard at Puntila Hall. It is Sunday morning. On the verandah Puntila is heard arguing with Eva as he shaves. Church bells are heard in the distance.

PUNTILA: You'll marry the Attaché and that's that. I'm not giving you a penny otherwise. I'm responsible for your future.

EVA: The other day you were saying I shouldn't marry if he's not a man. I should marry the man I love.

PUNTILA: I say a lot of things when I've had a glass too many. And I don't like your quibbling about what I say. And let me catch you with that driver just once more and I'll give you something to remember. There could easily have been strangers around when you came strolling out of that bath hut together. That would have made a fine scandal. *He suddenly looks into the distance and bellows*: What are the horses doing on the clover?

VOICE: Stableman's orders, sir.

PUNTILA: Get them out of there at once! *To Eva*: All I have to do is go away for the afternoon, and the whole estate's in a mess. And why are the horses on the clover, may I ask? Because the stableman's having it off with the gardener's girl. And why has that fourteen-month heifer been mounted so young that her growth is stunted? Because the girl who looks after the fodder is having it off with my trainee. Of course that leaves her no time for seeing that the bull doesn't mount my heifers, she just lets him loose on whatever he wants. Disgusting. And if the gardener's girl – remind me to speak to her – wasn't always lying around with the stableman I wouldn't have a mere couple of hundredweight of tomatoes for sale this year; how can she have a proper feeling for my tomatoes, they've always been a small goldmine, I'm not standing for all this stuff on my estate, it's ruinous I'm telling you, and that applies to you and the chauffeur too, I'm not having the estate ruined, that's where I draw the line.

EVA: I'm not ruining the estate.

PUNTILA: I warn you. I won't stand for scandal. I fix up a six-thousand mark wedding for you and do everything humanly possible to have you marry into the best circles, it's costing me a forest, you realise what a forest is? and then you start cheapening yourself with any Tom, Dick and Harry and even with a driver.

Matti has appeared in the yard below. He listens.

PUNTILA: I didn't give you that posh education in Brussels so you could chuck yourself at the chauffeur but to teach you to keep your distance from the servants, or else they'll get above themselves and be all over you. Ten paces distance and no familiarities, or chaos sets in, that's my inflexible rule. *Exit into the house.*

The four women from Kurgela appear at the gateway into the yard. They consult, take off their headscarves, put on straw wreaths and send a representative forward. Sandra the telephonist enters the yard.

THE TELEPHONIST: Good morning. Can I see Mr Puntila?

MATTI: I don't think he's seeing anyone today. He's not at his best.

THE TELEPHONIST: He'll see his fiancée, I imagine.

MATTI: Are you and him engaged?

THE TELEPHONIST: In my eyes.

PUNTILA'S VOICE: And I won't have you using words like 'love', it's nothing but another way of saying filth and that's something I'm not standing for at Puntila's. The engagement party's all fixed, I've had a pig killed, that can't be undone now, he's not going to trot quietly back to his trough again just to oblige me and go on eating merely because you've changed your mind, and anyway I've made my arrangements and wish to be left in peace on my estate and I'm having your room locked and you can do what you like about it.

Matti has picked up a long-handled broom and started sweeping the yard.

THE TELEPHONIST: I seem to know that gentleman's voice.

MATTI: Not surprising. It's your fiancé's.

THE TELEPHONIST: It is and it isn't. In Kurgela it sounded different.

MATTI: In Kurgela, was it? Was that when he went to get the legal alcohol?

THE TELEPHONIST: Perhaps the reason I don't recognise it is that things were different then and there was a face went with it, friendly-looking; he was sitting in a car and had the rosy dawn on his face.

MATTI: I know that face and I know that rosy dawn. You'd better go home.

Sly-Grog Emma enters the yard. She pretends not to know the telephonist.

SLY-GROG EMMA: Mr Puntila here? I would like to see him right away.

MATTI: I'm afraid he's not here. But here's his fiancée, would she do instead?

THE TELEPHONIST, *acting*: Am I mistaken, or is that Emma Takinainen who purveys sly grog?

SLY-GROG EMMA: What did you say I purvey? Sly grog? Just because I have to have a little alcohol when I massage the policeman's wife's leg? It's my alcohol the stationmaster's wife chooses to make her famous cherry brandy with, that'll show you how legal it is. And what's that about fiancées? Switchboard Sandra from Kurgela claiming to be engaged to my fiancé Mr Puntila, whose residence this is, if I am not mistaken? That's a bit much, you old ragbag!

THE TELEPHONIST, *beaming*: Look what I have here, you primitive distiller. What's that on my middle finger?

SLY-GROG EMMA: A wart. But what's this on mine? It's me's engaged, not you. With alcohol and ring too.

MATTI: Are both you ladies from Kurgela? We seem to have fiancées there like other people have mice.

Into the yard come Lisu the milkmaid and Manda the chemist's assistant.

MILKMAID *and* CHEMIST'S ASSISTANT *simultaneously*: Does Mr Puntila live here?

MATTI: Are you two from Kurgela? If so then he doesn't live here, I should know, I'm his driver. Mr Puntila is a different gentleman with the same name as the one you are no doubt engaged to.

MILKMAID: But I'm Lisu Jakkara, the gentleman really is engaged to me, I can prove it. *Indicating the telephonist*: And she can prove it too, she's engaged to him as well.

SLY-GROG EMMA *and* THE TELEPHONIST *simultaneously*: Yes, we can prove it, we're all of us lawful.

All four laugh a lot.

MATTI: Well, I'm glad you can prove it. To be honest, if there was only one lawful fiancée I wouldn't be all that interested, but I know the voice of the masses when I hear it. I propose a confederation of Mr Puntila's fiancées. And that raises the fascinating question: what are you up to?

THE TELEPHONIST: Shall we tell him? We've had a personal invitation from Mr Puntila to come to the great engagement party.

MATTI: An invitation like that could easily be like the snows of yesteryear. The nobs might well treat you like four wild geese from the marshes who come flying up after the shooting party's gone home.

SLY-GROG EMMA: Oh dear, that doesn't sound like much of a welcome.

MATTI: I'm not saying you're unwelcome. Only that in a sense you're a bit ahead of yourselves. I'll have to wait for the right moment to bring you on, so that you're welcomed and frankly acknowledged for the fiancées you are.

THE CHEMIST'S ASSISTANT: All we had in mind was a bit of a laugh and some slap and tickle at the dance.

MATTI: If we pick a good moment it may be all right. Soon as things get warmed up they'll be game for something imaginative. Then we could wheel on the four fiancées. The parson will be amazed and the judge will be a changed man and a happier one when he sees how amazed the parson is, but order must prevail or Mr Puntila won't know where he is when our confederation of fiancées comes marching into the room with the Tavastland anthem playing and a petticoat for our flag.

All laugh a lot again.

SLY-GROG EMMA: Do you think there'd be a drop of coffee to spare and a bit of a dance after?

MATTI: That is a demand which the confederation might get acknowledged as reasonable in view of the fact that hopes were aroused and expenses incurred, because I take it you came by train.

SLY-GROG EMMA: Second class!

Fina the parlourmaid carries a big pot of butter into the house.

THE MILKMAID: Real butter!

THE CHEMIST'S ASSISTANT: We walked straight up from the station. I don't know your name, but could you get us a glass of milk perhaps?

MATTI: A glass of milk? Not before lunch, it'll spoil your appetite.

THE MILKMAID: You needn't worry about that.

MATTI: It'd help your visit along better if I got your betrothed a glass of something stronger than milk.

THE MILKMAID: His voice did sound a bit dry.

MATTI: Switchboard Sandra, who knows everything and shares out her knowledge, will understand why I don't go and get milk for you but try to think out a way of getting some aquavit to him.

THE MILKMAID: Is it true that there are ninety cows at Puntila's? That's what I heard.

THE TELEPHONIST: Yes, but you didn't hear his voice, Lisu.

MATTI: I think you'd be wise to make do with the smell of food to start with.

The stableman and the cook carry a slaughtered pig into the house.

THE WOMEN *applaud by clapping*: That ought to go round all right! Bake it till it crackles. Don't forget the marjoram!

SLY-GROG EMMA: D'you think I could unhook my skirt at lunch if nobody's looking? It's a bit tight.

THE CHEMIST'S ASSISTANT: Mr Puntila would *like* to look.

THE TELEPHONIST: Not at lunch.

MATTI: You know what kind of lunch it's to be? You'll be sitting cheek by jowl with the judge of the High Court at Viborg. I'll tell him [*he rams the broomhandle into the ground and addresses it*] 'My lord, here are four impecunious ladies all worried that their case may be rejected. They have walked great distances on dusty country roads in order to join their betrothed. For early one morning ten days ago a fine stout gent in a Studebaker entered the village and exchanged rings with them and engaged himself to them and now he seems to be backing out of it. Do your duty, pronounce your judgement, and watch your step. Because if you fail to protect them a day may come when there's no High Court in Viborg any longer.'

THE TELEPHONIST: Bravo!

MATTI: Then the lawyer will drink your health too. What will you tell him, Emma Takinainen?

SLY-GROG EMMA: I shall tell him I'm glad to have this contact and would you be so good as to do my tax return for me and keep the inspectors in line. Use your gift of the gab to reduce my husband's military service, our patch of land is too much for me and the colonel's got a down on him. And see that our storekeeper doesn't cheat me when he puts my sugar and paraffin on the slate.

MATTI: You made good use of that opening. But the tax thing only applies if you don't get Mr Puntila. Whoever gets him can afford to pay tax. Then you'll be drinking with the doctor; what'll you say to him?

THE TELEPHONIST: Doctor, I shall say to him, I've those pains in my back again, but don't look so sad, grit your teeth, I'll be paying your bill soon as I've married Mr Puntila. And take your time over me, we're only on the first course, the water for the coffee's not even on yet, and you're responsible for the people's health.

The labourers roll two beer barrels into the house.

SLY-GROG EMMA: That's beer going in.

MATTI: And then you'll be sitting with the parson too. What'll you say to him?

THE MILKMAID: I shall say from now on I'll have time to go to church Sundays any time I feel in the mood.

MATTI: That's not enough for a lunch-time conversation. So I shall add this: 'Your Reverence, the sight today of Lisu the milkmaid eating off a china plate must give you the greatest pleasure, for in God's sight all are equal, so say the scriptures, so why not in that of Mr Puntila? And as the new lady of the manor she'll be sure that you get a little something, the usual few bottles of wine for your birthday, so you can go on saying fine things from your pulpit about the heavenly pastures, now that she no longer has to go out into the earthly pastures to milk the cows.'

In the course of Matti's big speeches Puntila has come out on to the veranda.

PUNTILA: Let me know when ycu get to the end of your speech. Who are these people?

THE TELEPHONIST, *laughing*: Your fiancées, Mr Puntila, d'you not know them?

PUNTILA: I don't know any of you.

SLY-GROG EMMA: Of course you know us, look at our rings.

THE CHEMIST'S ASSISTANT: Off the curtain-pole at the chemist's in Kurgela.

PUNTILA: What d'you want here? Kick up a stink?

MATTI: Mr Puntila, it mayn't be the ideal moment, in mid-morning so to speak, but we were just discussing how we could contribute to the engagement celebrations at Puntila Hall and we've founded a Confederation of Mr Puntila's fiancées.

PUNTILA: Why not a trade union while you're about it? Things like that shoot up like mushrooms when you're around the place. I know which paper you read.

SLY-GROG EMMA: It's just for a bit of a laugh and maybe a cup of coffee.

PUNTILA: I know those laughs of yours. You've come round to blackmail me into giving you something, you scroungers.

SLY-GROG EMMA: No, no, no.

PUNTILA: I'll give you something to remember me by all right; thought you'd have a high old time because I acted friendly to you, didn't you? You'd best clear out before I have the lot of you thrown off the estate and telephone the police. You're the telephonist at Kurgela, aren't you? I'll ring your supervisor and see if that's the sort of laughs they allow in the public service, and as for the rest of you I'll find out who you are soon enough.

SLY-GROG EMMA: We get it. You know, Mr Puntila, it was more for old times' sake. I think I'll just sit down in your yard so I can say 'I was sitting at Puntila's once, I was invited'. *She sits on the ground.* There, now nobody can say any different, this is me sitting. I needn't say it was on no chair but the bare soil of Tavastland about which the school

books say it's hard work but the work's worth while, though
not of course who does the work or whose while it is worth.
Did I or didn't I smell a calf roasting, and wasn't there some
beer?

She sings:

For the Tavastlander clasps his country to his heart
With its lakes and its trees and the clouds above its hills
From its cool green woods to its humming paper mills.

And now help me, girls, don't leave me sitting in this historic
position.

PUNTILA: Get off my land.

*The four women throw their straw wreaths on the ground
and leave the yard. Matti sweeps the straw into a pile.*

8

Tales from Finland

Country road. Evening. The four women are walking home.

SLY-GROG EMMA: How's one to tell what sort of a mood
they'll be in? When they've been on the booze they're full
of jokes and pinching your you-know-what, and it's all you
can do to stop them getting intimate and straight into the old
hay; then five minutes later something's hit their liver and all
they want is call the police. I think I got a nail in my shoe.

THE TELEPHONIST: The sole's half off.

THE MILKMAID: It wasn't made for five hours' walking on a
country road.

SLY-GROG EMMA: I've worn it out. Should have lasted

another year. A stone's what I need. *They all sit down, and she bangs the nail in her shoe flat.* As I was saying, you never know where you are with that lot, sometimes they're one way, sometimes another till your head spins. The last police sergeant's wife used often to send for me to massage her poor swollen feet in the middle of the night, and every time she was different according to how she was getting on with her husband. He was having it off with the maid. Time she gave me a box of chocolates I knew he'd sent the girl packing, but a moment later apparently he'd started seeing her again, 'cause however hard she tried racking her brains she just couldn't remember I'd given her twelve massages that month, not six. All of a sudden her memory had gone.

THE CHEMIST'S ASSISTANT: Other times it works out all right for them. Like Chicago Charlie who made a fortune over there, then came back to his relatives twenty years later. They were so poor they used to beg potato peelings from my mother, and when he arrived they served him roast veal to sweeten him up. As he scoffed it he told them he'd once lent his granny fifty marks and it was disturbing to find them so badly off they couldn't even settle their debts.

THE TELEPHONIST: They know what they're up to all right. Must be some reason why they get so rich. There was this landowner our way got one of the tenants to drive him across the frozen lake in the winter of 1908. They knew there was a break in the ice, but they didn't know where, so the tenant had to walk in front the whole seven miles or so. The boss got frightened and promised him a horse if they got to the other side. When they'd got half-way he spoke again and said, 'If you find the way all right and I don't fall through I'll see you get a calf.' Then they saw the lights of some village and he said, 'Keep it up and you'll have earned that watch.' Fifty yards from the shore he was talking about a sack of potatoes, and when they got there he gave him one mark and said, 'Took your time, didn't you?' We're too stupid for their jokes and tricks and we fall for them every time. Know why? 'Cause they look just the same as our sort, and that's what fools us. If they looked like bears or rattlesnakes people might be more on their guard.

THE CHEMIST'S ASSISTANT: Never lark with them and never accept anything from them.

SLY-GROG EMMA: Never accept anything from them: I like that, when they've got everything and us nothing. Try not accepting anything from the river when you're thirsty.

THE CHEMIST'S ASSISTANT: I've got a thirst like a horse, girls.

THE MILKMAID: Me too. At Kausala there was a girl went with the son of the farm where she worked as a maid. There was a baby, but when it all came to court in Helsinki he denied everything so as not to pay maintenance. Her mother had hired a barrister, and he produced the letters the fellow wrote from the army. They spelled it all out and could have got him five years for perjury. But when the judge read out the first letter, took his time over it, he did, she stepped up and asked for them back, so she got no maintenance. She was crying buckets, they said, when she came out of court carrying the letters, and her mother was livid and he laughed himself silly. That's love for you.

THE TELEPHONIST: It was a stupid thing to do.

SLY-GROG EMMA: But that kind of thing can be clever, it all depends. There was a fellow up near Viborg wouldn't accept anything from them. He was in the 1918 business with the Reds, and at Tammerfors they put him in a camp for that, such a young chap, he was so hungry he had to eat grass, not a thing would they give him to eat. His mother went to visit him and took some grub along. Fifty miles each way it was. She lived in a cottage and the landlord's wife gave her a fish to take and a pound of butter. She went on foot except when a farmcart came along and gave her a lift. She told the farmer: 'I'm off to visit my son Athi who's been put in camp with the Reds at Tammerfors, and the landlord's wife has given me a fish for him in the goodness of her heart and this pound of butter.' When the farmer heard this he made her get down because her son was a Red, but as she passed the women doing their washing in the river she again said 'I'm off to Tammerfors to visit my son who's in the Reds' camp there, and the landlord's wife in the goodness of her heart has given me a fish to take him and this pound of butter.' And when she got to the camp at Tammerfors she repeated her story to the commandant and he let her in though normally it was forbidden. Outside the camp the grass was still growing, but behind the barbed wire there was no green grass left, not a leaf on any of the trees, they'd eaten the lot. It's God's truth, you know. She hadn't seen Athi for two years, what with the civil war and him being in that camp, and he was thin as a rake. 'Here you are, Athi, and look, here's a fish and the butter the landlord's wife gave me for you.' Athi said hullo Mum to her and asked after her rheumatism and some of the neighbours, but he wasn't going to accept the fish and the butter at any price, he just got angry and said, 'Did you softsoap the landlord's wife for that stuff? If so you can bloody well carry it back. I'm not accepting nothing from that lot.' She was forced to pack her presents up again, even though Athi was starving, and she said goodbye and went back on foot as before except when a cart came along and gave her a lift. This time she told the farmhand, 'My boy Athi's in prison camp and he refused a fish and some butter because I'd softsoaped the landlord's wife for them and he's not accepting nothing from that lot.' She said the same thing to everybody she met, so it made an impression all along the way, and that was fifty miles.

THE MILKMAID: There *are* fellows like that Athi of hers.
SLY-GROG EMMA: Not enough.
They get up and walk on in silence.

9

Puntila betroths his daughter to a human being

*Dining-room with little tables and a vast sideboard. Parson,
Judge and Lawyer are standing smoking and having coffee. In
the corner sits Puntila, drinking in silence. Next door there is
dancing to the sound of a gramophone.*

THE PARSON: True faith is seldom to be found. Instead we
find doubt and indifference, enough to make one despair of
our people. I keep trying to din it into them that not one
single blackberry would grow but for Him, but they treat the
fruits of nature as entirely natural and gobble them down as
if it was all meant. Part of their lack of faith comes from the
fact that they never go to church, so I am left preaching to
empty pews; as though they lacked transport . . . why,
every milkmaid's got a bicycle; but it's also because of their
inborn wickedness. What other explanation is there when I
attend a deathbed as I did last week and speak of all that
awaits a man in the other life, and he comes up with 'Do you
think this drought's going to spoil the potatoes?'? When you
hear something like that you have to ask yourself if the whole
thing isn't just a waste of time.

THE JUDGE: I feel for you. It's no picnic trying to bash a little
culture into these bumpkins.

THE LAWYER: We lawyers don't have all that easy a time
either. What's always kept us in business has been the small
peasants, those rock-hard characters who'd sooner go on the
parish than forgo their rights. People still get something out
of a quarrel, but they're hampered by their meanness. Much
as they enjoy insulting each other and stabbing one another
and pulling down each other's fences, soon as they realise

that lawsuits cost money their ardour quickly cools and they'll abandon the most promising case for purely mercenary reasons.

THE JUDGE: We live in a commercial age. Everything gets flattened out and the good old institutions disappear. It's dreadfully hard not to lose confidence in our people but to keep on trying to introduce it to a bit of culture.

THE LAWYER: It's all very well for Puntila, his fields grow of their own accord, but a lawsuit's a terribly sensitive plant and by the time it's fully mature your hair will have gone grey. How often do you feel it's all over, it can't last any longer, there can be no further pleas, it's doomed to die young; then something happens and there's a miraculous recovery. It's when it's in its infancy that a case demands the most careful treatment, that's when the mortality figures peak. Once it's been nursed up to adolescence it knows its way around and can manage on its own. A case that has lasted more than four or five years has every prospect of reaching a ripe old age. But the in-between time! It's a dog's life.

Enter the Attaché and the Parson's Wife.

PARSON'S WIFE: Mr Puntila, you mustn't neglect your guests; the Minister's dancing with Miss Eva at the moment, but he has been asking for you.

Puntila doesn't answer.

THE ATTACHÉ: His Reverence's wife made a deliciously witty riposte to my Minister just now. He asked if she appreciated jazz. I was positively on tenterhooks to know how she would deal with that one. She thought for a moment, then she answered well anyway you can't dance to a church organ so it's all the same to her what instruments you use. The Minister laughed himself silly at her joke. Eh, Puntila, what d'you say to that?

PUNTILA: Nothing, because I don't criticise my guests. *He beckons to the Judge.* Freddie, do you like that face?

THE JUDGE: Which one d'you mean?

PUNTILA: The Attaché's. Let's have a straight answer.

THE JUDGE: Go easy, Puntila, that punch is pretty strong.

THE ATTACHÉ *humming the tune being played next door and tapping the time with his feet*: Gets into the old legs, eh what?

PUNTILA *again beckons to the Judge, who does his best not to notice*: Fredrik! Tell me the truth: how do you like it? It's costing me a forest.

The other gentlemen join in and hum 'Je cherche après Titine'.

THE ATTACHÉ *unconscious of what is coming*: I could never remember poetry even at school, but rhythm is in my blood.

THE LAWYER *since Puntila is violently beckoning*: It's a bit warm in here; what about shifting to the drawing-room? *Tries to draw the Attaché away.*

THE ATTACHÉ: Only the other day I managed to remember a line, 'Yes, we have no bananas'! So I have hopes of my memory.

PUNTILA: Freddie! Take a good look at it and let's have your verdict. Freddie!

THE JUDGE: You know the one about the Jew who left his coat hanging in the café. The pessimist said 'He's bound to get it back.' Whereas the optimist said 'Not a hope in hell of his getting it back.'

The gentlemen laugh.

THE ATTACHÉ: And did he get it back?

The gentlemen laugh.

THE JUDGE: I don't think you've entirely seen the point.

PUNTILA: Freddie!

THE ATTACHÉ: You'll have to explain it to me. Surely you got the answers the wrong way round. It's the optimist who ought to be saying 'He's bound to get it back.'

THE JUDGE: No, the pessimist. You see, the joke is that the coat is an old one, and it's better for him if he loses it.

THE ATTACHÉ: Oh I see, it's an old coat? You forgot to mention that. Hahaha! It's the most capital joke I ever heard.

PUNTILA *gets up lowering*: The hour has struck. A fellow like this is more than flesh and blood can bear. Fredrik, you have been avoiding my solemn question about having a face like that in the family. But I am old enough to make up my mind for myself. A person without a sense of humour isn't human. *With dignity*: Leave my house – yes, it's you I'm talking to – stop looking round as if you thought it might be somebody else.

THE JUDGE: Puntila, you are going too far.

THE ATTACHÉ: Gentlemen, I would ask you to forget this incident. You cannot imagine how delicate is the position of a member of the diplomatic corps. The slightest weakness, morally speaking, can lead to the refusal of one's *agrément*. In Paris once, up in Montmartre, the mother-in-law of the Rumanian First Secretary began hitting her lover with an umbrella and there was an irrevocable scandal.

PUNTILA: A scavenger in tails. A scavenger that gobbles up forests.

THE ATTACHÉ, *carried away*: You see the point: it's not that she has a lover, which is normal, nor that she beats him, which is understandable, but that she does it with an umbrella, which is vulgar. A question of nuance.

THE LAWYER: Puntila, he's right, you know. His honour is very vulnerable. He's in the diplomatic service.

THE JUDGE: That punch is too strong for you, Johannes.

PUNTILA: Fredrik, you don't realise how serious the situation is.

THE PARSON: Mr Puntila is a little over-emotional, Anna, perhaps you should see what's going on in the drawing-room.

PUNTILA: There's no danger of my losing control of myself, missis. The punch is its usual self and the only thing that's too much for me is this gentleman's face which I find repugnant for reasons which you can surely understand.

THE ATTACHÉ: My sense of humour was most flatteringly alluded to by the Princess Bibesco when she remarked to Lady Oxford that I laughed at jokes or *bons mots* before they're made, meaning that I'm very quick-witted.

PUNTILA: My god, Freddie, his sense of humour!

THE ATTACHÉ: So long as no names are mentioned it can all be mended, it's only when names and insults are mentioned in the same breath that things are beyond mending.

PUNTILA, *with heavy sarcasm*: Freddie, what am I to do? I can't remember his name; now he's telling me I'll never be able to get rid of him. O thank God, it's just occurred to me that I read his name on an IOU I had to buy back and that it's Eino Silakka; now will he go, do you think?

THE ATTACHÉ: Gentlemen, a name has now been mentioned. From now on every word will have to be most meticulously weighed.

PUNTILA: What can you do? *Suddenly shouting*: Get out of here at once and don't you ever let me catch another glimpse of you at Puntila Hall! I'm not hitching my daughter to a scavenger in tails!

THE ATTACHÉ, *turning to face him*: Puntila, you have begun to be insulting. To throw me out of your house is to cross that fine boundary beyond which scandal sets in.

PUNTILA: It's too much. My patience is giving out. I was going to let you know privately that your face gets on my nerves and you'd better go, but you force me to make myself clear and say 'You shit, get out!'

THE ATTACHÉ: Puntila, I take that amiss. Good day, gentlemen. *Exit*.

PUNTILA: Don't loiter like that! Let me see you run, I'll teach you to give me pert answers!
He hurries after him. All but the judge and the parson's wife follow.

THE PARSON'S WIFE: There'll be a scandal.
Enter Eva.

EVA: What wrong? What's all that din out in the yard?

THE PARSON'S WIFE, *hurrying to her*: My poor child, something unpleasant has occurred, you must arm yourself with courage.

EVA: What's occurred?

THE JUDGE, *fetching a glass of sherry*: Drink this, Eva. Your father got outside a whole bowl of punch, then he suddenly took exception to Eino's face and threw him out.

EVA: O dear, this sherry's corked. What did he say to him?

THE PARSON'S WIFE: Don't you feel shaken, Eva?

EVA: Yes, of course.

The parson comes back.

PARSON: Terrible.

THE PARSON'S WIFE: What's terrible? Did something happen?

THE PARSON: A terrible scene in the yard. He threw stones at him.

EVA: Did he hit him?

THE PARSON: I don't know. The lawyer quickly got between them. And to think that the Minister's in the drawing room next door.

EVA: Then I'm pretty sure he'll go, Uncle Fredrik. Thank heaven we got the Minister along. It wouldn't have been half the scandal otherwise.

THE PARSON'S WIFE: Eva!

Enter Puntila and Matti, followed by Laina and Fina.

PUNTILA: I have just had a profound insight into the depravity of this world. In I went with the best of intentions and told them that there'd been a mistake, that I'd all but betrothed my only daughter to a scavenger but now I'm quickly betrothing her to a human being. It has long been my ambition to betroth my daughter to a first-rate human being, Matti Altonen, a conscientious chauffeur and a friend of mine. So you are to drink a toast to the happy couple. What kind of response do you think I got? The Minister, whom I'd taken for an educated man, looked at me like something the cat had brought in and called for his car. And the others naturally followed him like sheep. Sad. I felt like a Christian martyr among the lions and gave them a piece of my mind. He cleared off quickly but I managed to catch him by his car, I'm pleased to say, and told him he's a shit too. I take it I was voicing the general opinion?

MATTI: Mr Puntila, suppose the two of us went into the kitchen and discussed the whole thing over a bowl of punch?

PUNTILA: Why the kitchen? We've done nothing yet to celebrate your engagement, only the other one. A bit of a mistake. Put the tables together, you people, make me a festive board. We're going to celebrate. Fina, you come and sit by me. *He sits down in the middle of the room while the others bring the little tables together to make one long table in front of him. Eva and Matti together fetch chairs.*

EVA: Don't look at me like my father inspecting a smelly breakfast egg. Not so long ago you were looking at me quite differently.

MATTI: That was for show.

EVA: Last night when you wanted to take me catching crayfish on the island it wasn't to catch crayfish.

MATTI: That was night-time, and it wasn't to get married either.

PUNTILA: Parson, you sit next the maid. Mrs Parson next the cook. Fredrik, come and sit at a decent table for once. *They all sit down reluctantly. Silence ensues.*

THE PARSON'S WIFE, *to Laina*: Have you started bottling your this year's mushrooms yet?

LAINA: I don't bottle them, I dry them.

THE PARSON'S WIFE: How do you do that?

LAINA: I cut them in chunks, string them together with a needle and thread and hang them in the sun.

PUNTILA: I want to say something about my daughter's fiancé. Matti, I've had my eye on you and I've got an idea of your character. To say nothing of the fact that there've been no more mechanical breakdowns since you came to Puntila Hall. I respect you as a human being. I've not forgotten that episode this morning. I saw how you looked as I stood on the balcony like Nero and drove away beloved guests in my blindness and confusion; I told you about those attacks of mine. All through tonight's party, as you may have noticed – or must have guessed if you weren't there – I sat quiet and withdrawn, picturing those four women trudging back to Kurgela on foot after not getting a single drop of punch, just harsh words. I wouldn't be surprised if their faith in Puntila were shaken. I ask you, Matti: can you forget that?

MATTI: Mr Puntila, you can treat it as forgotten. But please use all your authority to tell your daughter that she cannot marry a chauffeur.

THE PARSON: Very true.

EVA: Daddy, Matti and I had a little argument while you were outside. He doesn't think you'll give us a sawmill, and won't believe I can stand living with him as a simple chauffeur's wife.

PUNTILA: What d'you say to that, Freddie?

JUDGE: Don't ask me, Johannes, and stop looking at me like the Stag at Bay. Ask Laina.

PUNTILA: Laina, I put it to you, do you think I'm a man who'd economise on his daughter and think a sawmill and a flour mill plus a forest too much for her?

LAINA, *interrupted in the midst of a whispered conversation with the parson's wife about mushrooms, judging from the gestures*: Let me make you some coffee, Mr Puntila.

PUNTILA: Matti, can you fuck decently?

MATTI: I'm told so.

PUNTILA: That's nothing. Can you do it indecently? That's what counts. But I don't expect an answer. I know you never blow your own trumpet, you don't like that. But have you fucked Fina? So I can ask her? No? Extraordinary.

MATTI: Can we change the subject, Mr Puntila?

EVA, *having drunk a bit more, gets to her feet and makes a speech*: Dear Matti, I beseech you make me your wife so I may have a husband like other girls do, and if you like we can go straight off to catch crayfish without nets. I don't consider myself anything special despite what you think, and I can live with you even if we have to go short.

PUNTILA: Bravo!

EVA: But if you don't want to go after crayfish because you feel it's too frivolous then I'll pack a small case and drive off to your mother's with you. My father won't object . . .

PUNTILA: Quite the contrary, only too delighted.

MATTI *likewise stands up and quickly knocks back two glasses*: Miss Eva, I'll join you in any piece of foolishness you like, but take you to my mother's, no thanks, the old woman would have a stroke. Why, there's hardly so much as a sofa at her place. Your Reverence, describe Miss Eva a pauper kitchen with sleeping facilities.

THE PARSON *solemnly*: Extremely poverty-stricken.

EVA: Why describe it? I shall see for myself.

MATTI: Try asking my old lady where the bathroom is.

EVA: I shall use the public sauna.

MATTI: On Mr Puntila's money? You've got your sights on that sawmill-owner, but he isn't materialising, 'cause Mr Puntila is a sensible person or will be when he comes to first thing in the morning.

PUNTILA: Say no more, say no more about that Puntila who is our common enemy; that's the Puntila who was drowned in a bowl of punch this evening, the wicked fellow. Look at me now, I've become human, all of you drink too, become human, never say die!

MATTI: I'm telling you I just can't take you to my mother's, she'd hammer my ears with her slippers if I brought home a wife like that, if you really want to know.

EVA: Matti, you shouldn't have said that.

PUNTILA: The girl's right, you're going too far, Matti. Eva has her faults and she may finish up a bit on the fat side like her mother, but not before she's thirty or thirty-five, at the moment I could show her anywhere.

MATTI: I'm not talking about fat, I'm saying she's hopelessly unpractical and no kind of wife for a chauffeur.

THE PARSON: I entirely agree.

MATTI: Don't laugh, Miss Eva. You'd laugh on the other side

of your face if my mother tested you out. You'd look pretty silly then.

EVA: Matti, let's try. You're the chauffeur and I'm your wife; tell me what I'm supposed to do.

PUNTILA: That's what I like to hear. Get the sandwiches, Fina, we'll have a snug meal while Matti tests Eva till she's black and blue all over.

MATTI: You stay there, Fina, we've no servants; when unexpected guests turn up we've just got what's generally in the larder. Bring on the herring, Eva.

EVA, *cheerfully*: I won't be a moment. *Exit.*

PUNTILA *calls after her*: Don't forget the butter. *To Matti*: I like the way you're determined to stand on your own feet and not accept anything from me. Not everyone would do that.

THE PARSON'S WIFE *to Laina*: But I don't salt my field mushrooms, I cook them in butter with some lemon, the little button ones I mean. I use blewits for bottling too.

LAINA: I don't count blewits as really delicate mushrooms, but they don't taste too bad. The only delicate ones are field mushrooms and cêpes.

EVA, *returning with a dish of herring*: We've no butter in our kitchen, right?

MATTI: Ah, there he is. I recognise him. *He takes the dish.* I met his brother only yesterday and another relative the day before; in fact I've been meeting members of his family ever since I first reached for a plate. How many times a week would you like to eat herring?

EVA: Three times, Matti, if need be.

LAINA: It'll need be more than that, like it or not.

MATTI: You've a lot to learn still. When my mother was cook on a farm she used to serve it five times a week. Laina serves it eight times. *He takes a herring and holds it up by the tail*: Welcome, herring, thou filler of the poor! Thou morning, noon and night fodder, and salty gripe in the guts! Out of the sea didst thou come, and into the earth shalt thou go. By thy power are forests cut down and fields sown, and by thy power go those machines called farmhands which have not as yet achieved perpetual motion. O herring, thou dog, but for thee we might start asking the farmers for pig meat, and what would come of Finland then?

He puts it back, cuts it up and gives everyone a small piece.

PUNTILA: It tastes to me like a delicacy because I eat it so seldom. That sort of inequality shouldn't be allowed. Left to myself I'd put all the income from the estate in a single fund, and if any of my staff wanted money they could help themselves, because if it weren't for them there'd be nothing there. Right?

MATTI: I wouldn't recommend it. You'd be ruined in a week and the bank would take over.

PUNTILA: That's what you say, but I say different. I'm practically a communist, and if I were a farmhand I'd make old Puntila's life hell for him. Go on with your test, I find it interesting.

MATTI: If I start to think what a woman has to be able to do before I can present her to my mother then I think of my socks. *He takes off a shoe and gives his sock to Eva.* For instance, how about darning that?

THE JUDGE: It is a lot to ask. I said nothing about the herring, but even Juliet's love for Romeo would hardly have weathered such an imposition as darning his socks. Any love that is capable of so much self-sacrifice could easily become uncomfortable, for by definition it is too ardent and therefore liable to make work for the courts.

MATTI: Among the lower orders socks are not mended for love but for reasons of economy.

THE PARSON: I doubt if the pious sisters who taught her in Brussels had quite this sort of thing in mind.

Eva has returned with needle and thread and starts sewing.

MATTI: If she missed out on her education she'll have to make up for it now. *To Eva:* I won't hold your upbringing against you so long as you show willing. You were unlucky in your choice of parents and never learned anything that matters. That herring just now showed what vast gaps there are in your knowledge. I deliberately picked socks because I wanted to see what sort of stuff you're made of.

FINA: I could show Miss Eva how.

PUNTILA: Pull yourself together, Eva, you've a good brain, you're not going to get this wrong.

Eva reluctantly gives Matti the sock. He lifts it up and inspects it with a sour smile, for it is hopelessly botched.

FINA: I couldn't have done it any better without a darning egg.

PUNTILA: Why didn't you use one?

MATTI: Ignorance. *To the judge, who is laughing*: It's no laughing matter, the sock's ruined. *To Eva*: If you're dead set on marrying a chauffeur it's a tragedy because you'll have to cut your coat according to your cloth and you can't imagine how little of that there is. But I'll give you one more chance to do better.

EVA: I admit the sock wasn't brilliant.

MATTI: I'm the driver on an estate, and you help out with the washing and keeping the stoves going in winter. I get home in the evening, how do you receive me?

EVA: I'll be better at that, Matti. Come home.

Matti walks away a few paces and pretends to come in through a door.

EVA: Matti! *She runs up to him and kisses him.*

MATTI: Mistake number one. Intimacies and lovey-dovey when I come home tired.

He goes to an imaginary tap and washes. Then he puts out his hand for a towel.

EVA *has started talking away*: Poor Matti, you tired? I've spent all day thinking how hard you work. I wish I could do it for you. *Fina hands her a towel, which she disconsolately passes to Matti.*

EVA: I'm sorry. I didn't realise what you wanted.

Matti gives a disagreeable growl and sits down at the table. Then he thrusts his boot at her. She tries to tug it off.

PUNTILA *has stood up and is following with interest*: Pull!

THE PARSON: I would call that a remarkably sound lesson. You see how unnatural it is.

MATTI: That's something I don't always do, but today you see I was driving the tractor and I'm half dead, and that has to be allowed for. What did you do today?

EVA: Washing, Matti.

MATTI: How many big items did you have to wash?

EVA: Four. Four sheets.

MATTI: You tell her, Fina.

FINA: You'll have done seventeen at least and two tubs of coloureds.

MATTI: Did you get your water from the hose, or did you have to pour it in by the bucket 'cause the hose wasn't working like it doesn't at Puntila's?

PUNTILA: Give me stick, Matti, I'm no good.

EVA: By the bucket.

MATTI: Your nails [*he takes her hand*] have got broken scrubbing the wash or doing the stove. Really you should always put a bit of grease on them, that's the way my mother's hands got [*he demonstrates*] swollen and red. I'd say you're tired, but you'll have to wash my livery, I'm afraid. I have to have it clean for tomorrow.

EVA: Yes, Matti.

MATTI: That way it'll be properly dry first thing and you won't have to get up to iron it till five-thirty.

Matti gropes for something on the table beside him.

EVA, *alarmed*: What's wrong?

MATTI: Paper.

Eva jumps up and pretends to hand Matti a paper. Instead of taking it he goes on sourly groping around on the table.

FINA: On the table.

Eva finally puts it on the table, but she still has not pulled the second boot off, and he bangs it impatiently. She sits down on the floor once again to deal with it. Once she has got it off he stands up, relieved, snorts and combs his hair.

EVA: I've been embroidering my apron, that'll add a touch of colour, don't you think? You can add touches of colour all over the place if only you know how. Do you like it, Matti? *Matti, disturbed in his reading, lowers the paper exhaustedly and gives Eva a pained look. She is startled into silence.*

FINA: No talking while he's reading the paper.

MATTI, *getting up*: You see?

PUNTILA: I'm disappointed in you, Eva.

MATTI, *almost sympathetically*: Failure all along the line. Wanting to eat herring only three times a week, no egg for darning the sock, then the lack of finer feelings when I arrive home late, not shutting up for instance. And when they call me up at night to fetch the old man from the station; how about that?

EVA: Ha, just let me show you. *She pretends to go to a window and shouts very rapidly*: What, in the middle of the night? When my husband's just got home and needs his sleep? I never heard anything like it. If he's drunk let him sleep it off in a ditch. Sooner than let my husband go out I'll pinch his trousers.

PUNTILA: That's good, you must allow her that.

EVA: Drumming folk up when they should be asleep. As if they didn't get buggered about enough by day. Why, my husband gets home and falls into bed half dead. I'm giving notice. That better?

MATTI, *laughing*: Eva, that's first rate. I'll get the sack of course, but do that act in front of my mother and you'll win her heart. *Playfully he slaps Eva on the bottom.*

EVA, *speechless, then furious*: Stop that at once!

MATTI: What's the matter?

EVA: How dare you hit me there?

THE JUDGE *has stood up, touches Eva on the shoulder*: I'm afraid you failed your test after all, Eva.

PUNTILA: What on earth's wrong with you?

MATTI: Are you offended? I shouldn't have slapped you, that it?

EVA, *able to laugh once more*: Daddy, I doubt if it would work.

THE PARSON: That's the way it is.

PUNTILA: What d'you mean, you doubt?

EVA: And I now see my education was all wrong. I think I'll go upstairs.

PUNTILA: I shall assert myself. Sit down at once, Eva.

EVA: Daddy, I'd better go, I'm sorry, but your engagement party's off, good night. *Exit.*

PUNTILA: Eva!

Parson and judge likewise begin to leave. But the parson's wife is still talking to Laina about mushrooms.

THE PARSON'S WIFE, *with enthusiasm*: You've almost converted me, but bottling them is what I'm used to, I know where I am. But I shall peel them beforehand.

LAINA: You don't have to, you just need to clean off the dirt.

THE PARSON: Come along, Anna, it's getting late.

PUNTILA: Eva! Matti, I'm writing her off. I fix her up with a husband, a marvellous human being, and make her so happy she'll get up every morning singing like a lark; and she's too grand for that, and has doubts. I disown her. *Hurries to the door.* I'm cutting you out of my will! Pack up your rags and get out of my house! Don't think I didn't see you were all set to take the Attaché just because I told you to, you spineless dummy! You're no longer any daughter of mine.

THE PARSON: Mr Puntila, you are not in command of yourself.

PUNTILA: Let me alone, go and preach that stuff in your church, there's nobody to listen there anyway.

THE PARSON: Mr Puntila, I wish you good night.

PUNTILA: Yes, off you go, leaving behind you a father bowed down with sorrow. How the hell did I come to have a daughter like that, fancy catching her sodomising with a scavenging diplomat. Any milkmaid could tell her why the Lord God made her a bottom in the sweat of his brow. That she might lie with a man and slaver for him every time she catches sight of one. *To the judge*: And you too, holding your tongue instead of helping to expel her evil spirit. You'd better get out.

THE JUDGE: That's enough, Puntila, just you leave me be. I'm washing my hands in innocence. *Exit smiling.*

PUNTILA: You've been doing just that for the past thirty years, by now you must have washed them away. Fredrik, you used to have peasant's hands before you became a judge and took to washing them in innocence.

THE PARSON, *trying to disengage his wife from her conversation with Laina*: Anna, it's time we went.

THE PARSON'S WIFE: No, I never soak them in cold water and, you know, I don't cook the stalks. How long do you give them?

LAINA: I bring them to the boil once, that's all.

THE PARSON: I'm waiting, Anna.

THE PARSON'S WIFE: Coming. I let them cook ten minutes.

The parson goes out shrugging his shoulders.

PUNTILA, *at the table once more*: They're not human beings. I can't look on them as human.

MATTI: Come to think of it, they are, though. I knew a doctor once would see a peasant beating his horse and say 'He's treating it like a human being'. 'Like an animal' would have given the wrong impression.

PUNTILA: That is a profound truth, I'd like to have had a drink on that. Have another half glass. I really appreciated your way of testing her, Matti.

MATTI: Sorry to have tickled up your daughter's backside, Mr Puntila, it wasn't part of the test, more meant as a kind of encouragement, but it only showed the gulf between us as you'll have seen.

PUNTILA: Matti, there's nothing to be sorry about. I've no daughter now.

MATTI: Don't be so unforgiving. *To Laina and the parson's wife*: Well, anyway I hope you got the mushroom question settled?

THE PARSON'S WIFE: Then you add your salt right at the start?

LAINA: Right at the start. *Exeunt both.*

PUNTILA: Listen, the hands are still down at the dancing.
From the direction of the lake Red Surkkala is heard singing.

> A countess there lived in the northern countree
> And lovely and fair she was.
> 'Oh forester, see how my garter is loose
> It is loose, it is loose.
> Bend down yourself and tie it for me.'

> 'My lady, my lady, don't look at me so.
> I work here because I must eat.
> Your breasts they are white but the axe-edge is cold
> It is cold, it is cold.
> Death is bitter, though loving is sweet.'

> The forester fled that very same night.
> He rode till he came to the sea.
> 'Oh boatman, oh take me away in your boat
> In your boat, in your boat.
> Take me away far over the sea.'

> A lady fox loved a rooster one day.
> 'Oh handsome, I must be your bride!'
> The evening was pleasant, but then came the dawn
> Came the dawn, came the dawn.
> All of his feathers were spread far and wide.

PUNTILA: That's meant for me. Songs like that cut me to the quick. *Meanwhile Matti has put his arm around Fina and gone dancing off with her.*

10

Nocturne

In the yard. Night. Puntila and Matti making water.

PUNTILA: I could never live in a town. Because I like going straight out and pissing in the open, under the stars, it's the only way I get anything out of it. They say it's primitive in the country, but I call it primitive when you do it into one of those porcelain affairs.

MATTI: I know. You want to keep the sporting element.
Pause.

PUNTILA: I hate it when a fellow can't get any fun out of life. That's what I look for in my men, a sense of fun. When I see someone loafing around with a long face I want to get rid of him.

MATTI: I see your point. I can't think why all those people on the estate look so wretched, all skin and bone and chalky white faces and twenty years older than they should be. I bet they're doing it to tease you, else they'd have the decency not to show themselves around the yard when you got visitors.

PUNTILA: As if anyone went hungry at Puntila's.

MATTI: Even if they did. They ought to be used to hunger in Finland by now. They won't learn, they just aren't prepared to try. 1918 polished off 80,000 of them, and that made it peaceful as paradise. Because there were so many less mouths to feed.

PUNTILA: That sort of thing shouldn't be necessary.

11

Puntila Esquire and his man Matti climb Mount Hatelma

Library at Puntila's. Groaning and with his head wrapped in a wet towel, Puntila is examining accounts. Laina the cook stands beside him with a basin and a second towel.

PUNTILA: If I hear of the Attaché having any more of those half-hour phone calls to Helsinki I shall call the engagement off. I don't so much mind it costing me a forest, but petty thieving makes me throw up. And what are all those blots over the figures in the egg book: am I to keep an eye on the hens too?

FINA, *entering*: His Reverence and the secretary of the milk co-operative would like a word with you.

PUNTILA: I don't want to see them. My head's bursting. I think I'm getting pneumonia. Show them in.
Enter the parson and the lawyer. Fina makes a rapid exit.

THE PARSON: Good morning, Mr Puntila, I trust that you had a restful night. I chanced to run into the secretary and we thought we might drop in to see how you were.

THE LAWYER: A night of misunderstandings, so to speak.

PUNTILA: I spoke to Eino on the telephone, if that's what you mean; he has apologised and that's that.

THE LAWYER: Puntila, my dear fellow, there is a further point which you should perhaps consider. In so far as the misunderstandings that occurred at Puntila Hall concern your family life and your relationship with members of the government they are wholly your own affair. Unfortunately that is not all.

PUNTILA: Don't beat about the bush, Pekka. Any damage

that's been done, I'll pay.

THE PARSON: Unhappily there are some kinds of damage which cannot be repaired by money, my dear Mr Puntila. To put it bluntly, we've come to you in the friendliest spirit to discuss the Surkkala problem.

PUNTILA: What about Surkkala?

THE PARSON: We understood you to say the other day that you wanted to dismiss the man because, as you yourself put it, he was an undesirable influence in the community.

PUNTILA: I said I was going to chuck him out.

THE PARSON: Yesterday was quarter-day, Mr Puntila, but Surkkala cannot have been given notice or I should not have seen his eldest daughter in church.

PUNTILA: What, not given notice? Laina! Surkkala wasn't given notice.

LAINA: No.

PUNTILA: Why not?

EVA: You met him at the hiring fair and brought him back in the Studebaker and instead of giving him notice you gave him a ten-mark note.

PUNTILA: How dare he take ten marks from me when I'd told him more than once he'd have to be out by next quarter-day? Fina! *Enter Fina.* Get me Surkkala right away. *Exit Fina.* I've got this terrible headache.

THE LAWYER: Coffee.

PUNTILA: That's it, Pekka, I must have been drunk. I'm always doing that sort of thing when I've had one too many. I could kick myself. That fellow ought to be in prison, taking an unfair advantage.

THE PARSON: Mr Puntila, that will be it, I am sure. We all know your heart is in the right place. It could only have happened when you were under the influence of drink.

PUNTILA: How appalling. *In despair*: What am I to say to the National Militia? My honour is at stake. Once this gets around I'll be blacklisted. They'll stop buying my milk. It's all Matti's fault, my driver, he sat next to him, I can see the whole thing. He knows I can't bear Surkkala, and allowed me to give him ten marks all the same.

THE PARSON: Mr Puntila, there's no need for you to take this affair too tragically. Such things happen, you know.

PUNTILA: Don't tell me they happen. They'd better stop happening, or I'll get myself made a Ward of Court. I can't drink all my milk myself, I'll be ruined. Pekka, don't just sit there, do something, you're the secretary, I'll make a donation to the National Militia. It's the drink, that's all. Laina, it doesn't agree with me.

THE LAWYER: You'll pay him off then. He must go, he's infecting the atmosphere.

THE PARSON: I think we should leave now, Mr Puntila. No damage is beyond repair so long as one's intentions are good. Good intentions are everything, Mr Puntila.

PUNTILA *shakes his hand*: Thank you very much.

THE PARSON: Nothing to thank us for, we're merely doing our duty. Let's do it quickly.

THE LAWYER: And while you're about it it might be a good idea to find out about the past history of that chauffeur of yours, who makes no very good impression on me either. *Exeunt parson and lawyer.*

PUNTILA: Laina, from now on no drop of alcohol shall pass my lips, no, not one. I thought about it this morning when I woke up. It's a curse. I decided to go to the cowshed and make a resolution. I am very fond of my cows. Whatever I resolve in my cowshed stands. *Grandly*: Fetch the bottles out of my stamp cupboard, all of them, and all the alcohol left in the house, I shall destroy it here and now by smashing every single bottle. Never mind how much they cost, Laina, think of the estate.

LAINA: Right, Mr Puntila. But are you absolutely sure?

PUNTILA: That's disgraceful about Surkkala, my not evicting him, it's a frightful lesson to me. Tell Altonen too I want him right away. That fellow's my evil genius.

LAINA: Dear oh dear, they packed everything up once and

now they unpacked it again.

Laina hurries off. Enter Surkkala and his children.

PUNTILA: I said nothing about bringing your brats. You're the one I have to settle with.

SURKKALA: That's what I thought, Mr Puntila, that's why I brought them along, they can listen, it won't do them no harm.

Pause. Enter Matti.

MATTI: Good morning, Mr Puntila, how's the headache?

PUNTILA: Here the bastard comes. What's this I hear about you, up to all kinds of tricks behind my back? Didn't I warn you only yesterday I'd sling you out without a reference?

MATTI: Yes, Mr Puntila.

PUNTILA: Shut up, I'm sick of your insolence and smart answers. My friends have been telling me all about you. How much did Surkkala pay you?

MATTI: I've no idea what you're talking about, Mr Puntila.

PUNTILA: Trying to deny that you and Surkkala are as thick as thieves, are you? You're a Red yourself, managed to stop me getting rid of him just in time, didn't you?

MATTI: Excuse me, Mr Puntila, I was simply carrying out your orders.

PUNTILA: You must have realised those orders were without rhyme or reason.

MATTI: Excuse me, but orders aren't as easily distinguished as you might like. If I stuck to obeying the ones that made sense you'd sack me for idling.

PUNTILA: Don't put words in my mouth, you crook, you know perfectly well I won't stand for elements like that on my farm, agitating till my men refuse to go out on the heathland without an egg for their breakfast, you bolshevik. In my case it's mere alcoholic fuddle stops me giving him notice by the right date so that I have to pay three months' wages to be rid of him; but with you it's planned.

Laina and Fina keep bringing in bottles.

PUNTILA: This time it's serious, Laina. You can see it isn't just a promise but I really am destroying all the alcohol. I never went as far as that on previous occasions, I'm afraid, so I always had alcohol at hand when the weakness came over me. That was the root of all evil. I once read that the first step to temperance was not to buy alcohol. Too few people are aware of that. Once it's there, though, it must at least be destroyed. *To Matti*: As for you, I've a purpose in letting you watch, there's nothing could give you such a fright.

MATTI: That's right, Mr Puntila. Shall I take the bottles out into the yard and smash them for you?

PUNTILA: No, I'll do it myself, you swindler, just the job that'd be for you, eh, destroying this lovely liquor [*he holds up a bottle to inspect it*] by drinking the lot.

LAINA: Don't spend too long looking at that bottle, Mr Puntila, chuck it out of the window.

PUNTILA: Perfectly right. *To Matti, coldly*: You'll never get me to drink liquor again, you filthy fellow. All you care about is to have folk wallowing round you like pigs. True love of your work is something you just don't know, you'd never stir a finger if you didn't have to keep yourself from starving, you parasite. Making up to me, eh? Spending night after night telling me dirty stories, then leading me to insult my guests 'cause all you care about is seeing everything dragged into the mire you came from. You're a case for the police, you told me yourself why you were always getting dismissed, and didn't I catch you agitating among those females from Kurgela, a rabble rouser, that's you. *He starts absent-mindedly pouring from the bottle into a glass which his servant Matti has just thoughtfully brought him.* Your attitude to me is one of hatred, and you hope I'll fall for your 'That's right, Mr Puntila' every time.

LAINA: Mr Puntila!

PUNTILA: Don't bother me, there's nothing for you to worry about. I'm only checking up to see if the shop swindled me and to commemorate my inflexible resolve. *To Matti*: But I saw through you from the start and was only watching for you to give yourself away, that's why I got drunk with you but you didn't notice. *He continues to drink.* You thought you could lure me into a life of excess and make whoopee with me just sitting alongside you and boozing, but that's where you made a mistake, my friends have put the finger on you for me and very grateful to them I am, I drink this glass to their healths. I'm appalled when I look back at that life we led, those three days in the Park Hotel, then the trip to find legalised alcohol and those dames from Kurgela, what a life without rhyme or reason, when I think of that milkmaid at dawn trying to take advantage of the fact that I'd had a couple and she'd got big knockers, Lisu I believe she's called. You were always along of course, you rogue, all the same you must admit those were good times, but I'm not giving you my daughter, you swine, but you aren't a shit, I'll say that for you.

LAINA: Mr Puntila, you're drinking again!

PUNTILA: Me drinking? Is that what you call drinking? A bottle or two? *He reaches for the second bottle.* Destroy it [*he hands her the empty one*] smash it, I never want to see it again, you heard what I said. And don't look at me like Our Lord looking at Peter, I can't abide people who split hairs. *Indicating Matti*: That fellow keeps dragging me down, but you lot want me to rot away here till I'm so bored I start biting my toenails. What sort of a life am I leading here? Nothing but having to nag people and tot up the cattle feed day after day. Get out, you pygmies!

Laina and Fina leave, shaking their heads.

PUNTILA, *gazing after them*: Petty. No imagination. *To Surkkala's children*: Rob, steal, become Reds, but don't grow up to be pygmies, that's Puntila's advice to you. *To Surkkala*: Sorry if I'm meddling in your children's education. *To Matti*: Open that bottle.

MATTI: I hope the punch is all right and not peppery like the other day. Uskala needs careful handling, Mr Puntila.

PUNTILA: I know, and careful is my middle name. I always

make my first sip a very small one, so I can spit it out if
anything's wrong, if it weren't for being so careful I'd drink
the most unspeakable crap. For goodness' sake take a bottle,
Matti, I propose to commemorate the resolutions I've made,
because they are inflexible, which is a calamity all the same.
Here's to you, Surkkala.

MATTI: Does that mean they can stay, Mr Puntila?

PUNTILA: Need we discuss that now, when there's no one else
around? Staying is no use to Surkkala, Puntila Hall is too
small for him, he doesn't like it here and who can blame him?
In his shoes I'd feel exactly the same. I'd look on Puntila as
nothing but a capitalist, and you know what I'd do to him?
Shove him down a salt mine, that's what I'd like to do, show
him what work really is, the old fraud. Am I right, Surkkala?
No need to be polite.

SURKKALA'S ELDEST GIRL: But we want to stay, Mr Puntila.

PUNTILA: No, no, Surkkala's going and wild horses couldn't
stop him. *He goes to his desk, unlocks it, takes money from
the cashbox and hands it to Surkkala.* Less ten. *To the
children*: Always be glad you have a father like that, who'll
go to the limit for his convictions. You're his eldest, Hella,
you must be a support to him. And now it's time to say
farewell.

He offers his hand to Surkkala. Surkkala does not take it.

SURKKALA: Come along, Hella, we'll get packed. Now you
children have heard all there is to hear at Puntila's, let's go.
Exit with his children.

PUNTILA, *painfully moved*: My hand's not good enough for
him. Didn't you see me waiting for him to make a gesture
as we said goodbye, for some kind of word on his side? It
never came. The farm means nothing to him. Rootless.
Doesn't know the meaning of home. That's why I let him
go, like he insisted. A painful episode. *He drinks.* You and
me, Matti, we're not that sort. You are a friend and support
on my arduous path. Just looking at you gives me a thirst.
How much do I pay you?

MATTI: Three hundred a month, Mr Puntila.

PUNTILA: I'm putting you up to three hundred and fifty. Because I'm particularly pleased with you. *Dreamily*: Matti, one of these days I'd like to take you to climb Mount Hatelma, where there's that famous view, so I can show you what a splendid country you live in, you'll kick yourself for not realising it earlier. Shall we climb Mount Hatelma, Matti? It's not all that impossible, I'd say. We could do it in spirit. Given a chair or two we could.

MATTI: I'll do whatever you fancy, any day of the week.

PUNTILA: I wonder if you have the imagination?

Matti is silent.

PUNTILA *bursts out*: Make me a mountain, Matti! Spare no effort, leave no stone unturned, take the biggest rocks or it'll never be Mount Hatelma and we shan't have any view.

MATTI: Everything shall be done as you wish, Mr Puntila. And I realise an eight-hour day's out of the question if you want a mountain in the middle of the valley.

Matti kicks a valuable grandfather clock and a massive gun locker to pieces, using the wreckage together with a number of chairs to build Mount Hatelma in a fury on top of the big billiard table.

PUNTILA: Take that chair there! You won't get a proper Mount Hatelma unless you follow my directions, because I know what's necessary and what isn't and I have the responsibility. You might easily make a mountain that doesn't pay, in other words provides no view for me and gives me no pleasure, because you see all you're interested in is having enough work, it's I who have to give it a useful objective. And now I need a path up the mountain, and one that allows me to drag my sixteen stone up in comfort. Without a path I'd say stuff your mountain, so you see you don't really think. I know how to motivate people, I wonder how you would motivate yourself.

MATTI: There you are, mountain's ready, you can climb up it now. It's a mountain complete with path, not one of those

half-finished ones like God created in such a hurry 'cause he
only had six days so that he had to go on and create a whole
horde of servants for you to tackle things with, Mr Puntila.
PUNTILA *starts to climb up it*: I shall break my neck.
MATTI, *gripping him*: That's something you can do on level
ground if I don't prop you.
PUNTILA: It's why I'm taking you, Matti. Else you'd never see
the lovely country which bore you and without which you'd
be crap, so be grateful to it.
MATTI: I'm grateful to it unto death, but I'm not sure that's
enough, because the 'Helsinki Sanomat' says you have to be
grateful beyond death too.
PUNTILA: First come fields and meadows, then the forest.
With its fir trees that can survive among rocks and live on
nothing, you'd be amazed how little they need to get by.
MATTI: The ideal servants, so to speak.
PUNTILA: We're climbing, Matti; Excelsior! Leaving behind
us buildings and structures put up by human hands we enter
the pure realm of nature, which adopts a more austere
countenance. Shake off all your petty cares and abandon
yourself to the mighty sensation, Matti!
MATTI: I'm doing the best I can, Mr Puntila.
PUNTILA: Oh thou blessed Tavastland! One more pull at the
bottle, that we may see the full extent of thy beauty!
MATTI: Half a mo while I dash back down the mountain and
fetch up the plonk.
He climbs down, then up again.
PUNTILA: I wonder if you can see the whole beauty of this
country. Are you a Tavastlander?
MATTI: Yes.
PUNTILA: Then let me ask you: where else is there a sky like
the sky above the Tavast country? They say there are places
where it is bluer, but the moving clouds are more delicate
here, the Finnish winds are kindlier, and I wouldn't want a
different blue even if I could have it. And when the wild
swans take off with that rushing sound from the marshy

lakes, is that nothing? Don't you listen to what they say about other places, Matti, they're having you on, just stick to Tavastland, that's my advice.

MATTI: Yes, Mr Puntila.

PUNTILA: The lakes, for instance! Never mind the forests, so far as I am concerned, mine are over that way, I'm having the one on the point cut down; just take the lakes, Matti, just take one or two of them, forget the fish they're so full of, just take the way the lakes look in the morning and it's enough to stop you ever wanting to leave or you'd waste away in foreign parts and die of homesickness; and we've got eight thousand of them in Finland.

MATTI: Right, I'll just take the way they look.

PUNTILA: See that little tug with a bow like a bulldog, and the tree trunks in the morning light? The way they swim along in the tepid water, beautifully bundled and stripped, a small fortune. I can smell fresh timber ten miles off, can you? And talking of the smells we have in the Tavast country, that's a chapter on its own, the berries for instance. After it has rained. And the birch trees, when you come out of the sauna and get whipped with a stout bush, and even in bed next morning, how they smell! Where else do you find that? Where on earth is there such a view?

MATTI: Nowhere, Mr Puntila.

PUNTILA: I like it best when it goes all hazy, like those instants in love when you close your eyes and there's a haze round everything. Though I don't think you get that kind of love outside Tavastland either.

MATTI: Where I was born we used to have caves with rocks outside them round as cannon balls polished all over.

PUNTILA: I bet you used to creep inside? Instead of minding the cows? Hey, I can see some. They're swimming across the lake.

MATTI: I see them. Must be at least fifty head.

PUNTILA: At least sixty. There goes the train. If I listen carefully I can hear the milk churns rattling.

MATTI: If you listen really carefully.

PUNTILA: And I haven't shown you Tavasthus yet, the old place, we've got cities too, I can pick out the Park Hotel, they keep a decent wine there, I can recommend it. We'll pass over the castle, they've turned it into a women's prison for politicals, what business have they got meddling in politics anyway, but the steam mills make a nice picture at this range, they brighten up the landscape. And now what do you see to the left?

MATTI: Well, what do I see?

PUNTILA: Eh, fields! You see fields as far as the eye can reach, Puntila's are among them, particularly the heath, the soil's so rich there I can milk the cows three times a day once I've let them into the clover, and the wheat grows up to your chin and twice a year at that. Join in now!

> And the waves on the beautiful Roina
> Are kissing the milky-white sand.

Enter Fina and Laina.

FINA: Lawks!

LAINA: They've smashed up the whole library.

MATTI: We're just standing on top of Mount Hatelma enjoying the panorama.

PUNTILA: Join in! Where's your feeling for your country?

ALL *except Matti*:

> And the waves on the beautiful Roina
> Are kissing the milky-white sand.

PUNTILA: O Tavastland, blessed art thou! With thy sky, thy lakes, thy people and thy forests! *To Matti*: Tell me that your heart swells at the sight of it all.

MATTI: My heart swells at the sight of your forests, Mr Puntila.

12

Matti turns his back on Puntila

The yard at Puntila's. It is early morning. Matti comes out of the house with a suitcase. Laina follows with a packed lunch.

LAINA: Here, take your lunch, Matti. I can't think why you're going. Why not wait anyway till Mr Puntila's up?

MATTI: I'd sooner not risk having him wake. He was that pissed last night he was promising me in the early hours to make over half his forest to me, and in front of witnesses too. When he hears that he'll send for the police.

LAINA: But if you leave without a reference you'll be ruined.

MATTI: What's the good of a reference if he's either going to write that I'm a Red or that I'm a human being? Neither will get me a job.

LAINA: He won't be able to manage without you now he's so used to you.

MATTI: He'll have to soldier on alone. I've had enough. I can't take his familiarities after that business with Surkkala. Thanks for the lunch and goodbye, Laina.

LAINA, *sniffing*: Have a good trip. *Goes in quickly.*

MATTI, *after walking a few paces*:

> The hour for taking leave has struck
> So, Puntila, I wish you luck.
> I've met them worse than you and twice as tough
> You're half-way human when you've drunk enough.
> But matiness dissolves in boozer's gloom
> It's back to normal and the old 'Who whom?'
> And if it's sad to find out in the end

That oil and water cannot ever blend
Let's waste no tears, there's nothing we can do:
It's time your servants turned their backs on you.
They'll find they have a master really cares
Once they're the masters of their own affairs.

He walks rapidly away.

The Puntila Song

1

Old Puntila went on a three-day blind
In a Tavasthus hotel.
He left an enormous tip behind
But the waiter said 'Go to hell!'
Oh, waiter, how can you insult him so
When life's so gay and sweet?
The waiter replied, 'How am I to know?
I've been far too long on my feet.'

2

The landowner's daughter, Eva P.
A novel once did read.
She marked the place where it told her she
Belonged to a higher breed.
She turned to the chauffeur all the same
And gave his clothes a stare:
'Come sport with me, Mr What's-his-name
I'm told there's a man in there.'

3

Old Puntila met an early bird
As he strolled in the morning dew:
'O milkmaid with the milk-white breasts
Where are you going to?
You're going off to milk my cows
Before cockcrow, I see.
But the best thing for you now you've been roused
Is to come back to bed with me.'

4

The bath hut on the Puntila farm
Is the place for a bit of fun
Where a servant may go to take a bath
While the mistress is having one.
Old Puntila said, 'I'm giving my child
To be a diplomatist's wife.
He won't mind her being a bit defiled
If I'll settle his debts for life.'

5

The landowner's daughter wandered in
To the kitchen at half-past nine:
'O chauffeur, I find you so masculine
Come bring your fishing line.'
'Yes, miss,' the chauffeur replies to her,
'I can see you are ripe for bed.
But can't you see that I prefer
To read my paper instead?'

6

The league of Puntila's would-be brides
Arrived for the nuptial feast.
Old Puntila swore he would have their hides
And roared like a wounded beast.
But when did a sheep get a woollen shirt
Since shearing first began?
'I'll sleep with you, yes, but you're only dirt
In the house of a gentleman.'

7

The women from Kurgela jeered, it is said
When they saw how they'd been foiled
But their shoes and stockings were torn to a shred
And their Sunday was totally spoiled.
And any woman who still believes
That a rich man will honour her claim
Will be lucky to lose no more than her shoes
But she's only herself to blame.

8

Old Puntila thumped on the table, piled
With glorious wedding cake:
'How could I ever betroth my child
To this slab of frozen hake?'
He wanted his servant to have her instead
But the servant first wanted to try her
And finally said, 'I'm not having her.
She has none of what I require.'

Notes on the music

The Ballad of the Forester and the Countess *was written to the tune of an old Scottish ballad, the* Plum Song *to a folk tune.*

The Puntila Song *has been composed by Paul Dessau. During scene changes the actress playing Laina the cook comes before the curtain with a guitarist and an accordion player, and sings the verse corresponding to the scene just performed. Meanwhile she does various jobs in preparation for the great engagement party, such as sweeping the floor, dusting, kneading dough, beating egg whites, greasing cake tins, polishing glasses, grinding coffee and drying plates.*

Editorial note

Brecht's song provides no verses for scenes 4, 10, 11 nor (more understandably) 12. In case these scenes are played, the following verses in similar style and metre might serve the same function.

3a

He drove to the fair to hire some men
And quell his raging thirst
But he thought it a terrible insult when
A neighbour approached them first.
Old Puntila gave them his word and his hand

Till his servant said, 'All very fine
But they won't come unless they know where they stand.
You must sign on the dotted line.'

9
The stars in the Finnish summer night
Are a vision not to miss
And Puntila felt they were never so bright
As when he was having a piss.
'I detest black looks,' he said to his mate.
'They stab me like a knife.
'Why can't my men appreciate
'The joys of an outdoor life?'

10
Old Puntila stood on a lofty peak
To view the country round
And said, 'This landscape is unique
The economy too is sound.
We need to exploit our resources, my friend
And a thousand flowers will bloom.'
But his servant replied, 'Won't a lot depend
On who is exploiting whom?'

Notes and Variants

THE GOOD PERSON OF SZECHWAN

Texts by Brecht

1

THE GIRL

> In those distant days of loving-kindness
> Which they say are now forever gone
> I adored the world, and sought for blindness
> Or a heaven, the very purest one.
> Soon enough, at dawn, I got my warning:
> Blindness strikes the inquisitive offender
> Who would see the heaven's pure bright dawning.
> And I saw it. And I saw its splendour.
> How can scrounging crumbs make people happy?
> What's the good if hardships last for ever?
> Must we never pluck the crimson poppy
> Just because its blooms are sure to wither?
>> And so I said: drop it.
>> Breathe in the smoke twisting black
>> Towards the colder heavens. Look up: like it
>> You'll not come back.

2

THE MAN

> My enemy who 'mid the poppies moulders—
> I think of him when lighting up the drug.
> And my bull? I've harnessed his great shoulders
> And I've marched before a crimson flag.
> By midday I'd tired of strife and rancour
> Thought they offered nothing much to go on
> You meantime were being so much franker
> Saying they could be of use to no one.
> Why smite enemies? I have no doubt mine
> Nowadays could smite me without trying.
> Nobody grows fatter than his outline.
> Why, then, put on weight when you are dying?
>> And so I said: drop it
>> Breathe in the smoke twisting black
>> Towards colder heavens. Look up: like it
>> You'll not come back.

3

THE OLD MAN
  Ever since those distant days I've hurried
  Sown my millet, reaped it where it grew
  Lain with women, cried to gods when worried
  Fathered sons who now sow millet too.
  Late enough, at night, I got the lesson:
  Not a cock will crow, they're all ignoring
  My end – nor will the most complete confession
  Rouse a single god where he lies snoring.
  Why keep sowing millet on this gravel
  Soil whose barrenness can't be corrected
  If my tamarisk is doomed to shrivel
  Once I'm dead and it is left neglected?
      And so I said: drop it.
      Breathe in the smoke twisting black
      Towards colder heavens. Look up: like it
      You'll not come back.

> ['Der Gesang aus der Opiumhöhle,' GW *Gedichte*, pp. 90–91
> Brecht's typescript is dated by BBA 'About 1920.' This song,
> unpublished till after Brecht's death, is the origin of the 'Song
> of the Smoke' (pp. 19–20) and would appear to have been the
> first of his known writings on Chinese and Japanese themes.
> The opium motif will be found to recur in the Santa Monica
> version of the play (see pp. 325–30 and 336 ff.).]

FRAGMENT OF A STORY

However as the dearth increased and the cries of all living creatures
asserted themselves the gods grew uneasy. For there were many
complaints that there can be no fear of the gods where shortages are
excessive. And they said 'Were we to alter the world, which cost so
much effort to create, a great disorder would ensue. Therefore if we can
find people who are steadfast in time of dearth and keep our
commandments in spite of poverty then the world shall remain as it is
and there will be no disorder in it.'

Three of the highest thereupon set forth to discover god-fearing
people such as might keep their commandments and display resistance
in time of dearth.

And they came to the city of Szechwan, where they found a water seller who feared the gods, and he went around seeking a shelter for them. And he hunted round the city on their behalf for an entire day and could find no shelter.

And he said 'I thought that it would be simple, for these are among the highest of the gods, and it is only for one night. But there is not a house in Szechwan that will give them shelter.'

And he came back to them and comforted them, and went again and turned to a girl whom he knew by the name of Mi Lung to ask her for shelter.

And they saw that the measuring cup from which he sold water had a false bottom.

[From Werner Hecht (ed.): *Materialien zu Brechts 'Der gute Mensch von Sezuan,'* Frankfurt, Suhrkamp, 1968, p. 95. There described as 'probably written very early on.' The name Mi Lung never recurs.]

PRESS REPORT

A strange story has been reported from Szechwan province. Mr. Lao Go, a manufacturer of tobacco products in the provincial capital, has been standing trial for the murder of his cousin, a certain Miss Li Gung. According to witnesses this Miss Li Gung was known among the common populace of the slum quarters as a 'good person.' She even acquired the romantic sobriquet of 'angel of the slums.' Starting out as a simple woman of the streets, she was put in possession of a little capital by an alleged donation from the gods. She bought a tobacco shop, which however she ran on such altruistic lines that a few days later it was on the brink of ruin. Not only did she feed and maintain a number of persons from her extremely poor and overcrowded neighbourhood, but she also proved incapable of refusing lodging in her little shop to a family of nine with whom she was barely acquainted. Shortly before the débâcle a young man turned up describing himself to her numerous hangers-on as Miss Li Gung's cousin, and intervened so drastically as to put her confused affairs into comparative order. The following incident will provide an example of his methods. The family sent an adolescent boy out to steal bottles of milk from the neighbour's doorsteps. The cousin voiced no objection but called a policeman into the shop and chatted to him until the boy came back with the stolen milk. The visitors were forthwith taken off to the police station and Miss Li Gung was rid of them. The young lady for her part stayed away while her cousin was saving her business for her.

After her own return and her cousin Mr. Lao Go's departure, she resumed her charitable activities but on a very reduced scale. Instead she entered into an intimate relationship with an unemployed airmail pilot named Yü Schan whom she was locally rumoured to have saved from an attempted suicide. Unfortunately her hopes of making him a loan which would help him to secure a post as a mail pilot in Peking were cut short when her shop turned out not to be the little gold mine that people usually imagine such small concerns to be. There was a further threat to her shop in the shape of the methods employed by Mr. Feh Pung, the so-called 'Tobacco King of Szechwan,' a man not unduly inhibited by humanitarian scruples. When one of Mr. Feh Pung's shops opened in her immediate vicinity, selling tobacco fifty per cent cheaper, she once again bowed to outside advice and summoned her cousin to help. He did indeed . . . [A break in the typescript follows, during which there was presumably some mention of the other small tobacconists and their decision to unite.]

. . . On his first visit he had deliberately omitted to tell them of the threats already made to the shop by Feh Pung on the day of its opening; otherwise he would not have been admitted to their mutual aid association. While accepting their tobacco, which was intended to help him to hold out, he now nonetheless negotiated with Feh Pung and induced the tobacco king to make a special bid for the shop to the disadvantage of the other members. However, he was not anxious to effect his cousin's intended purchase of the desired post for her lover Yü Schan, even though the sale of the shop had put him in a position to do so. Apparently this Yü Schan had made it all too plain to him that he was counting on Li Gung's money. Rather than gratify Yü Schan's wishes her conscientious cousin arranged a sensible marriage between Mis Li Gung and the prosperous Mr. Kau, a barber. However, it seems that he had underestimated the extent of Yü Schan's power over his cousin. At any rate the pilot succeeded in gaining her complete confidence and persuading her to make a love marriage with himself. This marriage was much discussed in the neighbourhood, because it never came about. When the small tobacconists heard of Mr. Lao Go's plan to hand over the tobacco king Li Gung's shop, which had been kept afloat only by their joint efforts, they had little difficulty in persuading Li Gung to cancel it. Here her lover's power over her proved quite ineffective. Mr. Lao Go, sent for by the lover to make his cousin 'see reason,' failed to appear; then Li Gung realized how Schan's behaviour had hurt her, and made no secret of the fact that her cousin thought him a bad person and a fortune hunter; at which point the whole marriage blew up. Perhaps if the whole neighbourhood had not been so enchanted by its 'angel of the slums' it would by now have realised the amazing fact underlying the situation: that Mr. Lao Go was none other than Miss Li Gung herself. She was the conscientious 'cousin' whose sometimes equivocal manipulations made possible the good deeds for which people so admired her. However, it was to be a long time before Szechwan understood this. Unhappily the other tobacconists were not able to benefit from Li Gung's self-sacrifice. The short time spent on her efforts at marriage had been enough to make them doubt her loyalty. Undercutting one another's prices, they had handed their shops on a plate to the tobacco king, to the good old refrain of 'devil take the hindmost.' Li Gung meanwhile was forced to admit to her old friend Sun the water seller that she thought she was pregnant. The situation was desperate. Her shop was on the brink of total ruin. For the third (and, as it turned out, last) time her cousin appeared. His task was to rescue the shop on behalf of the expected child, object now of all the girl's love. The means selected by him were wholly unscrupulous. Taking every financial advantage both of the barber's admiration for his 'cousin' and the faith placed by many small people in the 'angel of the slums,' he organised a sweat shop of the worst sort in which her former friends and dependents were to process tobacco at starvation wages. Yü Schan, the child's father, was likewise roped into the rapidly booming business. Before her third disappearance Li Gung had promised his mother to find him a post where he might 'improve himself by honest work.' Under the strict hand of Mr. Lao Go he was made foreman in the new factory. The effect of such employment was to bring him into continual close contact with Mr. Lao Go. In the end this was to be Mr. Lao Go's downfall. Yü Schan had been led by an occasional small personal gift to believe that Mr. Lao Go was keeping his cousin locked up in a room at the back of the shop. He made an attempt at blackmail, which the tobacconist naturally rejected. Thwarted, he ended up by sending for the police, whereupon the back room proved to contain all Li Gung's clothing and personal possessions. The only way for Mr. Lao Go to answer the charge of murder was by making a clean breast of the true facts: that he and Miss Lil Gung were one and the same. Before the astonished eyes of the court, Lao Go changed back into Li Gung: the scourge of the slums and the angel of the slums were identical. Badness was only the reverse face of goodness, good deeds were made possible only by bad – a shattering testimonial to the unhappy condition of this world.

A poetic light is cast on the episode, which Szechwan regards as highly humorous, by the utterances of a water seller who claims that Li Gung's initial capital had indeed been a present from three gods, who told him that they had come to Szechwan to search for a good person, and also appeared more than once in his dreams to ask how the good person was faring. He claims that the three judges before whom the secret was finally unmasked were those same gods.

Whatever the real nature of the gods in question, they will no doubt have been somewhat surprised to find out in what way, in Szechwan, one sets about the problem of being a good person.

> [GW *Schriften zum Theater*, pp. 1157–61. Typescript is dated September 15, 1939, and in effect resumes the state of the story when Brecht abandoned it in order to write *Mother Courage*.]

WORKING PLAN

1. *swamped*

the little boat presented by the gods quickly fills with unfortunates to the point of capsizing / a family is given lodging / the former owners looked after / former suppliers arrive with demands / the landlady wants a guarantee /

2. *crisis and advertisement*

the cousin arrives to disentangle things / the family are handed over to the police / the suppliers paid off / the landlady placated / but as nastiness is neither a substitute for capital nor a shield against the powerful an advertisement must be drafted to get li gung a well-to-do husband.

3. *love*

quarrel about li gung's profession / she is off to an assignation with a well-to-do suitor / meets the unemployed pilot schan who is about to hang himself / comforts him / falls in love with him and buys him a glass of water from sun the water carrier /

4. *the flier has to fly*

sun's hand is broken / li gung tells of her love and buys a shawl / the barber falls desperately in love with her / but she discovers sun's wound and tries to find witnesses / without success / she offers to perjure herself / the carpet dealer and his wife overhear her talking to schan's mother about a job for schan which will cost 400 yen / they offer to guarantee the shop / the flier has to fly /

5. love triumphs

the cousin finds schan the money / sells the already mortgaged business to the landlady / gets to know schan and sees through him / talks things over with the barber / sun is disappointed / li gung should have a chance to do good / schan and the barber address the audience / li gung decides for schan /

6. the wedding

schan wants to get married and sell out / everybody is waiting for the cousin / the carpet dealers hurry in and are calmed by li gung / whenever li gung is present her cousin is not /

7. maternal joys

maternal joys / schan's mother / the guarantee / the garbage pail / the carpenter / li gung's little son will be looked after by her cousin /

8. the tobacco factory

the carpenter's children are hauling bales of tobacco / schan gets a job and distinguishes himself as foreman / song of the tobacco workers /

9. the rumour

rain / the landlady / schan makes a discovery / the monarchs smoke and the mob assembles / the police act /

10. the trial

the gods appear in the role of judges / the tobacco king is scared / the trial / the dénouement / the gods depart on a cloud /

> [From Werner Hecht (ed.): *Materialien zu Brechts 'Der gute Mensch von Sezuan,'* Frankfurt, Suhrkamp, 1968, pp. 22–23. This is a typical big structural plan, probably dating from the summer of 1940 and used for the main work on the play, with the ten scenes set out in ten vertical columns across a wide sheet of paper. Under each Brecht has pencilled further notes and suggestions, of which Hecht provides a photographic reproduction and a transcription.]

UNDATED NOTES

1. Elements of the 'Good Person of Szechwan'

The gods' investigative commission	0, 10
A person's only friend: himself. The double role	4a
The good one takes the matter in hand; the bad one takes the matter in hand	1,2/ 4,5/ 5,6/ 7/ 8
Evil must come that good may come of it	1,2/ 4,5/ 5,6/ 7/ 8
The 'cousin' is always supposed to arrive just for a moment, or just once more, but in the end only he is the only one.	1, 4, 7
The gods don't find a good person, this is the best they can find	9 / 10
Lao Go's realisation of Schan's badness fails to cure Li Gung of her love for him.	5
The way of the little people: either up or down	10
The good person on trial: the gods on trail	10

2. Scenic elements of the 'Good Person of Szechwan'

How hard it is for a believer to give his gods what they want	0
How quickly goodness destroys a life	1
How quickly toughness builds a life up again	2
The good person seeks a helper and finds one that can be helped	3
Unfortunately only the cousin can help the loved one	4
But the cousin reveals the loved one's evil side. This of course is no help to the lover	5
Where Li Gung goes Lao Go cannot go	6
To help Li Gung's little son the cousin must sacrifice many other people's little sons	7
When Li Gung makes a promise Lao Go keeps his word	8
Has Lao Go murdered his cousin Li Gung?	9
The gods cross-examine the murderer of their good person	10

3. The good deeds of Li Gung

(i)	Sheltering a family
(ii)	Rescuing a desperate man
(iii)	Giving false evidence for a victim
(iv)	Confidence in the loved one
(v)	Confidence is not disappointed
(vii)	Underwriting ambition
(viii)	Everything for the child

4. The misdeeds of Lao Go

(ii)	Landing a family in prison
(iv)	Discrediting the victim
(v)	Letting down the underwriters
(vi)	Planning a 'marriage of convenience'
(vii)	Acquiring cheap premises
(viii)	Exploiting children
(ix)	Exploiting the loved one (The Tobacco Queen)

5. It is bad

to kill	8. The children	
to blackmail	7. Schan	
to abuse	5. the old couple	9. Schan
to let down	5. the old couple	5. Sun
to ruin	2. the family	7. the carpenter, the old couple
to lead astray	2. the family	
to exploit	8. all the helpless	
to repress	9. Schan	
to lie to		
to fail to trust	9. Sun	
to despise	5. Schan	
to confuse	5. Sun	
to render unproductive	7. Caprenter	8. Schan
to make worse		
to neglect oneself		5.

[From Jan Knopf (ed.): *Brechts Guter Mensch von Sezuan*. Suhrkamp, Frankfurt, 1982, pp. 102–104.]

LI GUNG'S BIG SPEECH ABOUT THE PUNISHMENT IMPOSED BY
THE GODS FOR FAILING TO EAT MEAT

The battles for food
Caused dreadful crimes. The brother
Drove his sister from the table. Married couples
Grabbed the plates from one another's hands. For one bit of meat
Son betrayed mother. Thus a sect arose
Which believed fasting would bring salvation. They said
None but the abstemious would remain human. He who longed
    to eat
Would inevitably decline into an animal. For a while
The best of them looked on the riches of our universe
As noxious filth. Then the gods stepped in.
Angered by this contempt for their gifts, they proclaimed the
    death penalty
For abstention. You could watch
How the non-eaters collapsed and grew hideous
And he who failed to eat meat died. To escape this terrible
    malady
People who fell on their food all the more greedily
Crime increased.

> [From Werner Hecht (ed.): *Materialien zu Brechts 'Der gute
> Mensch von Sezuan'*. Suhrkamp, Frankfurt, 1968, pp. 93–4.
> Cut passage included with an incomplete working typescript
> of summer 1940.]

FROM BRECHT'S JOURNAL

making minor corrections to *The Good Person* is costing me as many
weeks as writing the scenes did days. not easy, given the definite
objective, to imbue the tiny sub-scenes with that element of
irresponsibility, accident, transistoriness which we call 'life.' moreover
in the end there is a basic question to be settled: how to handle the *li
gung – lao go* problem. one can either (a) extend the parable aspect so
as to have a straightforward conflict, *gods – li gung – lao go*, which
would keep it all on a moral plane and allow two conflicting principles
('two souls') to figure separately, or else (b) have a plain story about
how *li gung* masquerades as her cousin and to that end makes use of
the experiences and qualities which her gutter existence has brought out
in her. in fact only (b) is possible unless one is to abandon mrs. shin's
discovery (scene 7), her conversation with the pregnant lao go and the
whole theme of how this pregnancy makes the double game impossible

to maintain. the transformation scene before the curtain (4a) is not in any way mystical but merely a technical solution in terms of mime and a song. where the difficulty becomes acute is wherever *lao go* directly addresses the audience the question is whether he ought not to do this using li gung's voice and consequently her attitude too. at bottom it all depends on how scene 5 is handled. this is where lao go must make some remark to explain his change of attitude. however, he has no confidant, nor can he make a confidant of the audience – not as lao go. What is more, li gung's collapse at the end of that scene is harder to understand if the solution adopted is (b) rather than (a). the only possible explanation is that here too she is being addressed as li gung. when you come down to it the elements *good* and *evil* are too segregated for a realistic drama of masquerade. an occasional slip would be unavoidable. the most realistic scene in this respect is the ninth. A further consideration could be that li gung has to make strenuous efforts to play the part of lao go and is no longer capable of appearing unpleasant when dressed in her own clothes and before the eyes of those who know and address her as li gung. herein lies an important lesson: how easy it is for her to be good and how hard to be evil.

> [*Bertolt Brecht Arbeitsjournal*, vol. 1, 1938–42, Frankfurt, Suhrkamp, 1973, pp. 144–5. From the entry for August 9, 1940, roughly seven weeks after the completion of the first script and (obviously) before the changing of the characters' names. 'Two souls' is the Faustian concept also cited in *St Joan of the Stockyards*.]

THE GOOD PERSON OF SZECHWAN

Prologue

Three gods enter the city of Szechwan. They are looking for a good person, having heard a rumour to the effect that to be good on this earth has become difficult. Aided by an obliging water seller they make the acquaintance of a good person, to wit the poor prostitute Chen Teh. Even she, however, complains that she finds it almost impossible to respect all the commandments of the gods, because she is so badly off. In order to give her a chance, the gods make her a present of money, convey their best wishes and leave her.

1

The good Chen Teh uses the gods' present of money to fit out a small tobacco shop. Concerned from the outset to obey the gods' commandments, to help her neighbours, to put her own interests second and to satisfy every request, no matter how far-fetched, from her none too good-natured fellow humans, she finds her shop close to riun the very evening after it has opened. A family of eight has chosen to take refuge there. To keep out further cadgers her "visitors'" cynically advise her to invent a cousin who will supposedly be a hard man and the real owner of the shop. By bedtime there is no room in her own shop for Chen Teh, and she has to go away.

2

Next morning, greatly to the "visitors'" astonishment, the door opens and an extremely hard-looking young business man comes into the shop. He introduces himself as Chen Teh's cousin. Politely but firmly he invites the family to leave the premises, as this is where his cousin must conduct her business. When they prove reluctant to go he promptly summons the police, who gaol one or two of the family's members on some trivial charge. To justify himself to the audience he demonstrates that they were bad people: certain of the sacks which the family has left behind contain opium. – The friendly relations that have grown up between the cousin and the police bear fruit at once. A grateful policeman draws his attention to the flattering interest being taken in his pretty cousin by the prosperous barber Chu Fu from across the way. He is prepared to help set up an assignation in the public park. The cousin expresses interest: Chen Teh is clearly incompetent to run the shop without some protection, and he himself has to go off again and will probably not be able to come back.

3

We see Chen Teh in the park on her way to her assignation with the wealthy barber. Under a tree she sees, to her horror, a down-at-heel young man about to hang himself. He tells her that he is an unemployed pilot and is unable to raise the $500 needed to get him a pilot's job in Peking. A shower of rain forces Chen Teh to take shelter under his tree. A tender conversation ensues. For the first time Chen Teh samples the joy of a man-woman relationship unclouded by material interests. And before she goes home she has promised the pilot to help him get the Peking job. She thinks her cousin may be able to provide the $500. Radiant with joy, she tells her confidant the water seller that in setting

out to meet a man who might be able to help her she met a man she is
able to help.

Interlude

Before the eyes of the audience Chen Teh transforms herself into her
cousin Chui Ta. As she sings a song to explain how impossible it is to
perform good deeds without toughness and force she is meantime
donning costume and mask of the evil Chui Ta.

4

Chen Teh has asked her friend, the pilot Sun, to come to her shop. In
place of the girl he finds her cousin Chui Ta. The latter says he is
prepared to provide the $500 for the Peking job, which he reckons a
sound financial basis for Sun and Chen Teh. He has asked Mi Tzu to
come, a lady tobacco wholesaler who at once offers $300 for the shop.
Since Sun evidently has no hesitations the deal is soon agreed. He is
radiant as he pockets the $300. Admittedly there is the problem of
finding the remaining $200. The cousin's somewhat unscrupulous
solution is to make money from the opium which the family of eight
have left behind in Chen Teh's shop. Picture his horror, however, not
to mention astonishment, when it emerges as a result of a more or less
accidental question that the pilot is not thinking of taking the girl to
Peking with him. He of course breaks off all further negotiations. The
pilot is not so easily dealt with. Not only does he fail to return the $300
he has been given, but he also expresses himself easily confident of
getting the balance from the girl, since she is blindly obsessed with him.
Triumphantly he leaves the shop in order to wait for her outside. Chui
Ta, whom anger and despair have driven to distraction, sends for Chu
Fu the barber and tells him that his cousin's unbridled goodness has
been the ruin of her, so that she needs a powerful patron right away.
The infatuated barber is prepared to discuss the young lady's problems
'over a small supper for two.' As Chui Ta goes off 'to notify his cousin'
the pilot Sun smells trouble and reappears in the shop. When Chen Teh
emerges from the back room for her outing with the barber she is
confronted by Sun. He reminds her of their love; he recalls that wet
evening in the park where they first met. Poor Chen Teh! All that Chui
Ta has found out about the pilot's bare-faced egotism is washed away
by Chen Teh's feelings of love. She leaves, not with the barber her clever
cousin has designated, but with the man she loves.

5

At first light, following a night of love, a happy Chen Teh is discovered
outside a local teahouse. She is carrying a small sack of opium which
she proposes to sell so as to raise the extra $200 needed to get her flier
flying. In a kind of mime to musical accompaniment she and we see the
opium smokers leaving the teahouse after a night of indulgence, lonely,
stumbling, ravaged, and shivering. The sight of these wrecks brings her
to her senses. She is quite incapable of buying happiness for herself by
trafficking in such deadly poison. Sun will surely understand. He won't
reject her if she comes back to him empty-handed. Charged with this
hope she hastens away.

6

Chen Teh's hope has not been fulfilled. Sun has left her. In low dives
he is drinking all the money raised by the sale of the shop. We next see
Chen Teh in the yard, loading her few possessions on a cart. She has
lost her little shop, gift of the gods. As she takes down her washing she
becomes giddy, and a woman neighbour remarks mockingly that her
fine upstanding lover has no doubt put her in the family way. The
discovery fills Chen Teh with indescribable joy. She hails the pilot's son
as a pilot of the future. Turning round, she can scarcely believe her eyes
when she sees a neighbour's child fishing for scraps of food in the
dustbin; it is hungry. The sight brings about a complete transformation
in her. She makes a big speech to the audience proclaiming her
determination to turn herself into a tigress for the sake of the child in
her womb. That, it seems to her, is the only way to shield it from
poverty and degeneracy. The only one who can help is her cousin.

Interlude

The water seller asks the audience whether they have seen Chen Teh.
It is now five months since she vanished. Her cousin has grown rich
and is now known as the Tobacco King. Rumour however has it that
his prosperity is due to shady dealings. The water seller is sure he is
pushing opium.

7

The Tobacco King, Chui Ta, is sitting in solitude in Chen Teh's old but
newly smartened-up shop. He has grown fat. Only his housekeeper
knows why. The autumn rain seems to make him incline to melancholy.
The housekeeper pokes fun at him. Is the master perhaps thinking about

that rainy evening in the park? Is he still waiting for the pilot to reappear? The shop door opens and a decrepit individual comes in; it is Sun. Chui Ta is greatly agitated and asks what he can do for him. The ex-pilot brusquely refuses food and clothing. He wants just one thing: opium. Chui Ta, seeing in this unforgotten lover a victim of his own shady traffic, has just begged him to give up this suicidal vice when Wang the water seller appears with his regular monthly enquiry as to the whereabouts of Chen Teh. Reproachfully he informs Chui Ta that she herself told him she was pregnant, and swears that Chen Teh's friends are never going to give up enquiring about her, for good people are both rare and desperately needed. This is too much for Chui Ta. Without a word he goes into the back room. Sun has overheard that Chen Teh is expecting a child. He at once sees an opening for blackmail. Then he hears sobs from the back room; undoubtedly it is Chen Teh's voice. When Chui Ta reenters the shop Sun once again demands opium, and because Chui Ta refuses he goes off uttering threats. Chui Ta's secret is on the verge of being discovered. He must get away. He is just leaving the shop and Szechwan when Sun comes back with the police. A quick search reveals Chen Teh's clothing. The Tobacco King is taken away on suspicion of murder.

8

The water seller has a dream. The three gods appear to him and ask about Chen Teh. He is forced to tell them that she has been murdered by her cousin. The gods are appalled. During their entire trip across the province they failed to find a single other good person. They will return at once.

9

At the trial of Chui Ta the Tobacco King, which has aroused the entire neighbourhood, the three gods appear as judges. As it proceeds Chen Teh's good works are universally lauded and Chui Ta's misdeeds condemned. Chui Ta is forced to justify his harshness by his desire to help his unworldly cousin. He regards himself as her one genuinely disinterested friend. Asked where she is staying at that moment, he has no answer. When cornered he promises to make a statement if the court can be cleared. Once again with his judges he takes off his disguise: he is Chen Teh. The gods are horrified. The one good person they found is the most detested man in the entire city. It can't be true. Incapable of facing this reality they send for a pink cloud and hastily mount it in order to journey back up to their heaven. Chen Teh falls on her knees, imploring them for help and advice. 'How can I be good and yet survive without my cousin, Enlightened Ones?' – 'Well, do your best' is the gods' embarrassed answer. – 'But I've got to have my cousin, Enlightened Ones!' – 'Once a month, that will do.' And despairingly she watches her gods disappear into the sky, waving and smiling.

When the court doors are once again opened the crowd delightedly hails the return of the good person of Szechwan.

> [From Werner Hecht (ed.): *Materialien zu Brechts 'Der gute Mensch von Sezuan,'* Frankfurt, Suhrkamp, 1968, pp. 100–106. This outline, doubtless made for Kurt Weill, corresponds to the 'Santa Monica 1943' version of the play, as discussed below, pp. 336ff.]

ALTERNATIVE EPILOGUE

This Szechwan, as you must have understood
In which one can't survive and still be good
Has gone for ever. It had to disappear.
Yet cities can be found much nearer here
Where doing good can be the end of you
While evil actions help you to win through.
Dear audience, if you live in such a town
Make sure it's changed before it gets you down.
Earth has no happiness that can compare
With freedom to do good while you are there.

> [Written about 1953. From Jan Knopf (ed.): *Brechts Guter Mensch von Sezuan*. Suhrkamp, Frankfurt, 1982.]

Editorial Note

It was not till the spring of 1939, around the time of the German annexation of Czechoslovakia, that Brecht began a serious attempt to write this play which he had been ruminating for so many years. Locating it for the first time clearly in China, and already calling it by its final title, he outlined first a five-scene, then an eight-scene plan, the second of which goes:

Prologue
1. The whore gets a tobacco shop.
2. Her cousin has to rescue it.
3. The whore falls in love.
4. The cousin has to foot the bill.
5. The whore's one friend.
6. The whore's marriage.
7. Suspicion
8. Trial

But soon this simple plot grew too elaborate, the cousin's personality too simply bad, the whole play much too long. From Brecht's journal it sounds as if such writing as got done that summer was patchy, and certainly no complete script of this version is known to have survived. It looks as though there was to have been a subsequently eliminated character called Feh Pung, a large-scale tobacco merchant who wished to squeeze the heroine and other small traders out of business; nor did either the landlady or the family of eight figure in the story, the former being replaced by a male landlord, while in lieu of the latter the two prostitutes of scene 2 had a more elaborate role. The barber, for his part, would have been rather more likeable, since he was to have helped the heroine combat the tobacco merchant. The names all through differed from those in our version and were changed at a relatively late stage. Thus Shen Teh/Shui Ta was Li Gung/Lao Go; the pilot Yu Schan or Schan Yu; the water-seller Sun; Mrs Shin at first Mrs Si; and the barber Kau or Kiau. Finally in September, at the time of the German invasion of Poland and the allied declaration of war, the work ground to a halt. Within a fortnight of summing it all up in the 'Press Report' printed on pp. 317 ff., Brecht was hard at work on *Mother Courage* instead.

2 THE FINLAND VERSION

He picked up the threads again the next spring, after moving to Finland in April 1940. 'No play has ever given me so much trouble', he noted in June after he and Margarete Steffin had been working on it concentratedly for some six weeks:

> the material presented many difficulties, and in the (roughly) ten years since i first tackled it i made several false starts.
>
> the main danger was of being over-schematic. li gung had to be a person if she was to become a good person. as a result her goodness is not of a conventional kind; she is not wholly and invariably good, not even when she is being li gung. nor is lao go conventionally bad, etc. the continual fusion and dissolution of the two characters, and so on, comes off reasonably well, i think. the god's great experiment of extending love of one's neighbour to embrace love of one's self, adding 'be good to thyself' to 'be good to others,' needed to stand apart from the story and at the same time to dominate it . . .

The first complete script in the Brecht Archive dates from this period, but as it is one of Brecht's characteristic pasted-up typescripts, with many later additions and corrections stuck in and yet others written in by hand, much detective work will be needed before we know just what stages it went through. Originally the characters bore the earlier names (apart from Mrs. Si, who had already become Mrs. Shin), which Brecht at some point amended by hand. His journal suggests that this change was decided between August 9 and September 6, 1940, in other words at the last moment before he moved on to intensive work on *Puntila*. However, the addition of the three songs 'Song of the Smoke,' 'Song of the Eighth Elephant,' and 'Trio of the Vanishing Gods on their Cloud,' which were written in January 1941, suggest that the final amendments were probably made during that month. Thereafter it was re-typed and mimeographed, copies being sent to Switzerland, Sweden, and the U.S., with the text virtually as we now have it. Until the 1950s the play bore a dedication to Helene Weigel, Brecht's wife.

The most elaborate of the 'working schemes' used for the play is reproduced on pp. 320–21. Its pencilled additions include Li Gung's 'Praise of the Rain' in scene 3 (possibly the origin of the water seller's song on p. 37) and a sketch for the 'Song of the Defenceless of the Good and the Gods' (p. 48 f.). The January revision too seems too have been concerned (to judge from a journal entry of the 25th) with 'introducing a poetic element, a few verses and songs, this should make it lighter and less tedious, even if it cannot be shortened.' Besides this variation of its texture and the changing of the names it seems that Brecht's reworking of the draft completed the previous June concentrated on four main points: the treatment of the stocks of raw tobacco brought in by the family of eight, the exact details of Shen Teh's borrowings and payments, the direct addressing of the audience, and minor questions of local colour: e.g., should the characters feed on bread and milk or on rice and tea? 'i have taken care to avoid any element of folklore,' he noted at one point. 'on the other hand i don't want people to make a joke of yellow men eating white french bread . . . that would be using china as a mere disguise, and a ragged disguise at that.' What he was striving for rather, he said, was something equivalent to the imaginary London of *The Threepenny Opera* or the Kiplingesque Kilkoa of *Man equals Man*, both of which he considered successful 'poetic conceptions.'

3 ACCOUNT OF THE FIRST SCRIPT

To resume this 1940–41 script scene by scene, the chief points of interest are:

Prologue

Dated by Brecht June 11, 1940 and followed by a photograph of a Chinese water carrier.

1

Here as elsewhere the rice distributed by Shen Teh was originally milk. Sacks of tobacco are brought in by the 'elderly couple' on p. 13, also by the grandfather and the niece. The 'Song of the Smoke' (p. 19) was inserted with the title 'Song of the impoverished family.' The verse 'They are bad' was likewise a later addition (p. 15).

2

The details of Mrs. Mi Tzu's demand for the rent in advance (p. 28) were added to the script, as was the passage with the old woman (p. 30). All sums were originally in yen, not silver dollars.

3

At the start Brecht cut eleven lines in which young prostitute told Shen Teh that her family had seven sacks of tobacco with which to restart in business, and asked her to look after them. Thereafter the rain, Shen

Teh's references to her tame crane, her speech beginning 'There are still friendly people' (p. 36) and the verses 'In our country' (p. 35) and 'How rich I am' (p. 36) were all later additions to the script. The verse 'Hardly was a shelter' in the ensuing interlude (p. 40) was originally at the end of scene 1, where it was spoken by Shen Teh.

4

The episode where the two old people lend Shen Teh the rent money (pp. 44 f.) was certainly reworked, if not actually added to the script. The passage where Shen Teh hands the money to Mrs. Yang, proposes to sell her tobacco stocks and wonders how to raise a further $300 (from 'Of course you can have those now' on p. 47 to 'a pilot has got to fly, that is obvious' on p. 48) appears to be an addition too.

5

In various schemes for the complex finances of this scene it appears that Mrs. Mi Tzu was to buy not only the shop but also the sacks of tobacco left by the family of eight, who would then be reluctant to claim them. This was cut on the script. Brecht also deleted an appearance of the old woman early in the scene to inquire about her loan, substituting instead the exchange between Sun and Shui Ta (p. 53); both versions stress that there was no agreement in writing. Notes made after the change of names show Brecht concerned to reconcile Sun's more 'hooligan-like' features with his genuine keenness for flying. At that stage his boasting about his hold over Shen Teh was primarily intended to impress Mrs. Mi Tzu, not (as now) Shui Ta. The barber, too, was at this point to suggest turning his empty houses into a tobacco factory for the general benefit of the neighbourhood.

6

Brecht added Sun's references to the 'gremlins' (p. 64 f.) and the mention of the old couple (on p. 66). Shen Teh's demand that Sun repay the $200 is not in this script, and only appears in that of the Zurich production.

7

The first six lines, with their further mention of repayment, are not in the script. Shu Fu's gift of the blank cheque (p. 74) is not in the working plan, and it appears that the whole ending of the scene, with its installation of the factory in Shu Fu's sheds, was extensively worked over. Previously this development was to have been left to scene 8, while the sacks (subsequently bales) of tobacco would already have been sold in scene 5. The script specifies that Shen Teh's big verse speech on p. 75 should be accompanied by the music of the 'Song of the Defencelessness of the Good and the Gods', which would continue softly after its end. Her little rhyme about 'A plum off my tree' (p. 76) was added in revision.

8

Though the scene is dated May 21, 1940, the 'Song of the Eighth Elephant' (p. 88) was added in January. Most of the indications that Mrs. Yang's remarks were to be addressed to the audience were likewise additions.

9

Bears the dates May 23 and June 17 and seems to have been scarcely revised since.

10

Dated Helsingfors, May 29 and June 17, 1940, but bears signs of considerable subsequent reworking. Shen Teh's big speech (pp. 107 ff.) looks like a separate insertion, and the reference to her as 'strong, healthy and well-built' (p. 109) is added in Brecht's hand. Originally on this script the scene ended with 'Once a month: that will be enough' (p. 110), followed by the final quatrain. The gods' trio, initially with a slightly different first verse, was added in the January revision.

The epilogue is not included in this script, whose finally amended version is otherwise to all intents and purposes the same as the final text used in our edition.

4. THE ZURICH SCRIPT OF 1943

For the play's first production at the Zurich Schauspielhaus a duplicated script was made by the Reiss-Verlag of Basel. Sub-titled 'A Parable by Bertold Brecht', this again is very close to the final text, but includes a number of small dramaturgical changes due presumably to the theatre. Thus it runs most of the interludes into the immediately preceding scenes, puts an intermission after scene 5 and makes the following cuts:

1

The sacks of tobacco previously brought by the elderly couple were omitted.

6

Cut from Sun's 'Why not?' (p. 64) to the start of Mrs. Yang's next speech (p. 65).

8

Cut stage direction and Mrs. Yang's speech, following the song.

9

Cut from 'SHUI TA, *pitifully*' to '*in Mrs. Shin's arms*' (p. 91), also the stage direction and Wang's first speech in the interlude following.

10

Cut from 'Mr Shui Ta, on the other hand' to 'from straight perjury'. (pp. 102–3). Again, there was no epilogue.

5. THE SANTA MONICA VERSION

Even before the Zurich production Brecht had tried to arouse interest in the play in the U.S., but without yet attempting to modify it for the very different audience there. It was only later, when Kurt Weill thought he might be able to arrange a Broadway production, that Brecht in New York hurriedly made what he termed 'a szechwan version for here.' Though this has not been firmly identified, it could well be the 'story' printed on p. 325 ff., which was found inside one of the duplicated copies of the Finnish version, from which however it differs extensively. The full script embodying this story, typed by Brecht himself and marked 'only copy,' was headed '1943 version' and datelined Santa Monica 1943, so that it must have been written after his return there from New York at the end of May, probably once the main work on *Schweyk* had been completed. By September 20 Brecht's journal shows that Christopher Isherwood had read the play but was not interested enough to want to translate it as its author had hoped. Thereafter, as Weill began to think rather of making a 'semi-opera' of it, the new script was set aside and apparently forgotten, subsequent U.S. translations and productions being based, so far as we know, on the previous version. This seems surprising in view of Brecht's success not only in shortening and simplifying the play but also in shedding a more critical light on the heroine's goodness, and thus interweaving the ideas of good and evil as he wanted in the earlier journal entry printed on p. 332. The principal differences from our text are as follows:

Prologue

As before.

1

The stage direction for the entry of the elderly couple on p. 13 adds '*The wife and the shabbily dressed man are carrying sacks on their shoulders.*' Then there is a long cut from Mrs. Mi Tzu's entry (p. 17) to the nephew's 'Over the shelving' (p. 18), after which the former's exit speech, starting 'Well, I shall also be glad', and the wife's ensuing comment, ending 'all about you by the morning,' (p. 18) are likewise cut.

2

Unchanged up to where Shui Ta bows (p. 27–8). Thereafter the rest of the scene is different, thus:

SHUI TA: There's just one thing: aren't you going to take your sacks?

THE HUSBAND, *giving him a conspiratorial look*: What sacks? You know we didn't bring any sacks with us.

SHUI TA, *slowly*: Oh. Then either my cousin got it wrong or I must have misunderstood her. *To the policeman*: It's quite all right.

THE POLICEMAN: Get going, you! *he drives them out.*

THE GRANDFATHER, *solemnly, from the doorway*: Good morning. *Exit all, except Shui Ta.*

Shui Ta hastens backstage and brings out a sack.

SHUI TA, *showing the sack to the audience*: Opium! *He hears somebody approaching and quickly hides the sack.*

THE POLICEMAN, *reentering*: I've handed those crooks over to my colleague. Forgive my coming back. I would like to thank you in the name of the police.

SHUI TA: It is for me to thank you, officer.

THE POLICEMAN, *negligently*: You were saying something about sacks. Did those crooks leave anything here, Mr. Shui Ta?

SHUI TA: Not a button. Do you smoke?

THE POLICEMAN, *putting two cigars in his pocket*: Mr. Shui Ta, I must admit we at the station began by viewing this shop with mixed feelings, but your decisive action on the side of the law just now showed us the sort of man you are. We don't take long to find out who can be relied on as a friend of law and order. I only hope you will be staying here.

SHUI TA: Unfortunately I shall not be staying here and I cannot come again. I was able to give my cousin a hand just because I was passing through; I merely saved her from the worst. Any minute now she will be thrown back on her own resources. I am worried as to what will happen.

THE POLICEMAN: All you have to do is find a husband for her.

SHUI TA: A husband?

THE POLICEMAN, *eagerly*: Why not? She's a good match. Between you and me and the doorpost I had a hint only yesterday from Mr. Shu Fu, the barber next door, that he is taking a flattering interest in the young lady, and he's a gentleman who owns twelve houses and has only one wife and an old one at that. He went so far as to ask about her financial standing. That shows real affection . . .

SHUI TA, *cautiously*: It's not a bad idea. Could you arrange a meeting?

THE POLICEMAN: I think so. It would have to be done delicately, of course. Mr. Shu Fu is very sensitive. I'd say, an accidental meeting outside the teahouse by the city lake. There's a bath-hut there; I know because I had the good fortune to make an arrest there last week. Miss Shen Teh should be looking at the goldfish and in her delight could let drop some remark such as . . . well, what?

SHUI TA: Look at the pretty goldfish.

THE POLICEMAN: Brilliant. And Mr. Shu Fu could reply, let's say, for example . . .

SHUI TA: All I can see is a pretty face mirrored in the water, madam.

THE POLICEMAN: Perfect. I'll speak to Mr. Shu Fu at once. Don't think, Mr. Shui Ta, that the authorities have no sympathy for the honest businessman.

SHUI TA: Indeed I foresaw a black outlook for this little shop which my cousin regards as a gift of the gods. But now I see a way out. It is almost frightening how much luck one needs in order to live, what brilliant ideas, what good friends.

3

Up to p. 36 f. the first two-thirds of the scene are unchanged, except that on p. 33 and again on p. 36 Shen Teh 'has got' to marry the man she is meeting at the teahouse, not merely 'is going' to. Then from 'Have you got a friend?' at the end of Sun's speech (p. 36) to Shen Teh's 'And that was a raindrop' (p. 37) there is a cut and the following is substituted:

SHEN TEH: They say that to speak without hope is to speak without kindness.

SUN: I have no hope. I need 500 dollars to be human. This morning when a letter came saying there was a job for me the first thing I did was to get myself a rope; you see, it costs 500 dollars.

SHEN TEH: It's a flier's job? *He nods, and she slowly goes on.* I have a friend, a cousin of mine, who might be able to raise that amount. This friend is too cunning and hard. It really would have to be the last time. But a flier must fly, that's obvious.

SUN: What do you think you are talking about?

SHEN TEH: Please come tomorrow to Sandalmakers' Street. You'll find a small tobacco shop. If I'm not there my cousin will be.

SUN, *laughs*: And if your cousin isn't there nobody will be, is that it? *He looks at her.* Your shawl's really the prettiest thing about you.

SHEN TEH: Yes? *Pause.* And now I've felt a raindrop.

And so on as in our text, up to the end of the poem on p. 38. The scene then finishes thus:

WANG: Weren't you meeting somebody in the park who was going to be able to help you?

SHEN TEH: Yes, but now I've found somebody I am going to be able to help, Wang.

After that come the stage direction (*She pays* . . .) and her last laughing remark to Wang as we have them.

4

Is omitted, only the first six lines from Shen Teh's monologue about the city (p. 42) being kept and transposed to a new interlude before scene 7.

The interlude before the curtain which follows remains unchanged.

5

Instead of as on p. 50 Mrs. Shin's first speech reads:

MRS SHIN: I may be an old gossip, Mr. Shui Ta, but I think you should know what's going on. Once people start talking about how Miss Shen Teh never comes home before morning – and you know we have all the scum of the district hanging round the shop at crack of dawn to get a plate of rice – then a shop like this gets a bad name, and where do you go from there?

On page 50 for Sun's 'Oh boy. I'm going to be flying again' substitute 'Neat, very neat.' For 300 dollars (three times) read 500. For the two lines 'it was good of her' to 'or I'm stuck' read 'Nothing for it, we'll have to sell.' Then omit Shui Ta's next two sentences, (from 'Perhaps' to 'her business'), and for Sun's 'All to her credit of course' below substitute 'Really'. About a page further on delete Shui Ta's sentence about the 200 dollars and the rent, and for both mentions of 250 dollars (amount of Sun's pay in Peking) substitute 150 dollars. In Shui Ta's next speech, for 'the landlady' (p. 52) substitute 'the lady tobacco merchant' (*Tabakhändlerin*). The dialogue from that point reads:

THE LADY TOBACCO MERCHANT, *enters*: Good morning, Mr. Shui Ta. Are you really wanting to sell the shop?

SHUI TA: Mrs. Mi Tzu, my cousin is contemplating marriage, and her future husband – *he introduces Yang Sun* – Mr. Yang Sun, is taking her to Peking where they wish to start a new life. If I can get a good price for my tobacco I shall sell it.

THE LADY TOBACCO MERCHANT: How much do you need?

SHUI TA: 500 in cash.

THE LADY TOBACCO MERCHANT: How much did your stock cost?

SHUI TA: My cousin originally paid 1000 silver dollars, and very little of it has been sold.

THE LADY TOBACCO MERCHANT: 1000 silver dollars! She was swindled of course. I'll make you an offer: you can have 300 silver dollars for the whole business, if you move out the day after tomorrow.

SUN: All right. That's it, old boy!

SHUI TA: It's too little.

SUN: We'd consider that, certainly, but 300 isn't enough. *Like an auctioneer.* First-class tobacco, recently acquired, in admirable condition, price 1000 dollars F.O.B. Together with complete shop fittings and a growing clientèle, attracted by the good looks of the proprietress. The whole to be knocked down for only 500 dollars due to special circumstances. It's an opportunity that mustn't be missed. Now you're an intelligent woman, you know what life's about, it's written all over you. *He strokes her.* You know what love is, it's plain to see. The shop's got to go, selling below cost price due to hasty marriage – the sort of chance that occurs once in a business lifetime.

THE LADY TOBACCO MERCHANT, *not unaffected, but still firmly*: 300 dollars.

SUN, *with a sidelong glance at Shui Ta*: Not enough, but better than nothing, what? 300 in hand would give us room to turn around in.

SHUI TA, *alarmed*: But 300 won't get us the job.

SUN: OK, but what good is a shop to me?

SHUI TA: But everything would have gone, there'd be nothing to live on.

SUN: But I'd have the 300 dollars. *To the lady tobacco merchant.* It's a deal. Lock, stock, and barrel for 300 dollars, and our troubles are over. How soon can we have the 300?

THE LADY TOBACCO MERCHANT: Right away. *She pulls notes from her bag.* Here, 300 dollars, and that's because I'm glad to help where it seems to be a case of young love.

SUN, *to Shui Ta*: Write down 300 on the contract. Shen Teh's signature's already on it, I see.
Shui Ta fills in the figure and hands the contract to the lady tobacco merchant. Sun takes the notes away from him.

THE LADY TOBACCO MERCHANT: Good-bye, Mr. Yang Sun; good-bye, Mr. Shui Ta. Please remember me to Miss Shen Teh. *Goes out.*

SUN, *sits down exhausted on the counter*: We've made it, old boy.

SHUI TA: But it's not enough.

SUN: That's right. We need another 200. You'll have to find them.

SHUI TA: How am I to do that without stealing?

SUN: Your cousin certainly thought you were the right man to find them.

SHUI TA: Perhaps I am. *Slowly.* I took it that the point at issue was Shen Teh's happiness. A person's goodness, they said, doesn't have to be denied to that person and the same applies to his or her compassion.

SUN: Right, partner. O boy, I'm going to be flying again!

SHUI TA, *smiling and with a bow*: A flier has to fly. *Negligently.* Have you got the money for both your tickets, and enough to tide you over?

Thereafter the dialogue continues as we have it from Sun's 'Sure' (p.53) to the *Pause* on p. 54. Then Shui Ta continues:

I should like you to hand me back the 300 dollars, Mr. Yang Sun, and leave them in my custody until you are able to show me two tickets to Peking.

SUN: Why? You mean you don't trust me?

SHUI TA: I don't trust anybody.

SUN: Why specially me?
They look at each other.

SUN: My dear brother-in-law, I would prefer it if you didn't meddle in the intimate affairs of people in love. We don't understand one another, I see. As for the other 200 I'll have to rely on the girl.

SHUI TA, *incredulously*: Do you really expect her to give up everything for you if you aren't even thinking of taking her along?

SUN: She will. Even so.

SHUI TA: And you are not afraid of what I might have to say against it?

Then back to our text from Sun's 'My dear man' (p. 54), but with the following modifications. First of all Sun's exit speech (pp. 54–55) ends after *puts the box under his arm*'.

> And now I'm to go and wait outside the shop, and don't let it worry you if we're a bit late tonight. We're having supper together and we'll be talking about the missing 200.

Then Mrs. Shin's second sentence 'And the whole Yellow Alley' is cut, as is her speech following the poem (p. 55). Instead Shen Teh concludes the poem by saying 'Fetch Mr. Shu Fu the barber at once,' and Shin '*dashes off*'. About a page later there is a long cut from Wang's entry with the policeman (p. 56) to immediately before Shui Ta's 'I shall hasten to inform my cousin' (p. 58). Roughly two pages after that, Sun's 'But I can put up a fight' (p. 60) is followed by a new insertion 'Look me in the eyes. Do you really believe I can't be in love with you without a dowry?' before continuing 'They're wrecking' and so on as in our text. Finally, after Shen Teh's 'I want to go away with Sun' (p. 60) Sun says 'Bring your shawl, the blue one,' and '*Shen Teh fetches the shawl she wore in the park*' before Sun goes on 'We are in love, you know' and so on to the end.

The ensuing interlude (p. 61) is partly absorbed in the new interlude outside a teahouse (see below).

6

Is omitted, as is the interlude (pp. 71–3) which follows it.

Interlude Outside a Teahouse

This is mainly new. Carrying a small sack, Shen Teh addresses the audience as at the beginning of our scene 4 (p. 42), from 'I had never seen the city at dawn', but omitting the sentence 'It was a long walk' etc. After 'filling his lungs with fresh air and reaching for his tools' (p. 43) she continues:

And here is the Teahouse of Bliss where I am supposed to sell this little sack so that Sun may fly again. *She tries to enter, but guests are leaving. They are opium smokers, human wrecks, stumbling and freezing. A young man takes out his purse, finds it empty and throws it away. A hideous old woman escorts a very young drugged girl.* That's terrible. It's opium that has ruined them like that. *She looks at her sack in horror.* It's poison. How could I think of selling this? It doesn't even belong to me. How could I forget that too?

Then she goes into the monologue on p. 61, starting at 'In the tumult of my feelings', omitting the sentence 'How could I simply have forgotten two good old people?' and ending after 'he will understand' (p. 62) with:

> He would rather get a job at the cement works than owe his flying to a filthy deal. I must go to him at once.

7 [renumbered 6]

After the opening stage direction, which is as in our text, Mrs. Shin's speech is changed to read: 'There you are, your shop's gone and the whole district knows that for weeks that pilot of yours has been boozing away the money in the lowest sort of bar.' Shen Teh *says nothing*. Then Shin continues 'All gone, eh' as in our text (p. 73), down to Shen Teh's 'earn a bit as a tobacco sorter?' Then:

> *A child appears in the gateway to the yard.*
> MRS. SHIN, *shooing it away*: Clear out, you! *To Shen Teh*: Those gutter vultures only need to get one sniff of bankruptcy and before you know it they come around stuffing their pockets.
> SHEN TEH: Oh, let him look through my junk. He might find something worth taking.
> MRS. SHIN: If there's anything worth taking I'm taking it. You haven't paid me for the washing yet. Beat it or I'll call the police! *Child disappears.*

Shen Teh then asks 'Why are you so unpleasant?' introducing the poem as on p. 77. After it Mrs. Shin comments 'A pity your cousin didn't hear that,' and goes on 'What are Mr Shui Ta's trousers doing here?' etc., as on p. 73. After Shen Teh's 'No' seven lines further on there is another new passage:

> *Lin To the carpenter appears in the gateway.*
> THE CARPENTER: Good morning, Miss Shen Teh. There's a story going round the district that you have got permission for the

homeless to move into Shu Fu the barber's houses. Is that right?

MRS. SHIN: It was right. But now we've given Shu Fu the brushoff there ain't going to be no accommodation.

THE CARPENTER: That's a pity. I don't know what I can do with my family.

MRS. SHIN: It looks as if Miss Shen Teh will be in the happy position of being able to ask *you* for accommodation. *The carpenter goes out, disappointed.* There'll be a lot more of them coming along.

SHEN TEH: This is dreadful.

MRS. SHIN: You think you're too good for the barber, so the plague huts down by the river are going to have to be good enough for Lin To and his family. If you ask me you're not giving up that pilot of yours in spite of the bad way he has behaved to you. Don't you mind him being such a bad person?

SHEN TEH: It all comes from poverty.

Then she addresses the poem to the audience as on pp. 74–5, after which the text continues, with one exception, as we have it until after the plum rhyme that ends her big speech (p. 76). The exception is that the mention of the barber's cheque is cut; thus after Mrs. Shin's 'Let's only hope it isn't a little one' (p. 75) the speaker *laughs* and continues: 'Your pilot has fixed you good and proper. Landed you with a kid, that's what he's done!' Then *She goes to the rear* and so on. But once past the plum rhyme this version is different:

> *The child reappears in the gateway. It seems surprised by Shen Teh's play-acting. Suddenly she observes it and beckons it into the yard.*

THE CHILD: Where are you going?

SHEN TEH: I don't know, Ni Tzu.

> *The child rubs its stomach and looks expectantly at her.*

SHEN TEH: I haven't any more rice, Ni Tzu, not a grain.

THE CHILD: Don't go.

SHEN TEH: I'd like to stay.

> *The water seller is heard calling 'Buy water!'*

SHEN TEH: That's something I can still do for you. Come on, little man. *To the audience.*

Hey, you people. Someone is asking for shelter.

A citizen of tomorrow is asking you for a today.

To the child: Wait a moment. *She hurries to the gateway, where the water seller has appeared.*

WANG: Good morning, Shen Teh. Is it true that you're having to clear out of your shop?

SHEN TEH: That's not important: happiness has come to me, I am to have a child, Wang. I'm so glad you came; I had to tell somebody about it. But don't repeat that or Yang Sun may hear of it, and he won't want us. Give me a cupful.

He gives her a cup of water. When she turns round with it she sees the child and stiffens. It has gone over to the dustbin and is fishing around in it. It picks out something which it eats.

SHEN TEH, *to Wang:* Please go at once; I'm not well. *She pushes him out.* He's hungry. Fishing in the garbage.

Then *She lifts up the child* (p. 79) and makes her big verse speech as in our text, and the scene ends with 'for the last time, I hope' on p. 79.

A new, much shorter interlude follows in lieu of the present one (pp. 83–4). It goes thus:

The water seller walks slowly along before the curtain as if it were a street. He stops and addresses the audience.

WANG: Can any of you good people tell me where to find Miss Shen Teh, formerly of Sandalmakers' Street. It's five months since she . completely vanished. That was when her cousin suddenly popped up – must have been for the third time – what's more [?] there have been some queer business dealings in her tobacco shop, very profitable but dirty. *Softly.* Opium. The worst of it is I'm no longer in touch with the Enlightened Ones. It may be because I'm so worried I can't sleep a wink, so that I no longer have dreams. Anyway, if you do see Shen Teh, could you tell her to get in touch with me? We miss her badly in our district; she is such a good person, you see. *He walks worriedly on.*

8

Is omitted.

9 [renumbered 7]

This is the scene in Shen Teh's shop (pp. 90 ff.), but with changes. It starts thus:

The shop has been transformed into an office, with easy chairs and fine carpets. Shui Ta, fat and expensively dressed, is ushering out the elderly couple and the nephew who called on Shen Teh the day the shop was opened. Mrs. Shin, in noticeably new clothes, is watching with amusement. Outside it is raining.

SHUI TA: I tell you for the tenth time I never found any sacks in the back room.

THE WIFE: Then we'd better write to Miss Shen Teh. What's her address?

SHUI TA: I'm afraid I don't know.

THE NEPHEW: So that's it. The sacks have gone, but you've done all right for yourself.

SHUI TA: That indeed is it.

MRS. SHIN: Better watch your step. Mr. Shui Ta found jobs in his factory for some of your family, didn't he? His patience might suddenly give out.

THE WIFE: But the work's ruining my boy's health. It's more than he can take.

Shui Ta shrugs his shoulders. The elderly couple and the nephew go off angrily.

SHUI TA, *feebly*: Working in a factory unhealthy? Work's work.

MRS. SHIN: Those people wouldn't have got anywhere with their couple of sacks. That sort of thing is just a foundation, and it takes very special talents to build any real prosperity on it. *You* have them.

SHUI TA, *has to sit down because he feels sick*: I feel dizzy again.

MRS. SHIN, *bustling around him*: You're six months gone! You mustn't let yourself get worked up. Lucky for you you've got me. All of us can do with a helping hand. Yes, when your time comes I shall be at your side. *She laughs.*

SHEN TEH, *feebly*: Can I count on that, Mrs. Shin?

MRS. SHIN: You bet. It'll cost money, of course.

A smartly dressed man enters. He is the unemployed man who was given cigarettes the day the shop was opened.

THE AGENT: Our accounts, Mr. Shui Ta. From street-corner clients 50 dollars. From the Teahouse of Bliss . . .

SHUI TA, *laboriously*: Go away. Tomorrow.

MRS. SHIN: Can't you see Mr. Shui Ta isn't up to it?

THE AGENT: But we've got a little problem with the police in District Four. One consignment got into the wrong hands, Mr. Shui Ta.

MRS. SHIN: Can't you ever handle anything by yourself?

The agent starts to go, nervously.

SHUI TA: Wait! Hand over the money!

The agent hands over money and goes.

Then as in our text from 'SHUI TA, *pitifully*' down to 'They're watching the shop' (p. 91) after which Mrs. Shin says:

Have a drop of water, dear. *She gets some water.* Why don't you move out of this place and take a villa in a better district? Oh, but I know why. You're still waiting for that broken-down pilot. That's a weakness.

SHUI TA: Nonsense.

Enter a decrepit figure, the former pilot Yang Sun. He is amazed to see Shui Ta in Mrs. Shin's arms, being made to drink by her.

SUN, *hoarsely*: Am I disturbing you?

Shui Ta gets up with difficulty and stares at him.

MRS. SHIN: Mr. Yang Sun in person.

SUN, *respectfully*: Excuse me coming to see you dressed like this, Mr. Shui Ta. My luggage got held up, and I didn't want the rain to stop my calling on one or two of my old acquaintances, you see.

SHUI TA, *draws Mrs. Shin aside before she can open her mouth*: Go and find him some clothes.

MRS. SHIN: Chuck him out right away. I'm telling you.

SHUI TA, *sharply*: You do what you're told. *Mrs. Shin goes out, protesting.*

SUN: Woollen rugs. What riches. I'm told people are calling you the Tobacco King, Mr. Shui Ta.

SHUI TA: I've been lucky.

SUN: Oh, Mr. Shui Ta, it isn't just luck; you've earned it. Ah yes, some get fat and others get thin, that's it, isn't it?

SHUI TA: I take it that fate has not been kind to you, Mr. Yang Sun; but are you ill?

SUN: Me? No, my health is fine.

SHUI TA: Good. Damage to one's health is the only thing that cannot sooner or later be repaired, I would say.

Enter Mrs. Shin from the back room with clothing.

SHUI TA: I hope these things will fit you. Isn't that hat rather big?

Mrs. Shin tries a hat on Sun.

SHUI TA: Yes, it's too big. Get another, Mrs. Shin.

SUN: I don't want a hat. *Suddenly angry.* What are you up to? Trying to buy me off with an old hat? *Controlling himself.* Why should I want your hat? It's something else I need. *Ingratiatingly.* Mr. Shui Ta, would you grant just one favour to a man down on his luck?

SHUI TA: What can I do for you?

MRS. SHIN: It's written all over him. I can tell you what kind of favour he means.

SHUI TA, *beginning to understand*: No!

MRS. SHIN: Opium, eh?

SHUI TA: Sun!

SUN: Only a little packet, enough for two or three pipes. That's all I need. I don't care about clothes or food. But I've got to have my pipe.

SHUI TA, *in the depths of horror*: Not opium! Don't tell me you're a victim of that vice. Listen to me, those wretches who think it may help them escape their miseries for an hour or two are plunged in misery by it forever, so that in no time they need the drug not to make them happy but simply to reduce their worst sufferings.

SUN: I see you know all about it. That's how it is with me.

SHUI TA: Turn back at once! You must be ruthless and control your craving; never touch the drug again, you can do it.

SUN: All very well for you to say that, Mr. Shui Ta; you deal in it and know all about it. Your livelihood depends on us smokers not finding the way back.

SHUI TA: Water! I feel sick.

MRS. SHIN: You haven't been in form lately, not in your old form. *Mockingly*. Perhaps it's Mr. Yang Sun's fault for bringing the rain with him. Rain always makes you so touchy and melancholic. I expect you know why.

SHUI TA: Go away.

Then Wang's voice is heard singing, as on p. 93, but this time it is Mrs. Shin who comments: 'There's that bloody water-seller. Now he'll be nagging us again'. She then *goes out at a sign from Shui Ta* as his voice continues with his speech *from outside*, after which Sun says, pressingly:

We'll make a bargain. Give me what I asked for, and I'll shut him up. What business is it of his, where she is?

Then Wang enters, and with two minor changes the text is the same as ours up to Shui Ta's 'Have you dropped that?' on p. 95. The first change is the addition of the words '*as if transformed*' after 'SUN, *to the audience*' on p. 94. The second is the substitution seven lines on of 'left here rotting' for 'left here to work like a slave' and the addition of 'So that lousy water seller can't even recognise me' before '*He is losing his temper*'. Then after 'Have you dropped that?' the next four pages of our text are considerably changed and shortened, going on thus:

SUN, *cautiously*: Why do you ask that? Want to buy me a pilot's job? Now? What makes you think anyone can fly with hands like this? *He shows his; they are trembling*. Where's my fiancée? Do you hear me? I said, where is my fiancée Shen Teh?

SHUI TA: Do you really want to know?

SUN: I should think so.

SHUI TA: My cousin might be pleased to hear that.

SUN: Anyway, I'm concerned enough not to be able to shut my eyes if, for instance, I find that she is being deprived of her freedom.

SHUI TA: By whom?

SUN: By you.

Pause.

SHUI TA: What would you do in such an eventuality?

SUN, *crudely*: I'd say you had better meet my request and no arguing about it.

SHUI TA: Your request for . . .

SUN, *hoarsely*: The stuff, of course.

SHUI TA: Aha. *Pause.* Mr. Yang Sun, you will not get a single pinch of that drug out of me.

SUN: In that case perhaps your cousin wouldn't deny the father of her child a few pipes of opium every day and a bench to sleep on? Dear cousin-in-law, my longing, for the lady of my heart cannot be suppressed. I feel I shall be forced to take steps if I am to enfold her in my arms once more. *He calls.* Shen Teh! Shen Teh!

SHUI TA: Didn't they tell you Shen Teh has gone away? Do you want to search the back room?

SUN, *giving him a peculiar look*: No, I don't, anyway not by myself. I'm not physically in any condition to fight with you. The police are better fed. *He leaves quickly, taking care not to present his back to Shui Ta.*

Shui Ta looks at him without moving. Then he goes quickly into the back room once more and brings out all kinds of things belonging to Shen Teh: underwear, toilet articles, a dress. He looks lengthily at the shawl which Sun once commented favourably on in the park, then packs it all up in a bundle. Then he gets a suitcase and some men's clothes which he stuffs into it.

SHUI TA, *with the bundle and the suitcase*: So this is the finish. After all my efforts and triumphs I am having to leave this flourishing business which I developed from the dirty little shop thought good enough by the gods. Just one weak moment, one unforseeable attack of softness, and I'm pitched into the abyss. I only had to let that broken-down creature open his mouth, instead of instantly handing him over to the police for having embezzled $300, and I was ruined. No amount of toughness and inhumanity will do unless it is total. That's the kind of world it is.

On hearing sounds from outside, he hurriedly stuffs the bundle under the table. Somebody throws a stone outside the window. Voices of an excited crowd outside. Enter Sun, Wang and the policeman.

The scene then ends virtually as it does after their entry in our text (p. 98). The policeman in his first speech says 'we' instead of 'I' and omits the words 'received from your own firm.' Then in place of Mrs. Mi Tzu's speech Sun *'points at the bundle'* saying, 'He's packed his things. He wanted to clear out.' Finally Shui Ta's last speech is cut and he simply *'bows and goes out ahead of the policeman.'*

The interlude which follows (pp. 99–101) is as we have it.

10 [renumbered 8]

This is very largely the last scene as we have it, less the epilogue. Minor changes in the first part are:

P. 101, for Wang's first speech substitute 'I've collected as many witnesses as I could.'

Three lines below, for 'property owner' substitute 'lady tabacco merchant.'

P. 101 for 'THE OLD WOMAN' substitute 'THE YOUNG PROSTITUTE.'

Pp. 102–3, in the policeman's evidence cut the two sentences beginning 'There were some people' down to 'perjury.' P. 103, Mrs. Mi Tzu's evidence goes:

> As president of the United District Charities, I wish to bring to the attention of the court that Mr. Shui Ta is giving bread and work to a considerable number of people in his tobacco factories. This Shen Teh person, by contrast, was not in particularly good repute.

Five lines below, Wang steps forward with *'the carpenter and the family of eight.'*

There are also still slighter changes in the German which would not affect the translation. After the sister-in-law's 'But we had nowhere to go,' however (p. 104), the scene goes on thus:

SHUI TA: There were too many of you. The lifeboat was on the point of capsizing. I got it afloat again. There wasn't a single morning when the poor of the district failed to get their rice. My cousin regarded her shop as a gift of the gods.

WANG: That didn't prevent you from wanting to sell it off.

SHUI TA: Because my cousin was helping an airman to get back into the air again. I was supposed to find the money.

WANG: She may have wanted that, but you had your eye on that good job in Peking. The shop wasn't good enough for you.

SHUI TA: My cousin had no idea of business.

MRS. SHIN: Besides, she was in love with the airman.

SHUI TA: Hadn't she the right to love?

WANG: Of course she had. So why did you try to make her marry a man she didn't love, the barber here?

SHUI TA: The man she loved was a crook.

THE FIRST GOD, *showing interest:* Who was it she was in love with?

MRS. SHIN, *pointing at Sun, who is sitting like some kind of animal*: That's him. They say birds of a feather flock together. So much for the private life of your Angel of the Slums.

WANG: It wasn't the fact that he was like her that made her love him, but the fact that he was miserable. She didn't just help him because she loved him; she also loved him because she helped him.

THE SECOND GOD: You are right. Loving like that was not unworthy of her.

SHUI TA: But it was mortally dangerous.

THE FIRST GOD: Isn't he the one who accused you of her murder?

SUN: Of restricting her freedom. He couldn't have murdered her. A few minutes before the arrest I heard Shen Teh's voice from the room behind the shop.

Then from the first god's *'intrigued'* question (on p. 105) for nine lines, down to Shui Ta's 'Because you didn't love her,' the text is the same as ours, after which:

SUN: I was out of work.

WANG, *to Shui Ta:* You were out for the barber's money, you mean.

SHUI TA: But what was the money needed for, your worships? *To Sun*: You wanted her to sacrifice everything, but the barber offered his buildings and his money so that she could help the poor. Even to let her do good I had to promise her to the barber. But she didn't want that.

THE RESISTIBLE RISE
OF ARTURO UI

Texts by Brecht

INSTRUCTIONS FOR PERFORMANCE

In order that the events may retain the significance unhappily due
them, the play must be performed in the grand style, and prefer-
ably with obvious harkbacks to the Elizabethan theatre, i.e., with
curtains and different levels. For instance, the action could take
place in front of curtains of whitewashed sacking spattered the
colour of ox blood. At some points panorama-like backdrops
could be used, and organ, trumpet, and drum effects are likewise
permissible. Use should be made of the masks, vocal characteristics, and gestures of the originals; pure parody however must
be avoided, and the comic element must not preclude horror.
What is needed is a three-dimensional presentation which goes at
top speed and is composed of clearly defined groupings like those
favoured by historical tableaux at fairs.

['Hinweis für die Aufführung,' from GW *Stücke*, pp. 1837–38.]

ALTERNATIVE PROLOGUES

> Friends, tonight we're going to show –
> Pipe down, you boys in the back row!
> And madam, your hat is in the way –
> Our great historical gangster play
> Containing, for the first time, as you'll see
> THE TRUTH ABOUT THE SCANDALOUS DOCK SUBSIDY.
> Further, we give you for your betterment
> DOGSBOROUGH'S CONFESSION AND TESTAMENT.
> ARTURO UI'S RISE WHILE THE STOCK MARKET FELL
> THE NOTORIOUS WAREHOUSE FIRE TRIAL, WHAT A SELL!
> THE DULLFEET MURDER! JUSTICE IN A COMA!
> GANG WARFARE: THE KILLING OF ERNESTO ROMA!
> All culminating in our stunning last tableau:
> GANGSTERS TAKE OVER THE TOWN OF CICERO!
> Brilliant performers will portray
> The most eminent gangsters of our day
> All the hanged and the shot

Disparaged but not
Wholly forgotten gangsters
Taken as models by our youngsters.
Ladies and gentlemen, the management knows
There are ticklish subjects which some of those
Who pay admission hardly love
To be reminded of.
Accordingly we've decided to put on
A story in these parts little known
That took place in another hemisphere –
The kind of thing that's never happened here.
This way you're safe; no chance you'll see
The senior members of your family
In flesh and blood before your eyes
Doing things that aren't too nice.
So just relax, young lady. Don't run away.
You're sure to like our gangster play.

['Prolog (2)' from GW *Stücke*, pp. 1838–39. Written
subsequently to the first version of the play, which includes the prologue given in our text.]

Ladies and gentlemen, the management's aware
This is a controversial affair.
Though some can still take history as they find it
Most of you don't care to be reminded.
Now, ladies and gentlemen, surely what this shows is
Excrescences need proper diagnosis
Conveyed not in some polysyllabic word
But in plain speech that calls a turd a turd.
Never mind if you're used to something more ethereal –
The language of this play suits its material.
Down from your gallows, then! Up from your graves!
You murderous pack of filthy swindling knaves!
Let's see you in the flesh again tonight
And hope that in our present sorry plight
Seeing the men from whom that plight first came
Moves us not just to anger but to shame.

[BBA 174/131. Inserted at the end of the first version of

the play, but evidently written for a German audience after
the end of the Second World War.]

NOTES

1. Preface

The Resistible Rise of Arturo Ui, written in Finland in 1941,
represents an attempt to make Hitler's rise intelligible to the
capitalist world by transposing that rise into a sphere thoroughly
familiar to it. The blank verse is an aid in appraising the characters' heroism.

2. Remarks

Nowadays ridiculing the great political criminals, alive or dead,
is generally said to be neither appropriate nor constructive. Even
the common people are said to be sensitive on this point, not just
because they too were implicated in the crimes in question but
because it is not possible for those who survived among the ruins
to laugh about such things. Nor is it much good hammering at
open doors (as there are too many of these among the ruins
anyway): the lesson has been learned, so why go on dinning it
into the poor creatures? If on the other hand the lesson has not
been learned it is risky to encourage a people to laugh at a poten-
tate after once failing to take him seriously enough; and so on and
so forth.

It is relatively easy to dismiss the suggestion that art needs to
treat brutality with kid gloves; that it should devote itself to
watering the puny seedlings of awareness; that it ought to be
explaining the garden hose to former wielders of the rubber
truncheon, and so on. Likewise it is possible to object to the term
'people,' as used to signify something 'higher' than population,
and to show how the term conjures up the notorious concept of
Volksgemeinschaft, or a 'sense of being one people,' that links
executioner and victim, employer and employed. But this does
not mean that the suggestion that satire should not meddle in
serious matters is an acceptable one. Serious things are its specific
concern.

The great political criminals must be completely stripped bare
and exposed to ridicule. Because they are not great political

criminals at all, but the perpetrators of great political crimes, which is something very different.

There is no need to be afraid of truisms so long as they are true. If the collapse of Hitler's enterprises is no evidence that he was a halfwit, neither is their scale any guarantee that he was a great man. In the main the classes that control the modern state use utterly average people for their enterprises. Not even in the highly important field of economic exploitation is any particular talent called for. A multimillion-Mark trust like I. G. Farben makes use of exceptional intelligence only when it can exploit it; the exploiters proper, a handful of people most of whom acquired their power by birth, have a certain cunning and brutality as a group but see no commercial drawbacks in lack of education, nor even in the presence among them of the odd amiable individual. They get their political affairs dealt with by people often markedly stupider than themselves. Thus Hitler was no doubt a lot more stupid than Brüning, and Brüning than Stresemann, while on the military plane Keitel and Hindenburg were much of a muchness. A military specialist like Ludendorff, who lost battles by his political immaturity, is no more to be thought of as an intellectual giant than is a lightning calculator from the music-hall. It is the scope of their enterprises that gives such people their aura of greatness. But this aura does not necessarily make them all that effective, since it only means that there is a vast mass of intelligent people available, with the result that wars and crises become displays of the intelligence of the entire population.

On top of that it is a fact that crime itself frequently provokes admiration. I never heard the petty bourgeoisie of my home town speak with anything but respectful enthusiasm of a man called Kneisel who was a mass murderer, with the result that I have remembered his name to this day. It was not even thought necessary on his behalf to invent the usual acts of kindness towards poor old grannies: his murders were enough.

In the main the petty bourgeois conception of history (and the proletariat's too, so long as it has no other), is a romantic one. What fired these Germans' poverty-stricken imagination in the case of Napoleon I was of course not his Code Napoléon but his millions of victims. Bloodstains embellish these conquerors' faces like beauty spots. When a certain Dr. Pechel, writing in the aptly named *Deutsche Rundschau* in 1946, said of Genghis Khan that 'the price of the Pax Mongolica was the death of several dozen million men and the destruction of twenty kingdoms,' it made a great man of this 'bloodstained conqueror, the demolisher of all values, though this must not cause us to forget the ruler who showed that his real nature was not destructive' – on the mere grounds that he was never small in his dealings with people. It is this reverence for killers that has to be done away with. Plain everyday logic must never let itself be overawed once it goes strolling among the centuries; whatever applies to small situations must be made to apply to big ones too. The petty rogue whom the rulers permit to become a rogue on the grand scale can occupy a special position in roguery, but not in our attitude to history. Anyway there is truth in the principle that comedy is less likely than tragedy to omit to take human suffering seriously enough.

3. Jottings

Kusche: '. . . but at the very point where the projections unmistakably relate *Ui* to a specific phase of German history . . . the question arises: "Where is the People?"'

'Brecht has written, apropos of Eisler's *Faustus*, that "our starting point has to be the truth of the phrase 'no conception can be valid that assumes German history to be unalloyed *misère* and fails to present the People as a creative force'."'

'What is lacking is something or other that would stand for this "creative force of the People" . . . Was it all a mere internal affray between gangsters and merchants? Was Dimitroff (as it is simpler to give that force an individual name) a merchant?'

Ui is a *parable* play, written with the aim of destroying the dangerous respect commonly felt for great killers. The circle described has been deliberately restricted; it is confined to the plane of state, industrialists, Junkers and petty bourgeois. This is enough to achieve the desired objective. The play does not pretend to give a complete account of the historical situation in the 1930s. The proletariat is not present, nor could it be taken into account more than it is, since anything *extra* in this complex would be *too much*; it would distract from the tricky problem posed. (How could more attention be paid to the proletariat without considering unemployment, and how could that be done without dealing with the [Nazi] employment programme, likewise with the political parties and their abdication? One thing would entail another, and the result would be a gigantic work which would fail to do what was intended.)

The projected texts—which K. takes as a reason for expecting the play to give a general account of what happened – seem to me, if anything, to stress the element of selectivity, of a peep-show.

The industrialists all seem to have been hit by the crisis to the same extent, whereas the stronger ought to knock out the weaker. (But that may be another point which would involve us in too much detail and which a *parable* can legitimately skip.) The defence counsel in scene 9 [our scene 8], the warehouse fire trial, possibly needs another look. At present his protests seem designed merely to defend a kind of 'honour of the profession'. The audience will of course want to see him as Dimitroff, whether it was meant to or not.

As for the appearance of Röhm's ghost, I think Kusche is right. ('As the text now stands it makes a drunken Nazi slob look like a martyr.') [. . .]

The play was written in 1941 and conceived as a 1941 production. [. . .]

[From GW *Schriften zum Theater*, pp. 1176–80. Written for a proposed volume of the *Versuche* whose preparation was interrupted by Brecht's death in 1956. Since the play was first published in *Sinn und Form* only after that date, the characteristic East German criticisms voiced by Lothar Kusche (and originally made at a meeting between Brecht and younger writers in late 1953) must have been based on a reading of the script.]

Later Texts

1. Lessons of a pilot production at another theatre

Scene 1 [1a]

The members of the trust display the same gangsters' attitudes and costumes as we know from American films; two-tone suits, a variety of hats, scarves, and so on. This misses the point, essential to the story, that here we have old-established business-men who have been in the trade 'since Noah's ark.' These trust members are too much like parvenus, profiteers, so that the element of solid respectability – the bourgeois element – is lost. As a result their subsequent alliance with Ui, far from being worthy of remark, seems natural. Gangsters seeking out their own kind: *not* the bourgeois state turning to something it had expressly branded as its own mortal enemy – organized crime.

For the same reasons the crisis too is ill-founded, since people who make such an impression are used to running into money troubles, because their business (profiteering) involves risks.

Scene 2 [1b]

Ui, Roma, and Ragg emerge on to the apron from below stage and hurry past Clark one by one. In this way they formally announce themselves as gangsters emerging from a sewer man-hole and not, as the story demands, as gangsters offering their services to the trust in a particularly offhand and gentleman-like manner.

Scene 3 [2]. Dogsborough's Restaurant

Unless Dogsborough appears above all as an immovable, un-changeable, impregnable, rocklike fortress (i.e., solidly or im-movably set in an attitude which, to judge from the text, Brecht took from Hindenburg), the great turning point where he crumbles will not be properly brought out, Instead of a 'great personality' succumbing to an economic force we get an average personality doing what is only to be expected. The actor gave us a lively, forceful, decisive, far too young Dogsborough, with an agile mind and agile gestures. When he looked out of the window and succumbed to the house by the lake, he turned round at least two times in order to express his reservations, and in so doing destroyed the great instant of succumbing.

Similarly with Dogsborough's treatment by the trust people. They should not address him as if he were one of their own sort – i.e., in business jargon – but ought to deploy considerable human resources in order to get him to listen to them at all. They should all the time be confirming his reputation as honest old Dogsborough.

As to the identification of the characters with the Nazi leaders: Dogsborough bore no kind of resemblance to Hindenburg, neither of attitude, gesture, tone of voice, nor mask. The necessary degree of likeness to Hindenburg could only be achieved once one had taken in the inscriptions, and after the play had ended. The highly amusing way in which the course of the action instantly and directly alienates the gangsters into top Nazis was missed, or at any rate seemed vague and inexact.

The play was written against Hitler and the big shots of those times. No general conclusions can be drawn until this story, transposed into terms of the gang world, can be concretely recognized so as to allow people in subsequent times to generalize from concrete knowledge and detect fascist trends. To start off by generalizing – i.e., by making the characters identifiable not merely with Hitler and Hindenburg – makes the events less concrete and prevents any true historical generalization. This is particularly true of our own time, where the historical events are barely remembered and the top Nazis virtually unknown except from photographs. Brecht himself rejects such a discreet approach inasmuch as he uses allusive names (Dogsborough, Giri, Roma, etc.), and calls for prescribed similarities of voice, gesture, and masks. Without this, the work degenerates into a *roman à clef*.

Scene 4 [3]. Bookmaker's office

In the bookmaker's office the group of leaders – Ui, Ragg, and

Roma – associated with the other gangsters, with the result that their discussions degenerated into everyday conversation instead of being a crucial conversation between leading personalities; for the crisis would hardly be discussed before all and sundry. This was accentuated by the unrelievedly pliable, deflated, rubbery, unassertive attitude of Arturo Ui, who was in no way shown as a boss, but more as a passive plaything among strong men. Presented in such a wretched niggling light, his plans did not emerge as dangerous; what was shown was not so much the large-scale planning of lunacy as the actual lunacy itself. This meant that the Nazis' logical approach – which admittedly developed on a basis of lunacy and lack of logic – was never established, so that every subsequent action seemed more or less accidental and not thought up with a vast expenditure of effort. Hence Nazism emerged as haphazard and individualistic instead of being a system: a system based on lunacy and lack of system.

Puny swindles ought to be mightily pondered underhand actions conceived on a vast scale; instances of thoughtlessness realized by enormous thought.

Ui as a character

Ui was presented as a passive plaything in the hands of strong men (Goebbels, Göring, Papen). He has pathological features which ran unchanged right through the play. All through he gave evidence of exhaustion and lack of enterprise, needing to be prompted and jogged by Givola even during his big speeches. In this way the character was emasculated and the main weight of responsibility shifted to the strong men, but without any explanation why they in particular should be strong.

One of the dangerous things about Hitler was his immensely stubborn logic, a logic based on absence of logic, lack of understanding, and half-baked ideas. (Even the concentration camps were no accidental creation, having been planned as early as 1923.) Precisely Hitler's languidness, his indecision, emptiness, feebleness, and freedom from ideas were the source of his usefulness and strength.

The impression given in this production was that Hitler's feebleness and malleability were a liability to the movement, and that given greater energy and intelligence fascism would have proved much easier to put up with, since its shortcomings were here attributed to human weakness. [. . .]

[. . .]

The investigation [Scene 5]

The legal process failed to come across. It was impossible to tell who has convened the inquiry, who is being accused, what part is being played by Dogsborough, how far an appearance of justice still matters, what official standing Ui has there. This scene accordingly came across as a muddle, not as a bourgeois legal ritual that gangsters can use unchanged. Rituals and arrangements should therefore be portrayed with especial precision and care. Only the dignity of the traditional procedures can show the indignity of what is taking place.

The Warehouse Fire Trial [Scene 8]

This scene was not helped by the symbolic grouping which had the populace represented by Nazis who stood a few inches behind the centrally placed judges (pointing a pistol at their heads!).

The fact that the Nazis needed the seal of approval of the bourgeois court, along with its dignity and its traditions, was thereby made incomprehensible. Instead it became an unceremonious gang tribunal, and accordingly without any meaning as a court.

If all that is to appear is how the court's bourgeois traditions are flouted, then it becomes impossible to show how the bourgeois court, by the mere fact of its existence, flouts justice; how crime is an integral part of its traditional procedures; and how it is unnecessary for this tradition to be broken to make it criminal.

[From Manfred Wekwerth: *Schriften*, Arbeit mit Brecht, East Berlin, Henschel-Verlag, 1973, pp. 144–7. The production in question was that of the world première at Stuttgart under Peter Palitzsch's direction in November 1958, a pilot for the subsequent Berliner Ensemble production directed by Palitzsch and Wekwerth together.]

2. Two notes on the Berliner Ensemble production

(a) The historical references

After the third rehearsal we gave up trying to base the principal parts on their correspondences with the Nazi originals. The mistake became particularly evident in the case of Schall, who gave an extremely well-observed imitation of Hitler's vocal characteristics and gestures, such as we had seen a day or two before on film. The faithfulness of this imitation wholly swamped the story of the gangster play. What resulted was a highly amusing detailed parody, but of details from a play about Nazis. The more profoundly amusing point – the parallel between Nazis and gangsters – was lost, since it can only be made if the gangster story is sufficiently complete and independent to match the Nazi story. It is the distancing of the one story from the other that allows them to be connected up on a historical-philosophical, not a merely mechanical plane. We asked the actors to be guided by a strong sense of fun, free from all historical ideas, in exploiting their extensive knowledge of American gangster movies, then carefully on top of that to put recognizable quotations from the vocal characteristics and gestures of the Nazi originals, rather as one puts on a mask.

(b) About the music

The basic character of the music was dictated by setting the 'great historical gangster play' of the prologue within the colourful shooting-gallery framework of a fairground. At the same time it was the music's job to stress the atmosphere of horror. It had to be garish and nasty.

This suggested the use of pieces of music abused by the Nazis, e.g., the theme from Liszt's *Les Preludes* which they degraded into a signature tune for special announcements on the radio. The idea of playing Chopin's 'Funeral March' at set intervals throughout the long-drawn-out warehouse fire trial was suggested by Brecht. Tempi and rhythms of these themes were of course radically altered to accord with the basic character established for the production.

The orchestra consisted of just a few instruments: trumpet, trombone, tuba, horn, piccolo, clarinet, electric guitar, saxophone, piano, harmonium and percussion.

The sharpness and the fairground effect were furthered by technical effects in the course of recording on tape.

All music was on tape. For the first time the accompaniments to the three songs – Ted Ragg's song poking fun at the delay, Greenwool's soppy 'Home Song' and Givola's 'Whitewash Song' – were all reproduced from tape.

[Ibid., pp. 147–8, 'Probennotat,' and p. 150, 'Die Musik'. In this production Ekkehard Schall played Ui: an outstanding performance. The music was by the Ensemble's musical director Hans-Dieter Hosalla.]

SONGS FOR THE BERLINER ENSEMBLE PRODUCTION

1. Ragg's Song

> There was a little man
> He had a little plan.
> They told him to go easy
> Just wait, my little man.
> But waiting made him queasy.
>   Heil Ui!
> For he wants what he wants right now!

[Derived from the 'Was-man-hat-hat-man Song' in scene 7 of *The Round Heads and the Pointed Heads*, GW *Stücke*, p. 993.]

2. Greenwool's Song

> A cabin stands beside the meadow
> It used to be my happy home.
> Now strangers' eyes are looking out the window
> Oh, why did I begin to roam?
> Home, take me home
> Back to my happy home!
> Home, take me home
> Back to my happy home!

[Origin uncertain. Not by Brecht.]

3. Whitewash Song

> When the rot sets in, when walls and roof start dripping
> Something must be done at any price.
> Now the mortar's crumbling, bricks are slipping.
> If somebody comes it won't be nice.

But whitewash will do it, fresh whitewash will do it.
When the place caves in 'twill be too late.
Give us whitewash, boys, then we'll go to it
With our brushes till we fix things up first-rate.
Now, here's a fresh disaster
This damp patch on the plaster!
That isn't nice. (No, not nice.)
Look, the chimney's falling!
Really, it's appalling!
Something must be done at any price.
Oh, if only things would look up!
This abominable fuck-up
Isn't nice. (No, not nice.)
But whitewash will do it, lots of white will do it.
When the place caves in 'twill be too late.
Give us whitewash, boys, then we'll go to it
And we'll whitewash till we've got it all first-rate.
Here's the whitewash, let's not get upset!
Day and night we've got the stuff on hand.
This old shack will be a palace yet.
You'll get your New Order, just as planned.

[GW *Stücke*, tr. by Ralph Manheim, p. 936. This song origina-
ted as an appendage to Brecht's treatment ('The Bruise') for
The Threepenny Opera film, and was then taken into *The Round
Heads and the Pointed Heads*, where it is sung to a setting by
Hanns Eisler as an interlude between scenes 2 and 3.]

Editorial Note

Though *Ui* was among the most quickly written of all Brecht's plays we know little about its antecedents in his fertile mind. He himself spoke of it (in a journal entry for March 10, 1941) as inspired by thoughts of the American theatre and harking back to his New York visit of 1935, when he no doubt was made particularly aware of the Chicago gangs of the prohibition era and the films made about them by such firms as Warner Brothers and First National. The highly un-American name *Ui*, however, and its application to a Hitler-type leader, evidently originated slightly earlier when he was planning his never-finished prose work about the Tui's or Tellect-Ual-Ins, upside-down intellectuals whose ineffectiveness allowed such leaders to come to power. Walter Benjamin, making one of his visits to Brecht in Denmark in September 1934, noted that in addition to this more ambitious work Brecht was then writing a satire called *Ui* 'on Hitler in the style of a Renaissance historian'. This materialized in an unfinished and untitled short story set in classical Italy and describing an upstart city boss of Padua named Giacomo Ui, which can be found among Brecht's collected stories. Its style is deadpan, somewhat like that of the Julius Caesar novel which followed; its content is virtually the story of Hitler transposed into Roman terms. It resembles the eventual play in its depiction of the boss's rages, his aggressive ambitions, his currying of popular favour and even the way in which

> he was taught how to speak and walk by an old actor who had once in his heyday been permitted to play the mighty Colleone, and accordingly also taught him the latter's famous way of standing with his arms folded across his chest.

But the eight short sections of this story hardly get beyond establishing the character, and nothing is said about Hindenburg, the Reichstag Fire trial and the murder of Ernst Röhm, let alone the territorial annexations which were still to come. There are,

however, several allusions to that anti-Semitism which the play
curiously ignores (as do the notes on it) but which formed a
major theme of another play in mock-Elizabethan style dating
from 1934–35, *The Round Heads and the Pointed Heads* (which had
itself developed out of an adaptation of *Measure for Measure*
begun before 1933).

For years the three threads of gang warfare, the Ui-Hitler
satire, and the elevated Elizabethan style, seem to have lain
loosely coiled at the back of Brecht's mind before finally coming
together in the spring of 1941. A further element may have been
the example of Chaplin's *The Great Dictator*, even though Brecht
could hardly yet have seen the actual film. On March 10 he
roughed out a plan for ten or eleven scenes; by March 29 the
first typescript was complete; after which Margarete Steffin drove
him to tighten up the blank verse, another fortnight's work (all
this according to his journal). The complete play, virtually in its
present form, was ready about a month before the Brechts set out
on their trip to the United States, whose imminence had of course
helped to prompt it. There is thus much less than usual in the
way of alternative scripts and versions, most of the revisions,
such as they were, having been made directly on the first typescript. Many of them are primarily concerned with the iambic
metre of the verse.

However, it appears that the Cauliflower Trust originally contained another member called Reely, who appeared in lieu of
Butcher in scene 2. Dogsborough's first appearance was to have
been in his city office, not in the homely surroundings of his
restaurant, an amendment on the first script. In scene 3 Ui's first
speech was shorter, the present version only having been
established since the play's appearance in *Stücke IX* in 1957,
when not all Brecht's amendments were available. The first three
lines were as now, down to 'Is fame in such a place,' after which
the speech concluded

> Two months without a brawl
> And twenty shoot-outs are forgotten, even
> In our own ranks!

There were also differences in the wording of Roma's speech
which follows, though its sense was similar. In Scene 6, with the

old actor, Ui's and Givola's prose speeches were broken into irregular verse lines, and it was an afterthought to have Ui take over the Mark Antony speech from the actor and deliver most of it solo. The name 'Dockdaisy' too was an afterthought; to start with she was simply 'Mrs. Bowl' or 'the Person'. Clark's speech in scene 7, showing the trust's solidarity with Ui and his gang, was added at some point after the first script, together with Ui's ensuing speech down to where Clark is heard to applaud it (pp. 162–3). Then in the trial scene the playing of Chopin's Funeral March on the organ was an afterthought on the first script, as were all references to Giri's habit of wearing his murdered victims' hats (which echoes an incident at the beginning of *Happy End*, written in 1929). The first script ends with the woman's speech later shifted to scene 9 (i.e., immediately prior to the interval in the Berliner Ensemble production), this shift having been made after the play's publication in 1957. The epilogue was not in the first script.

When the play was finally staged by Palitzsch and Wekwerth in 1959 further changes were made, which were not included in the published text but were meant to take account of the changed public understanding of the historical background. According to Wekwerth, Brecht himself was long chary of staging this play in view of 'the German audience's lack of historical maturity'; he did not allow his younger collaborators even to read it until the summer before he died. They had to treat it as confidential, nor was it to be produced until they had first staged *Fear and Misery of the Third Reich* as an introduction to the tragic circumstances which it satirized. Thus warned, and well aware of the type of criticism voiced by Lothar Kusche (p. 357), the two directors now set to work to implicate Dogsborough and the industrialists more closely with Ui and to discourage German audiences from sympathizing with Roma. Ui accordingly was not referred to in scene 1a, and only entered the play once Sheet had refused to sell his shipping business in 1b. Dogsborough's packet of shares was given to him, not sold, while in scene 7 instead of seeming merely passive he was seen actually to give Ui his support. The episode with Goodwill and Gaffles was cut (pp. 146–8), to be replaced by a new section stressing the involvement of heavy industry. Roma was made to murder the journalist Ted Ragg, and scene 14 with his Banquoesque ghost was omitted; he still, however, emerged as a good deal less unpleasant than Giri and Givola. The name of Chicago was replaced by Capua or Capoha throughout. Finally an extra song was introduced, the 'Whitewash Song' from *The Round Heads and the Pointed Heads*, which Givola sang after the interval (pp. 364–5).

The main interest of the scripts, however, lies rather in the evidence which they give of Brecht's intentions with regard to the play. The title varies: once or twice it is simply *The Rise of Arturo Ui*, while the copy formerly belonging to Elisabeth Hauptmann is headed '*Arturo Ui*. Dramatic Poem. By K. Keuner' – Mr. Keuner (or Mr. Naobody) being the alter ego who features in Brecht's prose aphorisms, as well as figuring as a character in two of the unfinished plays. Elsewhere Brecht referred to *Ui* as 'the gangster play,' a title which he also tried rendering into English as *The Gangster Play We Know* or again *That Well-known Racket*. There is a table too, giving what he calls 'The Parallels', to wit:

Dogsborough = Hindenburg
Arturo Ui = Hitler
Giri = Göring
Roma = Röhm
Givola = Goebbels
Dullfeet = Dollfuss
Cauliflower Trust = Junkers (or East Prussian landowners)
Vegetable dealers = Petty bourgeoisie
Gangsters = Fascists
Dock aid scandal = 'Osthilfe' [East Aid] scandal
Warehouse-fire trial = Reichstag Fire trial
Chicago = Germany
Cicero = Austria

– Röhm having been Captain Ernst Röhm, chief of staff of the brownshirted S.A. or main Nazi private army, who was murdered in the 'Night of the Long Knives' in June 1934, while the Osthilfe scandal related to a controversial pre-1933 subsidy to the Junkers. There are also slightly varying versions of the historical analogies provided by the projected 'inscriptions'. Thus in the first script the inscription following scene 4 read:

In January 1933 President Hindenburg more than once refused to appoint Party Leader Hitler as Reich Chancellor. He was, however, nervous of the proposed investigation of the so-called 'Osthilfe' scandal. Moreover he had accepted state money for the Neudeck estate presented to him, but failed to use it for its intended objective.

After scene 8, the trial, there was a now-omitted inscription which read:

When Reich Chancellor Schleicher threatened to expose the tax evasions and misappropriation of 'Osthilfe' money, Hindenburg on 30 January 1933 gave power to Hitler. The investigation was suppressed.

That after scene 13 read as follows:

The occupation of Austria was preceded by the murder of Engelbert Dollfuss, the Austrian Chancellor. Tirelessly the Nazis continued their efforts to win Austrian sympathies.

– and the final inscription simply:

Perhaps there is something else that could stop him?

Further light on the play's topical meaning is given by the photographs stuck into the pages of Brecht's first script. Scene 2, with Dogsborough, is followed by a portrait of Hindenburg, scene 3 by a drawing of gangsters captioned 'Murder Inc.' In scene 6, with the old actor, there are four pictures of Hitler in his characteristic attitude with the hands clasped before the private parts, followed by two more with the arms folded and one captioned 'Hitler the Orator'. A further picture of Hitler speaking precedes the trial scene (8). In scene 10, following Givola's forgery of Dogsborough's will, there is a photograph of Hitler and Goebbels going over a document together, then at the end one of Hitler and Göring shaking hands. Scene 11 (the garage) is preceded by a picture showing Göring and Goebbels in uniform, while in scene 13 (Dullfeet's funeral) there is a photograph of a gangster funeral in Chicago.

MR PUNTILA AND HIS MAN MATTI

A Finnish Bacchus
by Hella Wuolijoki

'Enough of that,' said Madam Maria, laying her well-manicured white fingers on the table in a conclusive gesture. 'I insist that Farmer Punttila gets invited to my birthday. I am not having my daughter-in-law's father left out of the party.'

Toini sank her elegant teeth into her cake and passed the butter to her husband's father. He was a pillar of society: Consul, factory owner, engineer, and much more. 'All right. Then on your head be it, Mother. Nothing ever gets celebrated here without brandy, and Father will make such a fool of himself in front of your English guests that we shall never hear the last of it.'

The Consul said something inaudible behind his newspaper.

'Mother's just not thinking of the ghastly consequences there are bound to be,' said Maria's son, chief aide to his father and like him an engineer. 'But after all it's her birthday, and if Mother has set her mind on it there's nothing to be done.'

Maria smiled as she watched her sister-in-law distractedly shovelling sugar into her coffee. 'Leave a little space for the coffee, Hanna dear.' Miss Hanna pushed her cup aside. 'It's all very well for you to laugh, Maria, but you've never had to look after Farmer Punttila like I have.'

'Well, well,' said the master of the house, putting down his paper. 'That's not the worst of our worries. Fina, can you go and get me some hot coffee?'

Fina, the old parlourmaid in her neat white apron, gave a curtsey and disappeared.

'We must have something better for our foreign guests, either a proper butler or at least smarter servants than that rustic parlourmaid of yours.'

Madam Maria's coffee cup halted in mid-air, and this time her smile had more edge to it. 'You're quite wrong, Markus, if you think I'm going to turn our house upside down for your foreign guests, let alone make an Englishman's country seat out of it. Old Fina and my peasant girls will do their jobs properly and your guests can lump it. That's second nature to any well-brought-up visitor.'

'You win,' said the Consul, as he left the table. The engineer pushed his chair back. 'Mother, you really are impossible.' His wife folded up her napkin and put it in its sachet. 'Mother knows her own mind.' Maria and Aunt Hanna were left on their own.

'I like old Punttila,' said Madam Maria, 'better than I like his daughter. You shouldn't get so worked up, Hanna.'

Aunt Hanna peered venomously into her coffee cup. 'You ought to realise that Markus's position creates certain social obligations. And it is up to us to see that these foreign visitors get the right impression of our country.'

Maria gave a clear, disrespectful laugh, and Aunt Hanna went off in dudgeon.

❊   ❊   ❊

The evening before the birthday the main building of the home farm was lit up for the occasion, even though the lady of the house had gone to sleep following the usual eve-of-birthday serenade to which she had been treated. In the servants' hall sat the hosts' and guests' chauffeurs playing cards, while old Fina took them coffee. In the smoking-room the gentlemen sat over their brandies. They were noisy and at ease. The women were already asleep. Only Aunt Hanna went rustling round the house in her black satin, restless and ready to pounce. From the smoking room Punttila's voice could be heard topping the rest. While waiting for the serenade they had absorbed a few shots of brandy with their coffee, after which came further drinking.

The company was divided strictly according to language. On the sofa sat the English and Finnish bankers with their host, talking in English about the timber business and cursing the Russians for their dumping. By the porcelain stove, however, the prohibition laws were being treated with scant respect, the dominant figure being farmer Punttila, red as a brick, his hair ruffled, and around him the judge, the architect and the engineer. Every now and again Punttila went over to the foreign-language group and clinked glasses.

'So help me God,' said Mr Punttila, 'did I never tell you what happened to that landowner from Joensuu in Tavasthus when he celebrated his name day with Judge Tengbom? He left his coachman waiting for him outside the Park Hotel. The man was served his food and drink out there and slept with the hood over him. A week later they moved on to the City Hotel, where the landowner finally went to bed. Next morning his wife came to collect him. Didn't she look angry and hideous, and did she let him have it, hell! She sat down by his bedside with her tongue going like a millrace for hours on end. The old boy lay under the bedclothes quiet as a mouse, and when he finally got a chance to open his mouth he just whispered: "I say, Maria, fetch my cap from the Park Hotel and all your sins will be forgiven." You know old Tengbom, judge, don't you? A very good health to you Englishmen! My God, d'you know what Tengbom did then? Phew, what pretty girls that man had! What about giving the girls a bit of a song? At the tops of our voices now! Life's not all that bad under prohibition, is it? Do you Englishmen really know how to drink? Cheers to you, then!' A fresh bottle made its appearance on the table. Punttila and the judge struck up a resounding song.

Suddenly the smoking-room door sprang open, and there stood Aunt Hanna, a living reminder of life's blacker aspects. 'Come here, my girl, and sit on my lap,' called Punttila, stretching out a hand towards her. 'I suggest Johannes moderates his voice a bit,' said Miss Hanna, whereupon a marked silence descended. The banking gentlemen got politely to their feet, looked at their watches and were amazed at the lateness of the hour. And although Miss Hanna was offered a chair and sat down, one guest after another took his leave and the host went with them. Finally all that was left in the smoking-room was Punttila's group of drinkers. Then the brandy ran out.

'Bloody temperance home,' exclaimed the outraged Punttila. 'Markus's guests get treated no better than sawdust in this place. Have a heart, Hanna, and get us something to drink! We feel an exceptional urge to sing.'

'It is high time Johannes went to bed like the others, and he knows perfectly well that in this house all the alcohol is in my charge. The booze-up is over.'

Punttila thumped the table with his fist, but the rest of them drifted away. Aunt Hanna visited the card-playing chauffeurs with the same blistering success. Finally the whole house was quiet. The lights were put out, and the perpetual summer twilight revealed the solitary figure of farmer Punttila hunched over the empty glasses and bottles in the smoking-room.

'Bloody house, where they hang up the visitors' guts to dry like underwear!' Punttila's drunkenness was boosting his fiendish energy. He started feeling his way stumblingly through the darkened rooms till he found the door of Aunt Hanna's bedroom. Grabbing a chair he treated Aunt Hanna to a veritable serenade.

'Listen to me, you old squirrel, you old viper, don't you realise that farmer Punttila can get some aquavit into this temperance hotel if he wants to? Damme, Hanna, I'll show you how I can get liquor, and legal liquor at that!'

Punttila slammed the big front door behind him.

'Where is Punttila's chauffeur?'

But the yard was deserted. Dark and empty, the windows of the main house and its neighbouring buildings gazed down at the raging farmer. Nobody answered.

'Damn that for a lark, Punttila can find his own wagon.'

The doors of the garage where the guests' cars were slumbering were bolted. Punttila inspected the lock. 'Call that a lock? . . . God's sakes, I'll smash the whole place in!' A few resounding blows and the doors gaped open. Right at the front stood Punttila's Buick.

Firm foot on the accelerator, that's what it takes. A mudguard hits the door. Out, damned mudguard! What does one wretched mudguard cost? Johannes Punttila can get new ones any time he wants. Let's go!

The car followed a zigzag course from side to side of the road. 'I'll straighten out those curves, just watch me!'

In this way farmer Punttila pursued his narrow road to Heaven and rejoiced over each telegraph pole he managed to miss. 'Get out of my way!' he yelled at the telegraph pole at the entrance to the village, and lo! the pole evaded the car of so powerful a farmer.

The village was a fair size. How could one get hold of a prescription for alcohol?

But Punttila knew his way around. He stopped his car at the first hut he came to and started banging on the door as hard as he could.

'Haven't you a cow doctor in this village?' he yelled.

A sleepy old woman opened her window. 'What do you mean going round breaking down decent people's front doors, you drunken lout?'

'I'm just looking for the vet, my little dove,' said Punttila. 'I am farmer Punttila from Lammi, and all my thirty cows have scarlet fever.

So I need legal alcohol.'

'You sodden disgrace! You ought to be ashamed of yourself!'

'Hush, hush, my sweetheart, none of those nasty remarks or I shall smash up your dirty little hovel.'

After which farmer Punttila drove from end to end of the village promising to smash up their hovels, until he found the vet's house. There he leant on the horn of his Buick until the vet's grumpy and loud-mouthed wife opened an upper window. 'Go away! What do you mean by going round drunk, waking people up?'

'Please don't be cross, my darling. I am farmer Punttila from Tavastland, and back home my thirty cows have all got scarlet fever. I need legal alcohol.'

'My husband's asleep. Be off with you!'

'Is that the doctor's wife in person I'm addressing? I wish you a very good day. Kotkotkot, how pretty you are. Please tell the doctor right away that, back in his village, whenever farmer Punttila requires legal alcohol every vet in the place instantly prescribes him the correct dosage.'

The window slammed with a bang.

A renewed barrage on the door.

'Get out, man, I tell you!' and the angry face of the vet appeared at the window above.

'Why, there's the doctor himself. I am farmer Punttila from Tavastland, and my thirty cows have got scarlet fever. What's more I am the biggest bruiser in the whole of Tavastland, and when I want legal alcohol I get some.'

The vet understood his customer exactly and laughed. 'Ah well, if you are such a powerful gentleman then you'll have to have your prescription, I suppose.'

Punttila was most gratified. 'That's it. You are a true vet, ha ha. Come over to us some time and we'll celebrate in style.'

Punttila's car now headed for the chemist's. With one hand Punttila tended the steering wheel, with the other he brandished his prescription for legal alcohol.

The car halted outside the chemist's door. Then Punttila rattled the door violently till two furious women's faces appeared at the upstairs window.

'A very good morning to you. I am farmer Punttila from Tavastland and I've got thirty cows with scarlet fever and I urgently need alcohol.'

The chemist's assistant called down. 'You'd better clear off, an old soak like you disturbing folks' sleep.'

'The summer night was warm/As quiet slept the farm,' sang Punttila. 'Come down and open the door, my little turtledoves! Punttila wishes alcohol. Punttila is well aware that every second house in your village shelters an illegal still. But Punttila insists on having legal alcohol for his beloved cows. If I said my thirty cows had got glanders that, my darlings, would be a vulgar lie, but when I say that Johannes Punttila's cows are down with scarlet fever then it's as good as proven.'

The farmer went on arguing with the chemist's assistant till she opened up and got his alcohol. Back drove Punttila in the direction of the Consular estate.

Glug, glug, glug, went the schnapps bottle in his pocket, and Punttila's drunkenness was on the increase. The telegraph poles got more and more insolent and the road grew narrower and narrower.

'What a problem it is to get through,' sighed Punttila.

But he reached the estate with his honour unimpaired. Glug, glug, glug sang the congenial bottle as farmer Punttila reached Aunt Hanna's door, bottle held high.

'Do you know what I'm carrying in my belly, you miserable old maid? Legal alcohol, glug, glug, d'you hear the lovely music? Fancy thinking Johannes Punttila wasn't going to get his legal alcohol! Now we've something to lace our coffee with!'

The smoking-room was empty and the coffee cold. Punttila took a coffee with schnapps, but in the absence of company it didn't taste as it should. So Punttila went off to find some.

With some difficulty he located the judge's room. 'Hey, judge, look what I've brought you. Come on, just look,' said Punttila, and the judge looked blearily from his bed.

'You've got a bottle, so you have. And now good night.'

'I'm telling you it's a schnapps bottle, judge! Look at the official label, that means legal alcohol.'

The judge turned his face to the wall. 'The court will take a recess,' he murmured and promptly went back to sleep.

Punttila stood there wrapped in thought, observing the judge so prettily asleep between the white bedclothes.

'Too bad you aren't a woman,' sighed Punttila as he felt his way once more through the house. This time he and his bottle managed to locate the kitchen, from which sounds of early morning activity could already be heard.

*   *   *

The mistress of the house was accustomed to waking very early. Today she was fifty. She saw that it was a fine summer morning, thought a little about her life to date, and decided that thinking about it wasn't worth the trouble. She started listening to the sounds of the house. The silence had something menacing about it. She recalled the serenade and the company the previous evening, with Punttila's throaty and compellingly joyous voice following its own erratic path high above all the rest. She was aware of sinister premonitions and could feel the gnawings of conscience.

Madam Maria dressed rapidly and went downstairs. Familiar voices could be heard from the farm kitchen. There sat farmer Punttila with his fortified coffee. Across the table from him three beady-eyed ladies were sitting in judgement on him with severe expressions: Punttila's own two daughters with their golden hair and milk-white complexions, and grumpy Aunt Hanna. The three had gone through the entire litany of all Punttila's sins, from the first bottle to the last, but quite without success. Punttila sat there, his powerful body still buoyed up by the booze, with beaming face and rampant hair. Those fearsome females had caught him in that room, where he had been flirting with the cook and kissing the maid; for he had even been courting old Fina. 'Anyway, Fina, you're better than nothing.'

Punttila had told the story of his nocturnal adventures at least ten times over: how he had driven off to look for legal alcohol and threatened to smash the hovels in. He was overjoyed to see Madam Maria, and started telling it all over again. He was delighted to find that he made her laugh. Then some of the chauffeurs came into the kitchen, so the farmer had to repeat it all once more. The women took the opportunity to move into the dining-room for a council of war.

Maria's daughter-in-law Toini started sobbing: 'What are we to do with him?' 'Chuck him in the lake and drown him where it's deepest,' suggested Aunt Hanna. 'Then Auntie will have to winkle him out of the kitchen before she drowns him,' sighed the other daughter. The mistress of the house laughed: 'If only we could confine him to the kitchen.'

'You asked for it, Maria. Mind out for your dining-room when the guests come down to breakfast. How do you think it's going to look?' hissed Aunt Hanna.

Madam Maria looked out of the window: 'Keep your hair on, children. Let him be his own self, even if it's only when he's drunk.'

Aunt Hanna raised her hands to heaven. 'I wish you joy of whatever happens. Come along, girls.'

Meanwhile farmer Punttila was sitting in the kitchen, an arm round each of the two chauffeurs. 'Shut the door so those women don't disturb us again. Drink up, my boys, farmer Punttila has got legal alcohol. Punttila doesn't give a damn whether you're communists or socialists, so long as you do your job like clockwork. Yes, boys, chopping down the forests and ploughing the fields and digging out stones! That's proper work for a human being. In Punttila's young days there wasn't a bull that he hadn't wrestled on to its back. But don't imagine for one minute, boys, that they'd have let me go on working like that. I married my sawmill and my cornmill and got a couple of respectable daughters, and it's not done for Daddy to plough. It's not done for Daddy to tickle the girls and it's not done for Daddy to lie in the fields with his workers and eat the same meal. Damn it all, boys, nothing's done any longer as far as I'm concerned. But with you I can let my hair down. Listen, Jussi, here's a hundred marks for you. And one for you too, Kalle! And now we'll celebrate till the windows rattle. There'll be something for you, of course there's always something for you. There was that bathroom maid came and asked me to raise her wages because there wasn't enough for the kids. Of course I let her have it. Do you want more wages, boys, do you? But all they do at the sawmill is laugh and say I've had a drop too much. What business is that of theirs? Farmer Punttila gives and gives, because everybody must have it good, socialists, communists and the bourgeoisie. There's such a variety of us, we've got to get along together. Everyone can get along with Punttila.' And Punttila sang: '"Dear child, why sue me when you said/We always felt so close in bed?"

'You know, boys, why Punttila loves the entire world? The whole of humanity is good and nice. Have another coffee and schnapps. I shan't be able to take my sawmill and my steam mill and the estate into the grave with me, shall I? It's all got to stay here. Drink up, Jussi, drink, Kalle! We're all brothers in drink. There was a time when we fought to beat each other, and life was ugly, really ugly. But now it's possible to live again. The world is big enough, and there'll be enough for you and enough for farmer Punttila too. Cheers, Kalle!'

They went on cheerfully toping till the old housekeeper beckoned Kalle and Jussi into the back kitchen, after which Punttila again started mooching around, this time in the direction of the dining-room, which is two daughters at once left to dry their tears upstairs while Aunt Hanna went to the master of the house to ask for help.

In the dining-room Madam Maria waited for her guests, inwardly praying that they would sleep on until the Punttila problem had been painlessly deflected. To no effect. The English bank representative arrived first, since he was in the habit of getting up early despite the late night and the brandy.

When Aunt Hanna and her acolytes arrived back downstairs a strange performance greeted them. Beside the Englishman sat farmer Punttila, his hair unkempt, his face flushed by an inner dawn. He was alternately embracing the banker and embracing his bottle. At the end of the table sat Madam Maria telling the enchanged Englishman the story of Punttila's nocturnal escapades and how he had managed to get hold of his legal alcohol. Punttila patted the Englishman on the back and enthusiastically told him: 'You're just like a proper Finn, mate.'

The Englishman gave Punttila a friendly nod and laughed: 'A Finnish Bacchus!'

But Punttila thumped his barrel chest and asked: 'Did Maria go on to tell you that I threatened to smash all their hovels?'

In the golden morning light the silver shone, the cups clinked and old Fina in her snowy white apron poured coffee for Punttila and the bank director, while the village girl Selma handed round golden honey, jam and fragrant Finnish bread.

The Englishman approved heartily of what he saw of Fina, and said he couldn't stand those starchy English maids and menservants whom you had to address by their surnames. He envied his hostess.

*   *   *

In their bedroom that evening, when the celebrations were all over, the young engineer was talking to his wife, Punttila's daughter: 'Did you notice the way Mother, the Englishmen, Fina and your father were winking at one another? I have a feeling, Toini, that it was a conspiracy of the more tolerant and civilised element against ourselves.'

Madam Toini gave a yawn: 'Rubbish. I could have sunk into the floor when I saw that schnapps bottle glinting on the table. You can't imagine what embarrassments my sister Martha and I have always had to undergo when in society.'

Toini was overwhelmed by self-pity.

In the next room slept farmer Punttila, who towards evening had grown sober and silent. He lay there on his own, full of resentment against Aunt Hanna, who had taken their hundred mark notes away from Jussi and Kalle. Next time Punttila was planning to give the lads two hundred marks apiece, and to do so under Aunt Hanna's nose.

[From *Brecht-Jahrbuch 1978*, edited by John Fuegi, Reinhold Grimm and Jost Hermand (Suhrkamp, Frankfurt, 1978, pp. 96 – 106). Translated into German from the original Finnish by Margareta N. Deschner]

Texts by Brecht

A NOTE OF 1940

The reader and, more important, the actor may be inclined to skim over passages such as the short dialogue between judge and lawyer (about the Finnish summer) in the sixth scene, because they use a homely way of speaking. However, the actor will not be performing the passage effectively unless he treats it as a prose poem, since it is one. Whether it is a good or a bad poem is not at this point relevant; the reader or actor can make up his own mind about that. The relevant thing is that it has to be treated as a poem, i.e., in a special manner, 'presented on a silver platter.' Matti's hymn of praise to the herring in scene 9 is an even better instance, perhaps. There is more than one situation in *Puntila* which would undoubtedly seem crude in a naturalistic play; for instance, any actor who plays the episode where Matti and Eva stage a compromising incident (scene 4) as if it were an episode from a farce will entirely fail to bring it off. This is exactly the kind of scene that calls for real virtuosity, as again do the tests to which Matti subjects his betrothed in scene 8. To cite the casket scene in *The Merchant of Venice* is not to propose any kind of qualitative comparison; though the scene may fall a long way short of Shakespeare's it can still only be made fully effective if one finds a way of acting something like that demanded by a verse play. Admittedly it is hard to speak of artistic simplicity rather than primitiveness when a play is written in prose and deals with 'ordinary' people. All the same the expulsion of the four village women (in scene 7) is not a primitive episode but a simple one, and as with the third scene (quest for legal alcohol and fiancées) it has to be played poetically; in other words the beauty of the episode (once again, be it big or be it small) must come across in the set, the movements, the verbal expression. The characters too have to be portrayed with a certain grandeur, and this again is something that will be none too easy for the actor who has only learnt to act naturalistically or fails to see that naturalistic acting is not enough in this case. It will help him if he realizes that it is his job to create a national character, and that this is going to call for all his sensitivity, daring, and knowledge of humanity. One last point: *Puntila* is far from being a play with a message. The Puntila part therefore must not for an instant be in any way deprived of its natural attractiveness, while particular artistry will be needed to make the drunk scenes delicate and poetic, with the maximum of variety, and the sober scenes as ungrotesque and unbrutal as possible. To put it in practical terms: Puntila has if possible to be staged in a style combining elements of the old commedia dell' arte and of the realistic play of mores.

> [GW *Schriften zum Theater*, pp. 1167–8. This is the section bearing specifically on *Puntila* from the general essay 'Notes on the Folk Play' (or 'People's Play'), written in 1940, which will be included in Brecht's theatrical writings (and can meanwhile be found in *Brecht on Theatre*, pp. 153–7). It was originally prefaced by the words 'To take some instances from *Puntila*. . . .']

NOTES ON THE ZURICH PREMIÈRE

1

Instead of the conventional curtain falling like a guillotine to chop the play into separate scenes, back to the lightly fluttering half-height linen curtain with the scene titles projected on it. During scene changes this curtain was somewhat lit so as to make it come to life and allow the audience to become more or less aware of the busy preparations being made for them on the stage. In particular they saw the upper parts of the big wall sections as they were shifted in, and they saw the sun's disc and the moon's sickle being lowered on wires, not yet illuminated and therefore visibly made of metal; they also saw the various little clouds being changed around.

2

These emblems for sun, moon, and clouds hung, like inn or shop signs, before the high broad wall of birch bark that constituted the background of the *Puntila* stage. According as to whether it was day, half-light, or night the wall was lit strongly, feebly, or not at all; the acting area being fully illuminated the while. In this way the atmospheric element was established in the background, independently of the rest of the performance.

3

No use was made of coloured light of any sort. Provided the lighting equipment is up to it the light should be as uniform as for a variety performance which includes the display of acrobatics. Sharply defined spotlighting would blot out the faces. Areas of darkness, even if only relative, detract from the words issuing from them. It is a good idea to have photographs taken to find out what kind of lighting is liable to strain the audience.

4

Colour and contrast can be supplied by the stage designer without having recourse to coloured light. The colour scheme for *Puntila* comprised blue, grey, and white for the stage, and black, grey, and white for the costumes. On top of this the latter were strictly realistic, with particular respect for details (the village women's handbags; the farm workers working barefoot on Sunday in their best trousers, shirts, and waistcoats, etc.).

5

All working processes must be shown in proper detail. (An actress who happened to have a child's figure turned Fina the maid into a memorable character by showing her working late at the washing (6), carrying butter (7) and falling asleep exhausted during Mr Puntila's engagement party (9).)

6

The permanent framework consisted of the great birch bark wall at the back already mentioned with thin structures of gold rods on either side downstage. The sets were composed of separate elements, those in the first scene for instance being (a) a wooden panelled wall with table, chairs, tablecloth covered with bottles of red wine, and a dozen empties grouped on the floor; and (b) a potted palm (the luxury element). Elements like those of the sixth scene, with its courtyard gateway and its main entrance to the house, could be definitively placed during the rehearsals. A further luxury element was a trashy plaster statuette in the second scene, whereas the slaughtered pig of scene 5, suspended from a scaffolding made of carmine-coloured joists and a brass rod, was no luxury element since it told of the preparations for the engagement banquet and was to be carried across the courtyard in the next scene. Importance was attached to the beauty and ease of the elements and the charm of their combination. At the same time they had to be realistic. Though the car in scene 3 consisted only of a truncated forepart it had been made from authentic components.

7

That the various stage elements, the costumes and the props should all look worn not only contributes to realism but also relieves the stage of that new, untested look.

8

Meaning, spatial dispositions, and colour must be such that every glimpse of the stage captures an image worth seeing.

9

The German language has no term for that aspect of mime which is known to the English stage as 'business', and we tend to introduce it half-heartedly, in an embarrassed way. Our word Kiste [literally, 'box'] which we use instead, shows the contempt in which it is held. All the same, Kisten [pieces of business] are essential components of narrative theatre. (*Puntila walks dryshod across the aquavit* (1); *Puntila hires a woodcutter because he likes his eyes* (4); *the women of Kurgela see butter, meat, and beer entering their fiancé's house* (7), and so on.) Such things were of course played for all they were worth. This was greatly helped by the 'one thing after another' principle, which any dramaturgy founded on exposition, climax, and thickening of the plot is always having to disregard.

10

The decisive point is the establishment of the class antagonism between Puntila and Matti. Matti must be so cast as to bring about a true balance, i.e., so as to give him intellectually the upper hand. The actor playing Puntila must be careful not to let his vitality or charm in the drunk scenes so win over the audience that they are no longer free to look at him critically.

11

Among the play's nobler characters are the four women from Kurgela. It would be completely wrong to portray them as comic; rather they are full of humour. They would anyway have to be attractive, if only because their expulsion must be attributable to no other cause then their inferior status.

12

Possible cuts: Scene 4 (The Hiring Fair) is deleted. But parts of it are used in the following scene (Scandal at Puntila Hall).

Then scene 5 begins as follows:

The yard at Puntila Hall. A bath-hut, the interior of which is visible. Forenoon. Over the door leading into the house Laina the cook and Fina the maid are nailing a sign saying 'Welcome to the Engagement Party!'

Puntila and Matti come in through the gate, followed by a few workers.

LAINA: Welcome back. Miss Eva and His Excellency and His Honour are here, and they're all having breakfast.

PUNTILA: First thing I want to know is what's the matter with Surkkala. Why is he packing?

LAINA: You promised the parson you'd get rid of him because he's a Red.

PUNTILA: What, Surkkala? The only intelligent tenant I've got? Besides, he has four children. What must he think of me? Parson be buggered, I'll forbid him the house for his inhumanity. Send Surkkala here right away, I want to apologise to him and his family. Send the children too, all four of them, so I can express my personal regret for the fear and insecurity they must have been through.

LAINA: No call for that, Mr Puntila.

PUNTILA, *seriously*: Oh yes there is. *Pointing to the workers*: These gentlemen are staying. Get them all an aquavit, Laina. I'm taking them on to work in the forest.

LAINA: I thought you were selling the forest.

PUNTILA: Me? I'm not selling any forest. My daughter's got her dowry between her legs, right? And I've brought these men home because I can't stand those hiring fairs. If I want to buy a horse or a cow I'll go to a fair without thinking twice about it. But you're human beings, and it's not right for human beings to be bargained over in a market. Am I right?

THE WEEDY MAN: Absolutely.

MATTI: Excuse me, Mr Puntila, but you're not right. They want work and you've got work, and whether it's done at a fair or in church it's still buying and selling.

PUNTILA: Brother, would you inspect me to see if my feet are crooked, the way you inspect a horse's teeth?

MATTI: No. I'd take you on trust.

PUNTILA, *indicating the weedy-looking man*: That fellow wouldn't be bad. I like the look in his eye.

MATTI: Mr Puntila, I don't want to speak out of turn, but that man's no use to you, he'll never be able to stand it.

THE WEEDY MAN: Here, I like that. What tells you I'll never be able to stand it?

MATTI: An eleven-and-a-half-hour day in summer. It's just that I don't want to see you let down, Mr Puntila. You'll only have to throw him out when he cracks up.

PUNTILA: I'm going into the sauna. Tell Fina to bring me some coffee. While I'm undressing you go and fetch two or three more so I can take my pick.

He goes into the bath hut and undresses, Fina brings the workers aquavit.

MATTI, *to Fina*: Get him some coffee.

THE RED-HEADED MAN: What's it like up at Puntila Hall?

MATTI: So-so. Four quarts of milk. Milk's good. You get potatoes too, I'm told. Room's on the small side.

THE RED-HEADED MAN: How far's school? I've got a little girl.

MATTI: About an hour's walk.

THE RED-HEADED MAN: That's nothing in fine weather. What's he like?

MATTI: Too familiar. It won't matter to you, you'll be in the forest, but I'm with him in the car, I can't get away from him and before I know where I am he's turning all human on me. I can't take it much longer.

Surkkala comes in with his four children.

MATTI: Surkkala! For God's sake clear off right away. Once he's had his bath and knocked back his coffee, he'll be stone cold sober and better look out if he catches you around the yard. Take my advice, you'll keep out of his sight the next day or two.

Surkkala nods and is about to hasten away with the children.

PUNTILA, *who has undressed and listened but failed to hear the end of this, peers out of the bath hut and observes Surkkala and the children*: Surkkala! I'll be with you in a moment. *To Matti*: Give him ten marks earnest money.

MATTI: Yes, but can't you make up your mind about this lot? They'll miss the hiring fair.

PUNTILA: Don't rush me. I don't buy human beings in cold blood. I'm offering them a home on the Puntila estate.

THE RED-HEADED MAN: Then I'm off. I need a job. *He goes.*

PUNTILA: Stop! He's gone. I could have used him. *To the weedy man*: Don't let him put you off. You'll do the work all right. I give you my word of honour. You understand what that means, the word of a Tavastland farmer? Mount Hatelma can crumble, it's not very likely but it can, but the word of a Tavastland farmer stands for ever, everyone knows that. *To Matti*: Come inside, I need you to pour the water over me. *To the weedy man*: You can come in too.

(Unchanged from p. 246, line 8 to p. 249, line 16. Then:)

PUNTILA, *to Fina*: Now this is what I've decided, and I want you to listen so what I say doesn't get twisted around later as it usually does. *Indicating one of the labourers*: I'd have taken that one, but his trousers are too posh for me, he's not going to strain himself. Clothes are the thing to look out for: too good means he thinks he's too good to work, too torn means he's got a bad character. It's all right for a gardener, for instance, to go around in patched trousers so long as it's the knees are patched, not the seat, yes, with a gardener it has to be the knees. I only need one look to see what's a man's made of, his age doesn't matter, if he's old he'll carry as much or more because he's frightened of being turned off, what I go by is the man himself. Intelligence is no use to me, that lot spend all day totting up their hours of work. I don't like that, I'd sooner be on friendly terms with my men. *To a strongly built labourer*: You can come along, I'll give you your earnest money inside. And that reminds me. *To Matti, who has emerged from the bath hut*: Give me your jacket. You're to hand over your jacket, d'you hear? *He is handed Matti's jacket.* Got you boyo. *Shows him the wallet*: What do I find in your pocket? Had a feeling about you, spotted you for an old lag first go off. Is that my wallet or isn't it?

MATTI: Yes, Mr Puntila.

PUNTILA: Now you're for it, ten years' gaol, all I have to do is ring the police.

MATTI: Yes, Mr Puntila.

PUNTILA: But that's a favour I'm not doing you. So you can lead the life of Riley in a cell, lying around and eating the taxpayer's bread, what? That'd suit you down to the ground. At harvest time too. So you'd get out of driving the tractor. But I'm putting it all down in your reference, you get me?

MATTI: Yes, Mr Puntila

Puntila walks angrily towards the house. On the threshold stands Eva, carrying her straw hat. She has been listening.

THE WEEDY MAN: Should I come along then, Mr Puntila?

PUNTILA: You're no use to me whatever, you'll never stand it.

THE WEEDY MAN: But the hiring fair's over now.

PUNTILA: You should have thought of that sooner instead of trying to take advantage of my friendly mood. I remember exactly who takes advantage of it. *To the labourer who has followed him*: I've thought it over and I'm taking nobody at all. I'll probably sell the forest, and you can blame it on him there [*he points at Matti*] for deliberately leaving me in the dark about something I needed to know, the bastard. I'll show him. *Exit into the house, brooding.*

(Then unchanged from p. 250, line 13 on.)

[GW *Schriften zum Theater*, pp. 1169–73, and GW *Stücke*, pp. 1713–17, which originally were consecutive. Written in 1948 and first published in *Versuche 10*, 1950. For the Zurich première of June 5, 1948, the scene designer was Teo Otto. Puntila was played by Leonard Steckel, Matti by Gustav Knuth.]

NOTES ON THE BERLINER ENSEMBLE PRODUCTION

1. Prologues, inter-scene songs, and scene titles

Our new audience, being engaged in building a new life for itself, insists on having its say and not just accepting what happens on the stage ('That's how things are and what's to change them?'); it doesn't like having to guess the playwright's viewpoint. Prologues, songs during scene changes, and the occasional projection of scene titles on the half-curtain all make for direct contact with the audience. The actress playing the dairymaid, Regine Lutz, delivered a short verse prologue with a bunch of everlastings in her hand. For the Zurich production there were scene titles [examples as in our text are cited]. Prologues are to be found in the classic drama, scene titles however only in the classic adventure story. They put the audience in a state of mild suspense and lead it to look for something definite in the scene that follows. In the Berliner Ensemble production the scene titles were dropped in favour of the singing of the Puntila song. Annemarie Hase, playing the cook, stepped before the curtain carrying whatever household utensils she happened to be working with, thus making it possible to follow the various stages of the great Puntila engagement party. Her song was accompanied on the other side of the stage by two musicians who had appeared before the curtain carrying a guitar and a piano accordion. The song gave a running commentary on events at Puntila Hall as viewed from the kitchen, and by making them celebrated as it were, turned Mr Puntila's escapades into aspects of local history.

2. Some principles of the production illustrated

This play's satire is of a poetic kind. The director's task therefore is to translate its poetic features into memorable images.

At the beginning of the play, for instance, we encounter a Puntila of almost mythological grandeur. He is the triumphant last survivor of a veritable flood of spirituous liquors, in which all his drinking companions have drowned. [...]

The director accordingly must conjure up Puntila's moan of isolation and his berating of the inadequate judge; Puntila's encounter with a human being (Puntila is on the dining table demonstrating how one walks across a sea of aquavit when he catches sight of Matti. He has to clamber down and steer a wide course round the gratuitously large table in order to greet Matti and bring him back to the table); the revealing of his dreadful malady (Puntila formally creeps into the protesting Matti); Matti's ghost story (while he eats he recalls those who are being starved on the big landed estates); Puntila promoting Matti to be a friend and then consulting him about his own personal affairs (to solve his shabby problems Puntila keeps Matti up when he would much rather go home and go to bed); Matti leading a subdued Puntila out of the hotel (again a wide tour of the table, Puntila having confidingly and ceremoniously handed him the wallet containing his despised money).

3   The way people work

Showing how work is actually done is something the bourgeois theatre finds uninteresting; the usual solution is to botch up any old thing. It is essential that Matti, the chauffeur, should work deftly, whether he is changing a tyre as he talks to the landowner's daughter, or sweeping out the yard, or massaging Puntila, or dragging out the drunken judge. Likewise the kitchenmaid's serving of coffee, soaking of linen, and carrying of butter all have to be got right.

4. Puntila's drunkenness

The actor playing Puntila will find that his chief problem is how to portray the drunkenness which makes up 90 per cent of the part. It would seem unacceptably repellent were he to contribute the conventional drunk act, in other words to demonstrate a state of intoxication blurring over and devaluing every physical and mental process. The drunkenness played by Steckel was the drunkenness specific to Puntila, i.e. that through which the landowner achieves his semblance of humanity. Far from exhibiting the usual impairments of speech and physical movement, he displayed a rhythmical, almost musical way of speaking and relaxed, almost ballet-like movements. Admittedly a certain handicap was imposed on his inspiration by the weight of his limbs, which was too great for those superterrestrial motions which he had in mind. He ascended Mount Hatelma on wings, albeit slightly defective ones. Each of the monster's drunken gests – of meekness, anger at injustice, generosity in giving and taking, comradeship, and what not – was developed with gusto. Puntila abandoned his possessions like a Buddha, disowned his daughter as in the Bible, invited the Kurgela women to be his guests like some Homeric monarch.

5   Steckel's two Puntilas

Before playing Puntila in Berlin Steckel had played him in Zurich. There he played almost without makeup, and the impression gained by most of the audience was of a likeable man subject to the occasional nasty turn when in a state of sobriety, which state being tantamount to a hangover the turns seemed excusable. In Berlin, in view of these effects, he opted for a foully shaped bald head and made himself up with debauched and debased features. Only now did his drunken charm seem menacing and his sociable approaches like those of a crocodile. Nearly all German performances of this play, whether before or after the Berlin production, suffered from the same mistake as was made in Zurich.

6.   Socially based humour

There is little that a play like *Puntila* can take from the rag-bag of 'timeless humour.' True, even in 'timeless humour' there is a social element – the clown sets out brimming with self-confidence and falls flat on his face – but it has become overlaid to the point where the clown's fall appears like something purely biological, something that is humorous to all people under all conditions. The actors who perform *Mr Puntila and his Man Matti* must derive their humour from the prevailing class situation, even if that means there are one or two classes whose members will not laugh. When the happily reintoxicated landowner gets Matti to build him a Mount Hatelma from the billiard-room furniture, Matti does so with anger, because even in the depths of drunkenness Puntila did not omit to sack Red Surkkala. Relentlessly he demolishes gun cabinet and grandfather clock; this is going to be an expensive mountain. At each crash Puntila winces and his smile becomes forced.– In the village Puntila listens to the life stories of the Kurgela girls, but he does not listen properly because he knows what is coming and takes a long pull of 'legal alcohol' after every story. The humour is of a gloomy sort.– If the landowner takes the women's 'Plum' song as a personal tribute that is traditional humour and unexceptionable. But there is added depth if he appears somehow interested in folklore and adopts a knowledgeable expression. It shows up the cleft which is the theme of the play.– In scene 4 Puntila brings a group of agricultural workers back from the hiring fair. It is the one day in the year when they are able to find jobs, and Puntila has no use for them; he just wants company. He at once raises one man's hopes ('I like the look in his eye'). Then he breaks through the ring of workers surrounding him and hastens into the sauna in order to sober up enough to get the strength to throw the workers out. The cravenness of this flight into sobriety is a stroke of humour that can scarcely be achieved except by an actor with social understanding and socialist principles.

7. The women of Kurgela

From the outset the portrayal of those women of Kurgela whom Puntila invites to his estate when drunk and throws out when sober presented great problems. These are the noblest characters in the play, and in planning their costumes and makeup we hestitated a long time between the beautiful and the characteristic before realising that these are not really opposites. To give a fairy-tale quality to the story of the four early risers we started by making stylised costumes with very delicate colours, then thought them boring and plumped for naturalism without regard for beauty. This led to outsize boots and long noses. Then Caspar Neher intervened. Full of scepticism, he came to the rehearsals and produced a batch of scene designs that are among the most beautiful things which our generation has created for the theatre. He solved the problem of how to reconcile the women's naïve behaviour with their practical worldly wisdom by having them play a light-hearted game with the landowner. With jokes and a bit of play-acting they confronted the landowner as a body, as the legendary 'Women of Kurgela', biblical brides hoping for a dance and a coffee from their bridegroom on high. Neher made them don straw garlands, and he endowed the chauffeur Matti too with imagination, devising the broom which he sticks in the ground and addresses as the High Court at Viborg, and also uses to sweep up the garlands when they have thrown them down in the yard following their unpleasant reception. Now that their behaviour had been got right there was virtually no problem in making the costumes and makeup beautiful. The cut of the costumes remained realistic, but their contours were somewhat stressed and identical material was used for all of them. The faces were given a certain uncouth, peasant quality – we began by testing the effect of crumbled cement which we tried out on plaster casts – while a golden complexion was created by covering them with warm-toned pounded ochre. The big shoes, retained for one of the women, in no way detracted from the beauty which came above all from the dignity of these working women. Starting as poor guests, they became rich in kindliness, ready and willing to bestow their humour even on a landowner; from poetic figures they turned into real people with a feeling for poetry. Composed by a great painter, the groupings lent grace and power to their natural, realistic demeanour.

8.   Caspar Neher's Puntila stage

The symbolist stage of Expressionists and Existentialists, which expresses general ideas, is of no use to a realistic theatre, nor can we go back to the naturalistic stage with its crude mixture of the relevant and the irrelevant. A mere echo of the real world is not enough; it must be not only recognisable but also understandable. This means that the images have to be artistically valid and to display an individual handwriting. Wit and imagination are specially desirable in the designer of a comedy.

9.   The masks

Puntila, the Attaché, the parson, parson's wife, lawyer, and judge all wore more or less grotesque masks and moved in a foolish, regal manner. Matti, the women of Kurgela, the hired hands, and the agricultural workers wore no masks and moved normally. An exception was made for Eva, the landowner's daughter; she had no mask. Any suggestion that this amounts to symbolism would be unfounded. No hidden significance is intended. The theatre is simply adopting an attitude and heightening significant aspects of reality, to wit, certain physiognomical malformations to be found in parasites.

10. Is a play like *Mr Puntila and his Man Matti* still relevant to us now that the big estates have been got rid of?

There is an attractive kind of impatience which would have the theatre only present things in their current real-life state. Why waste time on an estate owner? Haven't we got rid of such people? Why show a proletarian like Matti? Don't we have more active fighters? Likeable as such impatience is, it should not be given way to. The fact that alongside those works of art which we have to organise there are certain works of art that have come down to us is only a valid argument if the usefulness of the latter can be proved, never mind how much time is needed to organise the former. Why can *Mr Puntila and his Man Matti* still be regarded as a play with relevance? Because not only the struggle but the history of that struggle is instructive. Because past eras leave a deposit in people's souls for a long time. Because the class struggle demands that victory in one area of conflict be exploited so as to promote victory in another, and in both cases the situation prior to victory may be similar. Because, like all pioneers, people who have been liberated from their oppressors may at first have a hard life, since they have to replace the oppressors' system with a new one. These are the sorts of arguments that can be adduced to show the relevance of plays like *Mr Puntila and his Man Matti*.

[1. 4 and 10 from GW SzT 1173–5, the rest from pp. 18–45 of *Theaterarbeit* (1950), for which these notes were written. They refer to the Berliner Ensemble production of 1949, in which Puntila was played initially by Steckel once more, and later by the comedian Curt Bois. Paul Dessau's setting of the songs was written for this. The last note is an answer to some of Brecht's East German critics.]

NOTES ON THE PUNTILA FILM

1 About the script for *Puntila*

As it stands the script doesn't seem right to me. It is true that it follows the general line which Pozner and I agreed on, but in the course of its realisation the story has lapsed into a genre which makes it not so much comic as ridiculous. It has become a drawing-room comedy in which the crude jokes of the play jar and seem merely crude. Nor is it clear *who* is telling the entire story or from what point of view. The film company, it would seem, and from the point of view of making a film. The Puntila tales have of course to be told from below, from the position of the people. Then characters like Matti and Eva Puntila can be seen in the right light. The present script turns Matti into a feeble, indefinite figure; it fails to bring out how despite and because of their master/man relationship he is in continual opposition to his employer in every line he says. What makes Eva Puntila 'love' him is not his muscles – it would be all the same if he had none – but the fact that he is a proper man, humorous, dominating and so forth. Nor of course must he for one instant imagine that Eva is the right wife for him or that Mr Puntila would really let him have her. His *test* is simply a way of deflating Eva and Puntila's romantic notion. It has to remain a game if Matti is not to be made into an idiot.

We have made a new outline, since I realise that the studio cannot wait. As the poetic material is already at hand the preparation of a new shooting script would be a remarkably quick business. Given the script as it is I would find it quite impossible to turn the new dialogue (which makes up at least half the total dialogue and is entirely naturalistic) into Puntila-German, because the situations are naturalistic and in my view false. Nor if this script were used could I under any circumstances allow the use of my name or the name *Puntila*. I am not by any means out to make difficulties, but neither do I wish to damage my reputation as a writer. I am sure you will understand this.

2 New story line for *Puntila*

1. Hotel Tavasthus

Surrounded by passed-out drunks and dead-tired waiters, a man is traversing a vast table covered with plates of meat and bottles: it is Mr

Puntila. He claims to be able to walk dry-shod across the sea of aquavit represented to him by the table top. Another man addresses him, and turns out to be his chauffeur whom he has left waiting outside for two days and a night. Feeling lonely and abandoned by his too easily intoxicated friends – the judge, the teacher, and so on – Puntila instantly becomes bosom pals with his chauffeur Matti and discusses with him his most intimate concerns, i.e. his daughter Eva's forthcoming engagement to an attaché. For this a dowry is required, so he must sell a forest. To postpone the decision Puntila has got drunk. They decide to have another look at the forest.

2. *Forest*

Puntila realises that the forest is too beautiful to sell. Sooner than that he will marry Widow Klinckmann, who is rich and the owner of the Kurgela estate, but whom he last saw fifty years ago. Off to Kurgela.

3. *Kurgela*

Rousing the sleepy domestics Puntila pushes his way through them into Widow Klinckmann's bedroom. One look is enough: the widow is too hideous to sell himself to.

4. *The Village of Kurgela Next Day*

Fleeing from Widow Klinckmann and avid for beauty, Puntila meets three young women, is upset by the sadness of their lives and instantly becomes engaged to them. He tells them to come to Puntila Hall on the following Sunday. The young women take this as a jest on the part of a well-to-do drunk gentleman, and laughingly promise they will come. The telephone operator, last of the three, advises him to drive to the hiring fair at Lammi, where he will meet another estate owner called Bibelius who wants to buy his forest. He will recognise him by his butterfly tie-pin. Since the forest has to be sold after all, Puntila decides to drive to Lammi.

5. *Hiring Fair*

The alcoholic effects are wearing off. Puntila gives vent to some intelligent and ill-natured remarks about servants. Drinks coffee laced with rum, and apologises to Matti. Discloses his malady and asks Matti for moral support. Engages four cripples because he likes them as people. Sees a fat man beating a horse and tells him where to get off. On Matti and the workers expressing their enthusiastic approval he learns that he has just beaten up the man who wants to buy his forest. This sobers him up, and he gets gloomily into his car without offering a lift to the labourers.

'Home,' he says curtly. 'I'm selling the forest to Widow Klinckmann.'

6. Puntila Hall

Preparations for the engagement party are in full swing. Pigs are being slaughtered, windows cleaned, and Matti is helping the cook to nail up a garlanded sign which says 'Welcome to the Engagement Party.' Miss Puntila would like to know what Matti thinks of her engagement to the Attaché. She herself has no use for him. With considerable ingenuity she induces Matti to help her stage a scandal in order to frighten off the Attaché, who is now staying at Puntila Hall. The scandal is staged (sauna) but clearly the Attaché must have enormous debts: he overlooks it. Puntila is very angry, takes his wallet from Matti, and threatens to tell the police. Eva blames Matti for not sticking up for himself like a gentleman.

7. Summer Nights in Tavastland

The combination of the feigned love scene with Matti and the erotic ambience of the summer night has put fresh thoughts into Eva's head. On the pretext of catching crayfish she takes Matti rowing to a somewhat notorious island. Once there however the thought that she is behaving like a milkmaid disconcerts her; she insists on catching crayfish and is eventually rowed back by a frustrated Matti.

8. Puntila Hall

Puntila turns his three 'fiancées' off the estate, then tells Matti to collect the entire stock of liquor so that it can be destroyed. Thousands of bottles are collected in an operation involving the entire staff. Puntila drinks extravagantly and sends Matti off to bring back his 'fiancées'. Beaming, he announces that in his view they are much better suited than certain other people to the sort of engagement party he has in mind.

9. Country Road

Matti drives off after the young women, but fails to persuade them to return.

10. Inside Puntila Hall

All the guests have arrived, including the foreign minister. Eva has locked herself in her room, so that the Attaché has to receive them on his own. Enter like a whirlwind a totally drunk Puntila, who throws the Attaché out. Thereafter he throws out the minister, parson, judge, and so on, and sends for the domestics. Matti on his return is offered Eva as his wife. Matti insists on testing Eva's matrimonial capacities. She shows herself incompetent to do her own housework. Eventually when Matti slaps her on the backside she takes it badly and runs off in tears. Left alone, Puntila hears his hired hands singing the Ballad of the Forester and the Countess. He resolves to show Matti what a beautiful country they live in, and with this object they climb Mount Hatelma.

11. In the Yard

Matti turns his back on Puntila.

[Brecht: *Texte für Filme II*, Frankfurt, Suhrkamp, 1969, pp. 636–40. The Puntila film, under the same title as the play, was made in Austria by Wien-Film with Alberto Cavalcanti as director and Curt Bois in the title part (which he had also played in the second Berliner Ensemble production), and was first shown in Brussels on March 29, 1955. Vladimir Pozner was one of the scriptwriters. A new musical score was written by Hanns Eisler, and the text of the Puntila Song somewhat varied for the purpose.]

Editorial Note

1. PRELIMINARY IDEAS

Though the Puntila theme was not Brecht's own it none the less struck
several familiar chords in his mind, among them being Faustian Man
(with his twin souls), Chaplin's film *City Lights*, and the ironic
discursive style of Hašek's *Schweik*. They may well moreover (as Jost
Hermand has suggested) have included Carl Zuckmayer's bucolic
'People's Play' of 1925, *Der fröhliche Weinberg* (The Cheerful
Vineyard), and the falsely jovial personality of Reichsmarschall
Hermann Göring. There is, however, no sign of such elements
coming together before Brecht met Hella Wuolijoki in 1940.
Stimulated, so it appears, by the Finnish Dramatists' League's play
competition, she then showed him her play *The Sawdust Princess*
together with the film treatment from which it derived, with the result
that by August 27 they had agreed to collaborate on a new version.
For her the theme went back to the early 1930s when (according to
evidence gathered by Hans-Peter Neureuter in the *Mitteilungen aus
der deutschen Bibliothek*, Helsinki, numbers 7, 1973 and 8, 1974), she
wrote the story based on the personality of one of her own relatives,
which she called 'A Finnish Bacchus'. This was worked up into a
treatment for Suomi-Film, which however was never made. Its central
character, says Margaret Mare in her edition of the play (Methuen,
1962), was to be

> Puntila, a Tavastland estate owner, who, mellowed by drink, went
> one night to the village and engaged himself to several young
> women with the help of liquor and curtain rings. Puntila has a
> daughter, Eva . . . who is wooed both by a young diplomat and by
> a chauffeur. She chooses the latter, and all ends well when he turns

out to be an engineer, masquerading in his own chauffeur's uniform.

Puntila himself was to marry 'Aunt Hanna', the owner of the house where he arrives drunk early in the story (and where he also confronts his village 'fiancées').

How far the play *The Sawdust Princess* was complete when Brecht first saw it is not entirely clear. Some commentators think that it was, but Brecht himself referred to it as a draft and in his journal (entry for September 2) describes it thus:

> hw's half-finished play is a comedy, a conversation piece. (puntila sober is puntila drunk plus a hangover, hence in a bad temper, the stereotype of a drinker. his chauffeur is a *gentleman* who had applied for the chauffeur's job after having seen a photograph of puntila's daughter, etc.) but there is also a film of hers which yields some useful epic elements (the mountain climb and the trip for legal alcohol). it is my job to bring out the underlying farce, dismantle the psychologically-orientated conversations, make room for opinions and for stories from finnish popular life, find scenic terms for the master/servant antithesis, and restore the poetry and comedy proper to this theme.

This was not, of course, the job as Hella Wuolijoki herself saw it, but in Brecht's view she was handicapped by a hopelessly conventional dramatic technique. A fortnight before, he had already tried to give her an idea of 'non-Aristotelian' dramaturgy while discussing a plan of hers to write a play about the early Finnish nationalist J. V. Snellman, a work which she never completed. Now he took over *The Sawdust Princess* and within three weeks had turned it into something very different from what he had found.

He started with a German translation which Wuolijoki, an excellent linguist, dictated to Margarete Steffin. From this orthodox four-act play he took the characters of Puntila, Eva (the Sawdust Princess of the title), the Attaché, the doctor, Fina the maid, and all the village women apart from the chemist's assistant. Initially he also took Kalle the pseudo-chauffeur, whom he turned into a genuine chauffeur and later renamed Matti, while from the treatment he took Aunt Hanna, first turning her into Puntila's housekeeper, then banishing her from the play altogether except in the shadowy form of the unseen Mrs Klinckmann. The setting and the Swedish-style place names – Tavastland or Häme in southwest Finland, Kurgela, Lammi, Tammerfors (Tampere), Mount Hatelma (Hattelmala near Tavasthus) and so on – are likewise taken from Wuolijoki, Kurgela indeed being the nearest sizeable town to her own Marlebäck estate.

A succession of plans shows Brecht isolating the crucial incidents in her story, switching them and building on them until he had the framework of a ten-scene play. One of the earliest gives Puntila the aristocratic 'von' and goes thus:

1. Mr von P. gets engaged to the churchgoers.
2. The league of Mr von P.'s fiancées.
3. Playing with fire (those who pretend to be in love fall in love).
4. Driving out the materialists.
5. Mr von P. sits in judgement.
6.
7. Climbing the mountain.
8. Mr von P.'s funeral speech.

Thereafter (it would seem) two new scenes were added at the start (the first being described as 'gethsemane/a chauffeur with dignity/the engagement'), while the centre of the play was left undetermined. According as to whether Puntila was to be mainly drunk or sober, Brecht now started marking the scenes 'd' or 's' – that is, in German 'b' or 'n', b(esoffen) or n(üchtern). Kalle's new role became clearer and something like the final play began to take shape:

1. puntila finds a human being and hires him as his chauffeur (d).
2.
3. puntila finds legal alcohol and gets engaged to the early risers. (d).
4. p engages his daughter to a human being/in the sauna/the league of mr von p's fiancées/kalle and eva conduct a test. (d and s).
5. p engages his daughter to an attaché/the attaché is uncongenial to him/k refuses to marry eva/puntila rejects her. (s and d).
6. judgement on kalle/kalle says goodbye to e/the mountain climb.
7. k leaves p and makes a speech about him.

Next the two main events of this scene 4, the engagement and the league of fiancées, are separated, the former being shifted to a separate scene immediately before or after scene 5. One scheme introduces 'p gets engaged to his housekeeper' as the theme of the last scene but one. Finally there is a characteristic big working plan in columns, such as Brecht used to pin up before starting to write in earnest:

1. p finds a human being.
2. p and his daughter.
3. p gets engaged to the early risers.
4. p engages his daughter to an attaché.
5. p at the hiring market.
6. kalle goes on strike.
7. the league of p's fiancées.
8. p engages his daughter to a human being.
9. p sits in judgement and climbs mount hatelma.
10. kalle turns his back on p.

Though two further scenes were to be added, initially as 7a and 8a, while 9 and 10 became run together, the above is in effect the play as Brecht first wrote it. He also kept before him three examples of what he called 'Puntila's way of speaking' (the passage starting 'I'd be ashamed', p. 254), 'Kalle's way of speaking' (a passage in scene 6 starting 'Your father's acting all for your best', p. 263), and 'the gentry's way of speaking' (the judge's passage in the same scene starting 'All those paternity cases', p. 259). Once these tones of voice had been fixed 'the work went very smoothly,' he noted, even though the tone was not original:

it is hašek's way of speaking in schweik, as already used by me in courage. the plan for the scenes was quickly settled. their length was predetermined and fairly closely kept to. the visit to the hiring fair was an afterthought; it took place a few days ago near here.

So he wrote in his journal on September 19, the day when he had finished the play and handed it to Hella Wuolijoki to read.

At first her reactions were far from favourable. 'She seems

extremely alarmed', says a journal entry five days later:

> it is undramatic, unfunny, etc. all the characters speak alike, not
> differently as they do in real life and in hw's plays. passages like the
> conversation between judge and lawyer in the kitchen are boring
> (something the finns are not unused to) and do nothing to further
> the plot. Kalle is not a finnish chauffeur. the landowner's daughter
> cannot attempt to borrow money from the chauffeur (but can
> presumably attempt to marry him, as in hw's play): it's all so epic
> as to be undramatic.

Brecht tried to encourage her, not least because she still had to
produce a Finnish text for submission to the jury. Though she
accepted something of what he said,

> the point i could not get across was that my scenes' gait and garb
> corresponded to the gait and garb of puntila himself, with all his
> aimlessness, looseness, his detours and delays, his repetitions and
> improprieties. she wants to bring on the women of kurgela earlier,
> immediately they have been invited, so as to make sure the audience
> has not forgotten them. she fails to see the beauty of having them
> virtually forgotten, not only by the audience but by puntila too,
> then making them pop up long after the morning of the invitation.

None the less she did embark on the translation, and only ten days
later seemed very happy about the whole undertaking. She told Brecht
(who again noted it in his journal) that the play was full of riches and
Puntila himself on the way to becoming 'a national figure'.

In the Finnish version published in 1946 (by Tammi of Helsinki)
the name Puntila is changed to Iso-Heikkilä and the title of the play
to *The Landowner Iso-Heikkilä and His Servant Kalle*, subtitled 'A
comic tale of Tavastland drunkenness in nine scenes' by Hella
Wuolijoki and Bertolt Brecht. An introductory note stresses this
aspect:

> Iso-Heikkilä's intoxication is in the nature of a divine dionysiac
> drunkenness. As a steadfast man of Tavastland, he never falters –
> an inner radiance like the brightness of early morning and an always
> human kindness and strength shine forth from his face. Alcohol is

only the magic potion which releases all the sources of kindness in the man, the landowner, Iso-Heikkilä.

'The structure,' she wrote, 'is entirely Brecht's. The idea of including epic tales in the scenes with the women was Brecht's. The stories themselves are entirely mine.' The change of name apart, this version is very close to Brecht's own first typescript dated '2.9.40–19.9.40 (Marlebäck)', though the latter also seems to include some later amendments. Then entitled simply *Puntila*, it was retyped by Margarete Steffin and given its final title; mimeographed copies were thereafter made and sent out by Reiss of Basel. Up to this point there were no songs embodied in the play, though those of Red Surkkala and Emma have been appended to the retyped copy, the former as an alternative to 'The wolf asked the rooster' (pp. 417–18 below). Then it was revised again after the Zurich première in 1948, when changes were made for Brecht's own production with Erich Engel for the Berliner Ensemble, the Puntila Song being written as late as 1949. Around that time the Munich publisher Kurt Desch acquired the stage rights, but at first he too simply duplicated the nine-scene version, which was described as 'after Hella Wuolijoki's stories' with no mention of her play; she is not named as co-author in any of the German texts, though Brecht in 1949 told Desch that she was to get half the royalties.

By 1950, when Suhrkamp first published the text (as *Versuche 10*), the play had expanded from the nine scenes of the early versions – or ten in those scripts where the epilogue was counted separately – to the present twelve. From the first, however, it included the scene with the hiring fair which had only figured in the last of the plans. The character of Surkkala introduced there was subsequently built up, being alluded to at various points and making a notable appearance also in scene 11. Like the village women's accounts of their lives in scene 3, their 'Finnish tales' in scene 8 were an evident afterthought on Brecht's first script, those now given to Emma being omitted from the 1946 Finnish version, possibly because of the censorship. As Aunt Hanna's role diminished from landowner to housekeeper (shedding the 'Aunt') and finally to nothing at all, around the end of the 1940s the shadowy Mrs Klinckmann was introduced to perform some of her original functions, and various references to Puntila's marrying her or selling the forest worked in. Meanwhile in the joint Finnish version

Hella Wuolijoki had given the Attaché an uncle to be the owner of Kurgela and speak some of the lines now given to the lawyer. The Kurgela location still survives in the play, even though without the aunt or uncle most of its *raison d'être* disappeared, its main bath-hut episode being shifted to Puntila Hall and run together with the sobering-up operation to form the present scene 5. Finally there was a change of balance in the relationship between Eva and Matti (Kalle), which Wuolijoki seems to have wanted still to treat as a conventional love story destined for a happy ending (see the last scene of the 1946 Finnish version). Something of her interpretation can be detected even in the first Brecht scripts (as in the detailed account of scene 9 below), a greater element of ambiguity and coolness being introduced later. Throughout, the unchanging pillars of the play were the first half of scene 1, scene 3, the bath-hut episode in scene 5, Matti's dialogue with Eva in scene 6, scenes 7 and 9, and the mountain-climbing episode in scene 11.

The detailed notes which follow are based on comparison of Brecht's first script (1940), the fair copy (1940–41), the joint Wuolijoki–Brecht version (published 1946), the *Versuche* text (1950), and the final text as we have it. Changes made for the Zurich production of 1948 are separately dealt with in Brecht's own note on pp. 385–9.

2. SCENE-BY-SCENE ACCOUNT

Cast

The first script includes the housekeeper Hanna and a doctor, has a peasant woman in lieu of Emma, and omits Surkkala and his children. The chauffeur is still Kalle, but becomes Matti on the fair copy. In the Wuolijoki–Brecht version of 1946 (which we will call the W–B version) Puntila is Johannes Iso-Heikkilä and his housekeeper is called Alina. There is an 'Agronomist Kurgela, a relative of Iso-Heikkilä's, owner of the Kurgela estate', while the attaché is 'Ilmari Silakkala, Kurgela's nephew, a foreign ministry official'. A note to the W–B version says: 'This all took place when Tavastland was still a cheerful place without a single war refugee.'

Prologue

In the first script·this is spoken by Kalle and omits eight lines in the middle. The W–B version has it delivered before the curtain by the whole cast and considerably alters the general sense. This is to the effect that a bad time can be expected in Finland, but one has to be able to laugh all the same. So the audience is invited to appreciate human character and take part in the wild excursions of master and man: never mind if the humour is broad and the element of mockery strong; the actors' work is only play. 'This drama was written in praise of Tavastland and its people.'

In the 1950 text the opening couplet went 'Ladies and gentlemen, the times are bad / When worry's sane and not to worry mad.' The present, slightly more optimistic version first appeared in 1952.

Scene 1

Brecht's original idea, which he amended in the first script, was to set the scene in a village tavern, with a landlord rather than a waiter. In the W–B version Iso-Heikkilä (whom we shall call Puntila for simplicity's sake) is discovered drinking with Mr Kurgela, at whose house Eva has been awaiting them for the past three days. It is he rather than the judge whom Puntila harangues and tells to 'Wake up, weakling' (p. 219), continuing 'I realise you're only drinking with me because I've got a mortgage on your estate.' The judge, by his own account, is more abstemious because of his job. The passage about walking on the aquavit is not in the first script or the W–B version; the latter, incidentally, has them drinking cognac.

After Puntila has described his attacks, ending 'Look at the lack of consideration I've shown you' (p. 222), Kalle asks what sort of state he is in when signing his highly profitable timber contracts. A state of senseless sobriety, answers Puntila:

> When I'm a human being and having a drink then I only discuss art. If a timber merchant came along asking 'Can't you bring the price down?' I'd say 'No, you rascal, today I'm only discussing art. Today I like nice people, whoever they are.'

Matti's long speech about seeing ghosts, which ensues, underwent some reworking, while after 'Mr Pappmann yelled and screamed at me' (p. 222) it originally went on:

> – saying he'd tell the police about me, and that I should go to the
> Pferdeberg and have a good look at the piles of Reds who were
> shot there because it was what they asked for.
> PUNTILA: I've got nothing against socialists [originally: Marxists]
> so long as they drive my tractor . . .

and so on as on p. 223.

In the fair copy the speech ends with a much longer excursion about
the Reds before going on to Puntila's 'So the only reason you lost your
job' (p. 223) as at present. In the W–B version much of the speech is like
a paraphrase of the present text, relating not to Mr Pappmann's estate
but to 'the agronomist's at Kortesoja' where the trouble was not so
much the food as the clock-watching and general stinginess. Probably
the whole speech derived from one of Hella Wuolijoki's stories.

In Puntila's speech the reference to Mrs Klinckmann (p. 223) is not
in the three early versions, which have him saying 'and I've got woods'
rather than 'I shan't give up my forest.' The first script made him
allude to the day when he 'married a papermill and a sawmill' in
explanation of his evident prosperity. All three early versions then cut
straight from Matti's 'no gulf' (p. 224) to Puntila's instruction 'Here,
take my wallet' (p. 225), the intervening dialogue about Mrs
Klinckmann and the sale of the forest only being introduced in the
1950 text. At the end of the scene the W–B version has the two men
wake the comatose Kurgela, who says he won't drive home as he is
frightened of Hanna. Puntila responds 'Down with all Hannas' and
gets Kalle to echo this.

Scene 2

The title of this scene on the first script, followed by W–B, was
'Puntila and his daughter Eva', on the fair copy 'Puntila is ill-treated',
and in the 1950 text 'Eva' as now. Originally Eva was discovered
reading, not munching chocolates, and the Attaché entered left, not
from an upper level.

The opening allusions to Mrs Klinckmann were added to the first
script, which originally started with the Attaché's 'I have telephoned
again.' His next speech, after 'it's got to be father' (p. 226) was

ATTACHÉ: Regrettable, yes.

EVA: Aunt Hanna is in such a bad mood. Imagine Father leading Uncle Kurgela astray.

ATTACHÉ: Aunt Hanna will forgive him. What disturbs me is the scandal.

– suggesting that, despite her changed role, Hanna is still being seen as part of the Attaché's family. Then on as on p. 226, up to Puntila's entrance. In all except the final text the latter 'bursts through the door in his Studebaker [or Buick in the W–B version] with a great crash and drives into the hall'; he also gets into the car again when preparing to leave. The allusions to Mrs Klinckmann on pp. 228–9 were to Aunt Hanna in the W–B version, where after 'And not getting a woman!' (p. 229) Puntila tells Eva 'I'm going, and Kalle's going to be your fiancé!'

After Eva's 'I won't have you speaking about your master like that' (p. 229) both the first script and W–B have Kalle saying that he is on the contrary sticking up for Puntila against Eva. He then asks Eva if she wants to get away, and is told he is being inquisitive. This leads him to discuss inquisitiveness, saying 'it was pure inquisitiveness that led to the invention of electricity. The Russians were inquisitive too.' Eva continues 'And don't take what he said' etc., as now, up to the present end of the scene. The W–B version prolongs this by making Eva reply to Kalle's last remark, 'You forget you're a servant.'

KALLE: After midnight I'm not a servant, I'm a man. (*Eva runs off*) Don't be afraid.

ATTACHÉ (*entering*): Who are you, fellow?

KALLE: Mr Iso-Heikkilä's chauffeur, sir.

The Attaché takes a dislike to him and threatens to check up on his past record. Kalle replies that he has been talking to the ghosts of departed ladies of Kurgela: 'I'm a sort of substitute bridegroom. Good night.'

Scene 3

The fair copy specifies at the outset that 'a tune like "Valencia" is being played'. In all three early versions Puntila starts by rousing a 'fat woman at the window', then the chemist's assistant, and has a bawling match with both before being sent on to the vet and picking up (virtually) the present text from p. 232. Emma appears after he has been given his prescription; in the first script and W–B she has no song; in the fair copy it is tacked on at the end of the play. Otherwise the rest of the scene follows very much as now, though each woman's description of her life is an evident addition to the original script. These accounts could well originate in stories told by Hella Wuolijoki, though in the W–B version there are some differences: thus the milkmaid does get meat, while the telephonist has 'enough money for pork dripping, potatoes, and salt herring' and gets a box of chocolates from the doctor.

Scene 4

In the three early scripts this follows the bath-hut scene, the present scene 5. The first script and fair copy limit Puntila's opening speech to 'I'm through with you', followed by the last sentence ('You took advantage' etc., p. 238). In the W–B version the setting is a 'hiring fair at Hollolan Lahei, a small park with a café, right. Left, a coffee stall with table and benches. Men are standing in scattered groups, the farmers are selecting labourers. Two stable girls giggling, left. Enter a fat man, left.' When the latter comments that there is not much doing, a labourer explains that people prefer to take forestry jobs, since the wages are going up there. Then Puntila enters, and the sense of what follows is much the same as in Brecht's script. In both, however, the proposed conditions of work are less bad than in the final version: the redhaired man is promised his meals and a potato patch, while the (first) worker is told that he will get wood delivered. In all three of these scripts Puntila's first speech after sitting down to coffee (p. 241) tells Kalle/Matti that he must control himself with respect to Eva, and it is this that Matti answers by 'Just let it be', after which the scene continues as now for about half a page. However, Surkkala (p. 242) is Salminen in the W–B version, and the reason why the parson wanted him thrown out was not because he was a Red but 'because he has a wife he's not married to, and appears suspect to the National Militia in various other ways.' All three versions of the scene end with Puntila's 'make me respect you' (p. 244).

Scene 5

In all three early scripts this precedes the hiring fair scene. All are headed 'Puntila [or Iso-Heikkilä] betroths his daughter to an Attaché', as in the plan. All omit the arrival of the labourers from the hiring fair and place Puntila's sobering-up process in the bath at the beginning of scene 6. They set the present scene not on Puntila's estate but at Kurgela

> *with a bath-hut that can be seen into. Kalle sits whistling beneath some sunflowers as he cleans a carburettor. Beside him the housekeeper [or in W–B the maid Miina] with a basket. It is morning.*

HOUSEKEEPER: Kindly have look at the door. Last night when you drove the Studebaker into the hall you ripped off the hinges.

KALLE: Can be managed; but don't blame that door business on me; it's him that was drunk.

HOUSEKEEPER: But if he sees it today he'll be furious. He always inspects the whole estate and checks every corner of our barns, because he holds our mortgage.

KALLE: Yes, he's fussy; he doesn't like things to be in a mess.

HOUSEKEEPER (*leaving*): The mistress is staying in bed with a headache because she'd just as soon not run into him. We're all nervous so long as he's here; he shouts so.

PUNTILA'S VOICE: Tina! Tina! [or in W–B, 'Miina!']

KALLE (*to the housekeeper as she tries to go*): I'd stay where you are; he's amazingly quick on his feet and if you try to get away he'll spot you.

PUNTILA (*entering*) [accompanied by Kurgela in W–B]: There you are; I've been looking all over the house for you. I'm tired of having showdowns with you people, you're ruining yourselves in any case; but when I see things like the way you preserve pork it sends me up the wall. Come Christmas you chuck it away, and the same goes for your forest and all the rest. You're a lazy crew, and you figure I'll go on paying till kingdom come. Look at the gardener going around with patched trousers; well, I wouldn't complain if it was his knees that were patched and not his bottom. If it's a gardener the knees of his trousers ought to be patched.

And the egg ledger has too many inkblots over the figures. Why? Because you can't imagine why there are so few eggs. Of course it has never dawned on you that the dairymaid might be swiping the eggs; you need me to tell you. And don't just hang around here all day!

(*The housekeeper leaves in a hurry*)

PUNTILA (*in the doorway*): Got you, boyo.

– and so into the episode with the wallet (p. 249). Then after Matti's third 'Yes, Mr Puntila' (p. 250) Puntila leaves and Eva appears (out of the bath-hut in the first script and carrying a towel) asking 'But why don't you stick up for yourself?' etc., thus cutting out the exchange between Puntila and the two workers. The Eva–Matti dialogue and the ensuing bath-hut charade then follow very much as in our text, but with the Kurgela housekeeper of course instead of Laina. In the W–B version Kalle has gathered from Eva's father that the attaché is to be got rid of, and so the six lines from Eva's 'that he must be the one to back out' to 'I'm crude' (p. 251) are missing, as is Matti's ensuing speech 'Well, suppose' with its allusion to Tarzan. Otherwise there are only very slight differences between all three versions and the final text.

Scene 6

The three early scripts have the title 'What Kalle [Matti] is and is not prepared to do.' As later, the scene is set in the Puntila kitchen, but begins with the sobering-up episode that was later shifted to scene 5 (pp. 248–9). Thus the first script:

> *Farm Kitchen at Puntila Hall. Kalle is trying to sober Puntila up by pouring cold water over his head. The weedy man is sitting in a corner. It is late evening.*

There is music. The scene starts with Matti's 'You'll have to bear with a few buckets' (p. 246); then after 'that fat man at the hiring fair' and before Fina's entry Puntila goes on:

> . . . by the car, he was just going to collect the piglet and missed it. That's enough buckets, I never have more than eleven. (*Shouts*)

Fina! Coffee!
(*Enter Fina*)
PUNTILA: Here's that golden creature with my coffee.
FINA: Miss Hanna says wouldn't you rather take your coffee in the drawing-room; Kalle can have his here.
PUNTILA: I'm staying here. If Kalle isn't good enough for her I'm having my coffee in the kitchen. Where is it?
FINA *goes and produces coffee from the stove*: Here you are, Mr Puntila.
PUNTILA: Is it good and strong? . . .

Then, after Kalle/Matti's 'No liqueur,' Puntila says to hell with his guests, Fina must hear the story of the fat man, which he then recounts, starting from 'One of those nasty fat individuals' (though 'a proper capitalist' is not in the early scripts). The rest of the episode is virtually as in our text except that after Puntila's second coffee (p. 248) Matti's speech about love of animals, with its reference to Mrs Klinkmann, is replaced by the exchange between him and the weedy man which is now on pp. 245-6 ff. immediately after Puntila has gone into the bath-hut. Thereafter it is Kalle who asks Puntila if the coffee was strong enough, and the remainder down to 'despise me when he's pissed' (p. 249) is as in our text.

The link between the sobering-up episode and the present beginning of the scene (p. 258) was simply a ring on the bell, leading Fina to say 'I forgot to say Miss Eva wants a word with you.' Then Hanna (or Alina) comes in – after the eighteen-line dialogue between Matti and Fina, ending with her sitting on his lap, which is all cut in W–B – and tells Fina to tidy the library and take the weedy man to the room where he is to spend the night prior to leaving; he must also return his 100 marks earnest money (most such sums being divided by ten in the course of revision). On his complaining that he has lost two days' work Hanna blames Kalle. Then the judge and lawyer (replaced by Agronomist Kurgela in W–B) come in, after which the rest of the scene continues much as in our text. However, the first two stage directions (pp. 260-61) describing Eva's would-be seductive walk were added later, while the third (on her re-entering on p. 261) originally read 'wearing sandals and pretty shorts.'

Scene 7

With the exception of Emma's last speech with its snatch of song (p. 273) and her action of sitting on the ground, this scene has remained essentially as it was when Brecht first wrote it, as envisaged in the preliminary plans. Among the small modifications incorporated in the 1950 version (and thereafter in our text) are the conception of the two-level set, the Sunday atmosphere with its bells, Puntila's phrase about the wedding costing him a forest (p. 266), the women's straw garlands and Matti's haranguing of the broom. In all three early versions Puntila's remark about forming a trade union (p. 272) is answered by Matti: 'Excuse me, Mr Puntila, it's not a trade union because there are no dues. So nobody's interests are represented. It was just for a bit of a laugh and maybe for a cup of coffee.' Finally in lieu of Emma's last speech the telephonist tells Puntila:

> But it's only a joke. You invited us yourself . . .
> EMMA: You have no right to say we wanted to blackmail you.
> PUNTILA: Get off my land!

End of scene.

Scene 8

This had no title before the 1950 version. In the first script it is unnumbered but inserted separately from scene 7, which suggests that it was added later; it is followed by a photograph of a peasant woman. In the fair copy it is numbered 7a, and in the W–B version 'Scene 7, conclusion, to be played on the forestage.' Emma's first tale (starting 'the last police sergeant's wife') is not in W–B; the telephonist's tale ('They know what they're up to') is delivered by the dairymaid; and the latter's 'Me too' (p. 275) is spoken by the peasant woman in the first script and by Emma in W–B. This is then followed by a comment from the telephonist 'What fools we women are,' which in W–B ends the scene. The first script adds Emma's long story (pp. 275–6) but gives it to the telephonist.

Scene 9 [8 in the early scripts]

Again the title and general sense of the scene have remained unchanged ever since Brecht's first plans, though a long section was cut out of its middle (which somewhat alters the picture of Eva) while the ending with Red Surkkala's song was tacked on to the fair copy. Originally the opening conversation was among parson, judge, doctor and lawyer (or agronomist in W–B); there was a slight redistribution and cutting of lines once the doctor had been eliminated. At first too the Attaché appeared accompanied not only by the parson's wife but also by Hanna/Alina, who delivered what are now the parson's wife's lines, sighed, and left.

The major change occurred after the parson's wife's reproachful cry of 'Eva!' (p. 282), before Puntila reappears. Here there enter, not Puntila at first but

> *the cook and Fina the maid with a great basket full of bottles. They clear the dining table and place them on it.*

EVA: What are you doing, Fina?

FINA: Master told us to reset the table.

PARSON'S WIFE: Are you saying that he came to the kitchen?

THE COOK: Yes, he was in a hurry, looking for the chauffeur.

EVA: Has the Attaché driven away?

FINA: I think so.

EVA: Why can't people say things for certain? I hate this awful uncertainty all round me.

FINA *laughing*: My guess is that you're not sorry, Miss Eva.
(*Enter Puntila and Kalle, followed by the doctor*)

PUNTILA: Hear that, Eva? There was I, sitting over my punch, thinking about nothing in particular, when suddenly I caught myself looking at the fellow and wondering how the devil anyone could have a face like that. I blinked and wondered if my eyesight had gone wrong, so I had another glass and looked again, and then of course I knew what I had to do. What are all you people on your feet for?

PARSON: Mr Puntila, I thought that since the party's over we ought to take our leave. You must be tired, Anna.

PUNTILA: Rubbish. You're not going to resent one of old Puntila's jokes, not like that pettifogging lawyer Kallios who keeps picking holes in everything I do and just at the very instant when I've realised my mistake and want to put it right; yes, the Attaché was a flop but I did a good job once I'd caught on, you'll bear me out there. Puntila may go off the rails, but not for long before he sees it and becomes quite human again. You found the wine? Take a glass and let's all sit down; I'll just tell the others there's been a mistake and the engagement party's going on. If that Attaché – scavenger, that's what he is, and I'm amazed you didn't realise it right away, Eva, – as I was saying, if he imagines he can screw up my engagement after weeks of preparation then he can think again. The fact is I decided a long time ago to marry my daughter to a good man, Matti Altonen, a fine chauffeur and a good friend of mine. Fina, hurry up and tell whoever's dancing in the park that they're to come here as soon as the dance is over; there've been some interesting changes. I'll go and get the minister. (*Goes out*)

KALLE: Your father's going too far, even allowing for him being drunk.

EVA: [illegible]

KALLE: I'm amazed you let him treat you like that in public.

EVA: I like being an obedient daughter.

KALLE: He's going to be disappointed, though. Maybe he can give your hand to anyone he chooses, but he can't give mine, and that includes giving it to you.

Eva answers 'Don't look at me' etc., on p. 283, down to Matti's 'it wasn't to get married', after which she continues:

I don't believe you. That wasn't how you held me at Kurgela. You're like Hulda down in the village, who had five illegitimate children with a fellow and then when they asked why she didn't marry him she said 'I don't like him.'

KALLE: Stop laughing, and stop telling dirty stories. You're drunk. I can't afford to marry you.

EVA: With a sawmill you could.

KALLE: I already told you I'm not playing Victor to you. If he wants to scatter sawmills around he can give them to you, not to me. He's human enough when he's stewed but when he's sober he's sharp. He'll spend a million on an attaché for you but not on a chauffeur.

(*Parson, judge, parson's wife and doctor have been standing as a group in the background and putting their heads together. Now the parson goes up to Eva*)

PARSON: Eva, my dear, I must speak to you like when I was preparing you for confirmation. [An illegible line is added.] Mr Altonen is welcome to stay, in view of his unfortunate involvement. Eva my dear, it is your hard duty to tell your father in no uncertain terms that he cannot dispose of you like a heifer and that God has given you a will of your own.

EVA: That would conflict with my obedience to parental authority, your Reverence.

PARSON: It is a higher form of obedience, an obedience that goes against accepted morality.

KALLE: That's just what I say.

PARSON: I am glad you have so much good sense. It makes the situation considerably easier for you, my child.

EVA: What's so hard about it? I shall say to my father in bell-like tones: I propose to do as you command. I am going to marry Kalle. Even if it means risking his saying in front of everybody that he doesn't want me.

KALLE: If you ask me, the problem's a lot simpler than that, your Reverence. I think he'll have forgotten all about it by the time he comes back here. I'll be the sacrifice and go into the kitchen with him, we'll have a bottle or two and I'll tell him how I've been sacked from job after job, that's something he likes hearing about.

EVA: If you do that I'll go into the kitchen too.

PARSON: I am sadly disappointed in you, Eva. (*He goes back to the others*) It's unbelievable. She's determined to marry the man.

DOCTOR: In that case it's time I went; I'd rather not be present; I know Puntila. (*Goes out*)

PARSON: All I can say is that I'd leave too if I didn't feel it my duty to drain this cup to the dregs.

PARSON'S WIFE: Besides, Mr Puntila would be displeased. (*The dance music next door suddenly stops. A confused sound of voices which likewise stops after a moment. The ensuing silence allows one to hear the accordion playing for the dancers in the park*)

KALLE: You're taking advantage of the situation.

EVA: I want my husband to be a man.

KALLE: What you want is a lively evening, never mind what anyone else may think. You're your father's daughter all right.

(Enter Puntila by himself, angry)
PUNTILA *(taking a bottle from the table and drinking from it)*: I have just had a profound insight . . .

and so on as on p. 282. Then there is a cut straight from his 'Fina, you come and sit by me' (p. 283) straight to *All sit down reluctantly* (thirteen lines below).

Thereafter there are only small differences in the scene at the table with Matti testing Eva. One is that Puntila's query 'Matti, can you fuck decently' (p. 284) down to Matti's 'Can we change the subject?' is not in the first script or the W–B version but was an addition to the fair copy. Then when Matti slaps Eva's behind both the first version and the fair copy have her evading the slap; she simply says 'How dare you,' etc. In the first version the scene ends with the exit of the cook and the parson's wife (p. 293). In the fair copy, however, Matti's immediately preceding speech continues after 'unforgiving':

It's only that the kitchen staff will be here in a minute; the music has stopped. You made Fina call them to hear about some new development. What are you going to say when they get here, led by Miss Hanna with her sharp tongue?
PUNTILA: I'll tell them that I've disowned my daughter for being a crime against Nature.
MATTI: You might do better to tell them that tomorrow.

Then he turns 'to Laina and the parson's wife' as on p. 292 down to their exit, after which one hears singing from the dance off:

The wolf asked the rooster a question:
'Shouldn't we get to know each other better
Know and understand each other better?'
The rooster thought that a good suggestion
Must have responded to the question
I'd say, seeing the field's full of feathers.
Oh, Oh.

The match asked the can a question:
'Shouldn't we get to know each other better
Know and respect each other better?'

The can thought that a good suggestion
Must have responded to the question
I'd say, seeing the sky's turning crimson.

The boss asked the maid a question:
Shouldn't we get to know each other better
Know and respect each other better?
The maid thought that a good suggestion
Must have responded to the question
I'd say, seeing her stays are bulging.
Oh, oh.

PUNTILA: That's meant for me. Songs like that cut me to the quick.

The last stage direction first appears in the 1950 text. Red Surkkala's song was added at the end of the fair copy, developing the theme of the first stanza of the above, then in the 1950 version supplanted it.

Scene 10

This is not in the W–B version but is included in the first script with no scene number or title. In the fair copy it is numbered 8a.

Scene 11 [9 in the early scripts]

In the first script the title is 'Puntila and Kalle climb Mount Hatelma', in the fair copy 'Puntila sits in judgement and climbs Mount Hatelma', in the W–B version 'Iso-Heikkilä condemns Kalle.' The setting in the first script is the

Library at Puntila Hall. Hanna, the old housekeeper, is writing out accounts, when Puntila sticks his head in, with a towel round it. He is about to draw back when he sees that Hanna has observed him, and walks across the room to the door. On her addressing him he is painfully affected and stops.

HANNA: Mr Puntila, I have to talk to you. Now don't pretend you've got something important to do, and don't look so pained. For the past week I've said nothing because what with the engagement and the house guests I've had my hands so full I didn't know where I was. But now the time has come. Do you realise what you've done?

PUNTILA: Hanna, I have a dreadful headache. I think if I had another cup of coffee and a bit of a nap it might help; what do you think?

HANNA: I think you've needed something quite different and been needing it a long time. Do you realise that his honour the judge has left?

PUNTILA: What, Fredrik? That seems childish.

HANNA: Do you expect him to stay in a place the foreign minister's been thrown out of? Not to mention the Attaché, who moves in the very best circles and will be telling everybody about you? You'll be left sitting at Puntila Hall like a lone rhinoceros. Society will shun you.

PUNTILA: I can't understand that minister. He sees I'm a bit boozed, and then goes and takes everything I say literally.

HANNA: You've always made a nuisance of yourself, but ever since that chauffeur came to the estate it's been too much. Twenty years I've been at the manor, but now you're going to have to make up your mind: it's the chauffeur or me.

PUNTILA: What are you talking about? You can't go. Who'd run the business? I've got such a headache, I think I'm getting pneumonia. Imagine attacking a man in such an inhuman way.

HANNA: I'll expect your answer. (*Turns towards the door*)

PUNTILA: You people grudge me even the smallest pleasure. Get me some milk, my head's bursting.

HANNA: There won't be any milk for you. The cook's passed out too, she was drunk. Here come the parson and the doctor.

PUNTILA: I don't want to see them, my health isn't up to it. (*Hanna opens the door to the two gentlemen*)

PARSON: Good morning, Mr Puntila, I trust that you had a restful night. (*Puntila mumbles something*) I ran into the doctor on the road; we thought we'd drop in and see how you were.

PUNTILA (*dubiously*): I see.

DOCTOR: Rough night, what? I'd drink some milk if I were you.

PARSON: My wife asked to be remembered to you. She and Miss Laina had a most interesting talk.

(*Pause*)

PARSON (*gingerly*): I'm very much surprised to hear Miss Hanna is thinking of leaving.

PUNTILA: Where did you hear that?

PARSON: Where? Oh, I really couldn't say. You know how these rumours get around.

PUNTILA: By telephone, I suppose. I'd like to know who phoned you.

PARSON: I assure you, Mr Puntila, there was no question of anybody phoning. What made me call was simply being upset that someone so universally respected as Miss Hanna should be forced to take such a step.

DOCTOR: I told you it was a misunderstanding.

PUNTILA: I'd just like to know who has been telephoning people from here behind my back. I know these coincidences.

DOCTOR: Don't be difficult, Puntila. Nothing's being done behind your back. We're not having this conversation behind your back, are we?

PUNTILA: If I find you've been intriguing against me, Finstrand, I'll put you on *your* back soon enough.

PARSON: Mr Puntila, this is getting us nowhere. I must ask you to consider our words as words of friendship because we've heard you were losing the valuable services of Miss Hanna, and it's very hard to imagine what the estate would do without her.

DOCTOR: If you want to throw us out like yesterday, go right ahead. You can put up a barbed-wire fence around the estate and drink yourself to death behind it.

PUNTILA (*with hostility*): So somebody did phone.

DOCTOR: Oh God, yes. Do you think everyone in Lammi just takes it for granted when you insult a cabinet minister under your own roof and drive your daughter's fiancé off the estate by stoning him?

PUNTILA: What's that about stoning? I'd like to know who's spreading that stoning story.

PARSON: Mr Puntila, let's not waste time on details. I fear I have come to the conclusion that much of what happened yesterday is not at all clear in your memory. For instance, I doubt whether you are aware of the exact wording of the insults which you hurled after our foreign minister, Mr Puntila.

DOCTOR: It may interest you to know that you called him a shit.

PUNTILA: That's an exaggeration.

PARSON: Alas, no. Perhaps that will make you realise that when you are in that deplorable condition you don't always act as you might think wise in retrospect. You risk incurring considerable damage.

PUNTILA: Any damage I incur is paid for by me, not you.

DOCTOR: True. But there is some damage which you can't pay for.

PARSON: Which money cannot repair.

DOCTOR: Though it's the first time I've seen you take things so lightly when somebody like Miss Hanna gives notice in the middle of the harvest.

PARSON: We should overlook such material considerations, doctor. I've known Mr Puntila to be just as understanding where purely moral considerations were concerned. It might not be unrewarding to take the matter of Surkkala as an example of the dangers of over-indulgence in alcohol, and discuss it with Mr Puntila in a friendly, dignified spirit.

PUNTILA: What about Surkkala?

All this long introduction, which was replaced by the present text in the 1950 version, takes us only to p. 296, after which the scene continues as now as far as Puntila's shaking of the parson's hand on p. 297, apart of course from the giving of Laina's lines to Hanna. Thereafter the parson, before leaving, begs Hanna not to abandon her employer but to go on acting as his guardian angel; to which she replies: 'That depends on Mr Puntila.' The doctor advises him to drink less, and the two men go out. Puntila's ensuing speech about giving up drinking ('Laina, from now on' etc.) is addressed to Hanna, not Laina, and is somewhat shorter than now. In the W–B version it follows straight after Hanna's statement that the cook was drunk (p. 419 above), the whole episode with the parson and the doctor/lawyer being thus omitted. To return to the first script, Hanna then replies:

Liquor and low company are to blame. I'll send for that criminal chauffeur, you can deal with him for a start. (*Calls through the doorway*) Kalle! Come into the library at once!

PUNTILA: That Surkkala business is a lesson to me; imagine my not evicting him. That's what happens once you let the demon rum get a toe-hold.

Surkkala's appearance with his family is omitted, Kalle/Matti entering at this point with his 'Good morning, Mr Puntila,' etc. as on p. 298. He then has to defend himself not to Puntila (and against the accusations of the latter's friends) but to Hanna, to whom he says that he was merely carrying out instructions and (as in the final text) could not confine himself to the sensible ones (p. 298).

HANNA: There's no need to top it all by being impertinent. They told me how you chased after your master's daughter at Kurgela and pestered her in the bath-hut.

KALLE: Only for the sake of appearances.

HANNA: You do everything for the sake of appearances. You put on a show of zeal and manage to get yourself ordered to force your lustful attentions on your employer's daughter and smoke Puntila's cigars. Who invited those Kurgela creatures over to Puntila Hall?

KALLE: Mr Puntila, down in the village at half-past four a.m.

HANNA: Yes, but who worked them up and got them to come into the house where the foreign minister was being entertained? You.

PUNTILA: I caught him trying to make them ask me for money for breach of promise.

HANNA: And then the hiring fair?

PUNTILA: He frightened off the redhaired man I was after and landed me with that weedy fellow I had to send packing because he scared the cows.

KALLE: Yes, Mr Puntila.

HANNA: As for the engagement party last night . . . You ought to have the whole estate on your conscience. There's Miss Eva sitting upstairs with a headache and a broken heart for the rest of her life, when she could have been happily married in three or four months' time.

KALLE: All I can say, Miss Hanna, is that if I hadn't restrained myself something much worse would have happened.

HANNA: You and she were sitting in the kitchen on Saturday night, do you deny that?

KALLE: We had a perfectly harmless conversation which I am not going to describe to you in detail, Miss Hanna, you being a spinster, and I don't mean that as an insult but as my personal conclusion based on certain pieces of evidence that are not relevant to the present discussion.

HANNA: So you're dropping your hypocritical mask, you Bolshevik. It all comes of your boozing with creatures like this, Mr Puntila, and not keeping your distance. I'm leaving.

Puntila then tells Matti/Kalle, in much the same words as now used to Laina on p. 297, to bring out all the bottles containing liquor so that they may be smashed. He follows with a shorter version of his speech on p. 299 down to 'Too few people are aware of that', after which Matti reappears with the bottles. The dialogue is close to that of our text, but with Hanna/Alina fulfilling Laina's role of trying to stop Puntila drinking, until he turns on her (p. 300) after his 'I never want to see it again, you heard.' Then instead of going on as in our text he says:

> And don't contradict me, woman; you're my evil genius. That gaunt face of yours makes me sick. I can't even get a drink of milk when I'm sick, and in my own house too. Because there you are, telephoning everyone behind my back and bringing in the parson to treat me like a schoolboy; I won't have it. Your pettiness has been poisoning my life for the last thirty years. I can't bear pettiness, you rusty old adding machine.

Then come four lines as in our text from 'You lot want me to rot away here' to 'tot up the cattle feed', continuing:

> I look across the table, and what do I see but you, you sleazy piece of black crape. I'm giving you notice, do you hear?
>
> HANNA: That beats everything. The two of you getting drunk before my very eyes!
>
> PUNTILA: Get out.
>
> HANNA: Are you trying to give *me* notice? Here's the man you promised you'd give notice to. You promised the parson himself. You were going to report him to the authorities. (*Puntila laughs, picks her up and carries her out, cursing him at the top of her voice*) Wastrel! Drunkard! Tramp!
>
> PUNTILA (*returning*): That got rid of her.

Matti/Kalle's speech 'I hope the punch is all right,' etc. follows as on

p. 300, together with Puntila's next speech as far as 'a calamity all the same.' Then instead of the reference to Surkkala and the half-page of dialogue with him and his family Puntila runs straight on:

> I always said it takes a certain inner strength to keep on the right path.
>
> KALLE: You always get more out of it if you wander off, Mr Puntila. Practically everything that's at all pleasant lies off the right path, you'd almost think the right path had been thought up on purpose to discourage people.
>
> PUNTILA: I say the pleasant path is the right one. And in my opinion you're a good guide. Just looking at you makes me thirsty.
>
> KALLE: I'd like to say something about yesterday's engagement party, Mr Puntila. There were one or two misunderstandings due to the impossibility of suppressing human nature, but if I may say so inhuman nature can't be suppressed either. You rather underrated the gulf between me and Miss Eva until I tickled her backside; I suppose it was because offhand you didn't see why I shouldn't go catching crayfish with Miss Eva just as well as the next man, which is an offhand way of looking at the sexes and one that doesn't get under the surface – as if only the intimate things mattered and not upbringing. As far as I know, though, nothing that happened at the party was so disastrous that you can't put it right, though all that came of it really was that the parson's wife now knows how to preserve mushrooms.
>
> PUNTILA: I can't take it tragically. Looking at it from the broad point of view, not from a petty one; devil take the woman, she's got a petty outlook, she's nothing. Eva will inherit the estate even if she makes a bad marriage.
>
> KALLE: Even if. Because so long as she's got the estate, and the cows yield milk and there's someone to drive the milk churns to the co-operative and they keep an eye on the grain and so on, nothing else counts. Whether it's a good or bad marriage isn't going to prevent her from selling her trees. You can chop down a forest even with a broken heart.

Then Puntila asks what his pay is, as on p. 301 (though the amount varies from script to script) and goes on, as in our text, to propose

climbing Mount Hatelma. After his 'We could do it in spirit' (p. 302)
Matti/Kalle interposes in the first script (not W–B):

> In spirit is always much the simplest way. I once got sore at an
> Englishman for parking his car so stupidly that I had to shove it
> out of the way with my drunken boss sitting in the Ford cursing
> me. In spirit I declared war on England, I defeated them in spirit,
> brought them to their knees, and laid down stiff peace terms; it
> was all very simple, I remember.

Then Puntila finishes with 'Given a chair or two we could' etc. (p.
302) and the dialogue continues virtually as we have it for some two
pages, omitting only the stage direction on p. 302 with its mention of
the billiard table. After Puntila's 'Are you a Tavastlander?' (p. 303),
however, Kalle gave details, e.g., from the first script:

> Originally, yes. I was born the other side of those forests in a
> cabin by the lake, and I grew up on bare stony ground.
> PUNTILA: Hold on, let's take it all in proper order. First and
> foremost, where else is there a sky . . .

– and so on as in our text to the end of the scene. In the W–B version
there are some cuts, and Kalle adds after his present concluding line
'Long live Tavastland and its Iso-Heikkilä!' after which the two men
sing the lines about the Roina once again. (These come from the
nineteenth-century poet Topelius, and the Roina is a lake in central
Finland.)

Scene 12 [10 in the first script]

Laina's second speech and both Matti's first two were additions on the
fair copy. In the first script, after Laina's 'until Mr Puntila's up' (p.
306) Kalle continues:

> I'm glad I was able to straighten out that business with the
> housekeeper. It got me a settlement of two months' pay, and she
> was so glad to be rid of me she gave me a decent reference.
> COOK: I don't get it. When you're in so good with the master.
> KALLE: That's just the problem. I couldn't have *him* writing a
> reference for me; I'd never get another job so long as I lived.

Then as in our text from Laina's 'He won't be able to manage without you' to her exit, after which Kalle flings a stone at one of the balcony windows and Eva appears in night attire.

> EVA: What's up? Why have you got your suitcase?
> KALLE: I'm leaving.
> EVA (*after a pause*): Why do you want to leave?
> KALLE: I can't stay for ever.
> EVA: I'm sorry you're going, Kalle.
> KALLE: I'll send you a crayfish for your birthday.
> EVA: I'd sooner you came back yourself.
> KALLE: Right. In a year from now.
> EVA: I'll wait that long.
> KALLE: By then I'll have my sawmill.
> EVA: Fine. I'll have learned how to darn socks by then.
> KALLE: Then it will work. Bye.
> EVA: Bye. (*Goes back into her room*)

The epilogue follows with some very slight variations.

The W–B version tacks this scene on to the preceding one by having Eva enter and call Puntila down from his mountain, after which he goes off with Fina and Laina, leaving her and Kalle alone. She asks 'Why have you got your suitcase?' as above, but the dialogue differs from that in the first script by having her press him to make it less than a year and suggesting that her father might give her a sawmill. Kalle says he will send her books, and she agrees to read them; then she comes close to him, forcing him to say 'Go away and lead me not into temptation.' He pushes her off, and the epilogue follows.